RED PLANET PUBLISHING PRESENTS

ADMIT ONE   ADMIT ONE

THE WHO
I WAS THERE

MORE THAN 400 FIRST HAND ACCOUNTS FROM PEOPLE WHO KNEW, MET AND SAW THEM

LIVE

FANS AND FRIENDS TELL THEIR UNIQUE STORIES FROM SHEPHERDS BUSH TO BRIGHTON

INCLUDING EVENTS FROM 1959 TO 2017

THE
WHO
I WAS
THERE

ADMIT ONE

Richard Houghton

RED PLANET

A catalogue record for this book is available from the British Library

This edition © Red Planet Publishing Ltd 2017
Text © Red Planet Publishing Ltd 2017

ISBN: 978 1 9113 4617 3

Printed in the UK by CPI

Red Planet Publishing Ltd,
Tremough Innovation Centre,
Penryn, Cornwall TR10 9TA

www.redplanetzone.com
Email: info@redplanetzone.com

Photo credits (with thanks)
Keith Rowley, 14 & 15; John Schollar, 17,18 & 19; Linda Walker, 29 31 & 32; Maureen Brown, 52 & 53; Chris Ferguson, 56; Howard J Payton, 82 & 83; Bridget Ward, 89; Bryan Bennion, 128; Bury Libraries Local & Family History & Archives, 166; Rod Blow, 218, 219, 221 & 222; Ric Siegel/Paul Brenton, 290; John Mears, 302, 303, 304 & 305; Rob Cranthorne, 323 & 327; Glenn Fearons, 379; Mark Fintz, 387.

Contents

13 August 1967,
Washington DC

**Memorial Auditorium
231**
17 August 1967,
Chattanooga, Tennessee

**Smothers Brothers
Comedy Hour
231**
17 September 1967, Los
Angeles, California

**Ballerina Ballroom
232**
6 October 1967, Nairn

**Beach Ballroom
234**
7 October 1967, Aberdeen

**Kinema Ballroom
235**
8 October 1967, Dunfermline

**New Century Hall
235**
21 October 1967, Manchester

**Coventry Theatre
236**
29 October 1967, Coventry

**Town Hall
237**
6 November 1967,
Birmingham

**Granada Cinema
238**
8 November 1967, Kettering

**Granada Cinema
239**
9 November 1967, Maidstone

**Cow Palace
240**
18 November 1967, San
Francisco, California

**Hollywood Bowl
243**
19 November 1967, Los
Angeles, California

1968

**Silver Blades Ice Rink
244**
8 January 1968, Bristol

**Assembly Hall
245**
11 January 1968, Worthing

**Starlight Ballroom
246**
11 February 1968, Crawley

**Royal Ballroom
246**
12 January 1968, Tottenham

**Sheffield University
246**
16 February 1968, Sheffield

**Winterland Ballroom
247**
24 February 1968, San
Francisco, California

**Marquee Club
248**
23 April 1968, London

**Stampede Corral
248**
10 July 1968, Calgary,
Canada

**Singer Bowl
249**
2 August 1968, Flushing,
Queens, New York City

**Jaguar Club
249**
10 August 1968, St Charles,
Illinois

**York University
252**
11 October 1968, York

**Adelphi Cinema
255**
9 November 1968, Slough

**Colston Hall
256**
10 November 1968, Bristol

**City Hall
257**
18 November 1968,
Newcastle

**Paisley Ice Rink
258**
19 November 1968,
Glasgow

**Bristol University
260**
7 December 1968, Bristol

**Bubbel's Club
260**
14 December 1968,
Brentwood

Wem Town Hall

262
Date Unknown, 1968, Wem

1969

**Mothers Club
264**
19 January 1969, Birmingham

**Newcastle University
265**
1 February 1969, Newcastle

**Central London Poly
265**
8 February 1969, London

**Lanchester College
266**
14 February 1969, Coventry

**Corn Exchange
266**
14 March 1969, Cambridge

**Casino Club
267**
22 April 1969, Bolton

**Strathclyde University
268**
25 April 1969, Glasgow

**Community Centre
269**
26 April 1969, Auchinleck

**Kinema Ballroom
273**
27 April 1969, Dunfermline

**Ronnie Scott's
273**
1 May 1969, Soho, London

**Merriweather Post
Pavilion
275**
25 May 1969, Columbia,
Maryland

**Royal Albert Hall
276**
5 July 1969, London

**Pier Ballroom
279**
20 July 1969, Hastings

**Whitburn Bay Hotel
279**
28 July 1969, Sunderland

**Winter Gardens
281**
2 August 1969, Eastbourne

Assembly Hall
282
7 August 1969, Worthing

Ninth National Jazz and Blues Festival
283
9 August 1969, Plumpton

Woodstock Festival
287
17 August 1969, Bethel, New York

Isle of Wight Festival
288
30 August 1969, Isle of Wight

Cosmopolitan Club
289
7 September 1969, Carlisle

Fairfield Hall
289
21 September 1969, Croydon

Grande-Riviera Ballroom
289
11 October 1969, Detroit, Michigan

Georgetown University
291
2 November 1969, Washington DC

Bristol Hippodrome
292
4 December 1969, Bristol

Palace Theatre
294
5 December 1969, Manchester

Regional College of Technology
295
12 December 1969, Liverpool

Coliseum Theatre
297
14 December 1969, London

City Hall
298
19 December 1969, Newcastle

1970

Winchmore Hill

301
4 January 1970, London

Bremen
307
27 January 1970, West Germany

Leeds University
307
14 February 1970, Leeds

City Hall
309
15 February 1970, Hull

Civic Hall
310
27 April 1970, Dunstable

University Central Hall
311
16 May 1970, York

Merriweather Post Pavilion
312
29 June 1970, Columbia, Maryland

Auditorium Theater
313
4 July 1970, Chicago, Illinois

Isle of Wight Festival
313
29 August 1970, Isle of Wight

Falkoner Centret Teatret
317
20 September 1970, Copenhagen, Denmark

Free Trade Hall
318
7 October 1970, Manchester

University of Sussex
318
10 October 1970, Brighton

Locarno Ballroom
319
13 October 1970, Leeds

Trentham Gardens
320
26 October 1970, Stoke-on-Trent

Hammersmith Palais
321
29 October 1970, London

Leeds University

323
21 November 1970, Leeds

Mayfair Ballroom
323
26 November 1970, Newcastle

The Lads Club
323
5 December 1970, Norwich

Futurist Theatre
328
6 December 1970, Scarborough

Mayfair Ballroom
332
15 December 1970, Newcastle

1971

Hurst
333
20 April 1971, Berkshire

Top Rank Suite
333
7 May 1971, Sunderland

Mayfair Suite
336
13 May 1971, Birmingham

Caird Hall
336
23 May 1971, Dundee

Assembly Hall
345
1 July 1971, Worthing

Center for the Performing Arts
346
2 August 1971, Saratoga Springs, New York

Public Music Hall
346
12 August 1971, Cleveland, Ohio

Mr Dee's Music Class
347
August 1971, Boston, Massachusetts

Oval Cricket Ground
349
18 September 1971, London

University of Reading
352

25 May 1978, Shepperton

Wembley Stadium
410
18 August 1979, London

Zeppelinfeld
413
1 September 1979,
Nuremberg, Germany

Madison Square Garden
416
13–18 September 1979, New
York City

Brighton Centre
416
10 & 11 November 1979,
Brighton

Riverfront Coliseum
417
3 December 1979,
Cincinnati, Ohio

The 1980s

Deeside Leisure Centre
417
28 February 1981, North
Wales

Arts Centre
418
16 March 1981, Poole

Capital Centre
419
22 September 1982,
Landover, Maryland

JFK Stadium
419
25 September 1982,
Philadelphia, Pennsylvania

Shea Stadium
419
12 & 13 October 1982, New
York

**Alameda County
Coliseum**
420
23 October 1982, Oakland,
California

Sun Devil Stadium
421
31 October 1982, Tempe,
Arizona

Tangerine Bowl
421
27 November 1982,

Orlando, Florida

**Mississippi Coast
Coliseum**
422
1 December 1982, Biloxi,
Mississippi

Astrodome
423
3 December 1982, Houston,
Texas

Carter–Finley Stadium
424
27 July 1989, Raleigh, North
Carolina

1990s & beyond

**Continental Airlines
Arena**
426
19 November 1996, East
Rutherford, New Jersey

MEN Arena
427
11 December 1996,
Manchester

Festhalle
428
6 May 1997, Frankfurt,
Germany

Ice Palace
429
15 August 1997, Tampa,
Florida

Madison Square Garden
430
4 October 2000, New York

Madison Square Garden
432
1 August 2002, New York

The Joint
433
14 September 2002,
Paradise, Nevada

Pimlico Racetrack
434
23 September 2006,
Baltimore, Michigan

Hollywood Bowl
434
5 November 2006, Los
Angeles, California

Arena di Verona
436

11 June 2007, Verona, Italy

Entertainment Centre
338
24 March 2009, Brisbane,
Australia

SECC
439
30 November 2014,
Glasgow

First Direct Arena
440
2 December 2014, Leeds

Mortlake Crematorium
440
8 October 2015, London

Motorpoint Arena
440
15 December 2015, Cardiff

SSE Arena
441
13 February 2016,
Wembley, London

Joe Louis Arena
442
27 February 2016, Detroit,
Michigan

Palacio de los Deportes
442
12 October 2016, Mexico
City, Mexico

Royal Albert Hall
444
30 March 2017, London

INTRODUCTION

How many guitars have been smashed by Pete Townshend? How many people have had their hearing permanently affected by the volume that The Who played at? How many people were on the receiving end of a prank by Keith Moon? If you've ever wondered about the answers to those questions, here's an opportunity to find out.

Perhaps more than any other band that emerged in the 1960s, The Who is the group most associated with live performance. This is due to their incendiary appearances, which often involved smashing up equipment on stage, hotel rooms off stage and – occasionally – each other on and off stage.

It is also testament to the phenomenal number of shows the original line up – Pete Townshend, Roger Daltrey, John Entwistle and Keith Moon – undertook between 1963 and 1978. They performed well over 1,600 times, and in compiling this book I have uncovered at least four performances, which were not documented before, so there may well be others.

Before The Who, Roger, Pete and John performed as The Detours. This book picks up the story of the band, renamed The Who, from May 1964 when Keith Moon joined the group. From their early days playing Motown covers, The Who were closely associated with the Mod movement and there are several stories from Mods who saw The Who in that period. But the band transcended teenage rivalries and their reputation as a singles group to become one of the biggest rock acts in the world, playing the Monterey, Woodstock and Isle of Wight festivals, and going on to headline arena and stadium gigs around the world from the 1970s onwards.

This is a slightly lop sided and incomplete history of The Who, for which I make no apology. The eyewitness accounts from people who have provided memories of seeing the band, have not been gathered on a systematic basis. But the book hopefully provides a new perspective on a familiar story.

Time and time again the character that emerges most strongly from these stories is that of Keith Moon. Perhaps more than any other member, he was the heartbeat of The Who. For a lot of fans, The Who ceased to exist when Keith died on 7 September 1978, and it is clear from reading the accounts of the many people who saw him behind his kit that he brought something to the band that no other drummer – however talented – could. Keith was a one off and, although the group has continued to exist in name, it isn't the same Who without Keith. Neither has it been the same Who since John Entwistle died in 2002.

That Roger and Pete carry on performing is to their credit, as The Who's songs continue to provide pleasure for thousands of people, and I have included memories of several post 1978 shows to reflect the longevity of their career. But to really understand The Who and the impact they had on the music scene, you have to go back to the mid 1960s, to the time when post-war Britain was still waking up to what the possibilities were, to the time when someone smashing their guitar on stage was truly shocking. The Who were loud, explosive and in your face. The memory of seeing them live is seared into the consciousness of everyone who witnessed those early performances.

I hope, in reading this book, the reader is transported back to a time before Ticketmaster and the need for Access All Area passes, to a time when a band as big as The Who could turn up with barely any fanfare in a place as small as Cromer in Norfolk and give a show that would be seared into the memories of those who witnessed it.

I would love to have been at the Trade in Watford or the Station Hotel in Wealdstone in 1964 to see the early Who strut their stuff. Until someone invents a time machine, this may be the nearest we'll get to experiencing The Who in their early days and witnessing their evolution into rock legends. Unless, like more than 400 people whose stories are in this book, you can say 'I Was There!'

ACKNOWLEDGEMENTS

I could not have embarked upon this book without reference to Joe McMichael and 'Irish' Jack Lyons' excellent *The Who Concert File* and Andy Neill and Matt Kent's equally excellent *The Complete Chronicle of The Who*, both of which are indispensable to anyone wanting to research the early history of The Who. But my labours have unearthed a number of previously undocumented performances that do not appear in either book, and which are noted within the text of this one, including shows at the Locarno in Stevenage, the Corn Exchange in Rochester, Laurie Grove Baths at Goldsmiths College, London and the Town Hall in Wem in Shropshire, along with suggestions of at least two others – at Whitchurch in Shropshire and at Portrush in Northern Ireland – about which I'd love to hear more details. I can be emailed at: thewhointhe60s@gmail.com

I am indebted to the staff of local newspapers up and down the land who enthusiastically helped in my appeal to find Who fans who wanted to tell their story. They did this by not only publishing my letter but often by an accompanying feature bringing back to life the night(s) that The 'Oo played their town or city. As with my book *The Beatles – I Was There*, I could not have done it without them. In particular I should like to thank:. Steve Hill from the *Aberdeen Press & Journal*; Stewart Ross from the *Dundee Courier*; Mike Hill from the *Lancashire Evening Post*; Colette Wartbrook from the *Stoke Sentinel*; and Mattie Lacey-Davidson from the *Watford Observer*.

I should also like to thank: Neil Cossar for his assistance in unearthing contributions for the book via his thisdayinmusic.com website; Maureen Browning for the numerous images she supplied; and vintagerock.com. I must also thank my many contributors, who made this exercise a fascinating trip back in time and who were good enough to share their memories of The Who with me.

Finally, I should like to thank Kate Sullivan, without whose typing skills, infinite patience and domestic goddesshood this book would still be a work in progress. And finally to Bill Houghton who at the tender age of four already knew the words to Sally Simpson.

Richard Houghton

EARLY DAYS

The founding members of The Who – Roger Daltrey, Pete Townshend and John Entwistle – grew up in Acton, London and went to Acton County Grammar School. Daltrey, who was in the year above Townshend and Entwistle, had moved to Acton from Shepherd's Bush. He had trouble fitting in at the school, and discovered gangs and rock and roll. He was expelled from school aged 15. In 1959 he started the Detours, the band that was to evolve into The Who.

Townshend's father, Cliff, played saxophone and his mother, Betty, had sung in the entertainment division of the Royal Air Force during World War II, and both supported their son's interest in rock and roll. Townshend and Entwistle became friends in their second year of Acton County, and formed a trad jazz group; Entwistle also played French horn in the Middlesex Schools' Symphony Orchestra.

He moved to guitar, but struggled with it due to his large fingers, so switched to bass on hearing the guitar work of Duane Eddy. After Acton County, Townshend attended Ealing Art College, a move he later described as profoundly influential on the course of The Who.

The Who at Shepherd's Bush in 1964

SHEPHERD'S BUSH

1950s, LONDON

In July 1962 Roger Daltrey, Pete Townshend and John Entwistle began performing as The Detours. Keith Moon joined the Beachcombers, a semi-professional London covers band, in December 1962.

I WAS THERE: KEITH ROWLEY

I grew up with Roger Daltrey. My grandparents in Percy Road, Shepherd's Bush, brought me up and Roger lived at number 16. I lived four doors away at number 22A. Roger lived there until he was 12 years old, when he moved from the family rented house to a nice council house in Fielding Road, Acton.

I remember our childhood vividly. Roger's father Harry owned an old taxicab and he often used to take me, Roger and my brother John to Lancing on a Sunday. Roger in them days was known as Trog and he would remember being one of the 'Percy Piddlers', which was the nickname for all the kids down our street. My

Roger Daltrey (far right), in 1958

brother is Roger's age. I'm about four years younger. My brother knew him very well too. Roger went to Westfield and then Victoria Junior School, which all three of us did. John remembers that Roger's nickname, Trog, came about because Roger could put his legs behind his head. John also says that Roger was kicked out of the school choir at Victoria Junior School as the music teacher said his singing was out of tune.

I know he supports Arsenal now but in the early days he just wasn't interested in sport at all. You could play in the street in them days and you'd only have to stop every fifteen minutes to let a car go past. He'd join in all the normal street games like Tin Tan Tommy with the can, and hide and seek. But if we stopped and put coats down and started playing football, then he wasn't interested. It always used to make me laugh. It'd be 'see you later, boys' and he'd just go in and sit on the wall and play on his mouth organ. So music was obviously in his blood.

He always wanted a guitar and he decided he was going to make one. Roger made his first guitar from a block of wood. He and my brother John used to sit on his doorstep in Percy Road working on

Roger Daltrey wrestles with his first car, in 1958

it using just a knife and sandpaper. There was a music shop just around the corner where Roger used to check his handiwork with a Stratocaster guitar, which was in the window. He used to go and peer through the window and get some ideas and then go home and gradually he'd finish making it. Any pocket money went to buying anything he could for it. It did play. He learnt on it.

My brother John remembers Roger took the guitar on a Boys' Club holiday to Plymouth and drove everyone crazy by continually playing 'All I Have To Do Is Dream' by the Everly Brothers and changing 'dream' to 'Jean' as that was his girlfriend's name. Roger could also play skiffle type Lonnie Donegan music very well and his singing wasn't bad either. I believe that he still has this guitar at home.

ROYAL BRITISH LEGION

DECEMBER 1962, HARROW

I WAS THERE: JOHN SCHOLLAR

I was the rhythm guitarist in a band called The Beachcombers. Our drummer had left and we were using the drummer out of Cliff Bennett and the Rebel Rousers when they weren't working. So we put an advert in the Harrow and Wembley Observer looking for a new drummer. We held auditions at the British Legion in Harrow Central and we had four or five drummers turn up, including Keith. His dad brought him. We tried to put him off because we were 21, 22 and he was about 16. That's a big gap when you're that age. It was like a little kid coming in. We said 'you're too young, mate' because he was quite tiny. And he waited until everybody had had a go and then his dad came over and said 'come on, let him have a go. Even if he's no good, it'll give him a bit of experience.'

Within minutes, he'd got all his kit in. He'd set it all up outside knowing that he was going to have a go. With the other drummers, we were lined up across the rehearsal room and the guys came in and sat in front of us, facing the band. But Keith pushed all our

A young Keith Moon with his pre-Who band, The Beachcombers

gear aside and set up where the drummer should be sat. We said 'what do you want to do?' and he said 'well, give us a couple and I'll see if I know 'em.' And we did 'Roadrunner', which he later used to do with The Who, and which The Detours used to do as well, and then we did a Shadows number which was real off-beat, called 'Foot Tapper'. He was absolutely superb and we all looked at one another in amazement. So we said to his dad 'well, it looks like he's in' and he said 'well, you'd better look after him because he's only a nipper.'

He was with us for about eighteen months. He completely changed the group. We used to do all the Elvis type ballads but Keith would rock 'em up. One time, Keith got hold of a duck call. We'd do 'Are You Lonesome Tonight?' and, when it got to a slow bit, Keith would

Now that's what I call a drum riser: before The High Numbers, the diminutive young Keith still scaled the heights get the duck call out and go 'quack quack.' Ron, our singer, used to go mad at him. One night Ron shouted out 'I've had enough of you' and Keith pulled a gun out and fired it at him. It was only a starting pistol but I thought Keith had shot him. When Keith left The Beachcombers, it was never the same. There was a big hole in the band. Not so much musically, but the fun side of it.

We did have some fun with Keith. We had red jackets, but we had gold ones before that. The suit that Keith inherited didn't fit him because the guy that left was bigger than Keith. And Keith said 'I've got a gold lame jacket' so he used to wear that. We were based in West London but we did quite a few American air force bases. We played Mildenhall in Suffolk and we got told off there for going and kicking the tyres on a B-47 bomber. We saw this plane and it looked close but it wasn't, because it was bloody huge.

The American military police were a bit heavy handed. They dumped us in the back of a jeep and took us back to the guard room. The policeman said 'how do we know you're not spies?' And we all had red band suits on so we said 'do you expect to see spies running around with bow ties and red suits?'

The Detours played the Oldfield Hotel in Greenford, West London, on almost 60 occasions in 1963, and a further 12 times in 1964. It was there that they played their first gig as The Who, on 20 February 1964. On 2 May 1964, in a pub on the North Circular Road, London, Keith Moon appeared with The Who for the first time.

OLDFIELD HOTEL

MAY 1964, GREENFORD

I WAS THERE: BARBARA HICKS

I used to go dancing at Greenford in the Sixties when the band were called something else. I can't recollect what it was. The place was always completely full and jumping, so I am not surprised they went places. I was about 20 and working at the BBC. I can't remember the price of admission but it was always packed. I was living in Denham in Buckinghamshire, so went on the bus and underground from Uxbridge.

Barbara Hicks saw The Who when they were still The Detours

FLORIDA ROOMS

10 MAY 1964, BRIGHTON

I WAS THERE: JOHN RITCHIE

I'd seen The Who about three or four times. The Florida Rooms in Brighton was an old aquarium where they used to play. I was a Mod and the Florida Rooms was part of the Mod scene in Brighton. There was a lot going on there. The Montpelier Rooms was another venue that used to be open around there, and the Tudor Bar too, which was also on Montpelier Road and which served Belgian lager – which was pretty strong old stuff in those days.

We all went off to Bournemouth one Easter weekend and then went to Torquay and my parents didn't have a clue where I was. We used to sleep in bus shelters and all sorts of things. We used to go to the Marquee Club in Wardour Street and all those sorts of places, including a club in Brixton called the Ram Jam Club. I think we went every Sunday from 1964 onwards until it shut in 68. I wouldn't dream of going there now, or anywhere like it. But they were different times.

I WAS THERE: HAZEL SMITH

I saw The Who in the Florida Rooms, which was next to the building that now houses the Sea Life Centre. My friend and I were packed in, standing very near the stage next to an enormous speaker. A very Mod Roger Daltrey had us drooling, and Keith Moon's drumming and gurning had us mesmerised. I put my tinnitus down to that concert, as I couldn't hear properly for a week afterwards after standing next to that enormous speaker!

MAJESTIC BALLROOM

24 MAY 1964, LUTON

I WAS THERE: FRANK ABBOTT

I was very fortunate in the early Sixties to be a regular visitor to the Majestic Ballroom in Mills Street, Luton and in a period of just over twelve months saw The Beatles, the Stones and, in May 64, The High Numbers. I can't remember too much about their set list although Moonie really stood out as a character. I have always thought that they played 'I Can't Explain' but on investigation it wasn't released until later so now I'm not so sure, although I do remember 'Bald Headed Woman'. All the top bands came to the Majestic at that time for a cost of about 5 shillings (25p) entrance fee. Those I particularly remember were the Dave Clark Five, Gerry and the Pacemakers, Billy J Kramer, The Undertakers and The Big Three, although my particular favourites were The Kinks who had just released 'You Really Got Me' in 64. It was an electrifying guitar riff, literally.

CORPORATION HOTEL

29 MAY 1964, DERBY

I WAS THERE: MICK SHELTON

I was a regular at the Corporation Hotel in Derby during the early Sixties. In fact, I like to think of myself as one of the small number of Mods who helped change the face of Derby's scene during that time. The Corp, as it was known, was our Friday night mecca and Roger Groome the landlord had run a successful jazz club there for many years. He had the vision to cater for the new generation and set up the Friday R&B scene after most of the farming community had gone home. The hotel was situated opposite the Derby cattle market and Friday

Mick Shelton: a Mod who changed the face of Derby's scene

was a busy day in the town. The open spaces where the cattle pens had been were ideal for the scooter boys to show off their Vespas and Lambrettas. I remember the night well when The Who played under the name The High Numbers, something they often did in their early days, especially when manager Kit Lambert was not sure what sort of reaction they would get. He need not have worried – they went down a storm. The venue also hosted The Moody Blues, The Pretty Things, Steam Packet with Rod Stewart and Long John Baldry, Jimmy James

The High Numbers featured in Record Mirror in 1964, shortly before the release of their 'Zoot Suit' single

HAILED as "the first authentic mod record," four hip young men called the High Numbers are out right now with "I'm the Face," backed with "Zoot Suit" — a Fontana disc. Two numbers penned by co-manager Peter Meaden.

How mod are this mod-mad mob? VERY mod. Their clothes are the hallmark of the much-criticised typical mod. Cycling jackets, tee-shirts, turned-up Levi jeans, long white jackets, boxing boots, black and white brogues and so on to the mod-est limits.

Says Peter Meaden: "After all, the Mod scene is a way of life. An exciting, quick-changing, way of life. The boys are totally immersed in this atmosphere. So they have this direct contact with thousands of potential disc-buyers.

SWITCHED

"And the reaction is already very strong indeed. Take places like the Scene Club in London. The fans are mad about the disc — both sides of it!" In fact, "Zoot Suit" was originally planned as the

HOW HIGH WILL THESE NUMBERS GO?

"A" side, being switched only at the last moment.

In a way, the High Numbers sound swivels directly round the vocals and harmonica-wailing of Roger Daltry. His blonde hair is styled in a longish French crew-cut and he buys clothes in the very latest styles. Currently he's modelling zoot-suit jackets. He digs the blues and Buddy Guy . . . and is glad he no longer has to work as a sheet metal worker.

Lead guitarist Peter Townsend originally wanted to be a graphic designer, having been to Ealing Art School. A near six-footer, he has cropped dark hair, piercing blue eyes — and says: "I admit to spending a fortune on bright

and in-vogue clothes. I go for the 'West Side Story' look and the Ivy League gear." Musically, he's for Bob Dylan and the Tamla-Motown-Gordy label.

AMBITION

On bass is John Allison. He went to school with Roger at Acton County Grammar School. "I used to be in an income tax office. This gave me an ambition: to get OUT of the tax office." John is certainly the most conservative of the group, really preferring classical music to most other kinds. He is an accomplished musician.

Come in, now, drummer Keith Moon. He's the youngest of the group — only seventeen. A Wembley resident, he went to Wembley Technical College and was a trainee representative before turning professional musician. Is the smallest of the group, too, has black hair and brown eyes — and says: "I spend all my free time listening to the music in various West End of London clubs."

Record Mirror colleagues are convinced the boys stand a good chance of getting away with "I'm The Face." And one thing is for sure: the phraseology is good and authentic. Mod, in fact.

Interesting to see how the disc sells.

and the Vagabonds, Zoot Money and his Big Roll Band and many more. It was a great time to be a teenager.

Other sources suggest that they were called The High Numbers up until 20 February 1964, then The Who until 3 July 1964, when they reverted to The High Numbers. They settled on The Who in early November 1964.

REGENCY BALLROOM

20 JUNE 1964, BATH

I WAS THERE: TONY CHURCHOUSE

They hadn't released any records. I was late arriving and my friends had said I'd just missed a great band, that played so loud 'you could feel it in your stomach.' Luckily they played a later set and so I can confirm this. During a break Roger Daltrey, Keith Moon and Pete Townshend were in the bar where we told them how we enjoyed what they played and had a drink with them.

During the conversation Roger Daltrey stated he enjoyed fishing and asked if there was anywhere he could go. A friend said he fished too and, if Roger liked, they could meet up the next day to indulge in a spot of fishing together.

RAILWAY HOTEL

30 JUNE 1964, WEALDSTONE

I WAS THERE: HAROLD MORTIMER

I was one of those who helped run the club at the Railway Hotel circa 1964. At the end of my teens in 1959 to 1961 I was a big fan of jazz both trad and modern, as well as folk and blues. My lifestyle at the time led to me spending a few months 'on the road' in Europe and when I returned to London towards the end of that year things were really developing on the music scene.

Bands were beginning to play old black American numbers in pubs and clubs. One of my earliest recollections is seeing Alexis Korner performing above the Roundhouse pub in Wardour Street with Charlie Watts on the drums and Mick Jagger doing vocals. When the latter pair subsequently formed The Rolling Stones, I was a regular visitor to Studio 51, aka Ken Colyer's Jazz Club, in Great Newport Street, where they belted out their renderings of Chuck Berry, Bo Diddley and Coasters hits.

Also at Colyer's were The Downliners Sect who had a good

Harold Mortimer who helped run the club at the Railway Hotel in 1964

guitarist named Jimmy Page. At the southern end of Wardour Street I used to see Georgie Fame and The Blue Flames at the Flamingo Club, and The Animals played at the 100 Club in New Oxford Street. Then there were The Yardbirds at the Crawdaddy Club in Richmond Cricket Club, while Manfred Mann played at Eel Pie Island in Twickenham.

My enthusiasm for such music led me to start looking out for records, both new and used, of the original artists, and it was around then that one of my friends, Tony Brainsby, who went on to become a music impresario, introduced me to Guy Stevens who had an absolutely enormous collection of R&B records. Guy used to deejay his discs back-to-back once a week at the Piccadilly Jazz Club in Ham Yard off Great Windmill Street, and I still remember the hypnotic effect the unfaltering rhythm of Chuck Berry's 'Run Rudolph Run' had on the dancers. Guy inspired me to seriously increase my own collection, to the point that I lived surrounded by shoeboxes full of 45s and cardboard boxes of LPs, fearful that they would all topple onto my bed and smother me one night. I still have a handful of them.

Another musician who played with Alexis Korner was Cyril Davies, and he formed a band that started doing a weekly gig at the Railway Hotel, Wealdstone. This was conveniently close to my home in South Harrow, so I became a regular there, going on almost any night a band was playing, and I became well acquainted with the small group of people of similar ages to myself who were running the club. The principal members were a pair of smartly dressed Jewish lads, one of whom I think was named Barney.

Now I can't remember if it was suggested to me or if I volunteered myself, but I ended up with the job of playing records before the band started and again during the interval. On paper I was the 'Entertainment Manager', earning £2.50 a night. I developed a successful knack of mixing sounds ranging from 'authentic' R&B such as Howling Wolf and John Lee Hooker, through mainstream Chuck Berry and Bo Diddley, to very early Motown. This was all put together before the night on a reel-to-reel tape recorder, and then I would sweet talk the band into letting me switch on their PA and lean the microphone against the tape recorder's speaker – all very high tech! Which leads me to The Who playing at the Railway once or twice before getting a regular weekly slot. This was about when they had just changed their name from The High Numbers. I particularly liked them because their covers of R&B material were well-played, they had dynamism and each member had charisma.

But what made them really outstanding as far as I was concerned was that three-quarters of the way through the evening they would go into an extended instrumental break, when Pete Townshend would turn round and fiddle with the controls on his amplifier before standing there rubbing his back against it while playing his guitar. This resulted in all sorts of weird and wonderful feedback noises, which Pete attempted to control, while Keith Moon rattled away on his drums and John Entwistle thumped up and down the notes on his bass guitar. It is something that you hear perfected on their record 'Anyway, Anyhow, Anywhere'. Pete's windmill arm movement developed around this time too. I was in the club the night Pete famously made a hole in the ceiling above the stage, but the accounts of him smashing up his guitar afterwards are an exaggeration. What I recall is Pete's look of alarm quickly turning into a guilty grin, while gasps of surprise followed by laughter spread through the audience.

Virtually my only other memories of The Who in the Railway are that for a small number of weeks Roger Daltrey was in the company of the singer Millie (of 'My Boy Lollipop' fame), and one night Chris Stamp, a tall and rather distinguished looking young man in a suit, came in with a stocky older and balding man; they stood near the entrance watching the band for about 30 minutes.

Many visitors to the club must remember 'Mad Mary', a lumpy and unattractive girl who always used to dance frantically on her own; no boy would be seen dead with her. There was occasional violence at the club, outside it mercifully, one particular incident being when the group called the T-Bones turned up half an hour late. A large group of lads had their revenge afterwards when the band were loading their equipment into their Transit van in the alley outside. On another occasion I was accosted by three Mods, one of whom practically stuck a gun up my nose (I think it was a starting pistol) on the landing of the stairs that led up from the club to the pub's bar. My response was to persuade a body-building friend who lived in the next road to me to accompany me the next night.

He was one of those people who could stand there rippling his biceps. While I was buying him a drink at the bar I quietly pointed out one of the Mods from the previous night. The face of the latter went white when he saw us looking, and without us saying anything he came over to grovel profusely. He was practically on his knees. He blamed drugs, the use of which was commonplace at the club. You got the impression that nearly everyone was taking blue amphetamine tablets.

The sessions finished at 10:30 p.m. Then it would take half an hour to clear up, after which a small number of us, usually including Pete Townshend and Roger Daltrey and sometimes John Entwistle, made our way to a late night coffee bar called the Kinkajou that used to be in St. Ann's Road, Harrow about three quarters of a mile away. Here we used to talk animatedly over Cokes and milkshakes till around midnight.

I recall one night when a guy called John Altman was in a bit of a disagreeable mood and started an argument with Pete, which ended in a scuffle outside. John threw Pete onto the snow covered pavement, at which I shouted 'cool it, man.' The shaken Pete misheard this and replied 'that wasn't cool!'

A girl of 17 was in charge of the cloakroom where people left their coats at the club; I often admired her leaning over the counter in her leather miniskirt. One night I spent the last bit of money I had getting a taxi to the club with my tape recorder and other bits and pieces, only to be told by the Irish landlord Mick when I got there that the club had closed at short notice. It had lost its licence. What was I to do now? I would not be paid and I had no money to get home. In stepped the cloakroom girl, who bought me a drink and paid my fare. In response to her act of charity I asked for a date. One thing led to another, and we have now been married for 47 years.

My wife is the youngest of three sisters, and her two siblings went to Ealing Art College where they got to know Pete Townshend. Consequently all three of the girls visited the Railway, which is how my wife ended up with an evening job there. The extent of the friendship was that Pete and his then wife Karen later set up a housing charity, all tax deductible, and bough a flat in Ladbroke Grove which they rented out to one of my sisters-in law. She still lives there today, although Pete sold out to a housing association some years ago.

If I have conjured up any vision of a musically hip, and well connected oldster, forget it. All that is long behind me. I've given up the long hair, I spent the last 28 years of my working life as a service engineer, and now I'm indistinguishable from any other old git of my age.

TRADE UNION HALL

11 JULY 1964, WATFORD

I WAS THERE: JOHN ALBURY

I was one of the many Mods who frequently attended the Trade Union Hall in Woodford Road, Watford around 1963 and 1964 to see The Who and many other bands in those wonderful years of our youth. Just about every weekend we turned up on our scooters, parked outside, paid around 2/6 (13p) for a ticket and joined the usually large crowd to see the bands attending.

The Who were regulars there, often alternating their appearances in Watford and the Railway Hotel a few miles away in Harrow and Wealdstone. They first appeared at the Trade on 11 July 1964 as The Who, with Keith, and I am pretty sure I was there as it was a day after my 18th birthday. They were back a week later and again I would have attended. They made nine or ten visits to Watford in 1964 as either The Who or The High Numbers and I must have seen them on four or five of those occasions.

If we did not see them in Watford for a while, we would sometimes ride over to Harrow and see them at the Railway Hotel in Harrow and Wealdstone. But Watford Mods did not venture to Harrow for too long and vice versa. There was a bit of bad blood there. At the Trade, I remember them playing as The Who, changing their name to The High Numbers, before changing back to The Who again, all in the space of a few weeks. Reputed to be the loudest band, they were responsible for my slight loss of hearing but we loved every minute of it! I can vividly remember Pete Townshend smashing his Stratocaster into the corner of an amplifier and finishing off the guitar on the stage floor. We all cheered!

On one of their visits, Keith knocked over his drum kit at the end of the session. It could have happened more than once at Watford, but I definitely witnessed at least one instrument breaking session there with guitar and drums broken! It got very frantic there during that summer, as it was an energetic, crowded and 'must go' place. It was certainly the best venue in Watford for bands at that time until things got a little less 'raw', when the Top Rank opened in the town and we started to sell our scooters and progressed to cars. I sold my final scooter in late 1965 and The Who had long departed small venues like the Trade. The Trade Union Hall was a fascinating place for music in the 1960s. It was only really a basic village hall type of place with wooden walls and floor but the acoustics always seemed good with some of the greats of the time appearing at the weekends. It was nearly always 2/6 (13p) in old money for the entrance fee so five shillings (25p) if you went twice over the weekend. It was band nights on Saturday and Sunday.

Sometimes the boss, Joey Seabrook – who later became Keith Richards' bodyguard – gave a couple of us regulars a free entry. A good guy was Joey – he looked after the locals! There was a painted backdrop to the stage which may have been a Swiss scene with a door to the backstage area on the left facing the stage. There may have been another door on the right but I cannot recall that. It was hot and very noisy but fantastic. The girls were wonderful and the music superb. There was no alcohol that I remember but there were two pubs just down Woodford Road, two minutes away, which we frequented during 'half time'. There were always rows of scooters up the left hand side of the hall or out on Woodford

Road and always the risk of bits being stolen off the bikes during the band performance as there was quite a market in the area for scooter accessories. It was a fantastic place where one grew up with music, atmosphere, great friends, the odd bit of Purple Heart taking, sometimes a little alcohol and a kiss or a little more on the way home! A wonderful period to grow up.

I WAS THERE: LINDA WALKER

I was a Mod in the Sixties and went to the Trade Union Hall every week. The Who played at The Trade quite a few times in 1964 and 1965 before and after they changed their name from The High Numbers. We knew they were terrific but never thought they would be still going now. The Trade was always packed with Mods and there were some fights, of course. There was no booze. You had to go to the nearby pub in the break.

It was always packed for them, and you just knew how good they were. Of course it was all Mods. Some Rockers did attend but they didn't stay long – thank God – as it was not their kind of music. Keith Moon was my favourite. He was crazy, but so good. At that time there were so many bands playing there – The Pretty Things, Rod Stewart and Steampacket, Long John Baldry, George Fame. I have photos of The Who at the Trade, although I have no idea why I never photographed Keith Moon. Maybe he had nipped out for a pint!

The Who played two shows at the Trade Union Hall (on 11 and 18 July 1964) and then changed their name to The High Numbers for six shows there from July through to October 1964 before reverting to The Who by the time of their return on 7 November 1964.

FLORIDA ROOMS

12 JULY 1964, BRIGHTON

I WAS THERE: DAVID GOODWIN

They were The High Numbers when I saw them at The Florida Rooms. They were part of the Brighton scene. They were one of a number of groups who would turn up to be part of the Mod scene in Brighton. That would be a Saturday night. That was more of a streetwise audience, whereas coming out into the sticks here you had the teddy boy slightly Rockerish sort of people. Rockers were still the country bumpkins, if you like. I don't think they went to see The Who. I think they just went out because it was a Sunday night out.

There wasn't much original material at the Florida Rooms. It was 'Dancing in the Street' and things like that. It was the same faces always. There were no speculative people. It was always the same crowd who went to Saturday night at the Florida Rooms. They wouldn't have come up to the Ultra Club in Hassocks on a Sunday night. The main faces from Brighton wouldn't have come to Hassocks. When I was at school there was a guy called Phil Towner who used to dep for Moon when they played at the Florida Rooms.

In Brighton, if you were a few weeks out of the fashion you weren't cool. It was really sharp. You had to be correct. I remember taking a girl down to the Florida Rooms. She had a Paisley miniskirt on and the girls were all pointing and laughing at her because it was six months late. You had to be just right to be accepted by the inner circle. Maybe it was only a hundred people.

The Who played the Florida Rooms 12 times in 1964 and, as The High Numbers, three times.

RAILWAY HOTEL

14 JULY 1964, WEALDSTONE

I WAS THERE: VALERIE DUNN (NEE WATSON

We used to see The Who, then known as The High Numbers, down the Railway Hotel Wealdstone, regularly on a Tuesday night. It was a great venue, a basement where we would also see Blues Incorporated with Rod (the Mod) amongst many others.

The Railway Hotel in Wealdstone was for some reason a gig that they seemed to come along to quite regularly. It was down in the basement down the steps. You could only get a

Valerie's membership card for the Railway Hotel's R&B club from around 1965

drink upstairs in the pub. It didn't have a bar downstairs. It had two entrances. The pub was really above it.

It was always a Tuesday evening that they had the various blues nights, when they had different bands playing. The High Numbers alternated with a few other bands, and another band who used to play regularly called Garry Farr and the T-Bones. He was the son of the boxer whose name was also Gary Farr. And you'd have Alexis Korner and Blues Incorporated on other Tuesday nights.

I lived in Harrow and it would be myself, my friend and my sister. The three of us would go down there. I went to Harrow School of Art and a lot of the art school lot would go down to the Railway Hotel and you'd see them all doing the amazing French jive, where they'd jive to the music. All the art students were a little bit older than me. I was always in awe of them, because at the time I was still at school although I did go on to art school the following year.

It was probably Long John Baldry who instigated the blues nights. He had a friend who was on the door to take the money, but he would always be standing there chatting. I think it was Long John that actually ran the music events because other than the Tuesday night blues, which was in the basement of the pub, (the pub itself was quite rough). I don't remember the landlord being particularly

Valerie Watson: Who fan, R&B lover and regular at the Railway Hotel pictured on the London Underground

interested. I just recall seeing people that were on the door at the basement of the pub on a Tuesday taking whatever it cost – a shilling – to get in.

When The High Numbers were on it was slightly more the Moddy feel whereas on other Tuesday nights it would be more bluesy. You'd get more lads coming down when The High Numbers were on and they'd all do a dance called the Puppet where they'd jump up and down. You'd see guys dancing more than girls when The High Numbers were on, where they'd put their arms up and bob up and down.

It was quite a small venue, and busy and packed. But standing at the front we'd watch Keith Moon because he would be such an entertainer. He was totally mad on the drums and completely gone. Pete Townshend would be swinging his arm around and getting feedback and John Entwistle was more in the background. He just got on and did his bit. And of course Roger Daltrey was up the front singing. They probably did two sets. It was great because it was very intimate. We were right up the front, close, watching them. They were loud and of course you had all the feedback from Townshend's guitar. It was a great atmosphere.

I probably saw them four or five times on a Tuesday night. The Railway was great because it was so close for us living in Harrow so it wasn't far to get home. After that it went back to just being a rough old pub.

The group appeared at the Railway Hotel 16 times in 1964, appearing as The Who on 30 June 1964 and 2 November 1964, but as The High Numbers on the 14 occasions in between.

I WAS THERE: VAL MABBS

I was born and brought up in Harrow, so I lived in the area where The Who played a lot. I was a Mod and, particularly from 1964, was very involved in the Mod scene. There was an awful lot going on in the area at that time.

I think the first time I saw The Who was actually when they were appearing at the Railway as The High Numbers. I'm sure I had seen them before that, but the earliest I had noted is mid 64 when they were at the Railway. I believe it was on the 28 July.

I remember us Mods gathering at the top of the hill in front of the pub, by the railway station, and there being a bit of chat about this band, The High Numbers, that were going to be on at the Railway that evening, and it being talked about them being The Who.

Quite a number of Mods had gathered there with their scooters. Then we all queued up at the pub. The frontage was right on the hill, and then you went down the slope at the side which took you down to the basement area at the back of the pub, where you went in to see the band. There was quite a long queue waiting to get in to see them.

Girls didn't have scooters, it was only the guys who had scooters. Sometimes they took you on their scooter, but having almost come off the back of someone's scooter once, it wasn't always a good idea. Not all of the guys were good at riding them! The Railway was only a train stop away for me, or a short bus ride. To see them at anytime, which I did quite a number of times, was an experience because they were quite different, and I saw a lot of bands at that time.

They were extremely loud, particularly in that venue because it was very small for the volume they created. It was always very dark. They had one small bit of red lighting in there and it was very smoky of course, because a lot of guys smoked then. It was quite trendy to do that.

It was a brilliant atmosphere. Some people might call it a seedy atmosphere but to me it wasn't. It was a good venue in that you were there with the band and the music was all around you. It was great – people danced and people just stood there and watched. It was very much part of the Mod scene. That pub has now gone. It was knocked down a while back and what's there now is called Moon House. I think it is quite nice that they've retained a little bit of the history there, although I'm not sure why it's specifically Moon as opposed to any of the others.

HARROW WEALD MEMORIAL HALL

SUMMER 1964, HARROW

I WAS THERE: MIKE BISHOP

I saw The Who several times when they performed at Harrow Weald Memorial Hall, North London. I believe that at this time they were still using the name The High Numbers when performing in Watford. I had several friends who saw them at Watford. I would guess they appeared at the Trade Union Hall in Watford, or 'down the Trade' as it was known. The Memorial Hall was quite small and, comparing it with other venues in the area, would have had a fire certificate for 200-300 people. It was rarely full because it didn't have an alcohol licence, (this put off most of my friends). The Railway Hotel Harrow was not far away and this was even smaller but had alcohol. Although I went there regularly, I don't remember seeing them there.

The audience at the Memorial Hall was almost entirely made up of Mods. As a rocker, I was almost alone but contrary to most stories about that time we weren't constantly fighting and there was never any problem. Many of the Mods came, like myself, from Borehamwood.

Other bands performing regularly at the Memorial Hall were Cliff Bennett and the Rebel Rousers, The Pretty Things and later, The Moody Blues. The Who were by far the most professional. The other bands came on stage and tuned their instruments, checked their sound balances, discussed what they were going to play and started off. The Pretty Things didn't even balance their speakers, which meant people moving around the hall to find a spot where the sound seemed OK.

The Who however, did all this unnoticed and unheard behind the curtains. The lights were dimmed and then the curtains opened simultaneously with the opening number. They then continued with their set without stopping or chatting among themselves. The same with their second set. I can't remember the songs they performed (possibly Benny Spellman's 'Fortune Teller'?), but I was struck by Pete Townshend's astonishing ability to play with the distortion that he deliberately induced with his speakers. I've never seen him do it on film or seen anyone else do it in such a controlled manner.

There is no other record of The Who appearing at the Memorial Hall.

GOLDHAWK SOCIAL CLUB

31 JULY 1964, SHEPHERD'S BUSH, LONDON

I WAS THERE: RICHARD WHITE

We were just a small band from south London called The Rivals playing the London circuit: a three-guitars, drums, two-a-penny band. We were semi-pro. We all had daytime jobs and we used to get the odd gig here and there. One day we were offered a gig in west London at the Goldhawk Club. They weren't The Who then. I think they were called The High Numbers. They were just absolutely amazing. I'd never heard such a dynamic band in my life and they seemed to have a cult following at the Goldhawk Club.

As people they were very friendly and approachable. They were quite complimentary about us, although I don't think we were anywhere near their standard! We were just a bog standard band from the time doing stuff like 'La Bamba' and rock classics that everyone did. They were in a different league altogether. They were doing a lot of American material at that time. They used to do a really powerful version of 'Ooh Poo Pah Doo'. They were really into the American stuff – R&B and soul type stuff. They used to give it the full Who treatment, with crashing guitar chords and Keith Moon thrashing around the drum kit. The Goldhawk Club was larger than a big house. It was more like a large back room of a pub. I think it was licensed, because I'm sure we had a drink with Pete Townshend afterwards. Pete complimented me on my bass playing. He said he liked it. He was a nice guy; I think he was the brains

The Rivals: the south London band who supported The Who at the Goldhawk Social Club

behind the band. He told me they'd worked on Roger Daltrey's voice. It was too high-pitched for them at one time and they wanted to bring it down a bit. They did it by getting him to sing into a tape recorder.

We used to bump into them later on. Roger Daltrey always had a crowd of girls round him. Keith was totally barmy. You'd be travelling somewhere by train and he'd be running through the railway carriages. He was very extrovert, but very likeable and very sociable. He loved talking to people and loved having a laugh. We met them quite a few times at places like the Marquee Club. They would see us and approach us, and that was after they had had hits. They were still the same guys we met at the Goldhawk Club; they were good guys.

HIPPODROME
9 AUGUST 1964, BRIGHTON

I WAS THERE: FRANK HINTON

They were called The High Numbers when I saw them. They

appeared at the Hippodrome as a support act when they supported Gerry and the Pacemakers. The other artistes were The Nashville Teens, Elkie Brooks – I remember both of them – and Valerie McCullam, whom I don't remember and have never heard of since. The High Numbers were at the bottom of the bill. All I remember is Daltrey tossing his microphone high and expertly catching it and Townshend striking his guitar in an aggressive windmill action. They are still doing it 50 years later. The audience, who hadn't come to see them, did not appreciate the mic tossing.

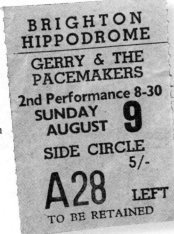

My friend says they often played in Brighton as The High Numbers and he saw them at the Florida Rooms. He said that the purple hearts he had taken at the time meant that he couldn't now remember anything at all about the gig. That isn't my excuse. I was a Mod by inclination – I followed fashion and wore the clothes – but I never took any drugs. I was never offered any and never even saw any.

OPERA HOUSE

16 AUGUST 1964, BLACKPOOL

I WAS THERE: SYD BLOOM

They were still called The High Numbers. They were backing Adrienne Posta and The Beatles and The Kinks. They were doing all kinds of Beach Boys stuff at the time. They looked a bit like The Beach Boys, that surfing stuff, largely at the behest of Keith Moon, I suspect.

When they came in the car park afterwards, I was talking to Pete Townshend and he was talking about Adrienne Posta and he said 'she started sniffing around The Beatles and got nowhere and then she started sniffing around The Kinks and got nowhere. And then, he said, 'she tried to park herself on us.' And that's how I remember what the line up was, because of Pete's anecdote. Otherwise I wouldn't have remembered.

I WAS THERE: STEVE GOMERSALL

When The Who were playing the Opera House at Blackpool as The High Numbers, John Entwistle was listening to The Beatles in his dressing room through the little PA speaker. The Fab Four were performing 'A Hard Day's Night' and John was allegedly singing 'It's been a hard day's night and I've been wanking like a dog' because he knew that the audience couldn't hear the words over the girls screaming.

I WAS THERE: WILLIAM WALTON, AGE 16

Myself and five boyhood friends embarked on a week's holiday in Blackpool. It was especially memorable as one of my friends' mums had managed to get us tickets to the Winter Gardens for a show featuring The Beatles. I believe it was on a Sunday. Unbeknown to us, on this same bill were The Kinks, The Hearts, Adrienne Posta and The High Numbers – later to become The Who. I can recollect being blown away by 'You Really Got Me' by The Kinks and also the on stage performances of Pete Townshend and Keith Moon. They sang 'I Can't Explain' and some other songs and the raw rock and roll on show that night totally eclipsed The Beatles, who I was never a great fan of. The memory of a packed house, mostly of hysterical females throwing sweets and other items when The Beatles were on, is something never to be forgotten.

CORN EXCHANGE

31 AUGUST 1964, ROCHESTER

I WAS THERE: KAY HUNT (NEE PETERS), AGE 15

Every Monday I went to the RSG club at Rochester Corn Exchange.

It was on Monday 31 August 1964 that I first saw them. At that time they were called The High Numbers. I wrote in my diary that they were fabulous and that I had got their autographs and a bit of Pete Townshend's plectrum that had broken off.

I got Pete, Keith and John's autographs but for some reason John signed his name 'John Brown'. Of course, at that time I didn't know any different as I didn't know their names. I gave my book to Roger Daltrey but he just pushed it away.

I remember standing, with my hands on the stage, enjoying the music with Pete Townshend ramming his guitar into his amplifier and Keith Moon going crazy playing the drums. One of his drum sticks broke and I tried to get it but another girl was quicker than me. As they finished their gig, Keith pushed his drum kit over and kicked it around the stage. They were certainly different from any other band that had been there before.

The appearance at the Corn Exchange in Rochester on this date is another previously undocumented gig.

RAILWAY HOTEL

JULY–OCTOBER 1964, WEALDSTONE

I WAS THERE: BRIAN CHATTERS

I was a student at Bristol University but my home was in Eastcote, Middlesex. In the summer of that year, a pal and I used to go and

Top: The High Numbers on stage at The Railway Hotel and (below) Roger Daltrey shows off his dance moves following the gig

see The Who regularly, on a Thursday if my memory serves me right, at the Railway Hotel just outside of Harrow and Wealdstone station when they called themselves The High Numbers.

I believe that some of the scenes in the documentary about the group were shot there (screened in early 1966). The Railway Hotel was a public house which had a room in a separate building where bands performed. The reason we went to hear them, apart from the usual reason – to chat up girls, was that they played a number of R&B songs. The ones that I remember the most were 'Heat Wave' by Martha and the Vandellas and 'Spoonful' by Howlin' Wolf.

They were beginning to appeal to the Mods at that time although the audience was very mixed. My pal and I were not Mods and we were not Rockers either. We did get some banter from some of the Mods who called us Rockers but it was always light hearted and fun. I do not recall any crowd problems, although the room in which they performed was always packed out.

The band did not smash up their equipment in those days – no doubt they could not afford to replace things! Pete Townshend played his guitar with his windmill action as he did in later times and Keith Moon was just as wild on the drums. There was one incident where he managed to cause his kit to fall apart and he asked if anyone had a screwdriver or knife. At that time, I carried a small penknife – nothing sinister about such things in those days and the blade was only about one inch long – so I offered it to Keith. He never returned it! They did not wear obvious mod clothes at the time. Their dress was very ordinary but I think Roger Daltrey may have worn paisley shirts.

The band played from about 8pm to 10.30pm with a short interval. Pubs closed at 10.30 in those days. They always played the same EP during the interval. It was called 'Singing the Blues' which featured 'It Will Stand' by the Showmen, 'Ooh Poo Pah Doo' by Jessie Hill, 'I Like It Like That' by Chris Kenner, and 'Mother-in-Law' by Ernie K-Doe. It gives you some idea of The Who's musical influences. I think they also featured 'Ooh Poo Pah Doo' in their act.

The Who performed as The High Numbers on fourteen Tuesdays at the Railway between July and October of 1964.

Henry Wright (second from right), drummer for Lulu and the Luvvers on the night they shared the bill with The High Numbers

KELVIN HALL

4 SEPTEMBER 1964, GLASGOW

I WAS THERE: HENRY WRIGHT

I was a drummer and I was lucky enough to be asked to join Lulu and the Luvvers that night. On the bill were The High Numbers, later named The Who, and the Paramounts, later called Procul Harum. Top of the bill was Dave Berry. I remember I thought The Who were exceptional and I had an argument with my mate that my wife remembers to this day. I thought they would be big and he didn't. I guess I won! After that, I would go and see The Who at the Marquee and once we played a TV date with them and Keith asked if he could use my drums, which he did. There was no damage to the drums but he broke my sticks. I also remember a night in London with my brother, Tommy from The Luvvers, Leslie Harvie and Pete Townshend going on a pub crawl in London. We ended up at the Scotch of St James where we proceeded to take the mick out of Brian Jones from The Rolling Stones. Good days.

CORN EXCHANGE

5 OCTOBER 1964, ROCHESTER

I WAS THERE: KEITH CRUST

Along with my mates, Malcolm Burch, Bob Thomas and Billy Price, I was at The High Numbers show at the Rochester Corn Exchange. We all parked our Lambretta scooters inside the building in front of the steps that went up to the ballroom! It was such a great night. Keith Moon smashing up his drums and Pete Townshend whacking his guitar on his amp! At the time, I had just bought a Vox guitar for £16, which was a lot of money then, and there was Pete Townshend smashing up a Fender Stratocaster!

I WAS THERE: KAY HUNT

After seeing them in August, the next time that I saw them was again at the Corn Exchange on 5 October. I wrote in my diary that they had changed their name to The Who. I can still remember after all this time how I felt watching The Who perform – they were truly very unique.

I WAS THERE: SHEENA POPE, AGE 18

I was 18 and a Mod. I saw The Who at the Corn Exchange a couple of times in 1964 with my friends Fred McDonald, Brenda LePage and her boyfriend Roger. It's a long time ago but I believe it was on Monday nights. It was difficult to get there at the time as I went to London to work each day. They were a great group, not the usual good-looking boys, but quite dramatic and loved by Mods. I think they were then called The High Numbers. It was pre The Who and I loved them!

Shena Pope after passing her driving test and no longer having to use her boyfriend's scooter

CORN EXCHANGE

28 NOVEMBER 1964, CHELMSFORD

I WAS THERE: BARRY THOMPSON, AGE 20

We had never heard of them before but they came to play at the weekly Saturday night dance. They used to have dances every Saturday night at the Corn Exchange at Chelmsford. In those days they didn't sell alcohol, they only sold soft drinks and you used to have to go in and pay your money. If you wanted to come out they put a mark on the back of your hand that you could only see under an ultra violet light. We used to go in and then nip out to the pub for a drink or two and nip back to the dance after.

Barry was only 20 when he saw The Who, but was still amazed by how young they seemed

We didn't know from one week to the next who was coming – this particular week I remember the Brighton riots were on with the Mods and Rockers, and they said that this group could come. When they were announced on stage the compere said 'we don't know who they are but here are The Who!' And they were fantastic, very young and very talented. They did quite a wide range of songs including 'Dancing in the Street'. I think we all knew that we were seeing something very rare and special as we all stopped dancing and stood and just watched in amazement. Pete whirled his arm like a windmill even in those days. They were absolutely amazing and I'm pretty sure that they'd gone through the stuff that they'd got and they were asking for requests and they'd play anything. They weren't very old. I don't know how old they were but I think that somebody had to drive them. I don't think that they could drive themselves. I mean, I was only 20 but they looked so young. But they were so good. You wouldn't believe how good they were for their age.

From memory, I paid something like half a crown to see them, which is about 12.5p, and you knew that they were going to be something special if they stuck together. They couldn't have got paid much for those gigs they were doing. When I saw them, they carried their own stuff in and carried their own stuff out and took it to bits. At Chelmsford Corn Exchange there were all sorts of people who used to come in those days. Georgie Fame used to play there regularly. He played there before he made his records and after he was famous for the same fee because people were loyal to him. When he was having his half hour break, he used to come to the pub. Jimi Hendrix came there, The Moody Blues came, John Lee Hooker, Howling Wolf. I saw them all there, just on Saturday night dances.

Sadly the Corn Exchange isn't there anymore – it's a shopping centre. That hall was so well used. They used to do roller-skating there on a Friday night and dancing on a Saturday and on Sundays nothing happened in those days as everything was shut. I love my music. My heart is in the 60s. My children, when I told them that I'd seen The Who before they'd made a record, were quite stunned. My grandchildren obviously know who The Who are and always say 'Grandad saw them before anybody'. They can't believe such a big band used to play such small venues.

MARQUEE CLUB

24 NOVEMBER AND 1, 8, 15, 22 & 29 DECEMBER 1964, LONDON

I WAS THERE: IAN GARNER

I used to live in south London in the Sixties and every Tuesday would go to the Marquee to see The Who. There was always a support group that usually received abuse from the audience, which was generally a 80/20 split between boys and girls. It cost seven and six (37p) to get in. Most of the lads seemed to be noting the chords that Pete was playing.

They were very loud as it was a small place and it seemed to me that Roger was out of it lot of the time. They did lots of covers – Tamla stuff, 'Heat Wave', 'Please Please Please', James Brown stuff – very well. I also saw them at the Wimbledon Palais and for some reason Roger didn't show up. However, it didn't seem to make much difference!

1965 This was the first year The Who entered the mainstream, thanks to the success of their first two singles. They made numerous appearances on radio and television, most notably on TV's *Ready Steady Go!*

The band performed continuously in the UK throughout the year, playing over 250 gigs, as well as shows in France and Scandinavia. Their act at this time consisted mostly of Tamla Motown and R&B covers, but more and more original material appeared as the year wore on. The instrument destruction that marked the band's early years was at its height at this stage.The Who's first single, 'I Can't Explain', was released on 15 January.

I WASN'T THERE: NIGEL SUTCLIFFE

I initially heard 'Carrot Springs' on Radio Luxembourg – that's what I thought 'I Can't Explain' was called at first – and I then found the Brunswick singles. I played 'Pictures of Lily' over and over. When I got *A Quick One* I played it on the school classical player the loudest I could in the assembly rooms. I was at St Bees School in Cumberland. It was a boarding school with enforced haircuts and fagging. I was 15 and starting to rebel.

I WASN'T THERE: LINDA SADLER

I attended Tottenham High School, a small girls' grammar school where behavioural standards were very high. Apparently a girl – whose name I can't remember – had been absent from school for a few days and somehow the school got information that she was at Keith Moon's flat in Finsbury Park. Our headmistress drove to the address and knocked at the door, which was opened by Keith. She asked for the girl, who came to the door dressed only in a pair of tights! She demanded the girl get dressed and she drove her back to school. It seems a bit unlikely now but the same headmistress apparently confronted Dave Clark when he held rehearsals at the Tottenham Royal ballroom, which was next door to our school. She asked if he could rehearse at a different time to avoid hordes of schoolgirls hanging round the door waiting for him to come out.

I WAS THERE: JOHN SCHOLLAR

Keith Moon rang me up one day and said 'I'm coming over.' And he came over on the bus from Wembley, because he never used to drive, and this was when he made his first record, which was 'I Can't Explain'. He came in and he'd got a pile of records under his arm. He was getting stuff in from the States at that time – Beach Boys, Jan and Dean – because we were both into all this surfing music. He put this record on an old Dansette record player and he said 'what do you reckon to this lot? Who do you think it is?' I said 'I know it's you, you daft sod.' I knew straight away it was him because I could tell by his drumming.

I remember when my dad was seriously ill and they told him to move out of London because of all the fumes. I rang Keith's mum and said 'oh, my mum and dad are moving Friday' and I gave her the address and said they wanted to keep in touch. A couple of nights after, there was a knock at the door and there was a Rolls Royce outside with a chauffeur in it and Keith came in with his wife. I said 'what are you doing?' He said 'I've come to say goodbye to your dad, mate.' He drove right across the other side of London to do that.

NEW THEATRE

17 JANUARY 1965, OXFORD

I WAS THERE: NIGEL MOLDEN

It was a Sunday concert at the New Theatre in Oxford. The band closed the first half of a show, which was headlined by PJ Proby. All that was known about them was the little that had been written in the *NME* about 'I Can't Explain', which was released at this time. The equipment had been set up stage right, presumably to facilitate the other performers on the show. My clearest memory is that they played considerably louder than any of the other bands. I also remember Roger Daltrey deliberately dropping the microphone onto the stage in a destructive kind of way. By the end of the short set, Pete Townshend was also thrusting the end of his guitar neck into the speaker stack, presumably to create a feedback effect. The band certainly made an impact on the music scene. Some eighteen months later we had at school a young French assistant. It was very unusual for popular music to be discussed at school but young Pierre was very keen to tell us sixth formers that his favourite group was 'Ze Woo'.

LOCARNO BALLROOM

3 FEBRUARY 1965, STEVENAGE

I WAS THERE: MAUREEN BROWNING

My sister and I saw The Who on many occasions, especially in their earlier years. We were also very lucky to know them fairly well and met

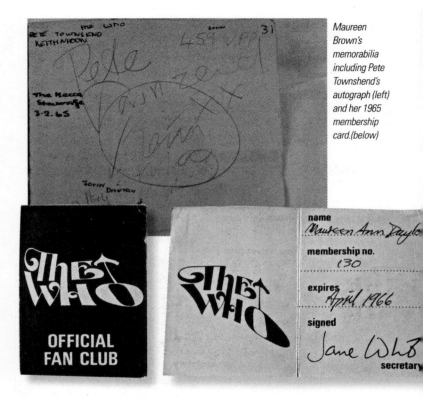

Maureen Brown's memorabilia including Pete Townshend's autograph (left) and her 1965 membership card.(below)

them many times, usually going backstage. My sister was three years older than me and we were very lucky that we had great parents who realised we loved music and bought us tickets for – and were 'teenager taxis' to and from – many a live show at what was one of the very best times for music.

I have many examples of their autographs in both my own and my late sister's autograph books, as well as signed photos. Some of the sets of autographs have John Entwistle signing as John Brown, a surname he used for a while. He also used the surname Alison for a time too, which I think was the name of a girlfriend.

John and Keith also wrote their addresses in my book, and they used to keep in touch and let us know if they were playing near us. Phone

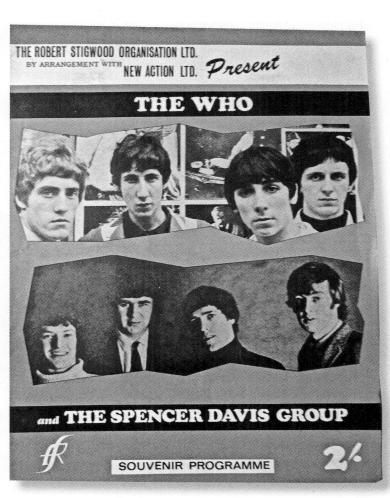

numbers were Belgravia 8989 and Wembley 1812 and various address are: 74 Kensington Park Road, London; 84 Eaton Place, Sloane Square, London; 134 Chaplin Road, Wembley. There is also a note from Feb 1965 that John's car reg was 459 VPP, but why that is in my autograph book I have no idea! I also have a small signature for John Daltrey, with a note I wrote saying he was their road manager.

I WAS THERE: CHRISTINE MACLEAN

I have searched my childhood diaries for references of when I went to see The Who. It seems like I was quite a fan! I lived near Stevenage New Town and most bands came to the Mecca, or Locarno Ballroom. I went to see The Who there in 1965 on Wednesday 3 February, Wednesday 14 July and Wednesday 3 November. I also saw them at the Bowes Lyon in Stevenage on Friday 18 June.

I WAS THERE: DAVID MACLEAN, AGE 15

'You going tonight?' 'Yeah, I'm going.' That's me and Snotty Glynn talking about seeing The Who at the Mecca Locarno Ballroom in, I don't know – maybe 1964? It was the first time they came

David Maclean, with his suspended bridge acoustic guitar

to Stevenage New Town, the Mod capital of North Hertfordshire. Snotty had seen The Who at the 100 Club in Wardour Street a couple of weeks before. Snotty was a proper Loona. He had all the gear – a two tone tonik suit from Mr John on Carnaby Steet, Hush Puppies and bright red socks, but no scooter. He couldn't afford one, not like Jenks and the gang, all covered in parkas and chrome. Me and Snotty met outside the Mecca around 8pm along with Jenks, Smithy and Clivey Bogbrush (on account of his hair). We were underage, but no one seemed to care, least of all the bouncers. Once inside it was really rocking with music blasting out from the Stones, Yardbirds, Kinks and – of course – Tamla Motown.

Squeezed right up front next to the stage surrounded by blokes and just a few birds, the band was the only thing on my mind and when they exploded onto the stage with 'I Can't Explain', the place erupted. Me and Snotty went crazy. I was a spotty 15 year old just teaching myself guitar and Townshend was God. I had never seen or heard anything like it. The Rickenbacker howled and roared into action, followed by great arching windmills from this guy from the streets. Totally original. He wore a brown and cream check jacket, or maybe it was the shirt, cream strides and brown alligator shoes. Smartly cut Mod with attitude – I couldn't take my eyes off him! What style! The set was loud, brash and unforgettable with the ritual demolition of drums, guitar and amplifier. What a night. I caught the 802 bus home to Bandley Hill with Snotty. That was the start of a Who love affair which continues to this day and includes *Live at Leeds* – and *Live at Leeds 2*!

The Who appeared on UK TV programme *Ready Steady Go!* more times than any other artist– a total of 18. Their first appearance on RSG! was their second ever TV performance, having been on *The Beat Room* in August 1964. They performed 'I Can't Explain' and one other number.

READY STEADY GO!

JANUARY 1965 - DECEMBER 1966, REDIFFUSION (ITV)

I WAS THERE: PETE WRIGHT

I was an apprentice toolmaker and I was outside working on my motorbike. My mum 'said *Ready Steady Go!* is about to start' and I said 'I must finish this off'. She went back indoors and came out again and said 'come and look at this crap that's on here now'. And it was The Who. I missed a bit of it, but they were doing 'Daddy Rolling Stone', it was so completely different from anything else I'd ever seen.

I got back to work on the Monday morning, at the apprentice

training school, and I said 'did you see that crap on *Ready Steady Go!* on Friday?' And someone said 'they're at the Locarno Wednesday night.' You could see the Locarno Ballroom across the railway line, out of our factory window. And so we went down there. I've still got my first wage packet. Three pounds three and a penny (£3.15) and there's no tax and no national insurance because I didn't make the threshold for those two things. And I'm standing there on £3 a week and I stood on tiptoe at the bar to make them think I was 18 and bought a light ale for 1/6 (7p), a big outlay, and he's smashing his bloody Rickenbacker to pieces. Those Rickenbacker guitars were £199. And that was it. The seed was sown. I've seen them over a hundred times since.

LE DISQUE A GO! GO!

3 MARCH 1965, LANSDOWNE, BOURNEMOUTH

I WAS THERE: CHRIS FERGUSON

I had a band called Nite People who were based in Bournemouth around the period that The Who played in Bournemouth. We played the whole of the UK and Europe. I met Keith at a party. He came to a friend of mine's 21st birthday. The both of us being drummers, we started chatting and it came from that.

Chris Ferguson of Nite People (left) at a party in Bournemouth

He had a girlfriend in Bournemouth – I think they eventually got married – and he kept coming down here and I went out on a couple of drinking sessions with him. He was a great guy and not as crazy as people made him out to be. That's as far as it went though and we never became big mates or anything.

Keith's girlfriend was Kim Kerrigan and lived in Bournemouth when he met her on 3 March 1965. She was to become Mrs Keith Moon.

TRADE UNION HALL

MARCH 1965, WATFORD

I WAS THERE: GORDON HEATH, AGE 17

I lived in Pinner during the Sixties and used to go to live gigs in the area to see mainly local groups. The term 'band' was not yet in use at that time, unless you were talking about one of the big bands like Ted Heath's. My nickname at school was Ted because of the Ted Heath Band's widespread fame.

I used to see The Who at a venue in Watford, near Watford Junction Station, where they played in the old Trade Union Hall, known as The Trade. If I remember, many gigs were on a Sunday evening. I would go on the train from Hatch End station where I would meet my friend Derek who travelled from Harrow and Wealdstone station. He would stick his head out of the window as the train came into Hatch End and I would run to jump in the compartment. This was in the days of individual compartments. It was also before we had cars. I didn't get my first car until I was 19, in 1966.

I had heard about The Who before I saw them and I knew they were going to be good as soon as the curtains opened for their set. Groups playing at the Trade all used their own sound equipment and the amount of amplifiers and speakers on the stage for The Who was more than I had ever seen before. They were stacked from floor to ceiling on both sides of the stage. When they played, the volume of sound was deafening.

I'm sure I am suffering from some hearing loss now because of going to those gigs. The notes from John Entwistle's bass guitar were so low that you didn't so much hear them as feel them through your body. Your chest seemed to vibrate on the inside. Keith Moon was the most manic drummer around at the time, and probably ever. Roger Daltrey would often carry a bunch of steel rings, about the diameter of a tambourine, which he would thrash against the mike stand in time with the beat. This was part of the violent undertone that was part of The Who's act.

Then there was Pete Townshend and his guitar. At some stage in the act he would stand in front of one the speakers, his back to the audience, take both hands off the guitar and push it against the speaker with his body. Somehow, he would make that guitar play itself. I assume the sound energy from the speaker was somehow causing the guitar strings to vibrate. Sometimes he would thrust the guitar really hard and I would be thinking about the cost of repairing or replacing the equipment, but Pete didn't seem to care. I never saw him smash up a guitar – I think that came later on in their career.

The sound that The Who made live was never even close to being captured on any recording. You just had to have been there to know what it was like. It's hard to remember details of individual gigs from so long ago but I do remember seeing The Who at The Trade not long after 'I Can't Explain' was released. They ended their set and the evening with that song and I remember walking back to the station with the sound of it ringing in my ears, it had been so loud. I decided I had to go out and buy the single, partly to try to help the boys get into the charts, because we considered them to be one of 'our' groups. I used to write on my records the date when I bought them and my copy of that single shows 13 March 1965.

As an aside, The Trade was always packed but it was well run, with plenty of doormen to make sure there was no trouble. But my friends and I did used to joke that if you got stabbed in there, it was so crowded that nobody would know until the end of the night when you fell to the floor.

Gordon buying 'I Can't Explain' on 13 March 1965 after hearing it played live would suggest a previously undocumented appearance at the Trade.

GOLDHAWK SOCIAL CLUB

20 MARCH 1965, SHEPHERD'S BUSH, LONDON

I WAS THERE: KEITH ROWLEY

I used to regularly watch The Who at the Goldhawk Club, Shepherd's Bush and I remember seeing them there on a Saturday night shortly after 'I Can't Explain' became a hit. Whenever they were down the Goldhawk Club I would go because that was just a ten-minute walk down the road for me. I was there with my fiancée at the time. They'd had a hit with that and being a local band it was absolutely jam-packed.

The Goldhawk Club was just a big house along a string of houses, a big terrace. They used to play in a room that was probably not a lot bigger than somebody's large front room. And it was absolutely rammed. You couldn't move to dance.

On this particular night some nutter suddenly started swinging a baseball bat around his head and you could suddenly have got another 50 people in! The group were looking on in horror but they suddenly went into 'I Can't Explain' and that helped defuse the situation and prevent what would have been a riot!

TRADE UNION HALL

21 MARCH 1965, WATFORD

I WAS THERE: VAL MABBS

The Trade was the Trade Union Hall, a working men's club which became known by us as 'the Trade' because it was a bit more trendy that way, I guess. My diary for Sunday 21 March 1965 says: 'Went to Trade. Queue right up past the station corner for The Who.' And then I've written: 'The Who were marvellous. Walls were running with water. So packed.' I remember this one very clearly. It was absolutely jam packed in there. Everybody was just watching them and the walls of the place were literally running with sweat.

At that point, they were doing their smashing up thing, because at the end of it, Pete Townshend would be whirling his guitar around, bashing it into the stack of amps behind him. As far as I'm aware they were real amps but they might not have been, because I think they used dummy ones at times. They'd have the whole stack of Marshall amps and they certainly produced the sound that indicated that they had quite a bit of power behind them. Pete Townshend would bounce the guitar off the stage, as he did, and it was just very different.

I also saw them there on a couple of other dates, 7th and 29th November 1964, where I noted seeing them but hadn't actually written a great deal about it. I saw them a number of times at the Trade.

For Watford, we would normally take the train because the Trade Union Hall was right next to Watford Junction station on the mainline down to Harrow & Wealdstone and Headstone Lane. There was a little pub almost opposite the Trade and that's where people used to gather and have a drink or stand around, even though we were too young really. Mods would congregate around the time of the gigs before going in. The whole Mod thing was a lot about standing around and being seen, wearing the right clothes and being a part of that movement.

I WAS THERE: MICHAEL WILSON

We were there! My girlfriend, now my wife, followed all the live bands in those days. They were exciting times. Moonie was a complete nutter – in the nicest possible way! Townshend also had his moments. We first saw The Who in Watford in the Trade Hall in Station Road near the train station.

Then a few weeks later they were at the college in Hemel. We used to get the bus from Abbots Langley to Hemel Hempstead with our crazy clothes on and our weird hair cuts. When we look around today, nothing much has changed. Great days!

PARR HALL

22 MARCH 1965, WARRINGTON

I WAS THERE: JOHN HEWISON, AGE 17

Every Monday there were top groups at the Parr Hall, including The Kinks, The Moody Blues, The Hollies, Them with Van Morrison, The Nashville Teens and many more. I was fortunate to see them and especially The Who. It was 50 years ago and memories are vague but I can still see Keith Moon completely trashing his drums very early in the set and borrowing the support act's drums.

I don't remember too much of their set but I do recall Pete Townshend and Roger Daltrey destroying their guitars and amps and leaving the stage in tatters, smoking and nearly in flames, with the crowd standing open mouthed in disbelief.

THE RHODES CENTRE

27 MARCH 1965, BISHOP'S STORTFORD

I WAS THERE: ADRIAN JAMES

They played with a supporting group, the Cops 'N' Robbers. They smashed their equipment. It seemed to start when Keith Moon broke a drum stick whilst playing, which he threw into the crowd. It was

Saturday, 27th March
Mark Gold Promotions present
THE WHO & COPS 'N' ROBBERS

Tuesday, 30th March
GRAND FINALS
of the Herts & Essex Beat Contest

MORNING COFFEES · LUNCHES · AFTERNOON TEAS
OLD HOUSE CAFE
High Street, (Windhill) **Bishop's Stortford**
Telephone: 4673
Everything home made, including cakes to order
Also a range of gifts for every occasion

STAR ARTISTES, BANDS AND SHOWS FOR EVERY OCCASION
BEAT GROUPS, WEST END FLOOR SHOWS, GALA ACTS
CHILDREN'S ENTERTAINERS, ETC.
FOR ALL ENTERTAINMENT
Wheeler Entertainments Ltd.
MANAGEMENT — AGENCY — PRODUCTION
Sawbridgeworth   SAWBRIDGEWORTH
2302   HERTS.

For details of advertisement rates in this Programme
telephone Bishop's Stortford 4735

Printed at R B W PRESS, Water Lane, Bishop's Stortford. Tel. 2976

FOR THE BEST IN LIVE
ENTERTAINMENT

★   ★   ★

RHODES CENTRE
BISHOP'S STORTFORD

★   ★   ★

Attractions for
MARCH 1965

During the interval Order your
TAXI from
F. W. PIGRAM

Bishop's Stortford 51634

It will then be at the door when you require it.

thrown back at him. Keith then seemed to kick over his drum set, standing on the bass drum and putting his stick through the drum skins. Pete was playing and getting feedback from the amps.

He started to bounce his guitar off the floor on the stage and also jammed his guitar into the amps and speakers until he broke his guitar. I have the flyers advertising the forthcoming attraction from October 1964 through to February 1966, with The Who's autograph on the April 1965 one.

I WAS THERE: JULIE KITCHENER, AGE 16

I went to almost all the concerts held at Rhodes that year but of course The Who weren't too famous then. The first 40 or 50 girls admitted on the door got in free so if a fairly well known group was coming we would queue from about 4pm, with rollers in our hair, get our hands stamped on admission at 8pm, disappear to my parents' house which was in the same road as Rhodes and then turn up for the evening all dolled up. Often the groups would arrive early to set up so we got to see them and maybe get autographs.

We were just lucky that this promoter, Alan Goldsmith, got these groups before they became really famous. We saw all the stars. When The Animals came it was five shillings (25p). Because it was such a lot of money we were allowed to pay it in two instalments. With The Who, we were frightened that they were going to smash up their guitars.

I WAS THERE: ANDY PEEBLES

I saw The Who at the Rhodes Centre in 1965. It might explain why I spent 46 years in broadcasting.

TOWN HALL

1 APRIL 1965, WEMBLEY

I WAS THERE: HELEN KAYES, AGE 18

I, and my now husband Peter saw them at the Harrow Tech College Rag Ball. They had probably been booked as an up-and-coming-but-not-yet-made-it band. But 'I Can't Explain' had just entered the charts so it was very exciting to see them. Donovan also played at the same event – he was also just breaking into the charts.

Helen Kayes and her husband-to-be, both saw The Who at Harrow Tech College Rag

DACORUM COLLEGE

7 APRIL 1965, HEMEL HEMPSTEAD

I WAS THERE: JOHN DEALEY

I was a big Who fan from the beginning. At school one of my friends had a copy of The High Numbers' 'I'm The Face' which of course was The Who in their previous life. I bought all the early singles and albums on Brunswick and then came the opportunity to see them live at the Dacorum College prior to the release of 'My Generation'.

I snapped up a ticket and was at the front, shoulders on the stage. What a performance! The entire place was going mad as Townshend smashed his speaker with his guitar for the ultimate feedback and there was Moon going berserk on the drums and a young Daltrey and Entwistle both doing their own thing.

We never had many live acts in town but when they did they played the Dacorum College, acts such as Them, The Undertakers, The Naturals and The Bo Street Runners. All of them were kicked into touch by the electric performance of The Who.

I WAS THERE: MICK LYNHAM, AGE 16

Hemel is split into areas and every area had a youth club. My mum ran Gadebridge youth club and she did the bookings at Dacorum College to raise money for the youth clubs, because the clubs had to be subsidised. It used to be about once a month that they used to have live acts down there. And it was my mother's job to book them through a booking agent. In the Sixties

The young Mick Lynham (centre) was lucky enough to have a mum who booked the bands for the local youth club

groups were coming out here, there and everywhere. Some lasted, some didn't. We used to go all the time to see different acts. They'd have a local group and a main act come out of London. We had Screaming Lord Sutch there. He was rubbish.

When my mum said 'we've got The Who booked' the first thing we said was 'who? Oh yeah, that's a new group that's out.' The Who were booked prior to them being super duper because

I think just literally the weekend that they appeared their record had gone to number one in the hit parade. They were under contract and were trying to get out of it.

Dacorum College is now being refurbished. And where The Who played was still there until several years ago but they've knocked a lot of it down. It was a very small venue. A little stage. Not very big at all. And the numbers we used to get wasn't thousands of people.Far from it. You're probably talking hundreds. But there was loads of people there.

They didn't smash up their equipment like they did later on in life. As they finished, they pushed the drums, kicked the drums over a bit, Keith Moon, and a few of the amps went over. But not all of 'em – far from it. And none of the stuff where they started sticking guitars through amps and stuff like that. My mum at the time thought 'oh my God. What's happening here?' Because she hadn't seen anything like it.

My sister actually went out with Keith Moon for a little while. She was a little bit younger than me, a bit of a groupie. She went to a few more of their gigs. I don't remember going backstage but my sister probably did with my mother. My mother would have been backstage while they were on. We were out the front. It didn't have a bar or anything. There was no drink. I certainly wouldn't have been allowed to drink even if there had been a bar. My mother would have been on top of me like a ton of bricks!

'I Can't Explain' appeared on the UK charts on 20 February 1965, reaching its highest position of number 8 on 17 April 1965.

I WAS THERE: SUE STOW, AGE 14

I saw The High Numbers and The Who. My first favourite record was 'I Can't Explain'. I played it over and over and would dance in my bedroom. When I got The Who's first album and joined the fan club, I was at odds with most of my friends as most were into the Stones or The Beatles. I was No 201 in the fan club.

Going to Dacorum College was brilliant. My Dad helped out in a local youth club and volunteered to help out that evening so I begged him to take me. We were first in the venue so I stood right at the stage. I could touch Roger Daltrey's feet but I only had eyes for Keith Moon – he was brilliant! They were loud and so exciting to watch, ending with the usual smashing of items on stage. My Dad wasn't impressed. It was an amazing evening.

Sue Stow, Who fan club member No 201, got to see them at Dacorum College in 1965

OLYMPIA BALLROOM

8 APRIL 1965, READING

I WAS THERE: NEIL CLARKE, AGE 18

I was in a group in the Sixties. We were the top group in Reading. First we were The Falcons and then we were The Dark Ages. We supported all the top groups at the Olympia in Reading – Manfred Mann, The Animals, The Searchers, The Rolling Stones and The Kinks, when 'You Really Got Me' was number one.

The Who played in early 1965. Their first record, 'I Can't Explain', was at number 10 in the charts. I spoke to their manager Kit Lambert and suggested that they plug in to our Vox AC50 amplifiers. Kit rejected this out of hand. I thought this was a bit big headed and was because they

Neil Clarke (far left), with Fender Stratocaster, and The Falcons, the group he was in, which supported The Who

were in the charts. We played the first half and then on came The Who. Needless to say, Keith's drums were flying everywhere and Pete broke his Rickenbacker in half. So I was glad they didn't use our amplifiers.

Pete was around 20 at the time and I said to Pete 'how can you smash a Rickenbacker in half?' He said 'we get the guitars on HP, pay the deposit and then we disappear.' I remember I bought my American 1964 Stratocaster for 100 guineas (£110) and sold it for £50. That guitar is worth £10,000 today.

STAMFORD HALL

9 APRIL 1965, ALTRINCHAM

I WAS THERE: JOHN BILLINGTON, AGE 14

I used to enjoy asking the old ladies who worked behind the record counter in the Co-Op in George Street in Altrincham 'can I have the latest by The Who? 'The who?' 'Yeah, The Who.' Or 'have you got Them?' 'Who's them?' Brilliant. They had no idea.

My friend had turned 15 in the April. He got me a job at Stamford Hall. 'The job' involved whatever Frank Bell, who was the promoter of the concerts, wanted. He was an ex professional boxer who was a PE teacher at Wellington Road school. He was a massive bloke and he used to stand on the door in a dinner suit with a white shirt and black bow tie. Basically, it was a youth club organisation but the turns that were on there were nothing great, not what you'd call recording artists or that type. But round about that time, that's when things started happening.

The Who was the second gig I worked. I only worked about five or six, because we never got

Young John Billington used to confuse the old ladies who worked in the Co-Op by asking them for records by The Who and Them

paid. Which was fair enough because at 14 years of age we shouldn't have been working, but we got a bottle of Coke and we had to do anything that Frank Bell asked us to do.

We had to work the door for a start. We had to take money. Frank used to stand blocking the entrance so there was never any mither of people diddling us or anything. It was advertised in the Altrincham

Guardian the week before they came on. The original advert went out on the 2nd of April, and it said members two and six (13p), membership free, new members three shillings (15p). Now they were on *Top of the Pops* on 1 April singing 'I Can't Explain' and most people would have gone to the concert not having seen the following week's *Guardian*, which came out on 9 April – the day of the concert – advertising a higher admission price of six shillings (30p) or 6/6 (33p) on the door, a 100% increase.

Would you believe that some people would not pay that entrance fee to see The Who? We were stood there and people were saying 'you must be joking, you can't. It was advertised as such and such' and we just looked at Frank Bell and he would say 'do you want to come in or not?' and people turned away. So, for a start, the place was only half full. And it was all down to the fact that they'd been on telly and he'd whacked the price up.

The Who were on at 9pm and the support group had to do a slot first and another slot afterwards, and another part of our job was opening and closing the curtains after each act finished. They were on ropes which you would have to climb up at the gym to do. I was about six foot two at 14 years of age and I thought I was pretty strong, but these bloody things moved about two inches every time I hung on them, so to try and get the things closed after The Who were finished – I never worked so hard in my life.

I'd never heard feedback. If I'd have got feedback at home, it was a mistake. The time Townshend spent just creating the most ridiculous noises, just standing right next to his amp and rubbing his guitar up and down the speakers and what have you, was just phenomenal. How long he'd had his amps I don't know. They were Marshall double stack 200 watt amps, one on top of the other with a Union Jack draped over them, and they draped the Union Jack over them because all the mesh covering the speakers had been ripped through him sticking his guitar into it.

The audience were just stood there with their mouths open after Keith Moon had finished the whole set by just kicking his drums off his little platform onto the ground floor level of the stage and Roger Daltrey was stamping on some of it.

You couldn't concentrate on what you were doing, trying to close the curtains, just seeing the chaos that was going on, and the audience. I don't believe anybody clapped as they went off – they just stood there in shock.

It's not whether you think it was entertainment. It was just so totally different from anything that had been and then, when he starts wrecking stuff you think 'actually I'm saving up to buy this and he's just destroying what he's got.'

He nearly had the thing on fire at one time. There was smoke coming out of it and him getting the feedback going again and then he'd lean back on it so that it almost fell over. Then he'd walk away from it and it'd be rocking backwards and forwards. His windmill bloody action and the fact that he could hit chords and hit the actual strings when he was doing it – we'd never seen anything like it before.

He had four input jack slots on his amp and, about a quarter of the way through their performance, he just turned around and punched down on the actual jack and snapped it off into the amp. Then he pulled his lead out, whacked another in the next available slot and then continued doing this during this show to keep doing it after every few songs.

After he'd done three, he walked straight to the side of the stage where the support group were all stood watching, pulled the jack plug in lead off the support band's bass guitar, walks back to the stage and rams that one in. And his final, final, final act of the concert is that he smashes that one.

And there's his arm coming down and I could see the bass guitarist's face and the lad going 'no!' Townshend bashed it up and walked off and the lad was going 'oh, what am I going to do?' He was nearly in tears. He just had no idea what he was going to do. They were due on next and no doubt he got another one off somebody else, but it was just total disregard by Townshend for absolutely anything.

The other thing that we'd never seen before was some guy singing and swinging a microphone out around his head and over the crowd and being able to catch it. And also knocking the microphone stand so it would fall flat beside him and then standing on it so that it'd shoot straight back in front of him.

Keith Moon just never stopped absolutely knocking seven shades out of his drum kit The whole night. John Entwistle never batted an eyelid The whole way through. He stood on the complete opposite side of the stage to me and just stood completely still. He played his bass and walked off amid the chaos when they finished as if nothing had happened.They did no more than 45 minutes and no encore, because obviously they kick over everything and just walk off and leave the roadie to pick it all up.

I couldn't actually class it as enjoyable music but as a spectacle it was just something else. I don't remember any of the tracks they played other than 'I Can't Explain', which they did twice, and perhaps Muddy Waters' 'I'm A Man'. Because my friend bought the first album the week after or whenever it came out, I recognised some of the tracks.

I would never have spoken to Townshend because he stormed off the stage. He didn't do any bowing or scraping or anything. He just went straight off. But I spoke with Keith Moon. He was just a dead genuine sort of a lad, he was dead friendly. Daltrey ran off and Keith Moon just clambers over his kit. He comes over and so I said 'you mind me asking something?' I asked how could Pete justify smashing stuff up like this? And he says 'oh, he's only bought that today. That guitar, he bought it in Altrincham.' Mind you, he hadn't broken it. He'd given it a good hammering but not broken it.

Keith said 'he buys one every time we go in. If they've got a music shop, he'll buy a guitar.' I said 'how the bloody hell can he afford that?' not knowing him and not knowing how much money they were earning. He said 'it's on HP. They'll never get the money off him.' The only other bloke I ever spoke to was Ronnie Wood. Some of these people were so normal it was unbelievable.

Keith Moon had a white t-shirt and a pair of jeans on. John Entwistle, as far as I remember, had on what I thought was a really good shirt, which was one with tab collars, and a black leather waistcoat. I remember he had Cuban heel boots. He wasn't quite a Mod, as The Who were promoting themselves as being a Mod band. He was what would have been known as a Rocker in those days, with big sideboards and the like, but it didn't matter what he wore or anything. The only thing I remember about Roger Daltrey was that he had a pair of loafers, like slip on shoes, that I really, really wanted.

I only did about six gigs because I got fed up with all the work when everybody else was in the crowd enjoying themselves. I thought 'this is ridiculous and I'm doing it for nothing.' I mean, it was usually only about three shillings (15p) to get in anyway.

I didn't recognised anyone else who was at the concert at all, in the crowd. Sometimes you used to see some guys from school or what have you but not that night. But in 1968 I met a friend who is probably my best friend now. And when The Who played in Manchester in about 2005 at the Arena, I got tickets for myself and my wife, but my wife was ill so I just asked him – do you fancy coming? Apart from being the best live concert I've ever seen – and I've see a lot of live concerts – this friend, who I'd been friends with the whole time, told me on the bloody tram into Manchester that night 'I've actually seen these in Altrincham, you know.' We've been mates for something like 40 years and we've never discussed that. I said 'I was working on the bloody stage that night.'

VICTORIA BALLROOM

15 APRIL 1965, CHESTERFIELD

I WAS THERE: JOAN ROWLAND, AGE 23

I have sometimes told people about seeing The Who at the Victoria Ballroom in Chesterfield and they cannot believe it. I was working for Top Rank in the same building. I went into our changing room and was confronted by these four scruffy lads crashed out and fell asleep on our settees. I was then told they were an upcoming group, but I had never heard of them.

As staff, we were allowed to attend performances if we chose to do so and so I rang a friend and she came down to join me. Later, these 'boys' went out to their old van to get out their instruments and they had obviously been sleeping on what looked like straw in the back.

I went to the ballroom and they began playing. Two things struck a chord with me. One of them was playing a guitar and made exaggerated circles with his arm as he plucked the strings on his guitar, and then they started smashing up their instruments. At which point I left, because it looked quite dangerous to me!

I may add that my husband has recently been to see The Who and thought their performance was great. To which I replied 'they've come a long way since Chesterfield then!'

OASIS CLUB

23 APRIL 1965, MANCHESTER

I WAS THERE: ADELE KAIN

My husband Pete and his cousin Sue were regular customers at the Oasis Club on Lloyd Street in Manchester in the 1960s. Being alcohol-free, the club was open to teenagers and Pete remembers that he and Sue were age 16 in 1965, when they paid a memorable visit to the Oasis. He said 'we were standing at the back and the manager was next to me. The manager didn't think much of the band that was on stage and he said to me "I wouldn't pay that lot in washers!" The band he was talking about was The Who.'

I WAS THERE: CHRIS PHILLIPS

My earliest memory of them is 1965 when they played the Oasis Club in Lloyd Street, Manchester. Oasis was a cellar club and everyone from The Beatles to the Stones played there. Going into see them one night we saw Moon and Townshend pull up in a car outside. Artists and punters used the same door. Daltrey wasn't with them as he was in the Nag's Head pub across the road with his Mod bird. I saw him there but didn't speak.

Anyway, we proceeded to go down the stairs and got about halfway down when I got charged in the back and tumbled to the bottom. There was a body on top of me clutching a bottle of Courvoisier brandy. It was Moony. He had his finger in the top of the bottle and it didn't break and he didn't spill a drop. He had a big smile on his face. 'Alright, mate – want a drink?' So I had a swig while he's still half on top of me!

TOWN HALL

26 APRIL 1965, BRIDGWATER

I WAS THERE: ROGER BOWERMAN

I lived near Taunton. I had read an article in the *Record Mirror* about a west London group, The Who, and the radical way they approached their music with amp abuse, use of feedback and other innovative sonic techniques. It was a pretty vivid exposition of what they were like live. The impression given was that they were an important west London group following in the footsteps of the Stones and The Yardbirds. So this was an opportunity to see and hear a promising band close up.

My friend Les had a car and we went over with our girlfriends. I'd never been to Bridgwater Town Hall before. I can't remember if there was a support or not. There wasn't a large crowd of interested people in front of the stage. We were able to watch them unimpeded.

Their performance more than lived up to the hype in the article. When we went in, 'I Can't Explain' was playing over the PA system and they came out and gave an amazing show. The sheer physicality and controlled aggression of their performance set them apart from any other bands I'd seen.

During 'I'm A Man', the singer walked off stage and didn't come back for some time. There seemed to be some tension between Pete and Roger. Pete shouted something to Entwistle along the lines of 'Where the fuck is Roger?' Pete had to keep going with all his antics to cover the singer's long absence with his repertoire of wind milling, blipping out morse with guitar's pick up selector switch and shoving the guitar into the amp covers. He was able to control the large amount of feedback he was coaxing through his Rickenbacker guitar to great effect. Pete also introduced 'Anyway Anyhow Anywhere' as their next single before performing it.

At the end, when they were packing up their equipment, I stood on a chair in front of the stage and, getting Pete's attention, asked if we could have autographs for our girlfriends, which he very kindly collected from the other members of the band. He seemed a very nice bloke.

I WAS THERE: MIKE TUCKER,

I still have my 1965 diary and the entry for Monday 26 April reads: 'Meeting xxxxx at Town Hall, The Who up Town Hall (going). Back to school, rotten day. Walked xxxx home from Town Hall.' As you can see, my diary tends to be more of a simple record of events rather than offering any sort of insight, but what do you expect from a 15 year old?

I remember them well. The Town Hall in Bridgwater had live music pretty much every Monday and many of the people playing there went onto to greater and long lasting things, so we were kind of spoilt for a small town in Somerset.

It was the time of my early Mod days and The Who fuelled that along with the Small Faces, who played there the following September. Like most 15 year olds, the interest was girls and music – in that order.

A thoroughly Mod teenager: Mike Tucker saw The Who in Bridgwater

TWO RED SHOES

6 MAY 1965, ELGIN

I WAS THERE: NEIL MUNRO

It all started for me by going to see The Beatles, because they were number one! Getting big names to Elgin and the north of Scotland was the work of one Albert Bonici. Later we moved to the Town Hall to see The Searchers, the Swinging Blue Jeans and Brian Poole and The Tremeloes.

The Two Red Shoes ballroom was owned by the Williamson family, a big recycling merchants whose business is still on the go. It could have been due to the size of the 'Boots', as the Two Red Shoes was called locally, but I remember The Who being quite loud.

I WAS THERE: TOM FORSYTH

I was the bass player of an Aberdeen-based band called The Delinquents. We played rock'n'roll standards and some Motown and we covered songs from the charts. Occasionally, we would rehearse at The Lads Club in Hutcheon Street. We would rehearse for a couple of hours in the evening and then throw open the doors and play a few numbers for the kids in lieu of payment for use of the hall. On the night in question, we had been rehearsing 'I Can't Explain', by a new band called The Who, which had charted recently.

At the end of the night, The Delinquents drummer, Stewart Kemp, and I were in the habit of going for a burger and a Coke at the café of the ABC Bowling Alley in George Street, which was near Stewart's home and quite near where I stayed. That night, when we walked into the café, Stewart stopped in his tracks and said 'that's Roger Daltrey of The Who!' I looked over and, right enough, there was Roger Daltrey sitting at the counter with John Entwistle.

Stewart and I went across to say 'hi' and started chatting, telling them of the coincidence that we had been rehearsing their song 'I Can't Explain' that night. I asked where the rest of the band were and Roger said that Keith was bowling. I looked down to the bowling lanes

The Delinquents: an Aberdeen band who briefly befriended The Who in May 1965 and who got a whiff of Keith Moon's pranks

and there was Keith throwing the bowls energetically, once on to the lane next to his. He seemed to be having a great time. Keith finished his game and joined us.

Roger bought me and Stewart a Coke and I asked what they were doing in Aberdeen. Roger said they were playing The Two Red Shoes in Elgin in a couple of days and that they had hired His Majesty's Theatre, the biggest and most prestigious theatre in Aberdeen, the next day to rehearse for a TV appearance the following weekend. I told them that the coincidence didn't stop at us doing their song that night; The Delinquents were playing Elgin on the same night as they were, although not at the Two Red Shoes but at the New Elgin Hall. Roger invited us to come along to His Majesty's Theatre the next day to watch the rehearsal and Stewart and I headed home buzzing.

Next day, I met up with Stewart and we headed for the theatre. We told the girl at the box office that the band had invited us along and she directed us down to the stalls. When we entered the auditorium, we were met by the fantastic sound of the band in full flow doing a song we didn't know. It turned out to be 'Anyway, Anyhow, Anywhere', which was to be their next single. We made our way down near to the front of the stalls and sat down. The band were sounding great, but a guy we took to be their manager was directing proceedings from the stalls. He would shout up directions, sometimes stopping the band to make a point. He was particularly keen to give Pete Townshend directions as to how to handle his guitar when rubbing it on his amp and controlling the feedback.

At the time, I wasn't sure who the guy was, but later worked out that it was probably Kit Lambert, although to this day I am not sure. When the rehearsal ended, Stewart and I went on to the stage for a chat and John offered to sell me one of his bass amps. I declined the offer as I had just bought a new Vox AC50 amp.

Keith and Stewart discussed drumsticks and Keith had some great advice. He reckoned that rather than buying expensive, high-end sticks it was better to buy packs of cheap practice ones, which were made of poorer-quality wood and broke easily. This meant that when a stick broke it could be thrown into the crowd and replaced by a stick from a bunch tucked into the top of the bass drum. This meant that the fan who caught the broken drumstick had a great souvenir of the gig. As we parted, Roger told us to look them up at The Two Red Shoes in Elgin after our respective gigs.

Next day, The Delinquents headed north and we played our set at the New Elgin Hall. I don't remember what the crowd was like, but I guess it was pretty sparse compared to the turnout for a chart band like The Who at the Two Red Shoes. At the end of the gig, we loaded our gear into the van and headed over to the Two Red Shoes. The doorman wouldn't let us in, but he sent someone to tell the band that we were there and Roger, Keith and John came out to see us. We chatted for a while and then we said we had to head off home to Aberdeen. As we were about to leave, Keith said: 'Hold on!' He came over and said 'see ya' as he threw a stink bomb into our van. What a hoot! What a stink! We laughed all the way back to Aberdeen, a distance of some 70 miles, with all the windows in the van wide open as we tried to clear the air. It was a hilarious end to a brilliant close encounter with a great band.

DE MONTFORT HALL

9 MAY 1965, LEICESTER

I WAS THERE: MITCH IRVING

I was in the audience when they appeared at the de Montfort Hall in Leicester on a package tour. The warm up group was The Naturals, then it was Marianne Faithful, followed by The Who and top of the bill were Tom Jones and The Squires – a really diverse collection, the like of which you could not even imagine today.

McILROY'S BALLROOM

18 MAY 1965, SWINDON

I WAS THERE: IAN TITCOMBE

I was a Mod in 1965 and saw probably all of the groups of that era, but obviously The Who were 'the' Mod group of the time. I caught all three of their shows in Swindon. The stand out memory is when they played at Swindon's McIlroy's ballroom for the second time, just as they were taking off as a major group. At that time they started their set with 'Heat Wave', the Martha and The Vandellas song, which was a favourite of mine and was a real 'grab you' number. At the end of the song the applause was nothing to shout about and Roger Daltrey came to the front of the stage, looked around and said 'I see that we are back in Swindon then!'

The Who only played Swindon twice, according to records

TOWN HALL

20 MAY 1965, KIDDERMINSTER

I WAS THERE: PETER STUBBS

I saw The Who in my home town of Kidderminster in West Midlands.

I do not know if this happened at all Who concerts in that era but Keith ended up with only his cymbals during the last couple of numbers. Great gig for sure!

The Who released their second UK single, 'Anyway, Anyhow, Anywhere' on 21 May 1965. It was released in the US on 5 June 1965. Although its guitar feedback wasn't the first to be heard on a record, it is thought to be the first solo with feedback

ASTORIA

22 MAY 1965, RAWTENSTALL

I WAS THERE: MICHAEL SMITH GUTTRIDGE

I played with The Avalons at the Astoria Ballroom in a little town called Rawtenstall in Lancashire. We were supporting a top group from London which had already had chart success and appeared on TV. They were The Who. The ballroom was packed and everyone was eagerly anticipating the headliners. We played our set, as did the other supporting group The Imps, and then enjoyed a very loud performance from The Who. But not before we had to do another set.

Keith Moon had gone walkabout in Rawtenstall, borrowing our drummer's jacket. Beforehand we'd been sharing a backstage area with them and they were a friendly lot. Keith was probably the friendliest whereas Pete Townshend kept himself apart a little bit. He was drinking red wine from the bottle, unaware that Keith had urinated in it!

Roy, our drummer, remembers that Keith gave him a handful of drumsticks, which he still has, and a beater for a bass/kick drum. He also got to play Keith's Ludwig kit as they stripped down his own and took it off stage to make room for The Who's. It was after Roy commented to Keith about the solid sound of his bass drum, that Moon put down to the beater, that he gave it

The Avalons supported The Who at The Astoria in Rawtenstall

to Roy and which Roy later sold with the drum kit. Crazy but generous.

The Who were using an old ice-cream van – the ones with the elevated roof – as their transport, which was quite interesting. One of their road crew offered to sell us a Vox 100 watt amplifier. This was something beyond our wildest dreams as we were using Vox AC30s and don't think we'd seen one so

The **AVALONS**

big. I think he wanted £100 for it. Apart from the fact we didn't have that kind of money, the amp was stencilled all over with the name of the TV show from which it had been 'liberated.'

David, our vocalist, remembers the night vividly and looking back he thinks even then they were a competitive lot, which gave rise to some of the tension. However, The Who were, and still are when they perform, a great rock band and it was a privilege to support them on that night more than 50 years ago.

PAVILION BALLROOM

27 MAY 1965, WORTHING

I WAS THERE: WENDY GREENE

I saw The Who on two occasions. Both times they were supported by my ex-husband's band Mo'Henry. Dave Greene was lead guitarist and at the second gig bought a Vox AC30 amp from The Who's roadie Cyrano, who received his nicknamed for his large nose (as in 'de Bergerac'). At the Worthing gig a girl had stolen Keith's target t-shirt and I was able to tell him which school she went to, though not a name.

Wendy Greene tried to help Keith track down a t-shirt thief

Dave Greene, whose band M'Henry supported The Who at the Pavillion Ballroom in Worthing

I WAS THERE: DAVE GREENE

We supported The Who that night. My only memory of that gig is that when we were packing away our gear at the end of the night. Keith and John and the roadie – Cyrano, I think – came and chatted with us. We were particularly impressed that they had some Vox AC100 amps, the most powerful you could get in them days, which I had seen The Beatles use but no-one else. One of the three aforementioned said 'you can buy one from us if you like.' At first, we thought they were pulling our legs, but when the price was mentioned – £15, I think – we quickly handed over the cash and the deal was done! I think Keith said they had ordered them in for a *Ready Steady Go!* appearance a night or so previously and had 'accidentally' forgotten to leave them in the studio. I seem to remember they got themselves quite a reputation for borrowing gear, mainly from Sound City, and then 'forgetting' to return it. I never knew if they just took a shine to us that night or whether it was a nice regular sideline they had going.

A few years later, in 1970, I had the pleasure of meeting Mr Moon again. I had only just joined a prog-rock band called Raw Material and we were playing in one of those private late night drinking clubs somewhere in Kensington area. We had just gone into our tiny 'dressing room' to take a break when who should walk in but

Moonie. 'Just come to say well done lads, and keep up the good work' or something along those lines. Then he handed over the bottle of Scotch he had been swigging from before disappearing into the night. I always thought what a great gesture that was. How many other people of his stature would have taken the trouble to say hello to a bunch of unknowns?

I WAS THERE: JANE MELHUISH

Growing up in Worthing, West Sussex as a teenager in the Sixties meant going to the Pier or the Assembly Hall on a Thursday night. All of the top groups played there, with the exception of the Beatles and the Stones. The Kinks, The Hollies, Amen Corner, Arthur Brown; they were all there. We took the 106 bus and bought ten No 6 ciggies. We paid five shillings (25p) for a lesser known group and 7/6 (37p) for a famous group.

Jane Melhuish didn't get much thanks for helping The Who shift their drums

We were friends with The Total, a local group who supported many of the bands, so we were allowed access backstage. I was there for The Who's performance in 1965. Pete Townshend smashed his guitar up, of course. It was an amazing performance. Afterwards we were backstage and, being a helpful girl, I carried some of the drums down to their van. Roger Daltrey said 'don't drop any of that!' Nice, eh?

LAURIE GROVE BATHS

DATE UNKNOWN, GOLDSMITHS COLLEGE, LONDON

I WAS THERE: JOHN STARKEY

The adage about those who grew up in the Sixties not being able to remember if they were there, doesn't quite apply in my case, as I was there and remember less that I would have liked, but I was not one of those who was into the excesses of the age. i.e. drugs, sex and rock and roll.

Laurie Grove Baths were Victorian public swimming pool and slipper baths in a narrow street located behind Deptford Town Hall. The main pool was surrounded by individual changing booths. The building had a gabled roof with partially glazed sections and was supported by metal rods across, from side-to-side and with vertical rods from these up to the roof apex. All this generated quite an echo chamber effect. The pool area was boarded over for social events and I don't think the pool underneath was drained out. I used to go swimming there during the day time on occasions.

Detailed recollections of The Who are sadly sparse, but I went to one of their live 'gigs' – I think we may have called them dances or hops in those days. This must have been in autumn 1964 or 1965. The event was organised by the Art School social secretary, who organised some very good events with live bands.

The Art School social events were even then what today would be called a bit edgy. The Bonzo Dog Doo-Dah Band played at a number of events while I was at Goldsmiths. I think the lead singer Vivian Stanshall was in the Art School at some time. The only other celeb alumni I was aware of then making their way in the world was Mary Quant.One of the Art School's early Balls led for a while to a ban on such events, as three summons were allegedly issued after one I attended – too much noise, selling more tickets than licensed for and no license for a stripper!

I remember the poster advertising The Who dance with the iconic O with its arrow pointing to 2 o'clock – an abbreviation for the male gender. I do remember that they smashed up all their kit at the end! The venue for this dance was comparatively small and it was standing only, but I don't remember it being particularly packed out. There was still room to walk about and dance nearer the stage.

The Moody Blues also played at this venue, organised by the Art School, some weeks or months later and one of their guitarists was wheeled across the boarded floor on an ambulance trolley after allegedly getting electrocuted on some of his equipment.Somewhere in my head I have a figure of £30 as the cost to hire The Who for this evening gig. I think this must have been before 'My Generation'. I particularly remember listening to this song, plus masses of others by groups at the time, on pirate radio stations. The stuttered 'f' s in 'why don't you all f-f-f-fade away' was chanted by us students in karaoke fashion and considered very daring. I don't think Kenneth Tynan had yet said the 'f' word live on television at that time. The Laurie Grove baths building still stands, but it is now used by the Art School and has been converted into a series of studios.

BOWES LYON HOUSE YOUTH CENTRE

10 JUNE 1965, STEVENAGE

I WAS THERE: MARY ABRA

I went to see them with my sister, Margaret Stanley (nee Abra). Margaret has found an entry in her diary on Thursday 10th June 1965: 'Went to see The Who. Cost me 5/-. Alan chucked me, almost lost my coat, nearly suffocated & crushed to death and my foot started to hurt.'

Poor Margaret. It doesn't sound as though she had a very nice time! I have nothing memorable to say. I just remember being there and I believe Keith Moon threw his drum sticks out to the crowd at the end of the performance.

This appearance by The Who at Bowes Lyon House is not recorded elsewhere.

MANOR LOUNGE

13 JUNE 1965, STOCKPORT

I WAS THERE: COLIN JOY

The most popular venue in Stockport was the Manor Lounge, approximately a mile away from the town centre. It was a former café set in the basement of the Wellington Picture House. It was unlicensed and could hold up to 1000 people. The roof was covered with egg boxes as sound-proofing to avoid annoying the picture-goers above and at the time attracted bands like The Who, Cream, The Yardbirds, Long John Baldry, the Small Faces and Pink Floyd, to name just a few.

All major gods of rock and roll now, but, then they were just bands we heard about and they would turn up and play un-announced. In fact, if you went into the pub just across the road, you'd find Pete Townshend or Freddie of Freddie and The Dreamers having a pint. The Lounge closed in 1967 as the Wellington became a bingo hall, as most theatres did in those days, and later a snooker or American pool hall as it is today. But as a music venue it was on par with, and was Stockport's version of, the Cavern Club in Liverpool.

The Who should have played the venue in May 1965 but had to cancel due to their van breaking down on the motorway. We had heard of the band through pirate radio. They were also from London and classed as Mods – the equivalent to Northern Rockers who were drenched in the Mersey Beat sound – so there was a lot of interest in going and seeing them. Although the Manor Lounge could hold a thousand people, there were probably about 400 to 450 there that night.

The band were dressed in typical plain shirts and trousers – not the late 1960s coloured types of the Carnaby era – and played a very sombre set of covers. They were not loud as they are today, but easy on the ears. The basic set-up was amplifiers and drums but no PA as we have today. Townshend had yet to master his trademark clock swinging guitar playing and the low roof meant Daltrey could not throw microphones around. Entwistle was, er, just John Entwistle – stood there looking bored and never moved. But highlight of the set was Keith Moon's enthusiastic drumming, emphasising all the words in the songs. The set was only short – approximately 45 minutes – but after they had finished the band stayed on stage shaking hands and signing autographs in appreciation for the reception they got from the audience. Most bands scarper out of the back entrance quick, but not The Who. They just stuck around with the crowd and even joined them in the pub just across the road.

Most of what they played were cover versions except 'I Can't Explain' and 'Anyway, Anyhow, Anywhere'. My brother remembers they started playing some of the same songs again later just to space out the set. It was a good night, but we never thought they would turn into the monster they are now!

BOWES LYON HOUSE YOUTH CENTRE

17 JUNE 1965, STEVENAGE

I WAS THERE: PETE WRIGHT

The Who were on *Top of the Pops* that night and they were being flown down from Manchester to Luton airport after they'd been on *Top of the Pops*. You could cut the atmosphere with a knife. The curtains were drawn. They had four TVs on the stage so we could watch *Top of the Pops*. The Who were the opening act on *Top of the Pops* because they wanted to get away, and they were using somebody else's instruments

BOWES LYON HOUSE YOUTH CENTRE, STEVENAGE

FRIDAY, 11th JUNE
DISC-SPIN with guest D.J. 1/6

SATURDAY, 12th JUNE
STEVENAGE DAY
Bowes Lyon House will be open to the public from
10 a.m. to 6 p.m. Admission 6d.
Morning Coffee 10 a.m. to 12 noon; Lunches 12 noon to
2 p.m.; Light Refreshments 2 p.m. to 4 p.m.; Teas 4 p.m.
to 6 p.m.

SATURDAY EVENING
BIG BEAT NIGHT
THE NIGHTSHADES of "Be My Guest" fame,
and "DISC-SPIN" with Shirley, 2/6

TUESDAY, 15th JUNE
FOLK NIGHT at 2/6
NATTERJACKS with guest artistes Shirley Hart and
Colin Wickie

THURSDAY, 17th JUNE
THE FABULOUS
WHO
of "I Can't Explain" fame
plus the "ENNI HOWS" and the "SYSTEM"
BIG BEAT RAVE at 5/-
Doors open 7 p.m.   Friday 6 p.m.

because, unbeknown to us, their gear was set up on the stage behind the curtains. The girls in the audience went absolutely berserk when The Who came on *Top of the Pops*. When they finished, a couple of these tellies were dragged out and just thrown over the balcony.

The heat was unbearable. It was about nine o'clock at night and this bloke comes on and he says 'I've had a phone call from the manager. The Who are with him. They're in his car and they're on their way.'

In the end the curtains opened and the audience went berserk again. I was looking at the group and they honestly looked terrified. And I've always thought 'is this the first time you've ever seen this adulation?' This was probably 'Anyway, Anyhow, Anywhere' when they were on. That was perhaps the first time they had that Beatles-type adulation. Being on the telly and the delay in them appearing allowing the atmosphere to build was what caused it.

FLORAL HALL BALLROOM

18 JUNE 1965, MORECAMBE

I WAS THERE: SYD BLOOM

I used to go to Manchester and all over watching them when they became The Who. I used to go down to the Oasis in Manchester and anywhere where they were on in the north, which was relatively infrequently. One memorable one is Morecambe Floral Hall because there was nobody there. The place was totally deserted and I was able to park right outside on the promenade. After quite some time, the ticket kiosk suddenly opened up and the old lady there clearly hadn't a clue who or what was happening but relieved me of the entrance fee and so I paid my money and went in.

The bar used to be at the back so I walked in the bar and there's nobody else in the place. Then I saw Roger Daltrey was there so I went 'alright? I was very querulous whether you where playing here.' He was clearly freaking out at the lack of interest in the band. He said 'I can't believe this. We were down at Eel Pie Island and they were queuing for two days to get in.' He bought me a drink and said 'come backstage with us.' So I went back to the dressing room for a chat and to meet the others.

John Entwistle was a really nice guy. He was extremely friendly and was musing at length about his surname, his suggestion being that his family's roots were presumably in the north. But Townshend was in another place. He was completely supercilious and aloof. I bet there weren't sixty people there that night. But Keith Moon still managed to pick a fight with somebody.

I WAS THERE: CHRISTINE BOWLES

My friend Anne and I saw The Who the first time they played in Morecambe. The audience consisted of about 50 or 60 people, as The Searchers were on at the Central Pier, the other big venue in Morecambe, and at that time they were much better known than The Who. So everyone else we knew went to see The Searchers. Anne and I had seen The Who on *Ready Steady Go!* and thought they were amazing so we went to see them.

Christine opted for The Who over The Searchers

Some boys we knew who were there said that they were sat with them in the bar before the show. We stood in front of the stage as in those days there were no barriers with security men, so it was as if they were playing just for us. I remember they played as if they were playing to 5,000 rather than the few dozen actually there.

I don't remember Pete Townshend smashing his guitar but I do seem to remember that his fingers were bleeding at the end. I think that they had just released 'Anyhow, Anyway, Anywhere' which soon went up the charts so the next time they came was to the Central Pier and it was packed.

They played at the Central Pier at least three times more and I went to see them every time and they are still one of the best live bands I have seen. Keith Moon often threw his drumsticks into the audience at the end and I once caught one. Unfortunately I no longer have this as my brother 'borrowed' it and I never saw it again.

I WAS THERE: TREVOR OWEN

At the time when The Who played at the Floral Hall, bands like The Beatles and the Stones made records and came to Morecambe. Everybody came to Morecambe and played at the Floral Hall and the Central Pier. Tom Jones and the Squires. Van Morrison – I even played on the same bill as him when he was with Them. There wasn't a fantastic amount of people in the Floral Hall that night. I'm sure it was a Friday night because it was always full on a Saturday. But the bulk of people used to go to the Central Pier on a Friday so it was always quieter on Friday nights at the Floral. Saturday nights it would be heaving, packed out.

I was in a band called the Milestones and myself and the drummer had been there in the afternoon getting the equipment set up. There was a cinema called the Empire. The Floral Hall was in the centre and Stocks Arcadia Café was above the lot. And there was another cinema at the other end called the Arcadian. Next to that was a really big fairground which is under development now. Right next to the Arcadian Cinema was the Cyclone, a big dipper, and a friend of ours used to work on there. And myself and Paul Wilkinson, the drummer, we took them on the Cyclone. We saw our friend Bish and he said 'yeah, go on.' We had about four goes round on the Cyclone. Because everybody used to have to pay, but Bish never used to come to take money off anybody he knew. That always sticks in my mind, going on the fairground with Keith and Roger.

I play keyboards and guitar. I went down to London for three months. The manager of The Who was going to get me work in Germany playing these air force bases but a lot of them had closed down. He had offices on

Edgware Road and he said 'I've got you a job in London for three or four months at a little place called the Plughole Club.' It was five dinner times and five nights. Tony Blackburn was one of the deejays, and Errol Bruce. They both worked on Radio Caroline at that time.

I was playing with the Arthur Brown Union, which became The Crazy World of Arthur Brown. He worked on the sewers in London, did Arthur. It was a good band. Carl Palmer was the drummer, out of Emerson, Lake and Palmer. A good band, doing soul stuff – 'In The Midnight Hour', which was in the charts at the time, and Otis Redding stuff. It was good. But I didn't like London. We ended up down there for three months. The worst three months of my life. I haven't been back to London since.

STARLITE BALLROOM

27 JUNE 1965, GREENFORD

I WAS THERE: CHRISTINE MACLEAN

The best gig I remember was in Ealing on Sunday 27 June. My three friends and I had the opportunity of a lift to the venue and back, so I am not sure exactly where it was but it was so exciting to be in a London venue! The room was filled with Mods in the latest fashions and all dancing the latest dance craze.

We got fairly near to the band, although we were not allowed to stay until the end. We were overawed by the experience and took that dance back to Stevenage and proudly showed off our new moves at the next opportunity. Luckily my boyfriend, later my husband, was also a Who fanatic and we have seen them at gigs big and small ever since and have never been disappointed by their performances.

MANOR BALLROOM

28 JUNE 1965, IPSWICH

I WAS THERE: JOHN MOORE

They played the Manor Ballroom in Ipswich – just about. It was the shortest set that I can recall there, lasting no more than 30 minutes. According to the promoter, Ron Lesley, he had booked them before 'I Can't Explain' hit the charts, so they only received a fee of £400.

They were doing the minimum possible to fulfil their contract, but it was enough to see what an amazing drummer Keith Moon was! Ron booked them in Ipswich again on 1 November 1965 at St Matthews Baths, no doubt at a much higher fee. My friends and I didn't go, in protest at the abbreviated nature of the earlier event.

I WAS THERE: DAVID GOODWIN

By the end of 1964, middle of 1965, the whole Mod scene was done. It wasn't cool anymore. But 18 months later there were still these people zipping around on chrome plated scooters with aerials on them. They weren't cool anymore, although they thought they were.

The genuine Mods were 1964, not 66. Although it got a lot of publicity it was not a large circle of people. The Teddy Boys, the Rockers, were a little bit older than the Mods. To me it was just an excuse for people to turn up and have a barney.

MANOR HOUSE CLUB

7 JULY 1965, MANOR HOUSE, LONDON

I WAS THERE: WENDY GREENE

After seeing them in Worthing, Dave (my husband) and I also went to the Manor House in north London to see them but I was taken ill. As we were leaving Keith Moon recognised me and waved and came to the dressing room door. A fan had cut a lump out of his and John's hair at the Worthing gig and I'd neatened it up. I kept the off-cuts until recently when I sold them along with their autographs and a picture.

I met Keith twice after, once at the Marquee and later when Dave was with professional band Raw Material in a London club. Keith bought us a bottle of brandy.

LOCARNO BALLROOM

9 JULY 1965, BASILDON

I WAS THERE: ROY KEBBELL, AGE 18

I travelled to Basildon from Southend with my two brothers on
an Eastern National 151 bus. It was a very exciting performance
with animated performances from Townshend, Daltrey and Moon.
Entwistle was quite impassive. When the band were not playing they
wandered around the ballroom and Townshend was just as surly then
as he appears to be today.

I WAS THERE: CHRIS STEVENS

I not only saw
them there
but was the
drummer
in one of
the support
groups, The
Premiers. The
other band
on the bill
was a more
accomplished
local outfit
called The
Monotones.

The Premiers: the teenage Canvey Island-based band which supported
The Who in Basildon

Our band was Canvey Island based and a bit of a 'youth club'
band, all very young at 15-16ish, so supporting The Who was a big
deal for us.

The previous year we won a local 'battle of the bands' competition
beating an embryonic Dr Feelgood, then known as The Heap
featuring Wilko Johnson, who later went on to make the *Going Back
Home* album with Roger.

ST GEORGE'S BALLROOM

11 JULY 1965, HINCKLEY

I WAS THERE: MERVIN WALLACE

Of all the groups that appeared at the St. George's Ballroom, more commonly known to us then as The George, the most eagerly awaited were The Who and The Small Faces. The night of 11 July 1965 will always be remembered by the 300 or so teenagers that were there for the first appearance of The Who.

The stage at The George was minute by today's standards, with even less space when there were three bands as on their return visit to The George on 26 March 1966. The stage was only a about a metre high from the ballroom floor, and dropped away about a foot on the band's side. Both Keith and Pete Townshend were, we suspected, drug fuelled for all of the performances we saw, but luckily all the mayhem was kept on the small stage, out of harm's way.

LOCARNO BALLROOM

14 JULY 1965, STEVENAGE

I WAS THERE: LYNNE WALTERS

I was a teenager living in Stevenage in the early to mid 1960s when The Who came to prominence. Stevenage was very much a town of Mods and every Wednesday we would go to the Stevenage Mecca as, for us, this was the best night of the week.

The Mecca was a traditional old fashioned

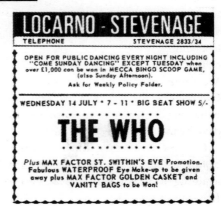

LOCARNO - STEVENAGE

TELEPHONE   STEVENAGE 2833/34

OPEN FOR PUBLIC DANCING EVERY NIGHT INCLUDING
"COME SUNDAY DANCING" EXCEPT TUESDAY when
over £1,000 can be won in MECCA BINGO SCOOP GAME,
(also Sunday Afternoon).
Ask for Weekly Policy Folder.

WEDNESDAY 14 JULY • 7 - 11 • BIG BEAT SHOW 5/-

THE WHO

Plus MAX FACTOR ST. SWITHIN'S EVE Promotion.
Fabulous WATERPROOF Eye Make-up to be given
away plus MAX FACTOR GOLDEN CASKET and
VANITY BAGS to be Won!

Keith Moon, in characteristic pose at the Stevenage Locarno

dance hall and Saturdays were over 21s night.

Wednesdays, however, were for teenagers and every other week there was a live band. It was an amazing time and in just over a year we saw The Rolling Stones, The Swinging Blue Jeans, The Hollies, The Dave Clark Five, Them and of course The Who.

The group was very much a Mod band then. They appeared there several times and were at their most anarchic and raw, with Pete Townshend smashing up his guitar and amplifier at the end of each night. Their following tended to be mainly Mod boys who liked to dance quite manically in a crowd, usually having taken a few pills to give them energy.

My most vivid memory of those concerts though is that two of my class mates used to get in the back of the van with The Who after the show, an activity the girls referred to as 'Who rolling'!

CHELTENHAM ATHLETIC FOOTBALL GROUND

16 JULY 1965, CHELTENHAM

I WAS THERE: MIKE CRAWSHAW

I was walking through town to the gig with a few friends. We were passing the old Waikiki Bar across the way from the Queens Hotel when a Transit van pulled up alongside us. Pete Townshend, whom we recognised immediately, stuck his head out of the door and said 'oi mate, where's this Athletic Ground we're playing then?'

We all joined in supplying instructions, the door slid shut and off they went. I always thought that if I'd been a bit sharper I could have said 'give me a lift and

Mike Crawshaw (right) ponders how much he likes The Who

I'll show you' but I was with my mates and they'd never have forgiven me! When we reached Albion Street, where the venue was situated, there was a mass of 'state of the art' scooters parked up as far as the eye could see. It turned out that many of these belonged to the London Mods who had come down to support their band. We were in awe!

The support band was the Hellions from Evesham which featured Dave Mason and Jim Capaldi who went on to play with Traffic and Steve Winwood. I have seen The Who many times since over the years, through their great and not so great times, and actually reminisced over this gig when I bumped into John Entwistle in a bar in Cheltenham not long before he died. He remembered the gig fondly.

I WAS THERE: ALAN CONDY

My girlfiend Mary, now my wife, and myself attended both the Cheltenham gigs they played in 1965 and still remember them. We both thought at the time and still think the same now – that The Who were the most exciting best live band we have ever seen. We also got see them at the O2 a couple of years ago and thought that was a pretty amazing gig too, with Keith and John playing along on the big screens. The support band on that occasion was The Yardbirds featuring Jimmy Page on guitar. I still remember wondering why he was playing his guitar with a cello bow.

I WAS THERE: JIM DILLON, AGE 18

It was a warm July evening and, if my memory serves me well, The Kinks and The Yardbirds were also on the bill. As an 18 year old, I was just exhilarated to be at a 'rugby club gig' although the significance was lost as to the historical importance of the occasion.

I remember drugs being bandied around. Although I didn't participate, we had a couple of drinks and I had a great evening.

Because of Keith Moon's reputation, we were all eagerly awaiting his performance with the drum sticks. We were mesmerised by the way he could juggle and play simultaneously. The Who were so iconoclastic that they were worshipped for the sheer audacity of their performance.

Jim Dillon caught The Who at their Cheltenham 'rugby club gig'

I WAS THERE: KEN DOUEL

It was an outside concert or dance organised by Cheltenham rugby club, hence myself and friends who were rugby players but at various Gloucester clubs went. The Yardbirds were also playing. The price was 10 shillings (50p) but being tight buggers we found a way in without paying. My memory of the whole event would have not been aided by plenty of

Ken Douel found a way to get into the Cheltenham gig for without paying

drink, which was the norm for weekend. The band members were in one of the marquees having a drink, which would have been no great thing as they were not famous then to the degree of having security. They were just a bunch of Sixties lads. I would have been the main guy wanting to go as I was music mad, especially about the blues aspect that both groups were playing at the time. It was the beginning of the era when youngsters were expressing themselves more on the dance floor. I loved the rock'n'roll and the jiving but you also had this music where you expressed yourself in the newer sound of The Rolling Stones and other groups.

I WAS THERE: MAURICE RUSSELL, AGE 20

There wasn't a very large crowd on that day. I went to the concert to see The Yardbirds who were the headliners. I stood near the front and I remember Roger Daltrey was wearing pinstriped trousers. A girl said to him 'I like your trousers', to which he shouted back 'they are pyjamas!' The Yardbirds were good – but The Who stole the show!

I WAS THERE: BRIDGET WARD, AGE 16

I have kept my ticket all these years, which still shows the little rip on the left which they did when you entered. The ground is unfortunately long gone with houses built there. I wasn't quite 17 and it was probably the first concert where we did not sit down. From what I remember we just stood around and danced in awe of the loud music. I remember thinking they were dressed strange and that the music was loud. It was wonderful!

I WAS THERE: CHRIS WATSON

The venue was the old rugby ground on Albion Street, just off Whaddon Road. The rugby club's long gone having moved to just out of Cheltenham at the Prince of Wales stadium. It was an evening rock concert, run by the rugby club with a makeshift stage outdoors. We were stood out on the field. I don't know what time it started – about half seven, eight o'clock – and it went on until nearly midnight. Three bands with The Who in the middle. The Ravens were a local girl band and they were not really very good, but I suppose you have a local band to open.

They were followed by The Who, who weren't the headline act. The Who created more interest than The Yardbirds, whose lead guitarist then was Jeff Beck. If that had been on tour round the country, The Who would have ended up headlining.

Their gig there was brilliant. I think 'I Can't Explain' was all they had put out at the time. They had a Mod following which was a new wave, a bit of a social phenomenon, a new way of dressing and things like that and The Who were right at the beginning of that. Some of the Mods got up on stage. I suppose I was a Mod, although I didn't get up on the stage area. They were doing the Mod dance to some of the music that was on that first album. They were doing the Motown thing. They performed 'Dancing In The Street'.

And The Who smashed their stuff up at the end, or most of it. They were doing that at most gigs, chucking the equipment around at the end. It was a very visual thing. At the time I hadn't seen anything quite like that. I was fascinated by them and I loved the music. This was the Mod era. A whole fashion industry came up with The Who, with the hairstyles and the different things, and everyone was dressing like that. The Who were the band that everybody followed if you were Mod. It was all very fascinating at the time, but none of the bands I saw were iconic at the time I saw them. Quite the opposite, they were just starting out. They're iconic now. But back then it was new – it was at the beginning of something different.

I WAS THERE: MIKE WILLIAMS, AGE 18

The gig was in the open air and The Who were the main support band. One of the other support bands was the Hellions, who had Jim Capaldi and Dave Mason in their ranks, both of whom went on to play with Steve Winwood in Traffic. I saw Keith Moon and Roger

Daltrey stood together by the gate, chatting about how big the crowd was. I was struck by how short in stature they were. When they came on stage, a few of the crowd shinned up the rugby posts to get a better view. We had never seen anything like this before and what followed was explosive. The Who wore all this coloured Carnaby Street gear, including bullseye logos, pop art, Union Jack – the lot.

The 18-year-old Mike Williams was impressed by The Who's Carnaby Street clobber – but also surprised at how short Daltrey and Moon were!

BRITANNIA PIER

1, 8, 15 & 22 AUGUST 1965, GREAT YARMOUTH

I WAS THERE: STEVE DUNN

I was the lead singer with a Yarmouth band called The Mi££ionaires and we appeared on several of the Sunday shows including three shows with The Who on the pier. We also played with Donovan, Tom Jones, David Bowie and Dana in 1965 to packed houses on both of the evening shows throughout the season. Robert Stigwood's agent originally employed us to do the 'soundings' at the Yarmouth Hippodrome for the upcoming Swinging Blue Jeans show at this venue and, as we were considered to be clones of The Hollies and Herman's Hermits at that time, Stigwood contracted us to play for the summer season.

The Mi££ionaires: Steve Dunn's band, which supported The Who

My memories of our participation in The Who shows are still vivid, with images of Keith Moon wrecking his drums and Pete Townshend demolishing one of the many guitars he destroyed on stage. The group members tended to be aloof with the rest of the artists, probably because they were so far ahead of us all both musically and culturally. We were all in many ways mimicking The Searchers, Freddie and The Dreamers, Herman's Hermits, etc. so in terms of originality we were way behind the image portrayed by Townshend, Daltrey and co., but we were really only budding 'stars' while The Who were already established as mega stars, even at this very early period in their career. They gave the impression that they couldn't care less what people thought of them, which in many ways explains why many of the youth of today have exactly the same attitude. Donovan was also blasé in this respect, but extremely shy in retrospect. The difference of course will always be The Who's incredible talent, which left us as musicians in awe of what they were capable of, both musically and in the way they presented themselves on stage.

Townshend had that something that Jagger has. It draws their audience towards them and in a guru-like way convinces fans that they are unequivocally the best, and to be loyally followed, leaving no doubt that the show they have just witnessed is a one and only life experience that no other person outside the theatre can be privy to.

I WAS THERE: REG GARROD

I worked at the Britannia Pier for ten years from 1965 as House Manager and then as Accountant and Deputy General Manager. The Who appeared in a number of Sunday night concerts during this period, doing two shows a night to an audience of 1,511 per show. My main memory during this period is the night the audience started to leave the auditorium because stink bombs were being let off in the theatre.

We asked our security man to go and investigate the source. Much to our surprise he came back to tell me the culprit was the drummer Keith Moon, who was throwing them into the audience from the stage. So our General Manager, John Powles, went and had words with their manager. The dressing rooms often contained broken equipment after the shows.

I WAS THERE: MICHAEL LADBROOKE

I was playing drums with one of the many local bands during this period. To get an opportunity to see a band like The Who on a fairly regular basis was almost too good to be true. My friends and I saw them every time they appeared in the town. We didn't have to queue to get tickets. They were still a bit of an acquired taste even then so there were always more middle of the road acts in Yarmouth on Sunday nights to attract other people. They didn't have their future reperoire of hits to play, so a few covers were included, mainly Motown and Beach Boys. However, much to our disappointment we never saw them smash any equipment. There were always plenty of holes in Pete Townshend's amps but obviously this was prior to arriving in Yarmouth.

I WAS THERE: PAULINE CATTON, AGE 16

I remember going for a day out with my family to Yarmouth in the Sixties. We got tickets to see Donovan and were devastated when he didn't turn up but we saw the support act, The Who. They were great but I remember my dad saying they were too loud. The audience demanded their money back and went to the box office after the show to receive it. So we saw The Who for free – and a great show it was.

The Who were contracted to play for four successive Sundays, performing two shows each time, and were co-billed with Donovan. When Donovan failed to appear on one date, The Who refused to play for longer than contracted and the second show was cancelled.

Pauline Catton got to see The Who for free, after Donovan cancelled

5TH NATIONAL JAZZ & BLUES FESTIVAL

6 AUGUST 1965, RICHMOND-UPON-THAMES

I WAS THERE: KEITH SHURVILLE

My mate John Fensome and I stayed with his sister in Blackheath for a week during the school summer holidays. Each evening ended in a visit to music venues. On the Monday night we went to the Marquee club in Wardour Street to see Long John Baldry and the New Seekers. Tuesday night was a slight change as we went to cinema to see The Beatles new film *Help!* before returning to the Marquee on Wednesday to see the Spencer Davis Group and another group I can't remember the name of. Stevie Winwood's renditioning of 'Georgia On My Mind' is still in my memory fifty years later.

At the interval we went outside to a pub as there was no alcohol in the Marquee and although we were only sixteen we were both over six foot so were served. In the street we stumbled across Eric Clapton who later came into the Marquee and jammed for over half an hour with both groups and Chris Barber. Thursday was a visit to Fairfields Hall in Croydon where we saw several groups although I can only remember The Byrds.

Our final night of an amazing week and the end of our adventure was at Richmond Jazz and Blues Festival. An unbelievable experience kicked off with the John Cotton Sound who were followed on stage by the Moody Blues. This wonderful music was then surpassed when The Who came on stage.

Keith Moon lived up to his reputation with some abrasive drumming and Pete Townshend smashed up his guitar. Roger Daltrey never stopped strutting his stuff while John Entwistle strummed his bass as if nothing else was happening around him. Surprisingly, The Who were not top of the bill and the final act that dragged the night past midnight were The Yardbirds with Keith Relf ending the set with 'Heart Full of Soul'. I believe the Tube station was informed the gig was running late and they held the Tube until everyone got on. What a night and what a week for two music-mad 16 year olds.

BLUE MOON CLUB

11 AUGUST 1965, CHELTENHAM

I WAS THERE: ALAN CONDY

The Blue Moon was our local Mod club. It was just a small club and I guess had a capacity of not more than a hundred. The stage was about 12 feet by 10 feet so was rather crowded with Keith's drum set and amps, but he was thumping and manic just as we liked it.

My claim to fame was that at this gig Roger powered his way to the stage past where I was at the bar – soft drinks only being served here – and trod on my foot. As I turned to see who'd done this, he snarled at me and stormed onto the stage. Best gig ever!

I WAS THERE: MIKE WILLIAMS

The club was the sister club to the Blue Moon in Hayes, Middlesex, which was owned by the Norman brothers, Eddie and John, and Bill Reid. It was on the top floor of a building, up two flights of stairs.

The first floor was a snooker hall and the ground floor was Burton's Tailoring, where we used to go to get measured up for our Mod suits. The club was very small and the condensation, low lighting and smoky atmosphere were far removed from today's modern venues. The sound was deafening. The story goes that they were unhappy at their appearance fee and decided to end their set half an hour early.

I WAS THERE: NELSON HAWKES

My late wife and I and our friends saw many groups at the Blue Moon including The Who. We thought they were 'dressed funny'. They appeared on the small corner stage and when Entwistle raised his guitar up it sometimes hit the low ceiling polystyrene tiles, which he then played up of course. It was a hot night and we had heard of The Who but they were not a huge band at that time and we were used to some relatively big names.

However, we all thought it was really rock and roll behaviour when Daltrey and Moon started to spray the dancers from those plastic lemon shaped Jiffy containers. We all rushed to the front – only to find Moon's still contained lemon juice! They refilled them, and after that initial shock, it was all water.

I WAS THERE: JANET JOHNSON

I was born and brought up in Cheltenham and in my teens I saw The Who perform at the Blue Moon Club. It was an iconic venue which we didn't realise at the time. Jimi Hendrix appeared there early in his career. I remember the evening The Who were there well, because I had my purse stolen!

I WAS THERE: CHRIS WATSON

The Who were completely defeated by the low roof and the small stage. They went through the repertoire again and smashed the stuff up and I remember that at the end Keith Moon was yelling at all the people at the front to keep back because he was slinging all the drums around. It was such a small stage that he was worried about the drums rolling off the stage.

I can remember him shouting 'move back, move back' and they were going through the repertoire of wrecking their stuff, but Townshend couldn't do the windmill stuff because the roof was too low.

ASSEMBLY HALL

19 AUGUST 1965, WORTHING

I WAS THERE: JOHN FEEST

Keith had a small kit and they had small amps. The support band was a local group called The Zabres. Looking back, they were magic days – as we only paid 6/6 (33p) to see them. Wonderful!

PAVILION BALLROOM

20 AUGUST 1965, BOURNEMOUTH

I WAS THERE: DICK IRISH

As it was a ballroom, if you wanted to see the group up close it was standing only around the stage, so quite a crush. Pete Townshend had a reputation for smashing his guitar at the end of their set, as had Keith Moon for demolishing his drum kit, so when this didn't happen at the Pavilion the audience were somewhat surprised. In retrospect I think Pete only destroyed his guitar when he would get maximum publicity for the band. The Pavilion Ballroom was a regular venue then with Bournemouth College putting on what are now classic Sixties bands.

I WAS THERE: SUSAN PAVITT (NÉE DEVEREUX)

I went with my then boyfriend Tony Reeve, who lived near Salisbury. I have to say I don't remember much about the actual gig but it has always stuck in my mind. Having only previously seen local bands play it must have seemed special although The Who were comparatively new at the time. We were able to dance as the gig was held in the ballroom rather than the theatre and I think there were a lot of people there.

The support act at the Pavilion Ballroom was a group called Davy Jones and the Lower Third. Davy Jones changed his name to David Bowie the following year.

I WAS THERE: PHIL PROWLES, AGE 16

The music scene in Bournemouth was becoming a real buzz and I was into bands at the time and we were going and seeing all different bands. When I went to see The Who I was amazed that there were only that amount of people. I was amazed by how few people there were there. I counted 30. They'd just brought out 'My Generation'and I thought to myself 'how can a band of this calibre' – they were all new then really – 'play to this amount of people? It's going to be different one day.' Of course it was. I don't know that they were popular.

I wish I'd kept the tickets, but I was only a young lad. You don't realise, do you, that you are sitting on history?

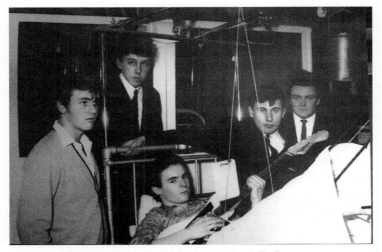

Phil Prowles went to see The Who with his fellow bandmembers in The Caymen

KING MOJO CLUB

29 AUGUST 1965, SHEFFIELD

I WAS THERE: DENNIS LAWSON

I can't remember seeing Pete smile, despite seeing the group on numerous occasions in the Sixties. I watched them many, many times in Sheffield, particularly at Peter Stringfellow's King Mojo Club, where I must have seen them six or seven times. I remember being at the Mojo Club when Pete got an electric shock from his Rickenbacker guitar and went backstage in some discomfort. The group continued as a threesome for a couple of songs and it was still a brilliant sound. Pete only came back when Stringfellow appealed for some rubber-soled shoes for him. Pete continued with a 12 string. Incredible!

The Who are recorded as only making three appearances at the King Mojo Club in Sheffield, which took place between May and November 1965.

SPA ROYAL HALL

4 SEPTEMBER 1965, BRIDLINGTON

I WAS THERE: GRAHAM PRICE

I played bass guitar in a group called Three Plus One. We played as support to all the big groups including The Who, Animals, Hollies, and Gerry and the Pacemakers. The Who were always popular in Bridlington and Scarborough, attracting two and a half thousand supporters per visit, which is not huge by today's standards but was a good crowd for the late Sixties and early Seventies. We supported them twice.

On one of these gigs, The Who had just had a full lorry load of equipment stolen and the road crew arrived with brand new Vox gear, Fender guitars and a set of Premier drums and proceeded to set up and test it to make sure it all worked, mainly at full volume! We were in awe at the sight of 500 watt Vox amps and speaker cabs and that unforgettable smell of new electrical gear warming up.

Later, after testing, etc., their manager arrived and said we had to
use their gear to avoid moving stuff around but we were not used
to this volume and managed to use our PA system. That was a 100
watt Marshall that was quite a rare sight and attracted interest from
the roadies and crew as it was early days for this gear.

Moonie appeared and proceeded to voice his displeasure at the
replacement Premier drum kit he was expected to play. He went
on to trash it and asked our drummer, Derek, if he could use his
Ludwig set. Derek agreed, but pointed out that we would like it
back in one piece as we had other commitments and couldn't afford
the cost of replacing it, which was about £1,000 in the late Sixties.
True to his word, Keith gave Derek's kit a good work out but no
damage.

The bass guitar that John Entwistle was playing was a new type
made by a maker unknown to me and was based on a lyre shape
with quite large horns. This was a big change from the Precision he
and I both usually played. It had a long neck and four extra frets
and long head stock that required hand wound longer strings not
available off the shelf so he told me he liked it so much he bought
two more guitars as he didn't want to be stuck if he broke a string.
His guitars travelled with him, hence not being stolen with the
rest. Following his death it appeared he had a collection of all the
guitars he had ever owned, a total of 300 plus – a few more than
Pete Townshend!

At the end of the show a brand new sunburst Strat was forced
through a Vox speaker cab by Pete and the neck got broken. An
article recently online had a sunburst Strat for sale with a later neck
fitted following repair and supposedly belonging to Pete. Could it
be, I wonder?

We later talked backstage with the group and the crew and laughed
about how busy they were kept with gaffer tape and screws, etc.
repairing 'wear and tear' to the kit. We spoke with many of the top
groups of the day. As a rule they were all friendly and spoke of how
they started out just like us with a Thames 15cwt van and playing in
pubs and clubs up and down the country for thirty quid a go.

I WAS THERE: JOHN HALL

I was the drummer in a band called The Roadrunners for a brief period of time. We supported The Who at the Spa with another group, Three Plus One. We played a kind of blues, a lot of the Stones, a lot of The Beatles and some of the Mersey chart sound. Quite popular sounds really. We had a bass, a rhythm, a lead, drums and a singer who used to do tambourine and maracas. And I used to harmonise with the singer with a microphone held between my legs! We were based in Driffield. I'm mentioned in Woody Woodmansey's recent book. That's my only claim to fame.

The bass player's brother and one of his friends were agents in a very non-profit making way. They may have been hoping to become profitable. But they would do all the bookings through agencies. We never got into that. We'd done one or two things at the Spa but supporting The Who was a massive event for us as a small group. I was 18 or 19 and from a country town, so it was a bit of a shock really.

I was massively excited but a bit awestruck and a bit dumbstruck by the way they performed and by the damage they used to do to their instruments. I can vividly remember some arguments amongst The Who themselves in the dressing rooms and backstage, where they were arguing that they were smashing more than they were earning. They were having a little bit of a discussion about that backstage.

We watched the performance partly from the wings and partly from the audience. They were massively talented but also destructive.

I had a set of Premiers. I thought they were good drums but I think Moonie always used Ludwigs, the top ones. I think he'd smashed some drums and looked at mine and passed on them and went to the other group who had Ludwigs. I think he did some damage to those. I think all would be rectified in the end with some money. My drums weren't the massive make that the others were.

I WAS THERE: DAVE WESTAWAY

I was a singer in a band that supported The Who in Bridlington Spa.

I think we got £25 for it. We got the gig because we were on the list. There were so many people who were used as residents at the Brid Spa and we were one on the list. In those days there used to be top line bands on every week and we were members of the Musicians Union, which you had to be to actually operate at Brid Spa, and so periodically they would call on us to support bands that were playing at the Spa.

I remember The Who smashing everything up. All our gear was all paid for on hire purchase, and we were paying quite a bit of our wages on hire purchase. And they had all this equipment and the finale of their show was smashing it all up so you can imagine how we felt.

I don't think they broke even or operated at a loss. Eventually they got on top of it but I know towards the end they were using a lot of equipment that didn't actually do anything. It was just used as a prop to smash up. They used to smash up the guitars up on a regular basis. It was quite a night. You were gobsmacked by the time they'd finished. They were an excellent band. They were the band at the time, the Mod band. As a band they were brilliant. But you know – the smashing up – we saw it from a different perspective because we were paying for everything. I suppose they indirectly were, but it was part of the show.

I WAS THERE: PAT RAMSHAW, AGE 11

As an innocent 11 year old, my best friend and I would stand outside the Spa by the stage door and collect autographs of the many bands who performed at the Spa. One such evening we were there, autograph book in hand, when our attention was diverted to the top of the slope leading down to where we were stood. At the top of the slope was a Mini emblazoned with a Union Jack. It was open topped and standing to attention were four people singing God Save the Queen as it descended down the slope towards us. What an entrance! The autograph book has long been lost but that image of The Who in that Mini will stay forever. I'm now a not so innocent 62 year old!

I WAS THERE: GORDON SYKES

All of us used to go to the Spa back in the Sixties, be it for The Rolling Stones, all nighters or The Animals, Hollies and so on. Brid Spa could hold quite a few folks in those days, all standing on the dance floor. It could be quite a crush, but great nights. I have two memories of The Who's visits – they played there in 1965 and 1966. One is of going for a drink before hand in a nearby bar and finding Moonie 'entertaining' several local girls. The other is of standing in front of the stage alongside a mate who was screaming at Townshend 'don't break it – give me the bloody guitar' as he repeatedly smashed it into the speakers.

IMPERIAL BALLROOM

11 SEPTEMBER 1965, NELSON

I WAS THERE: GEORGE GRIMSHAW

I grew up in Nelson and, being a baby boomer, entered my teenage years at just the right time to appreciate the advent of the British group scene. The Imperial Ballroom had been a top music

George Grimshaw from Nelson (wearing glasses)

venue throughout the Forties and Fifties, hosting many of the big bands on the circuit during those decades. When the Sixties dawned, the management were quick to begin booking the stars of the time, usually male singers from both sides of the Atlantic.

Then, in 1962, came the 'beat group' revolution when The Beatles burst on the scene with 'Love Me Do'. From then on we were treated to a chart topping act every Saturday. The venue was a Mecca for us and we still reflect how lucky we were to have such a ballroom in our small Lancashire cotton town.

I was fortunate to see The Who three times at The Imp, as the venue was affectionately known. You knew there was going to be a wall of sound as the roadies set up the stage with an array of speaker cabinets, many more by far than any of their contemporaries. I counted forty 12' or 15' speakers at the first gig. A wild night was assured when this band hit town. They had a reputation for their wild stage show, culminating in destruction of their instruments. With Moon the Loon on drums, you never knew what to expect. During one number he was hitting the drums so hard that one drumstick splintered and flew into the watching throng. At the end of one show, he kicked the entire drum kit off the stage and in to the audience. Bass drum, snares, cymbals all went rolling across the stage and ended up in the laps of the seated, screaming girls. There were always a number of large settees arranged around the front of the stage, mainly to act as a barrier to hold back the crowd.

Of course, Pete Townshend always got in on the act by destroying his guitars and amps. Fireworks were always guaranteed at their gigs. I always wondered how they managed to fund the replacements as they could not have been on mega bucks at the time, and electric guitars were not cheap, relatively speaking. The ballroom went into decline in the Seventies and eventually became a discotheque. It ended its days on 18 March 1976 when fire engulfed the cavernous aircraft hangar of a place. The Imperial Gardens housing project now stands where this great venue once stood.

Pete Grear's band, The Beathovens, who supported The Who at The Imperial Ballroom

I WAS THERE: PETE GREAR

I was in a band called The Beathovens and we played on the same bill as the support band to The Who twice at the Imp. Our bass player went into the dressing room and was given a pair of drumsticks by Keith Moon. Unfortunately he didn't sign them, but they are the genuine article. He still has them at home in Canada.

MARKET HALL

9 OCTOBER 1965, CARLISLE

I WAS THERE: ANDY PARK

A guy called Duncan McKinnon ran a company called Border Dances and he used to bring bands up to Scotland. He used to run them in Scotland Wednesday, Thursday and Friday and then Saturday was always Carlisle, at a place called the Market Hall. It was like a big barn. It held about 1,500 people and the sound was awful.

When I was 18, 19, I had an accident and ended up in hospital

CARLISLE JOURNAL, FRIDAY, OCTOBER 22, 19

Andy's Pop Talk

So that's where all that noise comes from !

THIS week I met the Peddlers, the Who, and the Three Pin Squares — three groups heading straight for the top but all very different !

Now take top recording group, the Who (hit records "Anywhere — Anyhow," and "I Can't Explain"). They really feature a terrific sound which comes straight from their drummer and lead guitarist, Pete Townsend.

He told me the secret of the really weird sound effects that are currently taking the charts by storm. By playing into the amplifiers the sound is fed back with a way-out note.

Pete has even been known to throw his guitar at the amplifier !

When the Who are on stage the impact is that of three or four juke boxes — all belting out rhythm at the same time.

But then, that isn't really surprising, as they use 93 amplifiers, valued in the region of £4,000 — more than double the number used by the average group.

After their great reception at the Market Hall they t me of their plans for future, which included concerts in Sweden the v next day.

Their new disc, Generation," which des its title is not a protest sc is due out later this mo and they'll appear in "Re Steady Go" and "Thank Y Lucky Stars" before Nov ber, too.

DISC OUT

"We'll Sing in the S shine" is just the record the Peddlers have been v ing for. Already it's in top 50, and this lively th some who hail from Li pool, told me when I them at the Market Hall they are keeping their fin crossed, and planning next disc, which will soo on release.

Another up - and - co group are the Three Squares, from Darling who are going to add to already good sound by ing a sax to the line-up in near future, after their disc, "Say Goodbye," is leased.

for ten months. I went in to hospital sport mad and came out pop music mad because I used to listen to Luxembourg and Caroline in hospital. When I came out, the local youth club wanted a band and, because I was pop music mad, I would go and find a band. And I found a band to do the village dance.

And this guy called Duncan McKinnon from Border Dances says 'I'll give you some posters to put up. Where would you be on Friday?' And I said 'I'll be in the pub.' He arrived with this other guy from a local newspaper and after a few pints I was offered the chance to go down to Liverpool to the Cavern Club to do a 'local guy goes to the Cavern' feature. In the end that never actually happened but I had a press pass and I could go anywhere I wanted. It was manna from heaven.

I started doing a column for the local paper. It was called Andy's Pop Talk and I did that for about three or four years. I interviewed Pete Townshend after the Market Hall gig and he talked about how he got his guitar sound and the group's plans to tour in Sweden. And then Duncan McKinnon said I should compere and deejay at the Market Hall. So that's what happened. That's how I got into it. I'm still doing it today.

If a band like Brian Poole and The Tremeloes were on the week before The Who, they would have a couple of speakers and couple of amps and that would be it. When The Who arrived, it took about three hours to set the equipment up. I've never seen as much equipment in my life. Just a wall of amplifiers. They had 93 amplifiers.

I can remember them being at the Market Hall because of the equipment more than anything. In them days, lads in bands were interested in the music but also in girls. The Who weren't interested in girls. They were more interested in what sound they could get. It took them a good two hours to get the sound right before they were happy. And Pete Townshend, instead of standing at the front playing out to the audience, he was more sideways, playing into his amplifier so that he could hear what it sounded like. I can visualise that now even after fifty odd years. There would be at least 1,200 people there. You could watch a different live band every night of the week in Carlisle then. Now today you'd be lucky if you got one a week.

PILL SOCIAL CENTRE

22 OCTOBER 1965, MILFORD HAVEN

I WAS THERE: KEVIN CROTTY

Together with three other lads from Pembroke Dock, we used to catch the 7pm Hobs Point to Neyland ferry and drive to Milford Pill every Friday. It was the best night of the week, returning home usually in the early hours on Saturday morning. I remember The Who so well for two reasons.

Firstly, Keith's drumsticks flying out of his hands. He had a quiver full of replacements which had all virtually gone by the end of the gig. Secondly, Roger changing a few words when he sang 'My Generation' from 'why don't you fade away?' to 'why don't you all fuck off?', much to the amazement of the Sunday school girls! It was brilliant and I will always remember it!

I WAS THERE: RAYMOND DONY

Whenever a big name came to the Pill, a friend of mine used to hire a bus to take us from Pembroke Dock round to Milford. This of course was in the Sixties before the Cleddai Bridge was built. A load of us went to see The Who and, as I was learning the guitar, I was so looking forward to seeing Pete Townshend in particular. They came on stage and boy were they loud!

Pete Townshend windmilled almost every song and Keith

Raymond Dony, a budding guitarist at the time, paid particular attention to Townshend's playing

Moon hammered his drums, throwing his broken drumsticks into the audience. I have to admit I was not impressed with the musical content of the act and the only thing I came away with was a headache.

I WAS THERE: PHILIP GOODRIDGE, AGE 16

I've seen The Who seven or eight times, three of which were with Keith and I saw them at the Isle of Wight festival. The first time I saw them was in Pill Social Centre. I had to ask my mum and dad if I could go and see them. I begged my mum. That's the way things were then. 16 then was young. The Pill Social Centre was a rough hole. You could guarantee a fight every time.

Pill Social Centre was like a community centre. There was no alcohol. They had a little coffee bar where you could buy soft drinks. They had people like The Hollies there, Lulu, Freddie and The Dreamers, The Searchers. They had people that were number one in the charts. I'd imagine 200 people would have been the capacity, max.

I thought it was going to be bouncing there but, honestly, I counted the people and there were genuinely only 16 people there. No one danced all night. People looked really bored and I was the only one in there that was interested. They played their set, and I can see it now. I had my elbows on the stage and I just watched them play there whole set. They played 'My Generation' and that sort of stuff. I thought they were amazing.

And when they finished, I stayed and watched them take all their kit down themselves and while they were putting their kit away I talked to them. I talked mostly to Roger Daltrey and he was really, really nice. I was a Mod then – well, I thought I was a Mod, anyway. He was amazing. He talked to me for ages. Keith Moon was bouncing off the wall. John Entwistle didn't say anything. Roger Daltrey was my hero. And Pete Townshend? Well, there he was. I had a drumstick and I had their autographs. I haven't got the autographs any more because I gave them to a girl I was going out with – or thought I was going out with!

I WAS THERE: LESLIE GUTCH

Despite being in the sticks the Pill Social Centre, located in Milford Haven in deepest west Wales, attracted more than its fair share of big name acts in the Sixties. I remember going to see the likes of Tony Rivers and The Castaways, Freddie and The Dreamers, Dave Dee & Co, The Pretty Things, The Hollies and, of course, The Who. Needless to

Les reckons his partial deafness is down to Townshend

say the joint was packed as The Who were already a big name act and obviously bound for super-stardom. I was positioned up against the stage, caught in an excited forward press when the band appeared. I was unable to move back and was stuck right next to a large Marshall amp that belonged to Pete Townshend and when he struck his first chord I was literally deafened. I could see the veins standing out on Daltrey's neck as he sang and I could see Keith Moon hitting his kit but all I could hear was a wall of noise coming from Townshend's amp. They were without doubt the loudest band to appear at the Pill in those heady days.

I also remember Keith Moon chucking several sticks into the crowd and kicking his kit all over the stage when they finished their set but no guitar smashing took place on that particular night. I was just twenty years old at that time but was left partially deaf in my right ear ever after. Many thanks, Mr Townshend!

The Milford Haven girls: Ruth Walters is second from left

I WAS THERE: RUTH WALTERS, AGE 16

I had got into music through The Beatles, who were a lifelong passion, but The Who were a different kettle of fish and a very exciting band. I only lived five minutes from the Pill Social Centre so me and my friends managed to see quite a few 'hit parade' bands at that time, such as The Hollies, Lulu, Peter and Gordon, Long John Baldry and PJ Proby. You didn't get big crowds to the events so there was no worry about getting in. It was a small stage inside and there was a small refreshments area – nothing fancy.

I remember Roger Daltrey as being very well groomed and dressed. He looked beautiful, in fact. I always remember his hair as being perfect in the then Mod style. Townshend too was immaculate in a long dress coat. I don't recall Entwistle as he wasn't my favourite, but Keith Moon was, as always, mad on the drums. They were all fabulous. They were all young and they were like gods to us girls. I remember that night in particular because I didn't have anything to wear so I had managed to get round my mother and she lent me one of my father's shirts.

She said it was Indian, but I think she meant she bought it from an Indian man. It was new and still in its box – a gold brocade shirt with a collar and with buttons down the front which I wore with brown trousers. As us girls crowded around the front of the stage gawping at the band – there were no bouncers in those days – Keith Moon threw a drumstick into the small crowd at the front. I grappled with another girl and I managed to get the drumstick. What a trophy! But in the process I tore my father's brand new shirt, which didn't go down well with my mother who confined the now torn shirt to the bottom drawer of the cupboard. I didn't care. I had my prize and was the envy of all my friends. That is why I always remember seeing The Who. They were a fabulous band and my Dad's shirt got torn!

THE RHODES CENTRE

23 OCTOBER 1965, BISHOP'S STORTFORD

I WAS THERE: RAY GREENALL

We used to go to the Rhodes Centre every Saturday night regardless of who was on and saw a lot of good bands in those days. The Who were obviously a big attraction.

I imagine some people probably didn't even get in, because you used to have to get there and queue in those days.

I was working in London at the time so you knew about The Who because of their London roots. What I remember of that night is that I was fairly near the front and I was down the right hand side. I lived in Sheering and the support band came from around there, because I seem to remember that the drummer of the band had invested every penny that he'd got in his set of drums.

Towards the end of the show, when The Who started to smash everything up, the roadies were bringing on spare kit for all of the people in the band. They were bringing on drums for Keith Moon. And I remember seeing this snare drum come on and Keith twirled his stick around his finger. I don't know why but I just happened to be watching him at the time and saw this snare come on. It was one of the bright red ones with sparkles on. He didn't attempt to play the snare at all. He knew straight away it wasn't his snare and he just stabbed straight through it. It was a very deliberate act. He grabbed his drumstick like a dagger and just stabbed straight through it. I can picture it now. I can picture him doing it. I didn't think any more of it.

And the show ended and we were parked round the back so we came out of Rhodes and turned left to go around the building and there was a dustbin area. And as we walked past the dustbins Keith Moon was lying in a heap in the dustbins clearly having been given a bit of a pasting. It turns out that one of the roadies or the manager for The Who had gone to the drummer of the local band and said 'we're running out of drums. Can we borrow your snare?' And he said 'yes' but he was a bit uncertain about it. And they said 'don't worry, if there's any damage done we'll pay for it in full.' And he said 'ok.' Well, it was his drum that got damaged and afterwards he asked for his money and they told him, not very politely, to eff off. So he took it out on Keith Moon.

They were banned from Bishop's Stortford after that. The town council banned them from ever appearing in Stortford again. Not that it did any harm to their career.

The Who released their third UK single, 'My Generation' on 29 October 1965. Reaching No. 2 in the UK, it was The Who's highest charting single in their home country.

STARLITE BALLROOM

29 OCTOBER 1965, GREENFORD

I WAS THERE: VAL MABBS

I have a diary note from 29 October 1965 saying that we queued for ages for The Who at the Starlite and paid 9/- (45p). They were there

Starlight Ballroom , Greenford, when it was the Sudbury Odeon

a few times, but on one particular occasion we were queuing in the foyer and I remember Roger came walking up and down the queue, talking to people and spreading the word a bit.

I had a conversation with him in later years, when I was working in the music business, and said to him how I remembered that he came along strutting up and down beside the queue. I think he took it in slightly the wrong way. I wasn't inferring that he was being arrogant. As the lead singer, Roger had to push himself out there, having characters like Moonie and Townshend behind him.

ST GEORGE'S HALL

6 NOVEMBER 1965, HINCKLEY

I WAS THERE: GRAHAM AUCOTT

I saw them twice at the George Ballroom in Hinckley, once at Granby Halls in Leicester, once at the Lanchester Polytechnic and once at The Belfry golf club. When we saw them at Granby Halls that was the first time I'd seen Daltrey swinging the microphone out and pulling

Lambretta lover Graham Aucott (right) with his Vespa-fancying brother

it back on the cord. They were on a raised up stage and it was a
good performance. The Belfry was also good, it was just the second
performance at the George Ballroom that wasn't so hot. Hinckley
is between Coventry and Leicester and there were Mods coming in
from both cities to the George Ballroom to see them. I was a Mod at
the time and had an original parka, it was an American one that had
jungle instructions on the inside. It used to stink when it got wet.

To get in the George Ballroom you went upstairs and could probably
get 500 in there. If you could get upstairs to the balcony you could see
out all over the other revellers and the bands but it was a poor stage
there. They sort of squeezed through a single doorway from the back.
Arthur Brown nearly set the place on fire with his horns because it was
so hard to get on stage.

I can't remember any trouble. You didn't argue with the bouncers
up in the George Ballroom. Being local lads we could get tickets. It
felt good. You'd go and park your scooter up somewhere in what
we used to call the Scoot Cave, which was the back of some shops

where there was a lot of robbery going on in those days. If you had wing mirrors on your scooter, somebody would come round and pinch 'em, and chrome racks and stuff like that. But then we'd come marching down and go straight in, hand the tickets in and we were in. Those from Coventry and Leicester were taking a chance and had to queue to get in. It was a good time to be alive.

TOP OF THE POPS

18 NOVEMBER 1965, MANCHESTER

I WAS THERE: DAVE HOUGH

I have never seen The Who but I have always enjoyed their music from day one. I bought all their music and also followed Roger Daltrey's career. My sister Linda, who now lives in Kent, was very close to The Who in more ways than one. She met The Who at one of the very early *Top of the Pops* television programmes and she and her friend got to know them well, to the extent that Linda used to babysit for Keith Moon for a long time. I think I'm correct in saying that Roger Daltrey brought her back home to darkest Deptford in London a few times.

The Who appeared on the BBC's flagship music programme Top of the Pops eight times in 1965.

EMPIRE POOL

19 NOVEMBER 1965, WEMBLEY

I WAS THERE: BRYAN BENNION

I saw the Small Faces, The Action and Benny King on different visits to the Dungeon in Nottingham. I had an Instamatic camera and regularly took photos. The first time I saw The Who was at the Dungeon in October 1965 but later that month I went down to London on my own to see The Who, Georgie Fame, The Kinks and Wilson Pickett at The Glad Rag Ball, at the Wembley Arena. I saw them again in 1966 at the Odeon in Derby.

The Who at the Empire Pool, Wemnbley

DOROTHY BALLROOM

23 NOVEMBER 1965, CAMBRIDGE

I WAS THERE: BOB SIMPSON

I remember that night very well, as I was the drummer in the support band The Tykes. The Who were very loud, although not as loud as Jimi Hendrix, whom we also supported there, and put on a great performance. I even had Keith Moon wander over to me at the end of the evening and offer to help me pack up my drum kit! He was stoned, with eyeballs the size of saucers. However it was not long before Roger Daltrey and a roadie came over and 'collected' him.

I have a copy of the ad from the *Cambridge News* advertising the gig. My girlfriend at the time added in 'The Tykes' because we only got the support gig the day before and had clearly missed the newspaper's print deadline.

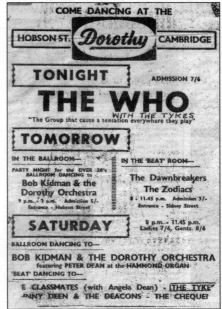

COME DANCING AT THE

HOBSON ST. *Dorothy* CAMBRIDGE

TONIGHT   ADMISSION 7/6

THE WHO

WITH THE TYKES
"The Group that cause a sensation everywhere they play"

TOMORROW

IN THE BALLROOM—
PARTY NIGHT for the OVER 20's
BALLROOM DANCING to
**Bob Kidman & the
Dorothy Orchestra**
9 p.m. - 1 p.m.   Admission 5/-
Entrance - Hobson Street

IN THE 'BEAT' ROOM—
**The Dawnbreakers
The Zodiacs**
8 - 11.45 p.m.   Admission 3/-
Entrance - Sidney Street

8 p.m. - 11.45 p.m.
Ladies 7/6, Gents 8/6

SATURDAY

BALLROOM DANCING TO—
BOB KIDMAN & THE DOROTHY ORCHESTRA
featuring PETER DEAN at the HAMMOND ORGAN
'BEAT' DANCING TO—
E CLASSMATES (with Angela Dean) - THE TYKE
NNY DEEN & THE DEACONS - THE CHEQUE

MY GENERATION

FIRST ALBUM. RELEASED 3 DECEMBER 1965

I WAS THERE: HARVEY KUBERNIK

Producer Shel Talmy's tenure with The Who was very brief. In those days producers and engineers were very involved in the mix. Often the bands would go home and would not even stick around for the mix.

Shel is not the guy that some of The Who and some of The Kinks have portrayed him as for decades. I think it has to do with an entry-level production deal or production contract. These things happen to people when they are young. As a producer and engineer, he brought very important technical aspects to the recording of that first album because he'd worked with some surf groups. And he really knew about a louder sound or mic position and stuff like that that I think influenced things like 'My Generation'. I don't think he's been given enough credit.

He was an engineer out here in Los Angeles. He had experience working at a place called Conway Studios where the engineer was called Bill Parr. The studios were very advanced out on the West Coast while some English studio engineers were still wearing white lab coats. Shel was a whizz kid. He either found The Who or he was assigned them – I was never quite sure how it worked. And he probably had a very good solicitor, with very good paperwork on The Who and The Kinks and a production agreement kind of situation.

No bands are ever happy with their first record. That being said, the producer as star was a pretty new concept in England. Mostly they were staff or they were record label people doing the supervision. I think Shel had a little bit more to do with it than just supervising the session. He did know a lot about mic placement and tape.

CORN EXCHANGE

4 DECEMBER 1965, CHELMSFORD

I WAS THERE: WHIZZ BATES

I saw The Who play twice at the Chelmsford Corn Exchange. Although at the time I lived in Romford, these days only a twenty minute ride away, back in the Sixties it would take about an hour to get there. There would be ten of us on our scooters and we would drive right up to the door.

The Corn Exchange was a lovely building – pampas grass each side of the stage and full to capacity with local Mods who chased us out of Chelmsford, I think because our fashion was more up to date.

Unless you were lucky enough to have seen The Who live back in those days, you have lost out. They were a very visual act – brilliant guitars and fantastic drumming from Keith Moon and, of course, fantastic singing from Roger. The added bonus, although it might sound mad these days, was the smashing up of the equipment at the end.

CORN EXCHANGE

8 DECEMBER 1965, BRISTOL

I WAS THERE: ANDY MUNDY, AGE 15

I was an early visitor to the music scene in those days. 1965 was pre the purpose built venues that we get today. I think most bands played in small market towns in market halls wherever they could. The Corn Exchange was very much a smaller venue that belonged to the city council. It only held three to five hundred people. It could have been like the Bristol Cavern.

All the bands played there, local and national. There was a triangle – bands would play the Marquee Club in London, then they would come on to Bristol Corn Exchange and the third location was in Birmingham and they used to do this route on a regular basis. Even the Stones played the Corn Exchange. A lot of the bands that turned up already had a top twenty hit and it was

absolutely fantastic. It was a dance venue – the bands would play
and the girls would throw down their handbags.

I saw The Who play there twice. Inside there's a number
of palladium type stone pillars and the stage was built around
four of these pillars with two of them to the front of the stage.
There were these enormous speakers at floor level all over the
stage. My recollection, from standing no more than ten yards
away, is of Pete Townshend finding these pillars very handy
because he used to enjoy smashing his guitar against them. Keith
Moon would obviously smash up his equipment. It wasn't long
after the war and most people were careful about looking after
equipment, whether it be a bicycle or your tools in your workshop
or whatever. But they used to smash up their equipment and you
used to stand there thinking 'you're never going to make it if you
don't look after your equipment.' But, of course, they did!

The people who used to turn up were the Mods and it was
more or less the same old faces that turned up. It was all smart
dress code, long leather coats and smart shirts and ties and that
sort of thing.

There were unlicensed and all that was on sale was coke and
fizzy drinks. Anadin and coke was quite popular with people in
those days to get their buzz. And then things like bombers came
on the market. Not that I took these things at all, but I knew
people who did. And they used to buy and sell and exchange them
outside (there were always a couple of police on duty but they
never had a clue what was going on!) The young people then –
and they still are today – are one step ahead of their elders and
the police and the press and the journalists, which makes the time
more and more exciting when you package it all up. Just doing
your own thing.

It all ended at the Corn Exchange in 1967 when the Locarno
and bigger venues opened where the bands could make more
money. They couldn't have made a bean out of playing at these
places because they didn't have the capacity. It's called St Nick's
Market, now and is an indoor market.

FEDERATION CLUB

13 DECEMBER 1965, NORWICH

I WAS THERE: TIM CLAXTON

I was there right at the front, I could have touched Roger Daltrey's feet! As a Mod born in 1950, they were 'my band.' They were everything I had hoped for, and more. I was shocked when Daltrey sang the F word in 'why don't you all fade away?' 1965, remember – heady stuff! But at the end, when I was expecting Townshend to break up another guitar, there was a bonus as Moon wrecked his drum kit as well.

The Who left the stage in turmoil with drums, cymbals and broken guitars strewn about. I loved it so much that even today, 52 years later, I can still recall those magic moments. I also shared them with John Entwistle, many years later in a Cotswold Hotel, and what a lovely man he was.

I WAS THERE: PAUL TAYLOR

I lived in North Walsham at the time and styled myself as a Mod, acquiring a Vespa Sportique – complete with fish-tailed parka, chrome crash bars, etc – on my 16th birthday in May of 1965. When The Who first hit the scene with 'I Can't Explain', I was joined in the fifth form at the Paston School by one Rob Bartlett whose family had moved from London to Sheringham. Rob had two older brothers, one of whom had attended art college with Pete Townshend, and I believe they knew the group back when they were still The High Numbers.

A few fellow local Mod friends and I went to see the group at the then Federation Club in Oak Street, Norwich. 'My Generation' was in, or had recently been in, the charts. The stage was only about one or two feet high and the crowd gathered on the dance floor immediately in front. This was prior to their guitar and drum smashing exploits. They performed very professionally and did not disappoint.

I WAS THERE: JOHN WARD

We saw The Who at the Federation Club on Oak Street. They were due to appear at St Andrews Hall, a much larger venue, about two weeks before but cancelled through illness. The warm up act was a local group called Lucas and the Emperors, a favourite of ours who played for an hour and a half. The Who came on and played for an hour.

I think the most memorable thing was the sound – it really made your body vibrate. We had not heard any groups as loud. The music was unbelievable, such energy. It was a great time for us. We were about to leave school and we had a real sense of freedom, all down to the music of the time. We were so fortunate to have lived through it. I remember the casual clothes – the shirts, trousers, winkle picker and chisel toed shoes. We carried our transistor radios around with us all the time, listening to the pirate radio stations.

John Ward

PAVILION BALLROOM

23 DECEMBER 1965, WORTHING

I WAS THERE: MALCOLM BALDWIN, AGE 21

My seat was in the gallery, which shook quite violently. I seem to remember it was very hot. The music was so loud that I thought the gallery would collapse. It was quite an experience – it was uncanny knowing that the music scene had changed so radically.

Loads of acts appeared in
Worthing, either at the Pier
Pavilion in winter or the
Assembly Hall in summer
and I saw many of them,
including the Small Faces,
Jimi Hendrix and Pink
Floyd. The best was,
of course, The Who.
I first saw them at the
Assembly Hall when
they had just released
'I Can't Explain' and the

Pete Smith nearly missed seeing The Who, as Keith Moon drove past saying 'they're not coming'

last time also at the Assembly Hall, when they
basically performed *Tommy*.

On one occasion, we were waiting outside when their van,
driven by Keith Moon, drove along the promenade and he called
out 'they're not coming' at which some people, not realising who
he was, started to walk away, much to Moon's amusement. We
also saw Pete Townshend driving himself along the seafront in an
old black Morgan hard top. They did perform, and I distinctly
remember them starting with 'Heat Wave' and ending with 'My
Generation', at which Moon threw both his drumsticks and his
drums over the top of his head and into the crowd.

PIER BALLROOM

24 DECEMBER 1965, HASTINGS

I attended their concert on Hastings Pier on Christmas Eve
1965. My enduring memory of the evening was that some idiot,
no doubt the worse for drink, attempted to climb on the stage
to accompany Roger Daltrey on 'My Generation'. Roger's

riposte was to thump him over the head with the mic, whereupon he collapsed back into the audience. I recently attended their concert at the O2 and could not help but notice that 90 percent of the audience were probably not alive when the band was in its heyday.

I WAS THERE: ANDRÉ PALFREY-MARTIN

Christmas Eve 1965 was the first time that The Who visited the 'Happy Ballroom' as it was known. The band had already had some successful singles and built up a reputation as an exciting live act. This tour was in support of their first album that had been released earlier that month. However, despite the 7/6 (37p) ticket price for the first 200 patrons, and 10/- (50p) after that, the hall was only half full. They were playing 'My Generation', which was always the last number. Everyone knew what would happen next and everybody was very hyped-up for it.

Bob Knights – general manager of Hastings Pier

Even Bob Knights, who was the general manager of the pier and who wanted nothing and nobody to cause problems – in his words it was 'my pier' and his word was law – sensed that Pete Townshend was just about to go into his guitar and amp wrecking routine. The song finished and in a flash Bob was on stage. He grabbed the microphone from Roger Daltrey and said 'Oh, look at the time. It's almost midnight and we have to be out by then. Can I have the curtains closed please, and many thanks to tonight's group, The Who, and to all you boys and girls out there in the ballroom. Go quietly, and take care as the deck is a little slippery with the frost.' The band were dumbstruck, but even they did as they were told.

1966 The band played nearly non-stop in 1966, with shows in the UK (over 200 live appearances), including short trips to European countries like France, Sweden, Finland, Denmark and Germany. March saw the release of 'Substitute', which would become one of the most performed songs in the Who canon, and 'I'm a Boy' (released in August) would also remain in their act for several years. Later 1966 shows would feature material from the *A Quick One* album, as well as the single 'Happy Jack'.

DOWNS HOTEL

2 JANUARY 1966, HASSOCKS

I WAS THERE: DAVID GOODWIN

I attended both Who gigs at the Downs Hotel (aka The Ultra Club) in Hassocks in West Sussex. I probably saw most of the Sunday night shows there over a period, starting with Georgie Fame and The Blue Flames, the Small Faces, Nashville Teens, The Birds, The Artwoods, The Yardbirds (who failed to turn up), The Hollies, Sounds Incorporated and others who I have forgotten.

I WAS THERE: KAREN TYRRELL

The Who played at the Downs Hotel, Hassocks, West Sussex twice as far as I know. I kept a diary throughout 1965 and 1966 and a note of who I saw there and also at a pub called The Pilgrim in Haywards Heath. Their support act on 2 January 1966 was a great band from Lingfield, Surrey called Johnny Fine and the Ramblers.

I remember being disgusted at the way The Who were famous for smashing up their instruments and made sure I disappeared into the bar towards the end so I didn't have to witness such unnecessary vandalism – other than that they were a great band of course!

The dances at the Downs were organised by two guys, Mick and Jim. I am sure Mick said he once played in Johnny Kidd and the Pirates. They used to run such brilliant nights on Sundays at the Downs Hotel in Hassocks and on Thursdays and every other Saturday at the Pilgrim pub in Haywards Heath. The Downs was demolished and the last time I looked the Pilgrim had been turned into a small supermarket! I couldn't even *think* about shopping there – what a let down for our lovely pub.

I WAS THERE: KEITH BRAINE

I saw them at the Downs and about three times down Brighton as well, at the Florida Rooms right by the seafront. When I saw them at the Downs there was a bit of an altercation.

The two people who ran the Downs were Pete Tree and Pete Shorland. They used to organise the groups and take the money on the door. Captain Brown actually owned the place. The Downs had a bar upstairs where all of the drinkers and the older kiddies sometimes were, and then you went to the side down a big wide hallway and into a big room downstairs.

It felt like it was underneath, you went to the side and then went in and it had a bar down there and of course nobody every asked you what age you were for drinking. Most Mods used to drink Merrydown and black.

It wasn't that big a place, but it used to get heaving. I don't know how much it was to get in because I got in free. Pete used to organise everything and one of their mates who was built like a shed house was on the door and there was never any trouble. Pete Tree, who was Jack the Lad, jack of all trades, used to write the music column for the local paper. His brother was lead guitarist for the group I was in so if ever we did perform we always got a brilliant write up even if we were shite. Pete Tree had the contacts and he used to get the groups down there – he got some groups who were on their way out, people like Eden Kane, Screaming Lord Sutch. He got the Small Faces, and a group that had done loads of shows called the Bo Street Runners, and another group who had just had one slight hit called the Mojos. There were several groups like that that had been down there, and then there was The Who. I'm afraid they weren't very good that night. Keith Moon impressed, but it was a very small venue compared to what they went on to do. And there was the altercation. At one time, they had one stage and then they had two little stages, one on side and one on the other.

Johnny Fine and the Ramblers were on one stage and The Who went on and Pete Townshend said something like 'get that load of shite off' and Johnny Fine did a hand gesture with his thumb above his lip and the other long forefinger up to his head, indicating 'large nose' if you know what I mean, and Townshend was a little bit upset, to say the least.

At the end, Townshend broke his guitar, because they used to break everything up. They still did there, even though it was a very small stage. The bass guitarist of our group got a bit of the head of the Rickenbacker and put it on his guitar. And people used to think – and to this day they still think – that it was a Rickenbacker bass guitar but it wasn't. It was Pete Townshend's headstock.

I was a Mod. I had my scooter. My mate was the flash one with the Vespa SS, which had just come out and I had the Lambretta. We used to go down to Brighton, to the Mods and Rockers, and didn't get up to much trouble. Just a bit of sugar in the petrol tanks of the motorbikes and things like that – nothing vindictive or anything!

I WAS THERE: ANDRE WELLS, AGE 18

I was an apprentice bricklayer working for a family firm in Plumpton. I was sort of a Mod, I had a scooter. You made sure you didn't go to coastal towns on bank holidays, otherwise you might have got caught up in trouble. Where I was brought up was only 15 minutes from Brighton, so you had to be a bit aware of what was going on at bank holidays.

The first time I saw them was at the Downs Hotel in Keymer and Hassocks, a small village in West Sussex. It was a basement part of the hotel and a bit scruffy. This is where I saw them smash all of their equipment. I didn't realise that was what they did. They broke it all up. They used to put a stamp on your hand which showed up in ultra violet light to make sure you paid if you went out.

COSMOPOLITAN CLUB

9 JANUARY 1966, CARLISLE

I WAS THERE: ALAN SEWELL, AGE 19

At the time I was a member of a six-piece band from Annan called

The Sad Eyes and we were a support act to The Who at the Cosmo. I played lead guitar and arranged some of our music. We played at the Cosmo most Sunday nights with many well known groups. We were originally called The Aztecs until Les Leighton – the owner of the Cosmo – suggested we changed our name to The Sad Eyes, as he reckoned we looked sad on our promotional photos!

On the night of The Who's performance, the venue was packed and

Former Aztec, Alan Sewell (far right), with his band

the audience noisy. Myself and other band members watched The Who's performance from both the 'sky top' bar and the bar behind the stage. My main memory is of Keith Moon's drums and cymbals crashing down from the upper tier of the stage onto all the equipment, and Pete Townshend smashing his guitar onto one of his amplifiers.

CO-OP HALL

23 JANUARY 1966, WARRINGTON

I WAS THERE: MIKE KELLY

We lived in a village outside Warrington called Burtonwood. Groups of us lads would get the bus from the village to the Co-op Hall. There was no alcohol served at the show and certainly no drugs around. As under age drinkers we would have a pint in the British Tar or the Three Pigeons on Tanners Lane prior to the Co-op Hall 'dance'.

Most weeks it was just records being played. The DJ was called Dave Warwick. I never heard of him for 40 years and then he popped up on local TV as Paul Burrell's agent (Burrell was the infamous butler to Lady Diana).At The Who performance I would guess there were no more than 150 teenagers and from memory it was a good show. I went onto see The Who again, at the original Isle of Wight festival. Happy days.

The Co-op Hall was a place of innocence and a good place for us village lads to meet savvy town girls. Some weeks later Fleetwood Mac appeared at the Hall. It was our Las Vegas.

IMPERIAL BALLROOM

29 JANUARY 1966, NELSON

I WAS THERE: IAN GASKELL

During the Sixties I was a regular attendee at the Imperial Ballroom in Nelson, which was known as the Imp. In January of 1966 I was eager to see my heroes, The Who. My abiding memory was the incredible volume of their performance – I had ringing in my ears for two days afterwards. I had managed to secure a place near the front and, for anyone who knows the venue, I was just behind the unforgettable sofas, so I was right at the front!

Ian Gaskell had ringing in his ears for two days after seeing The Who

The Who dutifully arrived via the revolving stage and I was struck by Pete Townshend's brown suit, which seemed out of character with the Pop Art reputation. Their set got louder and louder and the climax of the show was 'My Generation', Townshend windmilling his arms with predictable gusto! As Moon launched into his drum solo, I observed Pete disappear from stage only to return armed with what looked like his normal guitar. On a closer examination and being a guitar player myself, it became obvious that his

expensive guitar had been replaced by a cheap copy. He then proceeded
to destroy it against a fake Marshall amplifier which had been on stage
throughout the performance but not switched on. The frantic drumming
of Moon ended in a crescendo of smoke and sparks as the kit was finally
dispatched to drum heaven. Overall, an unforgettable evening.

BEACHCOMBER CLUB

30 JANUARY 1966, LEIGH

I WAS THERE: ROB DEE

In the late Sixties I was the DJ at the Beachcomber in Leigh and
Bolton along with being the all night deejay at the Twisted Wheel. The
Beachcomber was three clubs in Bolton, Leigh and Preston, which meant
that if they booked somebody in they could use them at all three venues
with a bit of luck. In those days you could do that kind of thing if you
had a tranny van, one band and do the three because they were within 10
miles of each other and it was – just do it, do the three gigs.

I was asked by the owners for some ideas on bookings. I had done
great gigs with The High Numbers, Wynder K Frog, The Exciters, Geno
Washington, The Drifters, Spencer Davis and The Action. Eddie, the
owner, backed my judgment and booked them all. We did three gigs with
The Who – Leigh, Bolton and Preston Beachcombers all in one night.

It was the height of the Mods vs Rockers thing and Keith was patently
a Mod at the time. At Leigh, someone threw a bottle at Keith Moon,
who promptly stood up from his kit and lobbed it back. He carried on
with blood streaming for last few numbers but it was getting a bit out of
hand and they all piled into their van as fast as possible to go to Bolton.
In Bolton the town centre was just absolutely jam-packed with people
who didn't know what was going on. It delayed them getting to Preston.

The first time I met The Who would have been when they were The
High Numbers. There was also a band called The Action. The Action
were what you would call the best white soul band in the country and
were so big in London, they had a massive following. The Who were
doing the same kind of numbers – basically white soul, a bit of Motown,

'Dancing In The Street', all that kind of stuff – but The Action were a better band at that and they were a big problem for The Who management because they were better than them.

They were so big that they were using the same signs as The Who –the Mod sign with the target and the arrows and that stuff. Reg, the singer, told me before his death about four or five years ago that they were paid off to disappear. The band were paid off with a lot of money by the

The souvenir programme from The Who's tour with The Fortunes, The Merseybeats and others

record label to disappear so that they could promote The Who. It was enough money to make it worth their while, about half a million quid or something. And The Action were a good band. They were a red-hot band at the time.

ODEON CINEMA

5 FEBRUARY 1966, SOUTHEND-ON-SEA

I WAS THERE: DAVE BRABBING, AGE 16

I had just started work as an apprentice engraver in Westcliff-on-Sea, when I bumped into an old school friend who asked me if I wanted to go and see Screaming Lord Sutch at the Southend Odeon as he had a couple of free tickets and back stage passes to meet him. These had been obtained by my friend's brother, who knew the then Odeon manager

Handbill for The Who's gig at Club A Go Go in Newcastle

Arthur Levenson. My friend and I were both big fans of Lord Sutch, mainly because he ran a pirate radio station which we always listened to just off the Essex coast at Shivering Sands. It was called Radio Sutch!

We met Lord Sutch backstage and he seemed quite a nice bloke, although a little bizarre. We also saw some of the other acts backstage who were just hanging around. They included The Merseybeats, The Fortunes and Graham Bond as well as The Who.

Although we didn't meet them the thing I most remember was Keith Moon who seemed quite mad – no surprise there! He was playing practical jokes on just about everyone who was around. We then went to watch the concert, which was both exciting and mad, with all the girls screaming. It was difficult to hear anything, as it was at most concerts in those days.

CLUB A GO GO

17 FEBRUARY 1966, NEWCASTLE

I WAS THERE: IAN DALGLEISH

The club was packed out, with the condensation dripping off

the walls. The Who put on an energetic performance and, as they finished their set, Moony kicked his drums over and hit Pete Townshend on the leg with his cymbal. This resulted in a fierce glare aimed at the drummer.

I enjoyed the set but most of the audience was not impressed, many preferring a more soul-based act (who were on the bill). So you could say they did not go down very well.

VOLUNTEER HALL

18 FEBRUARY 1966, GALASHIELS

I WAS THERE: KATH SYMONS

I was very young then but I do remember them playing and how exciting it was to see them in the flesh. I do not have any specific memory of that night, only that they appeared as they did on TV with Keith Moon and Roger Daltrey standing out for me. Keith was wild on the drums! It was a wonderful time for us teenagers in this very quiet rural area of Scotland, because there was a local promoter called Duncan

Galashiels gal: Kath Symons shows off her zippy motors

MacKinnon who brought lots of top bands to our local venues. I saw The Kinks, Jeff Beck and Rod Stewart before they became famous. With lots of local good bands, there was live music every weekend.

NORTHWICH MEMORIAL HALL

SATURDAY, FEBRUARY 19th   10/6d. (pay at door).
HARRY SCOTT presents —
Brunswick Chart Toppers — "My Generation" "I Can't Explain"

THE WHO

Plus — **THE SCORPIONS** :: **THE IMPERIALS**

Dancing 7.45 to 11.45 p.m. Doors close at 10.30 p.m.
LATE TRANSPORT to all the usual destinations — Flat Rate 1/6d.
SPECIAL TRIPS to the Hall — Book at your local Crosville Bus Station :
Crewe and Nantwich 4/- return; Sandbach and Middlewich 3/- return.
SATURDAY, FEBRUARY 26th : **THE MINDBENDERS**

MEMORIAL HALL

19 FEBRUARY 1966, NORTHWICH

I WAS THERE: PETER SCOTT

My father ran the Saturday night dances – that is what we called
them back then in 1966. I was still a schoolboy but was, due to the
family connection, the MC. My dad used to book his acts via Arthur
Kimbrell who ran the Midland Variety Agency. The Morgue as it was
called was the Memorial Hall, Northwich. Arthur begged my dad to
book a band called The Who for a 45 minute spot, I think, for £30,
promising him they would be in the charts when they appeared. True
enough, 'I Can't Explain' charted.

One of the fortunate things about the Sixties was that you were
able to see all the top bands at your local dance hall, and not like
today being in the middle of a field, half a mile from the stage
watching on a giant TV screen. Halls like the Morgue were found in
most towns where each week you would have a top act. I, like many
others, was able to see acts like The Beatles, Stones, Walker Brothers,
Original Drifters, Hollies, John Lee Hooker, Marianne Faithful,
Donovan, Dave Berry and The Who for between 7/6d (37p) and
10/6 (53p). The Morgue was licensed to hold 850 people but the
highest attendance was 2,350 for the Walker Brothers.

On the night The Who were on, we arrived at about 6pm as
normal. When I walked into the main hall the first thing to hit me

was the amount of equipment on stage. The stage was about five feet higher than the dance floor and on each side of the stage was a stack of speakers about fifteen feet high. Most bands of the time used to have one speaker sat on a chair each side. The band's amplifiers were set across the stage with the drum kit on the elevated platform.

The roadies had arrived early and set up. The problem with this was that every week there were also two local bands, on this occasion from Crewe and Liverpool. When this was explained to the road crew, they were quite happy for the support groups to use the equipment. Before the doors opened at 6.45pm, the roadies had a sound check. The whole place shook and vibrated while this took place, causing the hall manager Mr Lewis to threaten to not allow the show to take place. The roadies lowered the volume to his satisfaction, but I could see it was just a way of appeasing him and full volume would be on again later. The support groups had now turned up and were very happy to be able to use the equipment provided.

The crowd built up steadily through the evening. Quite a number of the lads used to come in and then get a pass out and go to the pub opposite which was called the Penryhn Arms, returning just before the main act who went on at 10pm. I used to go and see the act about fifteen minutes before this to chat about what was going to happen eg. how I would introduce them, etc. and find out their finishing number, if they would be doing an encore and other odds and sods. 'Don't let the girls grab you!' was my final bit of advice.

At about 9.58pm, we were stood behind the curtain. I asked the guys if they were ready, and then went out front and announced 'ladies and gentlemen, Harry Scott presents for your entertainment – sensational chart band The Whoooo.' The curtains went back and The Who struck up their opening number. The sound was incredible.

From the side Pete Townshend was playing in his own inimitable style, Entwistle was stood in his own way while Roger Daltrey was rasping out vocally and behind them was Keith Moon drumming manically. The crowd were in raptures. I have never heard that level of noise before or since.

One of my tasks, with the help of a lad called Keith Robinson, was to stand at the side of the stage and, when girls tried to get up, gently push them back into the crowd. Or, if people fainted, then between us we would get them out of the milling throng. The audience used to be very good in those days and gave us great assistance. The problem on this night was that it was impossible for Keith and I to take up our normal position owing to the noise. Neither of us wanted to end up deaf.

The lads were very good, never allowing themselves to be grabbed by the audience and we managed to stop any invasion of the stage.

The night went fabulously with the crowd loving the band and when I signalled for the boys to play their last number, everything seemed hunky dory. I think they finished with 'I Can't Explain' and the crowd loved it, but within seconds chaos erupted as the band – well, Pete Townshend and Keith Moon – went on a wrecking spree. Guitars were being used as sledgehammers on the amps and the drum kit was all over the stage. Needless to say the crowd loved it, no doubt never having seen anything like it before or since.

The curtains closed and I went on stage to wrap the spot up, absolutely gobsmacked. Composing myself I, as normal, thanked the band for the performance and was stunned when they appeared from behind the curtain to take a bow. Obviously no encore could take place as the stage was in chaos. A record was put on and we all left the stage. As we walked to the dressing room I was astonished to be asked by the band if I thought the crowd had enjoyed it and if I thought it a good show!

The lads went to change but, before they left, sought me out to say thanks for having them. Off they went into the night, leaving a very happy audience who had witnessed a fabulous gig. The chaos on the stage meant the final act had to rush to get their own equipment onstage for the last spot and it probably lasted 10 to 15 minutes as the hall had to be cleared before midnight to comply with the law, as you could not be open on a Sunday.

OASIS CLUB

20 FEBRUARY 1966, MANCHESTER

I WAS THERE: JOHN SANDERSON

I remember seeing The Who at the Oasis in Manchester around 1966.
They were late in coming on because no one could find Moonie.
He was eventually found in a bar near Piccadilly. He was brought to
the club and, because there was only one way in and one way out of
the club and it was packed to the rafters, we had to pass him over our
heads to the stage. But he hit the stage and he didn't miss a beat. The
stage looked like a scrap yard when they had finished – broken amps
and the odd Rickenbacker with no neck. Fantastic!

MAJESTIC BALLROOM

25 FEBRUARY 1966, WALLINGTON, SHROPSHIRE

I WAS THERE: DAVID BAGNALL, AGE 16

I have seen The Who live on five occasions and they are definitely my
favourite live rock band. The first time was at the Majestic Ballroom
in Wellington during the mid 60s but sadly Roger Daltrey didn't turn
up and we were told he was ill. They still put on a great show with
Pete Townshend taking over on vocals. In those days bands didn't do
particularly long gigs, but twenty minutes isn't very long.

I used to work for the local paper as a trainee photographer. The
owner of the venue was Dennis Boyle and he often used to let me in
for nothing to the gigs if I did a picture of them in the dressing room.
So I photographed people like the Small Faces and the Alan Price
Set in the dressing room. But sadly it didn't happen on this occasion,
possibly because Roger wasn't there and they just didn't want to
have their photo taken. It's only a small venue, and I suppose I was
easily satisfied in those days, but it was just great to see a band I was
already into so close up.

The Beatles weren't as good as The Who – there's something about
The Who live. The other thing with The Beatles was that it was a waste

of time going, because all you could hear was people screaming, which is awful really. But I don't think anyone screaming could drown out The Who anyway. You could be outside the venue and still hear it, which is why they're all deaf.

I WAS THERE: ADE FELTON, AGE 15

I was 15, 16 at most, and that night Roger Daltrey was not singing. He'd had a bad throat so they only did a short set. They tried to perform without him and they did literally just twenty minutes. In those days of course it was a dance hall, so you had bands that people danced to. There weren't really discos in that sense. So they only did about twenty minutes and then there was another band I can't remember, probably The Big Three from Liverpool or something like that.

I've got a feeling in the back of my mind that the support act was better. But I think, to be fair to them, Roger Daltrey had a bad throat and they wanted to fulfil the engagement but didn't have enough stuff to do more than twenty minutes without the lead vocalist. It was all of them singing, and it was obvious that it wasn't working. After twenty minutes they stopped. It was 'right we've done our set and we're off'.

I WAS THERE: BRYAN JOHNSON, AGE 20

I remember it well. I was with my younger brother and a friend. Roger Daltrey was ill and Pete Townshend did vocals. They were brilliant. But my best memory of the night was a drum solo by Keith Moon. People just watched him, it's a long time ago but I will never forget that drum solo.

STARLIGHT ROOM

26 FEBRUARY 1966, GLIDERDROME, BOSTON

I WAS THERE: NICK BASFORD

I was brought up in the Lincolnshire market town of Spalding, some 20 miles north of Peterborough, but between 1965 and 1967 the place to be on a Saturday night was Boston, 16 miles north of Spalding. Boston Gliderdrome was a superb venue and I saw The Who's one and only appearance at 'the Glider'. Boston Gliderdrome was a truly amazing institution. It started as a dance hall in the 1930s hosting swing and dance bands. By the early Sixtiess it was into rock 'n' roll, eg. Joe Brown, Billy Fury, Marty Wilde, etc. Tales are legendary about the performers having to make their way to the stage through a sometimes hostile audience dodging punches from local yobs and jealous boyfriends!

However, in November 1964 the 'new' Gliderdrome was unveiled. The old ballroom was now a huge bar with a counter at each end and a stage for local acts on the side. On the other side of the foyer, or the other wing of the building, was the new custom built Starlight Room with several hundred lights in the ceiling. During slow smoochy dances the 'stars' would come out.

There was a revolving stage so that as one group disappeared the next one came round. The amazing thing about the Glider was that here in a small market town in the Lincolnshire Fens was a dance hall capable of holding 3,000 people which hosted all the big names in popular music – Tom Jones, Sandie Shaw, Dusty Springfield, The Kinks, The Move, Manfred Mann, The Hollies and many more.

An unusual feature of this gig was that The Who appeared as a trio. Roger Daltrey was absent so Townshend, Entwistle and Moon performed as a threesome with Townshend doing all the lead singing. As far as I can remember they wore Mod style parkas just like hundreds in the audience, many of whom had travelled some distance. Daltrey was apparently suffering from laryngitis – at least, that was the official excuse!

I remember the local Spalding paper, the Lincolnshire Free Press, carried a piece on the concert and the reporter, speaking of the audience, referred to 'a sea of centre-parked heads.' I was never a big fan of The Who but despite the absence of Roger Daltrey they seemed to go down well with the crowd. They did all their big numbers like 'I Can't Explain' and 'My Generation' and, unlike the Small Faces, they didn't get pelted off with coke bottles!

TOWER BALLROOM

23 MARCH 1966, BLACKPOOL

I WAS THERE: HELEN PLANE

I saw The Who at the Tower Ballroom. Keith Moon was in the band. He cut himself and I did have the hanky with his blood on it. I didn't realise at the time it was that important so I have no idea where the hanky is! My cousin Wendy might have it!

I WAS THERE: COLIN STANLEY, AGE 16

Roger Daltrey banged the cymbal and cut his hand on the side and all the girls threw handkerchiefs up on the stage. He picked some up and wiped his hand on them and thrown them back into the audience. They were fighting over these handkerchiefs!

They were good, they were really good. I'm pretty sure 'My Generation' was in the charts. Every Sunday night had a group, I saw the Small Faces The Kinks, The Tremeloes, The Hollies, Lee Dorsey.

The Who went on with their equipment before Peter Jay and they absolutely blasted the place, and Peter Jay said 'we were embarrassed to go on after them.' They went on before him and he said 'fucking hell. How do we follow that?'

STARLIGHT BALLROOM

24 MARCH 1966, CRAWLEY

I WAS THERE: JULIAN DUNCALFE

I recollect seeing The Who at the Starlight Ballroom in Crawley for the price of seven shillings and sixpence (37p). They put a row of chairs in a semi circle around the stage to prevent people getting on it and I was asked to sit on one of them, just a few feet away from the speakers. Great gig!

I remember Keith Moon drumming with his flies open and occasionally tossing sticks into the crowd. The set ended with

Colin Stanley saw The Who at The Tower Ballroon, Blackpool

Townshend bashing his guitar into the speakers just in front of me and Moon kicking his drums all over the stage. All that teenage angst was expressed so brilliantly in their songs. I saw Hendrix in the same place and the same year for 12s6d (62p). Incredible really, as I was working on the petrol pumps in a garage in Crawley High Street earning 4s6d (22p) an hour plus tips, so it was amazingly cheap to see such great bands!

I WAS THERE: DAVID GOODWIN

I saw The Who at the Florida Rooms in Brighton but later on I also saw them at the Starlight Ballroom in Crawley where Keith Moon stood on my toe when walking past and brought us a drink and had a chat. He was utterly bonkers! I seem to remember that I might also have seen The Who at Chislehurst Caves in Kent.

ARCADE RECORD SHOP

HERTFORD

I WAS THERE: CHRISTINE SMITH, AGE 14

I was born in Hertford. I remember as a schoolgirl persuading a girlfriend whose name I cannot remember to go to the Arcade Record Shop in Hertford town centre to meet The Who after school. They were either opening the record shop or just promoting 'I Can't Explain' but they had only just come onto the pop radar and not many people really knew who they were.

My friend and I were the only people to turn up and I was given their autograph on a picture of the group. At the time I didn't know the significance of all this even though I loved their record. I think I may have discarded this in later years, going on to love Motown and rock steady. How foolish was I?

CORN EXCHANGE

25 MARCH 1966, HERTFORD

I WAS THERE: MAUREEN BROWNING

One of the most memorable gigs we saw was at Hertford Corn Exchange in 1965. Until a few years ago I wouldn't have been able to tell you the date, but just before my sister fell ill, we were in Hertford and saw the door to the Corn Exchange open, so we sneaked in and asked if we could have a look around. It is still a venue, but has changed since the Sixties. It was a high-ceilinged hall, but has now been split into two levels, and the bar is where the stage was, and vice-versa.

However, we got chatting to a chap there and told him why we were taking a nostalgic sneaky-peak, and he showed us a framed handbill, showing that it was 25 March 1966, started at 7.30pm and it cost 10/6d (52p) to get in! I was so pleased to know this part of my past. However, looking in my autograph books, I have put 13 March. The support act was the Modern Blues Six.

Also on that evening, they asked how we were getting home,

Maureen Browning (left) and her sister Marion

and we told them our parents were picking us up, but as they had our telephone number, they called our parents, who they had met before, and told them they would drop us off as they were going past Stevenage. So The Who drove us home! Could you imagine that happening today with even a B-list one hit wonder?

As I said, it was a very memorable gig, with them playing all their early music, plus the classic covers they always did in those days, 'Barbara Ann', 'Heat Wave', 'Daddy Rolling Stone', 'Shout and Shimmy' and, I think, 'Runaround Sue', 'See See Rider', 'Dancing in the Street' etc.

They were also on *Saturday Club* on BBC radio once, when Brian

Matthew was still presenting I think, and my sister and I sent in a request and it was read out! Our dad was a grocery shop manager and he gave us a paper till roll to write the request on, which ended up a few feet long, so that probably got it noticed.

Although I cannot prove the provenance (other than we obtained the pieces from The Who personally), when my sister died I found a small group of items, which we collected in those days. A broken Keith drum stick, a Pete guitar string, and an old 1d coin and plectrum from John, and a button from Roger's shirt – although for the life of me I can't recall how we got the penny and the button! My sister never left the family home, so they were buried and forgotten among loads of old stuff, but I recognised them immediately.

I think I still have The High Numbers single of 'Zoot Suit' and 'I'm the Face', but one thing I was very silly to give away to Capital Radio to auction for their *Help A London Child* charity in the mid Seventies was a single of 'I Can't Explain', with the cover signed by all four of The Who. I wonder what that would be worth today?

I WAS THERE: ALAN GOLDSMITH, AGE 25

I put The Who on at Hertford and I paid them £50 cash. Some so-called expert said that The Who never played in Hertford but they did and in fact I've got the press cutting where they went to the local record shop. I paid them £50 plus a percentage and there was this huge queue and the guy, the young guy with the clicker, was sitting on the stairs and obviously I was going way over the percentage so I had him thrown out so I didn't have to pay the percentage, that was one of the little tricks.

We didn't actually get too friendly with the acts because we were working, we were too busy with the big queue outside and getting on with running the show and making sure there was no fights and so on.

I used the name Mark Gold and it said 'Mark Gold Promotions' Present and, because we used to fly post everywhere in those days, everyone from the Council was looking for this Mark Gold to prosecute him, but he didn't exist, because it was really me.

We never put our names on the posters. The only people who put their names at the top were the people on a sort of ego trip. I was more focussed on the money side so I didn't go bankrupt. They all got carried away and wanted their name to go with the bloody acts, but no one was interested in who Alan Goldsmith was, they were interested in the act.

When The Who broke things up, and smashed bits of amplifiers and all the guitars, we just swept it up and put it all in the bin. It would be worth a bloody fortune now! I got on very well with Keith Moon, I liked him, although he was as mad as a hatter, he was a nice bloke. They were all OK. Pete Townshend was a bit distant, but we didn't getting chatting. You'd go to the hall, the band would turn up, you'd go up and say 'hi, you're on at 7.30' or 8.30 or whatever it was, they'd get on with setting up, tuning up and I'd go down to the front of the venue where there was a bloody great queue. I'd be getting ready for opening so they were doing their thing if you like at one end of the hall and I was doing my thing up the other end. I was basically keeping me eye on my money. It was licensed for four hundred but I wasn't very good at counting and I got six or seven hundred in there. I had nine hundred for Stevie Wonder!

The Who attracted a big Mod following then. It was all Mod, girls in the latest fashion. Before the Sixties and The Who, everything was very drab and then suddenly all the girls – you didn't see trousers – they were all in high heels and stockings and suspenders and Mary Quant and Mr Freedom, all the latest fashion and the hairstyles. Everyone throughout the world wanted to have the fashion that London and especially the English girls had. All the guys had Prince of Wales suits and were very fashionable from Take 6, Cecil Gee etc, and winkle picker shoes.

I think it will go down as one of the biggest social revolutions this country has ever seen, because it was a very suppressed and class-conscious society and we broke that mould. Suddenly girls were opening dress shops and coffee bars and people like me were promoting shows.

PAVILION GARDENS BALLROOM

9 APRIL 1966, BUXTON

I WAS THERE: MICK SHELTON

When they played at the Spa Pavilion in Buxton, the Derby Mods were en route to Manchester for a night at their beloved Twisted Wheel. It was obvious that we should stop off at Buxton to watch our heroes. With the band in full swing and the Derby boys showing off their dancing skills to the delight of the local beauties, it became apparent that the local boys, mainly Rockers, were not happy. A fight ensued, which was not unusual in those days. But what amazed me was when Roger Daltrey leapt from the stage, kicked one of our assailants and jumped back on stage, almost without missing a beat. Magic! Sadly we were removed from the premises but we went on to have a great night at the Wheel!

GAUMONT CINEMA

14 APRIL 1966, SOUTHAMPTON

I WAS THERE: ALAN BURDEN

My memory of The Who with Keith Moon playing was a concert at the Mayflower Theatre in Southampton, which was called the Gaumont back then, where the whole balcony was moving and my ears were whistling for a week after the concert!

GAUMONT CINEMA

22 APRIL 1966, DERBY

I WAS THERE: MARGARET ADAMS, AGE 15

The Odeon was then called the Gaumont. Do I remember? Wow – yes I do! My father would send his apprentice to the box office at 7.30am the day it opened to get my friend and I front row seats. That

The Who in 1966 at the Gaumont Cinema, Derby

accomplished, our next task was to get the afternoon off school. We both had dental appointments, ie. we forged letters to our teachers. Then it was down on the bus to join the other fans around the Gaumont to wait for the groups to arrive.

We had written to the fan club, of which we were members, to get a letter to go backstage. The previous week we went to the manager of the Gaumont with said letter, but he was having none of it; disappointed yes –deterred no. On the afternoon of the gig we showed the letter to the assistant manager who organised for us to go backstage after the first show and meet our idols.

We could not believe our luck. We got personalised autographs, which I still have. Backstage, I remember Keith drinking something, Pete eating something and Roger being really kind and making sure we had everybody's autographs. It's all a bit of a blur. The show? I can't remember a lot apart from 'My Generation' and not believing we were really there. I don't remember smashed guitars, but it was the first show of the day. I remember Pete windmilling. And, yes, I have dined out on this experience for 50 years.

I WAS THERE: TRICIE DELAHAY

I went to their concert in 1966 at the Odeon. Also on the tour were the Merseys. It was a magical evening and I had gone on a coach group so we were all excited teenage girls. I will never forget the evening. When they sang 'Substitute' the roof virtually lifted off!

I WAS THERE: PHIL DOXEY, AGE 14

I was two months short of my 15th birthday and I lived in Cromford at the time. All I can remember is that I thought there was at least three acts so possibly The Moody Blues or Spencer Davis Group as well as The Who. We sat in cinema seats, a few girls screamed and tried to run to the front, but were immediately ushered back to their seats. Also The Who smashed some equipment. Funnily

enough I have not seen The Who since but my wife bought tickets for my 65th birthday to see them in Sheffield.

ODEON CINEMA

23 APRIL 1966, ROCHESTER

I WAS THERE: DERMOT BASSETT

Keith Moon was the first thing I noticed about The Who. One evening in early 1965, on a long forgotten TV programme, I saw The Who for the first time. Saw? Fell in love with, more like. I didn't know it at the time, but it was the start of a lifelong obsession. I'd never seen or heard anything like it before and who was that drummer? At school the next day the big discussion seemed to be 'did you see that drummer on TV last night?' It was just over a year later that I got to experience him and them live, at Rochester Odeon, both houses of course. Other highlights came and went. Seeing what people call the 'Pictures Of Lily' drum kit, but what I remember Keith calling 'the engine' live for the first time, shining in the lights as the curtains came back at Maidstone ABC in 1967. Especially as Keith had beaten The Tremeloes' drum kit into submission in the first house!

CORN EXCHANGE

30 APRIL 1966, CHELMSFORD

I WAS THERE: JILL CARMAN-STEWART,

I went to see The Who at the Corn Exchange when I was 15. I ended up backstage and Roger asked me where the best pub was in Chelmsford to go to and I walked with then to show them all! Roger wrote his autograph in red biro on my arm – I was so excited, but when I returned home my mother was horrified and scrubbed it off as she said I would get blood poisoning! I was so upset as I couldn't show it off to my friends!

I WAS THERE: MARION PARKHURST, AGED 15

My friend Linda and myself saw The Who in Chelmsford. I would have been there against my parents' knowledge – my Dad is now 94 and none the wiser! The hall was packed but we had a great view. Roger had trouble keeping his words in sync with the guitars when he sang 'My Generation'.

Keith was breaking drumsticks and throwing them into the crowd. After being jumped on and shoved about, I managed to catch one, but unfortunately have since lost it during one of my many house moves. They went on to smash their equipment, which I found a bit frightening. Me and Linda hung around for a while after and stood staring at Keith as he sat all on his own, wearing a huge brown fur coat, on the front of the stage. We didn't have the nerve to speak to him. What an amazing night. We went home on the backs of scooters.

NME POLLWINNERS' CONCERT

1 MAY 1966, EMPIRE POOL, WEMBLEY

I WAS THERE: JOHN WALLACE

The New Musical Express used to do an annual awards event and get all these bands on – you'd get all these awards, best single, best newcomer and so on. I can't even remember why The Who were there, but they were with people like Herman's Hermits, and Wayne Fontana and The Mindbenders and all sorts of other people. We saw them on television in black and white.

The stage was set up so you had these plinths for the drums kits because there were so many musicians coming on and doing their bit. They'd come on and do one, maybe two, numbers and then they'd disappear. God knows how they managed the PA in those days because they were so technical about stage set up. I remember there was a bank of guitars on these stands, running along the side of the drum platform. Keith Moon decided to trash the kit and he actually damaged other people's guitars, which was spectacular. Everybody was outraged!

I WAS THERE: DERMOT BASSETT

I'd seen them only eight days before. This time, Keith was on a very high drum riser and finished their two song set by kicking his drums off the front of the riser. With just the Stones and The Beatles to follow, Keith wasn't going to be upstaged by anyone!

ARCADIA BALLROOM

8 MAY 1966, CORK

I WAS THERE: JEAN KEARNEY

We didn't get to see them, but me and my pals did 'stalk' them around various hotels in the city. We were a group of very giggly schoolgirls phoning various hotels asking if The Who were staying there with the predictable responses: 'The Who?' 'Yes, The Who', 'Who do you want to speak to?' 'The Who'. And round and round it went. We never did find out where they were staying.

CORN EXCHANGE

11 MAY 1966, BRISTOL

I WAS THERE: JOHN HARRIS

I'd been gripped by the picture of Pete Townshend with a row of smashed Rickenbackers hanging on his bedroom wall, and had been fired up by the energy and power and mayhem and freedom in the TV footage of 'Anyway, Anyhow, Anywhere' and 'My Generation'. We licensed them to break all the rules and we loved it. But nothing prepared me for the sheer impact of seeing The Who live for the first time.

The Corn Exchange was the premier Bristol venue for blues-based and emerging music, run by the enterprising Uncle Bonnie each Tuesday, under the unlikely title of the Bristol Chinese R&B Jazz Club. It was a superb place to really listen to a band – not too large, with a small projecting stage surrounding a couple of pillars, so you could get very close to the action.

John Harris, seated, with house mates from university

We learned about the forthcoming acts from posters at the Corn Exchange itself, and through word of mouth. There were no tickets in advance, so to be sure of getting in you needed someone to bag a place for you near the front of the queue, which often stretched right round the block. A hundred or more of us pressed ourselves tight against the stage to watch The Who setting up two or three yards in front of us. This was the first time I'd seen double-cabinet Marshall stacks – a far cry from the standard Vox AC30s used by other bands. When Pete Townshend tested the system with a power chord, it was so very loud that all one hundred of us found we had thrown ourselves back several feet in shock as if we were a single being.

I'd listened to every track on the first LP again and again, dissecting each one to try to understand what made this strangely different music so exciting. What The Who played that night I can't now recall. Still vividly with me is the sheer energy, the driving forcefulness and the volume. The set was so loud in that small venue that my ears physically hurt, and to be able to bear it I had to move to the side and stand on a table. I clearly remember my ears ringing continuously for five days afterwards.

Would they smash all their gear at the end? In the event, for the final number Pete swapped his Rickenbacker for an old solid-body guitar, which he aimed repeatedly at the nearest pillar on the stage, glancing it off – the marks were still visible months later – before finally bouncing it robustly against the floor. Keith kicked his drums over and Roger did his trademark microphone swirling. But it was enough. We'd glimpsed The Who in destructive mode and we were happy.

The drive, imperiousness, rebelliousness and intensity of The Who blew me away. Their stage show became even more commanding and powerful later in the Sixties but, for me, the rawness, the edge, the unbridled power of this first experience of The Who live was just extraordinary.

I WAS THERE: JOHN RUDGE, AGE 15

It was my first experience of the might of The Who. We joined the queue at the back of the Corn Exchange and didn't think we'd get in. I can't remember how much it was to get in but I seem to remember it was expensive – ten bob (50p)? As I recall, it was announced Keith Moon could not play that night. My mate has confirmed this as he was with me. Keith was apparently ill and his place was taken by Viv Prince of The Pretty Things.

All I remember is that it was amazing. I vividly remember Pete saying 'now this is song from our new album – our only album' and they played 'A Legal Matter'.

PAVILION BALLROOM

12 MAY 1966, WORTHING

I WAS THERE: SONIA JOHNSON

My friend and I were very much part of the pop scene in Worthing during the Sixties. We worked in a shop for low pay, so these evenings were the highlight of our week. We saw many great groups, and dancing and fashion were our lives. I remember seeing The Who in the early days when they had recorded 'I Can't Explain'. My main memory of them is from a later date. There was always a small group of girls hanging around the front of the stage hoping to be noticed. I was typical of a lot of girls then. Long blonde hair and very short skirt. It was getting near the end of the evening when one of these girls came up to me and said that I had been invited back to the band's hotel room. I declined the offer and went off to get my bus.

URY PALAIS DE DANSE

TODAY (SATURDAY), MAY 14th

RNING   TASKER SCHOOL OF DANCING
10-30 — 12 noon   JUVENILE LESSONS, 7—14 YEARS
TERNOON   Admission 2/-

2 — 4-30 p.m.   'TOP OF THE POPS'
ENING   Admission 1/6

BIG BEAT PALAIS NITE!
JACK VENET ENTERPRISES present Hit Recorders of
"My Generation" and "Substitute"
THE WHO
+ BRUCE & THE SPIDERS + THE IN-CROWD
with Allan 'Doc' Merwin, D.J.
6-30 — 11 p.m.   Admission 8/6
NDAY   TEENAGERS' POPULAR NITE!
Presenting SOME OTHER GUYS
7-30 — 11 p.m.   Admission 2/-
DNESDAY   TEENAGERS' SENSATIONAL NITE!
Presenting the Fab BO-RAYNORS
7-30 — 11 p.m.   Admission 2/-
URSDAY   OLD TIME DANCING
7-30 — 11 p.m.   Admission 2/-
DAY   BENSONS ROUNDERS TEAM
SELECT MODERN DANCING
8 p.m. — 1 a.m.   Licensed Bars   Admission 2/-

PALAIS DE DANSE

14 MAY 1966, BURY

I WAS THERE: CHRIS (CJ) SMITH

I went with my mates hoping for a great and explosive set! I think they had just released 'I'm a Boy' on Pete Townshend's Reaction imprint/ label. The Who often ended their set by trashing the equipment. On this occasion they didn't. Pete Townshend settled for ramming his Rickenbacker

Chris' John Entwistle's autograph on that Jackie poster

back into the big Marshall stacks behind him throughout the set. I wish I could remember the set list but I can only remember 'Substitute' and 'A Legal Matter' and a couple of other tracks off their first Brunswick album although they may have done 'Barbara Ann' and/or the 'Batman' theme off the *Ready Steady Who EP.* The most significant thing about the gig is that Roger Daltrey was absent, leaving Townshend to handle vocals. I found out years later that Daltrey had been sacked around this time – from his own band! I remember talking to John Entwistle just before they went on, asking him for plectrums to which he replied 'I don't use them lads', so we asked to look at his fingers which, due to this, were as hard as nails. I also got his autograph on a picture I took with me from some girl's magazine like *Jackie*. I still have it.

I WAS THERE: PHIL SPENCER, AGE 17

I recall it being 7/6 (37p). Townshend was smashing the equipment and finally his guitar. Can you imagine seeing that live in such a small venue, which was packed? I'm informed that they were a trio as Roger Daltrey couldn't appear. I don't remember this myself as it was a long time ago but I do remember where I stood! This was only four days before the 'Judas' concert at the Free Trade Hall where I was horrified by Dylan's strident and distorted second half. I loved The Who since first hearing 'The Kids Are Alright', 'Anyway, Anyhow, Anywhere' and 'I Can't Explain'. The Rocking Vicars were active locally and recorded a version of The Who song but called it 'It's Alright'. I don't know why.

I WAS THERE: TED TUKSA

Roger never turned up. I have heard different reasons as to why he never showed, but would love to know the truth. Pete had to do all the singing. I don't know if he was annoyed that Roger wasn't there, but the equipment was completely destroyed.

It's not clear why Roger didn't show up at the Palais de Danse on the 14th but six days later on Friday 20 May 1966 Keith and John arrived two hours late for a gig at the Corn Exchange in Newbury to find that Roger and Pete had gone on stage without them, borrowing the bass player and drummer from support group the Jimmie Brown Sound. A fight ensued, in which Keith received a black eye and a broken ankle. Moon told a journalist at the gig that he and John were quitting. Keith missed the next few shows, only returning to the drummer's stool on Wednesday 25 May 1966.

FLORAL HALL

21 MAY 1966, SOUTHPORT

I WAS THERE: SUE McGOWAN (NÉE GREEN)

I was present at two of the three Who concerts at the Floral Hall in Southport circa 1966. On the first occasion I went with a group of school friends and on the second with a boyfriend. There was no advance booking in those days; most people were older schoolchildren and young working adults who could not afford to pay in advance. Very few people were older than about 19. You paid on the door from the wages you received – in cash.

Advertising was by posters which appeared around the town perhaps a month before the performance, which gave us time to save up. Prices for bands like The Who were 8/6 (43p) compared with perhaps two shillings (10p) for a lesser well known band like Pink Floyd! Very few people had their own transport and so most people were dependent on the last bus or train. There was never any trouble, and no alcohol. Soft drinks were available. The first half of the evening was devoted to dancing to records played over the sound system followed by a break, followed by The Who. Most people gathered around the stage. There was no seating.

They always finished by smashing up their instruments whilst Keith Moon drummed insanely! Many people found the smashing up quite scary. I know that I did. The band looked so much older than us. Some of the 'big' acts, like Long John Baldry and Chris Farlowe, ended by coming off stage and dancing with the audience but The Who never did.

I WAS THERE: DAVID MELLING, AGE 19

It must have been a Saturday night. I went with my girlfriend at the time, her friend and the friend's boyfriend. They were the only band on. There were between one hundred and two hundred people there, not many people there really. It was good.

We were stood on the dance floor, there were bleacher seating towards the rear and a number of people were sat down on the bleacher seats. But we were just stood on the dance floor about twelve feet from the stage. We weren't dancing, we were just stood there listening to it. They didn't smash their instruments. They played 'I Can't Explain', that's the only one I can remember them playing.

Keith was a real character, he was really, really, good. I don't remember him throwing the drumsticks out into the audience. He might have just thrown them up into the air at the end of it. Each member of the group was memorable but he was particularly good. He was very energetic.

LOCARNO BALLROOM

23 MAY 1966, BLACKBURN

I WAS THERE: DAVID ALMOND

I remember them playing in Blackburn Mecca – the Locarno –

and one of them broke his arm and someone stood in for him. I remember, because they only played for about half an hour and it was only a little cellar club.

I WAS THERE: ADRIENNE JENKINSON, AGE 15

The venue was at an under 18s night at the Locarno Ballroom, Blackburn aka the Mecca. The Who were fantastic and on the up at the time. Roger Daltrey and Peter Townshend were on stage. Keith Moon was absent so another guy was drumming.

They played a good tight set of their earlier hits including 'My Generation' and no guitars were smashed! They were just as good live as in the recording studio and they were very gracious towards their appreciative audience. Afterwards Roger was modestly collecting cables from the stage. I remember a girl shouting: 'Hey, Roger! Have you any fags?' He hadn't but smiled through those blue eyes as he willingly signed my autograph book. Ten minutes later we discovered that Pete Townshend was going to leave via the back door. We dashed around and managed to obtain his autograph as well. Pete was quite shy, very obliging and polite. The Who were without airs and graces, a hard working and talented band who put on a fantastic show.

I WAS THERE: JIM PITTS

I do remember it. I've always remembered it. I've mentioned it a couple of times to people of my age who didn't go. Even they remember it, and wish they'd have gone. The thing that sticks in my mind is that Keith Moon didn't turn up that night. It was the day after they played Rawtenstall. I was looking

Jim Pitts was disappointed not to see Keith Moon behind the drumkit on The Who's visit to the Locarno Ballroom in Blackburn

forward to seeing Keith Moon throwing himself around on the drums.

In Blackburn there was a coffee bar where all the buses gathered and set off from and it was called the KJ Coffee Bar that was known as the Mod place in the 1960s. Everybody tended to meet up there and then get into the pubs that you could get into at that age. You had to be very careful – 'don't go in no rough pubs and keep your nose clean.' And then we'd go off to the Mecca and we could get in OK. It was just the start of us going out drinking at 16 years old, like you did in them days.

There were definitely Mods in Blackburn at that time and I remember seeing all them there, jumping around. They used to have a set Mod dance. They were all grouped together, all cliquey. I think they were over to the left hand side of the stage. I remember looking down and thinking 'oh. That's such a body and such a body' who were the main Mod people. We weren't quite old enough – they'd be about 18 where I'd be about 16 and two years was a big difference. At that time we'd only just started going out and they'd been going out for a couple of years. They were the faces of the time, of the era..

I remember there were rumours about a fall out between the band but I don't remember them announcing that on stage. I might be wrong on this but I have a feeling that it was that guy who stood in for The Beatles when they did a bit of a tour, Jimmy Nichol? I was looking forward to seeing Keith because he was a one-off kind of drummer. Everyone else tended to stay on the stage. Even with The Rolling Stones, Charlie didn't tend to jump around very much. Not like Keith Moon. Obviously I was looking forward to seeing the rest of the band as well. I'd seen them on the television, on *Ready Steady Go!*.

They had balconies in the Meccas and the Locarnos and I was on the balcony leaning over so I was pretty close, right over the top of them, watching them play. It was a good show. I remember Pete waving his arms around, the windmilling that he did and Roger Daltrey jumping around like he did on *Top of the Pops*.

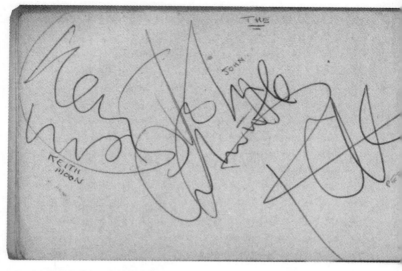

SOUTH PIER

28 MAY 1966, BLACKPOOL

I WAS THERE: TONY BEADEN

I was at the South Pier in Blackpool at the same show as my friend Neville Lee, collecting autographs, and met the group. I helped to carry some of Keith Moon's drums to the theatre and also got their signatures in my book. My recollections of the group was that they were very nice lads and very pleasant to talk to. If my memory serves me I think Cliff Bennett and the Rebel Rousers were on the same bill.

I WAS THERE: NEVILLE LEE

In the 1960s I was an autograph collector. In the spring of 1966 The Who played a concert at the South Pier, Blackpool. As a collector I was there and, whilst I did not see the concert, I was outside and obtained a number of fully signed pictures of the band from magazines such as *Fabulous*. None of these pictures seem to have

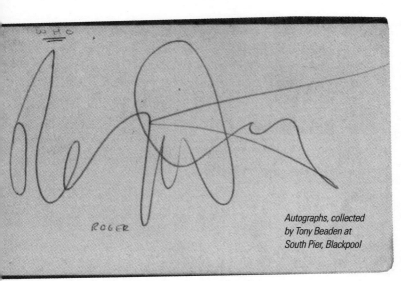

Autographs, collected
by Tony Beaden at
South Pier, Blackpool

survived the years and I have only one set.

What I do remember is they were all happy to sign all my pictures and those of the two or three others who were there and I particularly remember how pleasant Keith Moon was. After signing everything that was requested of him, he chatted on for a while before heading off with the other wild man drummer, Viv Prince, to the bar.

I WAS THERE: SYD BLOOM

I used to roadie for a few bands. I was the only one who could drive at our age. One of the bands was the Rockin' Vickers, (featuring a pre-Motorhead Lemmy), who were quite big in the north and supported The Who at South Pier. Because I used to bang on and on about The Who, they actually recorded a version of a Who song. Pete Townshend slightly rewrote 'The Kids Are Alright' for them to do it as 'It's Alright' in a very plodding pedantic way. They released that as a single – largely, I suspect, at my behest because I just used to annoy everybody about The Who.

Because it was the season – because it was Blackpool – they had to do two houses, 6.20 and 8.45, which was anathema to most bands.

A mate of mine came out to see them and said 'I thought you said they were good?' He said 'The Rockin' Vicars blew them off stage.' I said 'you're kidding me'. The Who just blew the place apart for the second half. They just weren't trying for the first house.

HIT HOUSE

7 JUNE 1966, COPENHAGEN AND FYN'S FORUM, ODENSE

I WAS THERE: HARRY KERSHAW

I was the bass player and main vocalist in a Danish band called the Excheckers during the Sixties. We were scheduled to play two gigs with The Who in 1966 at Hit House in Copenhagen and Fyn's Forum in Odense. The gig in Fyn's Forum went terribly wrong and the place was wrecked whilst The Who were on stage. After the gig had finished, Roger Daltrey had pulled a chick and because girls were not allowed in his hotel and maybe to avoid getting ribbed by the other members of the band I said he could come to my apartment in Copenhagen with her. He stayed the night and we chatted in the morning — he was a nice guy.

CITY HALLS

17 JUNE 1966, PERTH

I WAS THERE: SANDRA BOYLE

We were Mods and they were heroes of ours. We lived in Dundee but often travelled through to Perth to see bands. If we missed the milk train home we had to hitch-hike. They were absolutely fantastic and at the end of the show me and my friends Evelyn and Betty met Roger Daltrey and John Entwistle and got chatting to them. Keith Moon was up on the balcony and obviously away with it as he was playing imaginary drums! Roger and John asked if we would like to go to a party in Edinburgh, where they were staying.

Only being 17 or 18, and quite innocent, we said we couldn't as we had to get the milk train home as we were working the next day! I didn't have anything for an autograph but Roger Daltrey wrote on my arm with a little drawing and his name. I didn't wash it off for a week, until it was starting to be too faded to read. My then boyfriend (now husband) was jealous and wouldn't speak to me.

He remembers a girl called Diane Low running onto the stage and launching herself at Pete Townshend to land a kiss on his cheek. It was funny as he is about 6' and she was only about 5'2'. He took it well. Great times. The Kids Were Alright!

MARKET HALL

18 JUNE 1966, CARLISLE

I WAS THERE: GORDON RAE

I recall seeing The Who at the Market Hall and at the Cosmo Club in Carlisle. They arrived in a black limousine and they took Roger Daltrey to the infirmary after he strained his voice and vocal chords. No wonder they put up a great performance both times.

COLLEGE OF FURTHER EDUCATION

25 JUNE 1966, CHICHESTER

I WAS THERE: ZIGGI JANIEC, AGE 19

In 1966 the Chichester College of Further Education was in existence for just a year or so, and had formed the basis of a students union by each department offering a student to sit on the fledgling committee. I had some previous experience in running dances and had spent some time managing a local R&B group called The Nightmares so was asked to run as social secretary. We would have a dance each term and book three bands for each event. We used some local schoolboy bands and also from an agency called The Beat

Ziggi Janiec helped promote The Who's show at Chichester FE College. Ticket sales were boosted by a guy who 'knew a printer....'

Ballad and Blues Agency at Worthing. Dances were always a sell out and live music was still the preferred choice.

Our nearest competition was the Guildhall in Portsmouth and venues in Brighton. I booked The Who from a London based agency called the Mayfair Agency about three months before the event for a magnificent price of £400 and they were contracted to do two 3/4 hour spots during the evening. At the time of booking, the band were not in the charts, but when it came to the day of the dance, they were actually climbing up the charts with 'My Generation' and were in great demand.

The tickets were so in demand that people couldn't get tickets. So a guy on the committee said he knew a printer. I don't want to imply that the fire safety rules were broken, but in those days things weren't that serious, and Health and Safety hadn't even been invented. Basically we had a hall that could hold 400 and The Who at that time were playing to huge, huge capacities. It was apparent to me that they were not too interested in doing a small gig such as our college dance, as we had a hall capacity of 400 – stretching to 500 if no one was looking!

Suddenly, when your number climbs up the charts, you're in demand and the next thing you know you're all over the place, up and down the country. They turned up and they honoured the contract. We felt that they weren't all that happy and I just assumed they weren't happy because they could have been somewhere else playing for a larger fee and to a larger audience. Their choice of where to play had changed and was much more enhanced in the three months since we'd signed the contract. All that came to dance had a great time and the organising committee were pleased with the feedback.

We raffled about six of their LPs which were signed. Keith Moon was very entertaining and the most animated of the band, as you can imagine. The language was blue during the setup and performance, which was something not encountered before on previous dance gigs here. They didn't smash their equipment. Sometimes I dine out on this thin claim to fame but my dear wife, who was there at the time, does get bored with it.

I WAS THERE: CHRIS WEBB, AGE 17

I remember seeing the posters in the college advertising the concert. Many of the students did not believe The Who would come to do a show there but I still bought a ticket and if my memory is right the tickets cost 10 shillings (50p). Well The Who did turn up and did a brilliant show to what I thought was a small audience. During the show some bullies gatecrashed the show and started picking on some of the audience including me and the friends I was with.

They probably thought that guys dancing and enjoying the band without girlfriends in tow was not right. What a mistake to make! Not only did they get a rebuff from some of the people they were trying to intimidate but Roger and Pete stopped the group playing and warned these thugs that if they did not stop and leave then they would come and sort them out along with their helpers! Needless to say, when the penny dropped their bravery vanished and they left with their tails between their legs never to be seen again.

Many years later I managed to get tickets for The Who's concert at a music festival at Beaulieu in the New Forest, sadly without John Entwistle or Keith Moon who had long since passed away. The cost of those tickets was over £30 but well worth it as the show that Roger and Pete put on was still fantastic. I look back on my teenage years and my early twenties and know it was a very special time in this country's music scene. How lucky I was to enjoy so much of it.

BRITANNIA PIER

26 JUNE 1966, GREAT YARMOUTH

I WAS THERE: DON WALKER

In the early to mid Sixties I was an apprentice at Rolls Royce Derby and thinking my early influences were getting rather stale. Then I heard 'I Can't Explain' and this turned the light on for me. A group of friends from Derbyshire went to Great Yarmouth on holiday and we saw that The Who were playing at the Britannia Pier during our stay. Donovan was headlining, although he failed to turn up, along with Dana whose best attributes were her breasts and not her singing. A local group also featured but I seem to remember they were not very good.

When The Who came on the place erupted with the audience yelling 'smash your guitar, Pete'. He did not. When Donovan failed to show, we all expected The Who to come on again but no luck, as the crap local band finished the night. After their first song, the place was empty. Leaving the show we came across a Ford Thames van that would not start. My mate Stu, being a motor mechanic, dived in to fix the problem. Of course it was The Who's transport. What a night – and what memories!

I WAS THERE: JOHN BULLOCK

I only saw them on stage once at Great Yarmouth's Britannia Pier. It was a Sunday evening concert and I cannot remember the other artists who appeared that night. All four members of The Who were by then at the top of their game and the music was very loud and vibrant. The one outstanding memory of that night is Keith Moon aiming one of his drumsticks at the first few rows of the stalls at the finish of 'My Generation". The stick flew pass many ears – we were sitting in row C! If only I had picked up the stick it would have been worth a couple of shillings. My wife-to-be, Mary, was a fully blown Mod so The Who was the group to be associated with. She still loves them today and enjoyed watching Pete and Roger perform 'Baba O'Riley' at Glastonbury in 2015.

CIVIC HALL

16 JULY 1966, BARNSLEY

I WAS THERE: LESLIE SIMMONS

We moved up to Barnsley from London about 1964, and my Dad was the manager of the Civic. He used to get a budget and he would be able to get big bands. He'd had a lot of trouble with the fire brigade and the amount of people they were getting into the Civic. He had a meeting with them and the fire officer said he was going to put two firemen on the front door and he was going to use a clicker to allow only so many people in that night. Now, my Dad had gone top dollar for The Who and he worked it out that, however many people were allowed in, it wasn't going to be enough to cover the bills. His office used to overlook the front of the Civic so he left the doors shut as long as he dare. There was a massive queue all the way down and they were banging on the doors asking to be let in and he wouldn't let them in. At the last minute he opened the doors and the fireman was trying to click everyone in and they were just piling straight by him so he wasn't able to count them properly. I don't know how many were allowed in that day but whatever the fireman was going to let in wasn't going to cover the cost of hiring The Who.

Dad left it to the last minute so there was a big pile up of people and they stormed past the fireman. I think there was a paying in point a bit further on. So they couldn't actually count how many had come in.

He used to have a photo on his office wall of him with Johnny Kidd and the Pirates, I can remember him booking Genesis. During the Seventies, as I grew up, I got to see Nazareth and the New Seekers.

I WAS THERE: JAMES BRADBURY, AGE 15

Who fans of that time were all quite a trailblazing bunch. We were very young and didn't have any money, hence I didn't attend the Civic Hall, which sat around 850 at the time. We used to spend our evenings not doing homework but walking around the town drinking coffee and pretending to smoke cigarettes at the Aloha coffee bar, so named after the recent popularity of Elvis's Blue Hawaii film. I even used to take out my father's Ronson Variflame lighter which, when turned up to full, gave a very impressive display! Mind you, it used quite a bit of gas and I had to secretly refill it when I got home. Great bragging rights though.

Whilst I was not at the Civic Hall when The Who played, I was a fan well before this. I can remember following them to the Broadway Bowl, around a mile or so outside Barnsley town centre, where I got my copy of 'My Generation' signed by John Entwistle and Keith Moon. They were there having an after gig drink in the bar. We did have sufficient spending money for a regular visit to the Broadway and that allowed us into the bar to get the signing, as there was a friendly guy on the premises who we 'knew'.

Naturally, I still have the record and sleeve. I was an early buyer of many 7' singles before the LP, as it was called then, was released. My friends and I constantly played 'I Can't Explain', etc until our parents could take no more. We were drinking cider back then – very trendy. Well, we were up to speed with those fast moving days. Wonderful memories!

I WAS THERE: GLENN FEARONS, AGE 15

I was in the audience at Barnsley Civic to see The Who. The parents of my girlfriend at the time owned a shop and she seemed to get these tickets, for The Who, the Small Faces, The Kinks, Canned Heat and everything like that. She used to take me along. I remember it was a great concert but one thing sticks in my mind. I remember watching Keith Moon, because I've always been a fan of drummers. He just seemed to finish every number, have a rub down with a towel, reach for a bottle of beer from a crate, open it, drink that and off he'd go again.

I WAS THERE: DENNIS LAWSON, AGE 18

I was the bass player in a group and had won a competition in

Barnsley for local groups of being the warm up band at the Civic Hall. We were students in the local grammar school, in the sixth form. We'd moved away from the Shadows stuff and got into the sound of The Who. They were our idols at the time so to get the chance to actually be on the same gig – well, can you imagine? It was unbelievable. We were the warm up band and people were trickling in as we were playing.

In those days we had the de rigeur Vox AC30 amps which all the local groups had. We were in front of the curtains with about two foot of stage, almost jumping into the orchestra pit.

We came on at 7.30pm and played to an audience of about a dozen, growing to about 50 people 45 minutes later. The Who were our idols then – as they still are now – and we finished with three Who songs – 'Substitute', 'The Kids Are Alright' and, believe it or not, 'My Generation'. Our drummer Paul White even scattered his drums at the end. Can you imagine the reaction of the small number in the audience?

We didn't think for one moment that any of The Who would be there because there was another act to follow us, a group called Christie who went on to have a hit with a song called 'Yellow River'. Before that they were called The Outer Limits.

We went backstage and there's Pete Townshend and it's like 'my God, what have we done?' Can you imagine our reaction? Pete Townshend, who had got there earlier than the rest of the group, was standing there. 'Cheeky bastards' was his opening gambit. I think – I hope – I detected a twinkle in his eye.

And then Roger Daltrey comes in with his long golden locks in those days and curly hair. Two women on his arms. 'Guess what these bastards have been doing?' said Townshend.

So we were absolutely in awe. And then Moonie came in and was straight up the curtains. The Civic Hall is really old fashioned, really tall. They have the pantomimes there and everything and they've got these massive curtains that are about twenty foot tall and Moonie being Moonie, he just shot straight up them and he's leaping about twenty foot in the air. Fortunately this is behind the scenes and the audience couldn't see it. The rest of the band were acting like it was completely normal. Keith then leapt, actually leapt, twenty foot back onto the floor and landed on all fours. His eyes were like saucers. I think he'd probably had a glass of Pepsi or something.

We were lucky enough to meet the group properly that night, Pete Townshend giving Rod Senior, our lead guitar, a master class on how to get maximum effect and reverb by using open strings wherever possible in his chords. He said to him 'don't play the chords. Don't play a D there. Play both strings.' And just the slightly different sound that it made, you began to appreciate some of the sounds that that guy was hearing even in 66. This was very effective on the intro to 'Substitute'.

He even allowed us to stand in the wings by the curtain two or three yards away. Wow! What an experience! He smashed his guitar on stage, of course, and handed it to Rod as he left the stage. I was beside Pete Towshend for the full act. He played all the way through and I was about two or three yards away. I was just totally mesmerised. I remember what Moonie was like when he was going. He was the only guy I saw at the time who had two bass drums. How he was playing two bass drums God only knows, and he got these beats going with two bass drums. It was absolutely fantastic.

We had said to Pete Townshend beforehand 'will you be smashing your guitar up?' And he said 'it all depends what mood I'm in.' And he did. He smashed his guitar and afterwards we said 'that guitar, that Rickenbacker, in our local shop is £333. How much do you get paid for this?' They got paid £400 for the gig. We got paid £20. And he said 'oh, I don't make any money. This is just stuff for the fans.' In those days they didn't make anything. All the money was made on the records.

There was a guy there called Chris Stamp and I thought he was a roadie. He was moving all this stuff. And I was talking to him and I said 'do you want a hand?' and he said 'no, I can manage.' And I later found out he was their co-manager.

And he was moving this stuff around and talking about this girl he was after called Chrissie Shrimpton. She'd been going out with Jagger and he was after her. It was like we were looking into a goldfish bowl filled with mid Sixties pop stars. You had to pinch yourself.

Sue Riley, for whom
The Who at the Civic
was her first gig

I WAS THERE: SUE RILEY, AGE 14

I went to see them at the Civic. I remember going with a friend from school, and maybe her older sister. I think we were up on the balcony and I can remember having a really good view. I can just remember being completely star struck as it was my first concert. I had pin ups of them, Keith being my favourite as I thought he was the best drummer ever.

I still have a scrapbook with clippings in from *NME*, *Jackie*, etc. They are all yellow with age and the Sellotape has made marks. I looked to see if there was any mention of Barnsley but I couldn't see any, although there was mention of tours and some of the songs they sang, including 'Barbara Ann', which I was surprised at.

I WAS THERE: MIKE TONRA

I have a traditional gentleman hairdresser's shop in Sheffield Road, Barnsley. But back in 1966 I was on stage at the Civic to witness The Who's only appearance in Barnsley. I was doing DJ work and local radio broadcasts and I was part of a team of six compering shows at Barnsley Civic Hall. This gave us all access backstage to any of the concerts. I got paid between 2/6 (13p) and 5/- (25p) depending on the size of the audience.

The manager of the Civic was a John Simmons who had come up from London. He had big ideas about booking artists at the Civic Hall and I think the only three bands that we didn't have, and it was only because we couldn't get bums on seats to make it a viable proposition, were The Rolling Stones, The Beatles and The Hollies. They were the three bands at the time that we couldn't really afford to pay because of the seating capacity.

They were riding on the crest of 'My Generation' although, if memory serves me right, if they didn't have a hit in the top ten or the top twenty the agent could negotiate a better deal to get them. I think some of the bands who came and were in the top ten got more money because of the chart position.

The auditorium was packed with screaming teenage girls and their lads, with an atmosphere of excitement and anticipation on the back of The Who's recent chart and LP success with 'My Generation'. Pete Townshend was next to me as I looked out through the tabs, with Roger Daltrey, John Entwistle with his bass guitar strapped on, and a fired up Keith Moon behind his drums.

Prior to the concert, I took my copy of 'My Generation' to their dressing room and asked them to sign it. I was awestruck and, whilst I was hopeful, I was also expecting rejection. But amazingly each signed as I took it round them. I later sold their autographs, something I now regret.

Their performance consisted of all their well-known hits up to that time, R&B standards and a self-penned instrumental – The Ox. It was a sensational night, and I was standing just a few feet away from Pete Townshend when he started smashing his amplifiers. During the finale, Pete approached his amp and rubbed his guitar against it to achieve maximum feedback and then attacked the soft front of the speaker in an axe-like movement with his guitar as Keith did his utmost to destroy his drum kit.

When the manager said 'quick, he's going to push the speakers over,' the crew, manager, agent, compere and team were all standing behind the speakers because they were going to fall. They were all stacked up and Townshend was going at the speakers like he had an axe. He just swung it and smashed it into the front, right at the end, and the amplifiers were all down. Keith Moon was smashing his drum kit up in a frenzy. It was mayhem. This is what the kids had come to see. That's what there was excitement about – the destruction which they were witnessing. Keith, wet through from his exertions, was the last to exit the stage, walking off through his kit and the debris from the mayhem. It was a typical night for a Who concert, or so I was told.

There were two girl Who followers backstage with us as the set finished. They were from Wythenshawe in Manchester. We had chatted with them throughout the concert. One was called Sue. A little later, we were all in the dressing room and Keith enquired about late night action in Barnsley. There was none at this time, other than Barnsley Bowl, which was a bowling alley off Dodworth Road, behind what is now the main Ford Polar Garage. I told Keith this and it was agreed he would follow me in my Mini with me taking the two girls. He did, and we had a couple of frames of bowling together, with my main attention moving from Keith to Sue!

I think Sue was a groupie. I didn't want to say that, but I think she used to follow them around like they did in those days. She told me that she was John Entwistle's girlfriend. Well, I didn't know whether to believe it or not. But it was the carrot which got me to take her back home over the Pennines. I had a Mini, one of the first Minis that came out, and we went back to Wythenshawe with the promise of meeting up with some of the members of the group.

This was also a fib to get me to take her home, because she must have had some sort of public transport to get her from Manchester to Barnsley. She actually lived in Wythenshawe. Your testosterone is riding very high when you are 19 but she was very, very attractive and we started with a friendship, and her mum and dad asked me to come over. So I kept going over to Manchester hoping for – ahem, well you can imagine what I was hoping for – but it never transpired because every time I went over, well the parents were really friendly but they were good Catholics.

So every time I went over to visit them and stay with them, we got separate rooms. It was the Swinging Sixties but some people were not swinging! Eventually the miles and the driving back in the early hours of the morning just got to me and I thought 'oh, sod it. I've had enough of trailing over to Manchester.'

One thing other that sticks out in my mind is that she was the first girl I met who wore tights. Up to then it was all stockings and suspenders in Barnsley, and tights were just something which a young fella had never come across on a woman. They were wearing Mary Quant knee high boots, Mary Quant haircuts and Mary Quant mini skirts, and tights came in with all this fashion.

So she was actually the first lady that stuck in my mind. She never showed them to me but she told me she wore them. It wasn't jaw dropping but funny to meet somebody of the opposite sex wearing something different to what you'd been used to. I sound like an old fuddy duddy but it was part of the social change, the way people dressed. I've got books of the Swinging Sixties and you can see them in the PVC skirts and the Bob Dylan hats, the corduroy hats and the Levi jeans. It was all part of the generation thing. I would imagine that she's a grandmother now. I mean, she was a lovely girl. I'm sure somebody would have snapped her up.

SPA ROYAL HALL

23 JULY 1966, BRIDLINGTON

I WAS THERE: PAUL JENKINSON, AGE 14

I was the drummer with 21st Century who supported The Who. It was eye opening, to say the least. We were on first, The Who were the main band and then there was a band on afterwards called the Mandrakes. Robert Palmer was their lead singer – he was from Scarborough originally. We were pals – they were from Scarborough,

we were from Bridlington
– and we used to meet up.
We'd both be playing at
gigs round and about.

The rest of 21st
Century were a lot
older than me. They
were in their late teens,
early twenties. They had
a rock and roll band
at the time and their
drummer happened
to break his leg one
Saturday afternoon
and I just got a bang
on my door saying
'Oh, we understand that
you've got a drum kit and do you want to join a band?' And
I said 'Yeah, I do'. We did two gigs that night, one at the Seabirds
in Bridlington and one at the Golden Gloves which was one of the
first nightclubs in Bridlington. And they never asked the other guy
back.

I never really wanted to be a full-time musician. I had a family
business I wanted to go into, so I was only in it for the fun. The
Who was a complete eye opener. You'd heard rumours about them
wrecking gear and seen little bits on TV about them wrecking stuff,
but when you saw it first hand it's like 'wow!' When they arrived I
can remember the roadies ripping all the cellophane off the Premier
kits, because I had a red glitter premier kit myself at the time, and so
did Moonie. They were ripping all the plastic off, all the amps and
everything.

They finished their act with 'My Generation' and they literally
destroyed everything on stage. There was nothing left at the end of
the gig. It was all mashed. John Entwistle smacked his guitar right on
the top of the amp and, as he walked downstairs into the changing

rooms, he just chucked his guitar – which was in half obviously, it was all held together by the strings – and said 'Here, fix that if you can'.

I think Moonie was in a Bentley and they were staying at the Windsor Hotel in Bridlington. I never saw it myself but somebody said that he smashed it into the back wall of the car park. Townshend got in an Austin 1800 and just revved it until it seized up. It was absolute carnage.

Bridlington at that time was an unbelievable place because it was the largest dance hall on the east coast of England. You could get 5,000 people in there at any one time. And everyone played there – Little Richard, Roy Orbison, Ike and Tina Turner, Three Dog Night. Everybody that was around at that time, used to play at the Spa. Free played here twice. Interesting times, and it was exciting and for a 14 year old, it was just crazy.

I WAS THERE: BILLY LESTER

My group The 21st Century was based in Bridlington during the mid Sixties and appeared at the Spa Royal Hall on numerous occasions supporting top artistes and groups during that period.

Having already appeared with The Who in a previous line up as The Corvettes the year before we were invited to appear again with The Who and, after meeting them for a sound check in the afternoon, they allowed us to use their PA system and invited us back to their hotel for drinks and a game of darts.

The evening concert was a sell out, with The Who living up to their reputation as a visual rock concept, and the audience were treated to a brilliant performance by them as they tirelessly and powerfully went through their hit songs – 'Substitute', 'I'm A Boy', 'My Generation', etc.

During the afternoon soundcheck, however, I had noticed a roadie taping up a red Rickenbacker guitar that was all smashed up and wondered why? I decided to stand in the wings of the stage to watch them perform. Towards the end of their show, dry ice was blown across the stage and I noticed a roadie appear next to me and subsequently proceed to squat behind Pete Townshend's Marshall stack.

When Pete started to 'attack' his speaker with his regular guitar, the roadie began to rock the stack to and fro. Amidst the dry ice this seemed like Pete was hitting the Marshall with his guitar. However, then a second roadie appeared next to me and swapped the regular guitar for the taped up version with Pete. The audience could not see this because of the amount of dry ice onstage acting like a smoke screen.

Pete then proceeded to smash this guitar on the stage floor and the guitar fell apart from the red tape whereupon Pete threw the guitar into the frenzied crowd followed by the two roadies diving in to retrieve it. Even top paid rock stars cannot afford to smash their guitars up every night!

This was followed by Roger Daltrey twirling his microphone above his head before hurling it into the audience. Keith Moon then kicked all of his drum kit all over the stage, causing mayhem, and then threw his drum sticks into the crowd before falling back off his drum stool, not realising that there was a six foot drop from his drum platform to the stage floor. Fortunately, he was uninjured and walked off the stage looking a bit dazed.

I asked the The Who if we could call and see them off from their hotel the next day and they agreed. The first car out of the hotel car park was a white Aston Martin driven by Roger Daltrey. Secondly followed a bottle green E-Type Jaguar driven by Pete Townshend and, lastly, a Rolls Royce Silver Shadow containing a grinning Keith Moon and John Entwistle with their own chauffeur as neither had a driving licence at the time.

We watched as they waved and disappeared down the road. Even though they would soon forget us, we knew we would always remember them.

QUEEN'S HALL

28 JULY 1966, BARNSTAPLE

I WAS THERE: PETER GLEAVE, AGE 16

A gang of us would go to the Queen's Hall every week to see a chart act. The Who were head and shoulders above the other acts. They were that good the fighting in the audience actually stopped. But at the end of the show a bare chested Roger Daltrey came out from behind the curtain and offered to take a heckler outside!

I WAS THERE: PETER REVELEY, AGE 18

I was at that concert, or 'dance' as we thought of them in those days, with a mate from Appledore and a number of school friends from Bideford Grammar School – Richard Ashley, John Blackmore, Neil Cooper, Martin Petherbridge and Richard Mendham.

I remember the event well, not least for the fact that after the interval Mendham came back to the dance floor rather dishevelled. When asked what had happened he commented 'just had a fight with that daft drummer in the bar' – Keith Moon of course! I don't remember the exact reason for the fight but I have a vague recollection it was about a girl.

I WAS THERE: MARILYN SMYTH, AGE 18

I remember seeing them perform in Barnstaple at the Queens Hall, when it was more of a dance hall, rather than a theatre. I saw them before I left home age 18, when they were fairly unknown. Incidentally, my brother has researched the family tree and shows that we are in fact related to Roger Daltrey! My maternal grandmother was a Daltrey before her marriage.

Marilyn Smyth remembers the Queen's Hall in Barnstaple as a dance hall

SHERWOOD ROOMS

23 AUGUST 1966, NOTTINGHAM

I WAS THERE: TINA SEARCY, AGE 16

My friend and I were at the front of the queue to go in very early. We found a stray dog and so we took him to the police station on Canal Street. When we got back, the queue was 15 people deep. They were brilliant even though the instruments got broken as they always did.

DREAMLAND BALLROOM

25 AUGUST 1966, MARGATE

I WAS THERE: JOHN SANDERS

During the mid-Sixties, the Dreamland Ballroom had a weekly dance on Sunday nights with a top-line act. I particularly remember Brian Poole and The Tremeloes and especially their version of 'Twist and Shout'. But on 25 August 1966 there was something special. So special that it was held not on a Sunday but a Thursday night. It was The Who electrifying that iconic ballroom. Of course we had heard about

The Who but we were not prepared for what happened. The music was so loud and so powerful that we were all entranced. Nobody was dancing – apart from on the spot as we slowly but surely pushed forward to be nearer the stage and nearer certain deafness.

John Sanders: 'we were all entranced'

At least one of the strings on Pete Townshend's guitar broke mid number and Pete snapped. He smashed his guitar over the top of one of the amplifiers, snapping off the headstock. Picking up another guitar he seemed to get lost attempting to slot back in with the others and then he totally lost it, kicking and pulling over parts of Keith Moon's drum kit. Despite this, Roger Daltrey continued playing which seemed to provoke Pete even more, which resulted in him thrusting his guitar into amplifier after amplifier trying to stop the music. By the time that they left the stage it was just piles of rubbish. The atmosphere in the ballroom was one of shock, with everyone slowly and quietly leaving to go home, none of us stopping to collect souvenirs from amongst the mess!

LOCARNO BALLROOM

2 SEPTEMBER 1966, BASILDON

I WAS THERE: BARBARA WEBBER

My friend at the time, Chrissie, had asked me to make up a foursome. I had only left school the previous summer. I worked in a bank in London and my pay was £510 per annum, so with the train fares and paying mum for my keep there wasn't much left for me. I had bought work clothes but had only a few 'going out' clothes so I wore a dress that I had the summer I left school. It was yellow, silky and sleeveless and had black stripes round it. I must have looked like a demented wasp but thought I looked 'the bee's knees'!

We went to Basildon Mecca, as it was then. The place was packed, but to be honest The Who had never floated my boat. I was more into Motown and soul. But then the concert began – we started at the back where the boys could prop up the bar but soon I was itching to get down the front. Chrissie wouldn't leave her man so off I went and, hanging on the front of the stage, I saw the guitars being smashed, drum kit falling over and, with the incredible music, the crowd going wild. It was quite an eye opener for this country girl. I don't think I saw my date again as I had spent all the gig at the front. It still wasn't my sort of music but I could see what all the fuss was about.

DOWNS HOTEL

11 SEPTEMBER 1966, HASSOCKS

I WAS THERE: MICK BLACKBURN

I can remember seeing them at the Ultra Club in Hassocks, a venue I rarely missed on a Sunday night. I first saw The Who at the Florida Rooms in Brighton, now part of the Sea Life Centre, where they played regularly as The High Numbers. I only remember them playing once in Hassocks and at the time I helped set up equipment for local band The Dominators, who were playing that night as support band. We commented on the state of their amplifiers, especially Pete Townshend's, which was covered with a Union Flag to disguise the many attacks it had received from Pete's guitar.

At this gig Pete managed to break the neck off the guitar and as it was of no further use he left it behind. Rescued at the end of the show by The Dominators' lead guitarist, it was subsequently repaired and used for many gigs afterwards. When I think back at all the now famous bands that played in Hassocks on a Sunday night, it reads like a Who's Who of the music industry, if you'll excuse the pun.

I WAS THERE: JOAN BROWN

We saw The Who at The Downs Hotel, in Hassocks, owned by a

chap called Captain David Brown. The hotel was knocked down years ago. We also saw The Hollies, the Small Faces and lots of other great groups of the Sixties at the Downs. And, yes, Pete Townshend did smash up his guitar at the end of the evening and it was quite wild.

I WAS THERE: RICK DIVALL

I was playing in a local band and we supported The Who at one of their gigs that year. We started off as Rob and the Dominators, but Rob left so we became a harmony band as none of us would admit to being a singer. The Downs Hotel was owned by Captain Brown.

Every Sunday there would be a top singer or band playing there, The Hollies, Goldie and the Gingerbreads, The Animals, The Yardbirds, John Mayall's Bluesbreakers, Long John Baldry, etc. Some of it is a bit vague as there was no breathalyser in those days and a lot of beer was always consumed, which also accounted for a lot of brawls on the night.

The Who turned up very late which meant we had to play much longer than expected which was annoying especially as they got paid massively more than us. The Who smashed up their gear which was expected and one of Pete Townshend's pickups flew off the stage where one of my friends managed to retrieve it. It has been on one of his guitars ever since.

I WAS THERE: GRAHAM GORING

I played in The Dominators with Rick Divall and Mick Hobby at the gig at the Downs Hotel, Hassocks with The Who. I didn't know until I turned up at the gig and saw that poster that we would be backing The Who!

I remember Keith Moon arriving in his white Roller and parking it haphazardly. On The Who's last number I saw Pete Townshend change his guitar from behind his equipment and bring out a Rickenbacker. At the end as usual, he smashed it against his Marshall stack, a bit went flying, there was a scrabble and luckily I managed to grab a guitar pickup. The Downs Hotel had a basement where about one to two hundred could be accommodated. That used to be our local Sunday

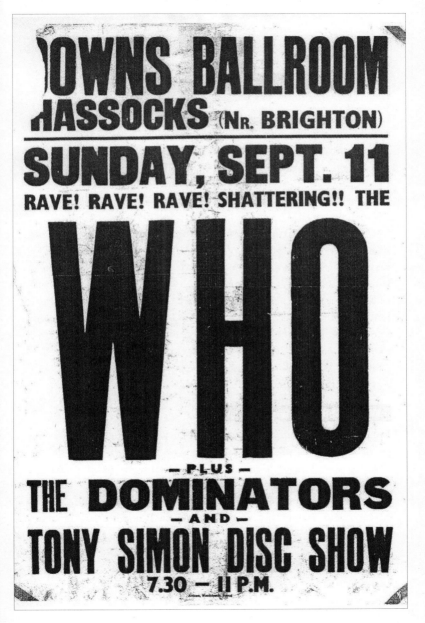

night place where we could see some big name bands. I cried for years when they knocked it down.

I WAS THERE: DAVID GOODWIN

When they came back a few months after their first appearance at the Downs, they did a very powerful performance, which was top notch. The difference in the two performances was astonishing. The second time at the Downs was a complete performance. It was 'Substitute' and all those songs. They did 'I Can't Explain' and I think they did 'I Can See for Miles'. It was a more professional performance, like they would give at a theatre rather than a 250 capacity dance hall.

There was a family who were just thugs who just ruined an evening for everybody. You'd look at your watch and come half past nine, twenty to ten, you moved out of the way and let them have their fight with somebody or other. By ten to ten they'd have given somebody a nosebleed, got blood all over their white shirt and it would all calm down again.

You knew if you went out in our area they would have a fight with someone. To me they were pretty ghastly thugs who just wanted to fight people. But they got the girls. I'd seen these guys acting as bouncers to The Who.

I WAS THERE: MARIANNE HOBBY

My husband was in a group from Haywards Heath in the Sixties and his group, The Dominators, played on the same bill as The Who in 1966. The group members were Rick Divall (bass guitar), Dave Fotheringham (drums), Graham Goring (rhythm guitar) & Mick Hobby (my husband – lead guitar). I wasn't there that evening and, in fact, my husband and I hadn't yet met. Sadly, my husband died in 2011. I know Graham collected a pick-up from one of the smashed Who guitars.

I WAS THERE: JOHN RITCHIE

I lived about 6 or 7 miles away from the place. It's such a small, sleepy little town, Hassocks, but it all happened in those two or three years. When I think back about it now and I tell my children it's almost unbelievable how good it used to be there. It was a pretty good venue. It was a hotel run by a gay ex-RAF captain who had connections with show business, a guy called Pete Shawland. Him and two other guys used to get all the people there. And it was downstairs and the bar was at the top of the place. It was a residential hotel at one stage. The stage was probably eighteen inches high and the people on the dance floor were all right there. That's how close everybody was to everything that was going on.

They had everybody there apart from The Beatles and the Stones. People used to come from miles around to go there. It was the place to go. Everybody appeared there on a Sunday evening. We saw John Mayall, The Hollies were there, The Who were really good. That's when they used to smash up their gear and it was all going into the crowd, people had never seen anything like it. Long John Baldry used to serve behind the bar. Because he was also gay and was a friend of this guy's. If you had a pound you could get extremely drunk. It was the highlight of the weekend, to be honest.

GAUMONT CINEMA

15 SEPTEMBER 1966, HANLEY

I WAS THERE: PHIL BOWER, AGE 16

I went with two friends to watch The Who specifically, although I remember there was good supporting acts including John Walker of the Walker Brothers. We caught a bus to Hanley and before we went to the show we called into the (now demolished) Vine for a few drinks, in spite of us being underage. Not being used to the beer I fell asleep during the first part of

the show, but was woken up when The Who came on – they were so loud. They were brilliant and we enjoyed the performance climaxing in Keith Moon kicking over his drums and Pete Townshend smashing his guitar on the bits of drum kit left. In truth, having seen The Who on TV, the smashing-up was one of the main reasons we went to watch them.

I WAS THERE: SANDRA BROWNSWORD, AGE 16

I saw The Who twice – once at the Kings Hall, Stoke-on-Trent on 19 March 1966 when I got all four autographs. The second time I saw them was later the same year at the Gaumont Theatre, Hanley. They were on the same bill as the Walker Brothers.

I again obtained Keith Moon and John Entwistle's autographs. They arrived in a Bentley, registration number LLF 905. My main memory is the sheer volume of their performance and the memorable 'My Generation'.

I WAS THERE: MIKE JONES, AGE 16

My first 45 was 'I Can't Explain' and my first album was *My Generation*. I heard from my cousin, Tim, who lived in Wellington at the time, that they had appeared at the Majestic but I didn't go to see them. What I also heard at the time was that they'd also played at Wem Town Hall but it hadn't been good value for money as they had only performed three songs. What used to happen during the mid Sixties to early seventies was that acts would have two bookings in one night and the archives might show that they appeared at, say, Wellington but earlier in the evening played a short set somewhere else – not too far away.

I first saw The Who in Hanley at the Gaumont Theatre just as 'I'm a Boy' was released. The support act was Cream! I then went on to see them a number of times between 1967 and 1969 at the Civic Hall in Nantwich. The hits had pretty well dried up and they were on comparatively hard times but still amazing. I saw them before the hall was extended and then later when it had been extended. I remember Pete Townshend commented on how much better the venue was.

I went with a mate, Bill, who managed to get thrown out just as the curtains opened for the opening chords to 'I'm a Boy'. So, Bill and I were 65 in May of this year and what do you buy a guy who has everything? I managed to buy a mint copy of the Reaction label single of 'I'm a Boy' and framed it and gave it to him. A reminder of what he had missed all those years ago! I'd forgotten the lyric 'my name is Bill and I'm a headcase'. He drew this to my attention and asked if it was a comment on his mental state. I guess it was.

I WAS THERE: TERRY VICKERS

My mother worked at the Hanley Gaumont cinema, which is now the Regent, and at the time loads of artists played at this venue when they were on tour. I was in my early teens but my Mum managed to wangle a job for me on the stage for most of the concerts. All I had to do was to stand in the wings and then walk across the stage with the tabs [curtains] before and after each act, pulling back the microphones etc. out of the way. Although it was an unpaid job, I was at an age when I would have willingly paid for the privilege of being there during those times. A few things stick in my mind about the night when The Who appeared at the Gaumont.

If I recall it was the last night of the tour and the management of the Gaumont were very concerned that Keith Moon would do something crazy after their final stint. In the event, apart from sending his drums flying over the stage, he only managed to burst a bag of sugar or possibly flour onto the stage, which came as a relief to the management. He also wore a motorbike crash helmet that he had borrowed from another guy working back stage towards the end of their act.

As I was to the right of the stage, I was alongside Pete Townshend during the concert and I noticed that there was a pre-prepared cut in his speaker cabinet into which he inserted his guitar at the end of their act although the audience thought that this was part of the 'smashing up of the equipment' at the end of each gig which had become their trademark!

During an interval, I asked Keith Moon for his autograph and asked him if he had a spare drumstick to give me as a memento. He then led me backstage where he has a sports bag crammed with new drumsticks and invited me to pick whichever one I wanted!

After the show I was outside the Gaumont with my mother and a few other employees waiting for our lift home when from the stage door around the corner appeared Keith and John Entwistle, dressed in their garish stage attire of satin trousers and shirts etc, walking down the street and heading towards us. The walk soon changed to a gallop as they began to be chased by a couple of girl fans. A Bentley then drove past us and a short time later the car headed back up the street with Keith, John and the two girls all inside as it then sped out of sight!

ODEON CINEMA

16 SEPTEMBER 1966, DERBY

I WAS THERE: CARL CHESWORTH

Between 1965 and 1967 I was on the projection staff at the Odeon before transferring to the Superama/Odeon Pennine in Colyear Street. We would often present these 'one night only' stage shows. The Who were supported by the famous variety theatre artiste Max Wall.

On this show, I was working on the stage. I usually helped operate the two follow-spots up in the projection room and I can remember Max Wall being booed off the stage during his famous Professor Walloski routine and the tour's manager asking me to bring the curtain down on him as the audience were becoming threatening. The show's compere was pushed back on stage to quell the restless audience and the following act had to make a quick entry! This would be for the second house at 8.40pm, as I remember taking my autograph book that evening and being able to talk with Max Wall.

To this day, I'm sure there were tears in his eyes as he signed my book for me and said that television had ruined him, as in his Variety days he could tour the halls for weeks on end with his various sketches but once on television, everyone had seen him. He cut a very sad and dejected figure as he shook my hand and walked out of the theatre stage door.

The Who lived up to the audience's expectations and, as expected, smashed all their instruments up at the end of the show. I was sent on stage during this mayhem, on both sides of the footlights, to retrieve the Odeon's microphones and stands. What a night that was!

I WAS THERE: BARBARA ZOPPI, AGE 16

I was on the front row and I met Pete Townshend afterwards. I managed to get front row tickets by going early. I lived on a farm but I'd go to my friend's on my bike, getting the workman's bus and going and sitting on the very cold steps. We were first in the queue as usual when it opened at 9am and we paid very little for tickets. It was no more than five bob (25p), possibly less. I can remember it was the loudest thing I've ever heard. And to meet Pete Townshend afterwards – he was so quiet and polite after seeing him smashing his guitar. It was scary as well.

Roger was driven off by an attractive brunette in a low blue sports car. Pete came down the steps in the dark looking like a flasher, wearing a flasher mac and carrying an old battered brown suitcase and very quietly and politely asked us the way to the Midland Hotel, a few streets away. He admired my friend's little fur jacket and the gold star on her face.

QUEENS HALL

14 OCTOBER 1966, LEEDS

I WAS THERE: BARRY LEONARD

Myself and my mates saw The Who at the Queens Hall along with many other bands of the time. If I remember rightly, I think it was the first all-nighter they did and DJ Jimmy Savile was the man in charge on stage. Yes, loony Moon did smash up the drum set when they had done but what a night to remember.

I WAS THERE: CHRIS SMITH

The Queens Hall was a huge tin can and the sound would echo but that didn't worry them. They played one hit after another and

I can't remember any introductions at all. They looked exactly like they did on telly in their mod gear. Did Townshend wear his Union Jack jacket? I'm not sure. Anyway, they were totally impressive and put on a professional performance despite the sound problems. The third time I saw The Who it must have been 1973 or 1974. I was sitting on the second to front row at the Marquee Club in London. At the end they smashed up a lot of equipment. Keith totalled the drum kit and Pete broke his black Gibson 335 into splinters. A piece landed at my feet and picking it up found it was the piece with the yellow Gibson guarantee. It was like viewing a war zone up close and personal. I gave the guarantee splinter to a painter friend who is a big Who fan, so he could do a Peter Blake type Who collage.

CITY HALLS

18 NOVEMBER 1966, PERTH

I WAS THERE: JAN TAVENDALE

That Friday night my friends and I had been at our usual Girl Guide meeting which, was typically followed by going to our village chip shop. During the chat there, hanging about on the shop doorstep and pavement, someone mentioned that The Who were playing at the dance at Perth City Hall. We decided we should go!

One of the boys agreed to drive us in his baby Austin car – I don't think we gave him much choice. Then all we had to do was run home to change out of our Girl Guide uniforms and gather again a few minutes later at the car. I still remember my arrival home in a rush – my dear father welcoming me in, thinking that was me home for bed earlier than usual, only to hear that I was going straight out again and that we were all going in X's car and to a dance at the City Hall 15 miles away!

I still remember his caution (well, his quiet word 'no') as I quickly ran on upstairs to my bedroom to get changed into my mini kilt and my mother's pre-war shirt, made from black-market silk bought by her in Germany just before war broke out. When I came back downstairs, my

Jan Tavendale (left) with her brother Tommy and her bedroom walls covered with pop posters

beloved dad quietly handed me a ten-shilling (50p) note and told me to have a good time. And we did!

Entry at the door was 7 shillings and 6 pennies (37p) – no advance booking, no waiting months for the exciting event, no sitting in numbered seats! My memory is that we danced. It wasn't a concert. We watched Keith Moon knocking his drums around and we danced – not just like the dancing in the aisles you can see at a concert today. The way I remember it was that they were just the band at the dance that night, albeit a particularly exciting band that we already knew about. In 2016, my husband noticed The Who were playing in Glasgow on my birthday, so he bought two tickets as a present, which meant it was both a celebration on the actual day and a reminder of my youth! It was slightly more expensive than the 37.5p spur of the moment that I (or rather, my Dad) paid in 1966. And required slightly more advanced planning.

MARKET HALL

19 NOVEMBER 1966, CARLISLE

I WAS THERE: IAN REED

As a penniless art student, and with only money for beer, I was in the bar of The Crown and Mitre Hotel in Carlisle with friends. It was the plushest hotel in town. We knew The Who were performing in the Market Hall but we had no tickets. The four lads standing next to us asked if we were going to gig and were we art students. It was The Who!

We explained the situation and Roger said he always wanted to be an art student and was sympathetic to our plight. 'Come with us and you can get in if you pretend to be part of our team to set up on stage!' We spent the entire performance standing in the wings and must have had the best 'seats'.

SPA ROYAL HALL

26 NOVEMBER 1966, BRIDLINGTON

I WAS THERE: DAVE CARMICHAEL, AGE 17

I didn't really class myself as anything but I wasn't a Rocker. I was nearer a Mod but I was playing in bands so I was a band type person. The band was called That Feeling and we played soul music – Wilson Pickett, James Brown, Sam and Dave etc. I played lead guitar. We played the stuff of the time that was in the charts, or had been in the charts, in the Sixties.

Dave Carmichael, on lead guitar, with his band That Feeling

There was a big dance floor in the Spa. It's quite a high stage and we were stood right near the front at one side on the right hand side, where Pete Townshend was stood. It was great. I can't remember all of the concert, but I remember at the end where Pete Townshend smashed his guitar to bits. I can't remember what he was using, probably a Rickenbacker, but for the last number he changed his guitar for a Fender Telecaster. They sang the song and at the end they got all the feedback going and he got his guitar off, got it in his hand and was banging the neck against his big amplifier stack. He started smashing it into that and all bits came flying off the guitar.

And some of it landed on the floor. And there's a metal ferrule that's part of the tuning peg at the end of the guitar neck. One of those came off and landed near me on the floor. So I picked it up. And I've still got that to this day. I got a part of his guitar.

I WAS THERE: SUE ROBERTS (NEE SCOTT)

I saw The Who at Bridlington. I was a massive fan. My lasting memory of that performance is being right at the front of the stage and waiting to catch one of Keith Moon's drumsticks when he threw them in the audience at the end of the concert, as he usually did.

However the drumsticks didn't make it that far this time as Keith, after a manic drum finale, kicked the drums over and promptly fell off his stool, knocking himself out and was carried off the stage by his roadies.

I WAS THERE: DAVE WESTAWAY

I was a singer in a band that supported The Who in Bridlington Spa. I remember The Who smashing everything up. All our gear was paid for on hire purchase, and we were paying quite a bit from our wages, they had all this equipment and the finale of their show was smashing it all up so you can imagine how we felt. I don't think they broke even or operated at a loss. Eventually they got on top of it but I know towards the end they were using a lot of equipment that didn't actually do anything.

Dave Westaway on vocals with his band

It was just used as a prop to smash up.

I WAS THERE: JOHN LESSENTIN, AGE 17

I was on lead guitar and vocals with a band called Three Plus One and we supported The Who on their second visit to Bridlington Spa during 1966. The Spa manager was John Stephenson who was also our manager, hence we got to support all the top bands at the Spa. A crowd of around 5,000 were standing in the hall by 8pm. Tickets were 7/6 (37p).

At 3pm twin wheelbase Transit vans arrived with all the gear. First in on the stage was the drum roadie. He was about to hammer blocks of wood with sixinch nails into the stage to secure the bass drums when John, the Spa's manager, said 'you are not hammering nails into my stage', the roadie replied 'Either I do, or The Who won't play tonight'. So he nailed the blocks to the stage.

Around 8pm I knocked on The Who's dressing room door with three guitars. Pete opened the door and grabbed the guitars and pretended to smash them. They were autographed by all the band

Three Plus One supported The Who at the Spa Royal Hall

who also autographed a piece of paper for me. Our roadie then grabbed a pack of Izal toilet paper and copied The Who's signatures and sold them to the crowd for a shilling each.

The Who also allowed my band to play 'I Can't Explain' and 'Anyway, Anyhow, Anywhere'. The Who took to the stage at 9pm. They were very loud and a roadie was holding Pete's speaker stacks to stop them moving across the stage due to the volume. They finished at about 10.30pm. The drums were smashed, fireworks let off and Pete smashed his Telecaster to bits against a concrete pillar. We stood at the side of the stage and I grabbed the headstock and the first three frets with the strings hanging off. It was a hell of a night. Bridlington Spa is now limited to 3,300 people after a health and safety risk assessment. There was none of that in 1966.

IMPERIAL BALLROOM

17 DECEMBER 1966, NELSON

I WAS THERE: DAVID ALMOND

We were called The Beathovens and we played with The Who twice at the Imp, in December 1966 and again in November 1967. The albums they had out at the time were *A Quick One* and *The Who Sell Out*.

We got the gig through an agency. The first time we played with them there was with a band called the Rockin' Vickers. And the Rockin' Vickers reckoned The Who nicked the song 'The Kids Are Alright' from them. We were in the downstairs dressing room when The Who all came in. On the wall the Rockin' Vickers had written 'who are The Who anyway?' and Pete Townshend borrowed a pen and wrote underneath 'if you don't know now you never will'.

I went to the upstairs dressing room looking for my mates who I was playing with, and Keith Moon was sat at the end of the room drinking vodka and lime-juice. He poured me a drink and I talked to him for about twenty minutes. He talked a lot about drums, about Premier, and sponsorship. I think he was sponsored by Zildjan cymbals, and the kit he had at the time was the one with 'Pictures Of Lily' on it. He was just relaxed. He wasn't drunk. When I was up there (in the upstairs dressing room) I think Daltrey and Townshend were downstairs and Alan Parr, who was in my band, who spent a bit of time talking to Townshend about guitars.

They had these smoke bombs from Brocks Fireworks which were taped to the backs of their amps. They set these off part way through one of the songs and filled the place full of smoke. They were just normal smoke bombs like they probably use as warnings on ships. We got some off them and later, when we played a gig at the local swimming pool in Darwen, we used the smoke bombs and got complaints.

1967 This was the first year the group performed in North America, playing short performances at New York City's 58th Street Theatre as part of shows promoted by disc jockey Murray the K. A return trip saw the band tour the United States and Canada over three months supporting Herman's Hermits, highlighted by their six-song set at the Monterey Pop Festival in June.

MARINE BALLROOM

6 JANUARY 1967, MORECAMBE

I WAS THERE: DAVID SCOTT

I was in the Morecambe area and I actually transported quite a few of these groups round the Floral Hall and Central Pier and various pubs and clubs. I didn't see The Who at the time. I think it was too much money for me to get in. My wife Susan saw them at the Pier. They came, and they were stopping at the Clarendon Hotel on the promenade towards the West End of Morecambe. She says they didn't smash anything up.

I WAS THERE: CHRISTINE

Pete Townshend had been in a car accident on the way to the gig but, instead of cancelling, as most bands would have done, they played with Roger Daltrey on guitar and drafted in a guitarist from a local group called the Doodle-Bugs, who were their support act.

I WAS THERE: IAN WARD

I was there on one occasion when The Who came to Morecambe. I was there, as lead singer of the Doodle-Bugs. We were the support group to many chart topping bands and solo artists who performed at the Pier and the Floral Hall. We must have been playing on other nights when The Who came to Morecambe. I do remember them coming once or twice besides the night we were there playing with them.

When The Who came to town, Pete Townshend didn't make it. The rumour on the night was that he'd been involved in an accident on the motorway, but it later turned out that he'd gone with Eric Clapton to an awards ceremony and spent the day with him. We shared a dressing room with them and the local band or orchestra were in the other room.

John Entwistle asked our lead guitarist Mike Dickinson if he would stand in for Pete. With only ten minutes notice and a quick run through of The Who's set list, Mike did a great gig with them. It was Mike's fifteen minutes of fame, although it lasted 45 minutes. And then they said 'you'd better go because we're going to blow everything up.' I can distinctly remember Keith Moon's drum kit coming from the back of the stage onto the dance floor. You thought they were smashing their gear but I think there were guitars that were screwed together that they would just use on one song. The guitars were built to be smashed.

Few places could outshine Morecambe in the Sixties. Blackpool, perhaps, but you didn't have the groups at Blackpool. Most of the pubs had bands in – it was a magical time. It wasn't just a summer season thing. It was all year round. You used to get people coming down from Scotland. They used to come down for the weekends, and we used to attract the people from Barrow. They used to make the journey by train. They used to come over for a punch up, but it was all good fun. The Floral Hall had a revolving stage, we called it the Revolting Stage. We came round on the stage to open the night and you'd have a set of locals on one side and a set of visitors on the other side and all hell would let loose sometimes when they'd had too much to drink.

And it was hard work lumping all the gear. We didn't have a roadie and the pier was extremely long in Morecambe. We used to put the gear on a cart and pull it for about 20 minutes until we got to the dance hall. Get a cold winter's night with the snow and the tide coming over the top and it was fun. It all adds to the glamour of it.

FESTIVAL HALL

13 JANUARY 1967, KIRKBY-IN-ASHFIELD

I WAS THERE: MARIAN WRIGHT, AGE 16

This brings back memories of my 16th birthday. Having always preferred rock music, it was a 'must have' ticket and no one that night was disappointed. I bought four tickets – for me, my friend and two guys from a group called The Tea Set who played regularly at our local miners welfare club. The arrangement was that they would pick us up from my home.

As the time wore on and they hadn't arrived, it was assumed they were not going to turn up so we went to get the bus. As it pulled up we saw the guys' van pull out of the street but there was nothing we could do. When we got to the Festival Hall, we sold their tickets, with enough profit to cover our expenses, and met the guys inside. The Who were amazing. The quiet one – no one ever remembers his name – did his thing. Keith Moon was crazy and his drums came off the stage in the final song. Pete Townshend's arms were twirling round as fast as a windmill and he smashed his guitar in the finale.

But for me the star was Roger Daltrey. The way he moved, his voice and his stage presence were amazing, as was the fact that he never competed with the outlandish behaviour of the others. He was completely confident in his own abilities. We got the full on Who experience and I love the fact that they are still rocking!

KINGSWAY THEATRE

25 JANUARY 1967, HADLEIGH

I WAS THERE: JENNY RAWLINGS

One of the supporting groups was Sounds Around and I was going out with the chap who knew them well and drove their van. I didn't get to meet them. I seem to remember all the girls connected to Sounds

Around were only interested in them. However, the founder member and keyboard player for Sounds Around was named John Pantry who was a recording engineer for LBC Studios in London and worked with the Small Faces, the Bee Gees and possibly The Who. He hosts – or did – Premier Christian Radio.

LOCARNO BALLROOM

26TH JANUARY 1967, BRISTOL

I WAS THERE: MIKE PARRY

For my sins I was a Bristol Mod back in the mid to late Sixties. What a night it was! I don't know what the crowd capacity was at that venue then but it was packed. Eventually I found my way upstairs and climbed on a table with my head touching the ceiling. It was all worth it. The Locarno had a revolving stage and, as soon as they started warming up with their double stack Marshalls, they drowned the records being played out to the dance floor.

They played probably for about 45 minutes until midway through 'My Generation' when all hell broke loose! Before any of this, however, Daltrey had been dragged off stage and into the audience and the remainder of the group had carried on as if nothing happened!

During the performance Townshend had already got through two guitars. The third went into one of the amps at the end, the drum kit came off the stage in bits and after all this mayhem they coolly walked off the stage with broadcast message to the crowd 'that was The Who!'

ROYAL LINKS PAVILION

11 FEBRUARY 1967, CROMER

I WAS THERE: CHARLES THIRTLE

Through work circumstances I was fortunate enough to be one of

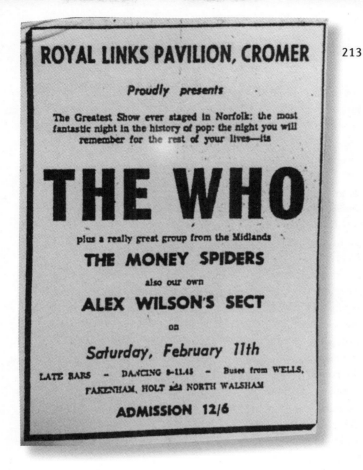

several hundred fans to see The Who perform at the Royal Links
Pavilion, Cromer. My connection with the Links came about when
I was employed by the Eastern Daily Press in their advisement
department at Cromer, handling weekly display copy for the Links
which was then under the co ownership of brothers Nigel and Rod
Blow. The distinct advert format, based on cave-man character
FLO (Fab Links Organisation) was created by local man Ian Foster.
However, this image was omitted from The Who avert so that a bold
type face could be set across the entire two column width. The text
declared: 'The greatest show staged in Norfolk: the most fantastic
night in the history of pop: the night you will remember for the rest
of your lives.' My goodness, it certainly ticked all of those boxes.

The Pavilion on Overstrand Road was the ballroom of the former Royal Links Hotel and lent itself admirably as North Norfolk's venue for top-notch bands of the 1960's and 70's. Often I was asked to help out as part of the crowd control team, the night of The Who gig being no exception.

Two balconies situated either side of the dance floor had stairs leading directly onto the stage. My station for the night was at the top of one of the flights to prevent over enthusiastic fans gaining access to the stage below. I reckon this position afforded me the best view to the action in the house, near to and directly above the band, and I was being paid to do it!

The atmosphere was electric and when The Who shaped up to play the crowd went wild. The band gave their all to every number played, notably 'My Generation' and their latest release, 'Happy Jack'. The stage reverberated to Keith Moon's drumming breaks, Pete Townshend performed his famous windmill arm action on lead guitar, John 'Thunderfingers' Entwistle (voted at one time the greatest bass guitarist in the world), excelled with his unique typewriter style of playing, and Roger Daltrey's wild man antics with his microphone – long lead and gaffer tape for twirling, completed this outrageous yet thoroughly absorbing scene.

During the final number a roadie fixed flares to the backs of the amps. When they were lit, all hell broke loose. The band kicked and threw their equipment around and smashed their guitars. Seriously unbelievable to watch. It may have been their gig finale, but I thought then as I still do 'what a bloody waste!' After the show, I believe this larger than life quartet stayed the night at the Danish House Hotel in nearby Overstrand with a quiet drink or three.

Sadly the Royal Links Pavilion is no more. It was destroyed by fire on 5 April 1978. The last high profile band to perform there was the Sex Pistols on Christmas Eve 1977. Now housing stands on this revered site where perhaps ghosts of famous rock bands still strut their stuff. The night The Who rocked at Cromer Links was the best gig staged there ever.

I WAS THERE: ROD BLOW

It was probably one of the biggest nights in the history of the Links in its day and one that we well remember. The Links was one of those places where we didn't realise what we were involved in when we started it. It just sort of grew on us so quickly in those heady days of the Sixties and it just became an absolute monster.

The Who were with us in February 1967. We'd had over the years many big names but none at the time as big as The Who. We had to put on the biggest back up in terms of facilities and people that we'd ever done.

It was the most we'd ever paid for a group. The money now seems quite small and insignificant compared to many but in its day it was a massive amount, and it frightened the life out of us to do it. But we did it and never regretted it. We booked all our groups in through Robert Stigwood and we had to pay £600 for forty minutes for The Who.

That meant with all the add ons – because we had two other groups on the night as well – it cost us round about £1,000 to open the doors, which to us was a massive amount of money to commit to.

The Links became an absolute institution. You almost didn't have to advertise it. But obviously we did. We only advertised the gig in the normal way. We did this poster round every week and put posters in shop windows, coffee bars, pubs, etc. We did a hundred posters every week. It was a whole day and a whole evening of putting up posters.

And we had the usual adverts running in the EDP and the North Norfolk News and that was all we had to do because everybody knew what was going on. Everybody knew who we'd got coming. The kids were all our friends and we used to talk with them and they'd say 'what about that group? What about this group?' It was very much a family affair. And the kids were fantastic.

And the buses we ran in, we did those for free which wasn't unusual in Norfolk. But what we used to do is we paid for the coaches to come in from various areas and they'd usually be full up after the second or third week. You'd get 40 or 50 kids coming in and the only condition we made was that the coaches had to arrive at eight o'clock.

That way you'd got that number of people in at the door paying the

The Who in full flight at the Royal Links!

money which meant that you'd got your audience right from the start of the night instead of waiting for people to drift in. And we would have up to eight to ten coaches coming in from all over Norfolk. It was a brilliant system. It meant we were fully operational right from the word 'go'.

In those days the ticket price at the door was five shillings (25p) every Saturday night and that always included at least two groups – a local one and a national known one. When we put The Who on, we did our sums and we estimated with the number that we could get in that we would have to charge 12/6 (62p), which was a huge amount of money bearing in mind that your average teenager then was earning probably £3 to £4 a week. It was quite a large percentage of their wage to come to us. But we did it and we got about the best part of two thousand kids through the door that night. Health and safety would have a nightmare today. It was just absolutely steaming. We would laughingly say that we shoved the kids out the back door to get some more in at the front. And at 2,000 in the door we made a small profit but it was a small profit. It was a brilliant, brilliant event.

One of the memories of The Who was the road leading up to the Links, which is the Overstrand Road out of Cromer. It's quite a wide road up the hill and the queue to get in was halfway down into Cromer, which absolutely terrified us. I went over to pick up my fiancée at the time (she became my wife) because she used to do the door. When we drove up the road at about seven o'clock with the doors opening at eight, there was this queue for several hundred yards down the Overstrand Road towards Cromer, we thought 'oh my God. How are we going to cope?'

We had to think on our feet. We had to get two or three bouncers to stand on the door to help my wife where she used to sit while she took the money. And let ten or a dozen people in at a time. We'd never had to do it before. It was just a whole new ball game. She was having to funnel the money into cardboard boxes because the till on the door wouldn't hold it. She literally had two cardboard boxes for the notes to go in and the change went into the till. But it all worked and we got through it.

God knows what the temperature was in the hall with that number of people in. It must have been quite frighteningly high. But when you're young you don't notice that sort of thing. You just get on with it, with the excitement of the night. From my point of view, I was quite amazed that Roger Daltrey turned up on his own in the late afternoon between 5 and 6 o'clock. He was just so natural and normal and pleasant and asked would it be all right if we set up a television which he'd brought with him? Because he was fascinated with The Monkees who were on television then at tea-time.

We set a TV up in the changing room, and he and I sat in there on our own for the best part of a couple of hours talking about how things

were going and then watching The Monkees!

He wanted a bottle of vodka so I got him a bottle of vodka. And there he sat. He didn't get plastered, but he had a drink. And it was just so natural and normal, two people talking, which was extremely pleasant. And obviously I was quite honoured at the time. Then the rest of the guys turned up, one by one, in various classy cars. I remember one was a Bentley Continental and one was a Lincoln Continental. And that was the start of the night. We were just absolutely flooded with people. The main thing we regret about the night and about The whole Links

Rod Blow (left) on DJ duties at the Royal Links Pavillion, Cromer

event in a way was the fact that we didn't save what would now be fairly valuable memorabilia. There was no such thing as that in those days. We just had no trouble. That was the amazing thing in those days. You used to have the odd bit but you didn't have any trouble. You didn't have the fights that you'd have today. You probably couldn't stage it today.

I stood on the corner of the stage whilst The Who did their performance and some of the photographs show how close the kids were. They were literally just touching Roger Daltrey's feet, which you were able to do in those days. The noise was absolutely phenomenal and it was a wonderful, wonderful night. We breathed a sigh of relief when it was all over, because the tension was quite immense when you saw that number of people and realised that we'd got to control it and make it work. And we did. It went fantastically well. The only thing that went wrong was The Who's minders said to us 'the boys will want something to eat and drink afterwards. Where can they go?' This is North Norfolk. Everything had shut up and gone.

So we rang up our local country club, called North Repps, and spoke to George Hoy, who we knew. And we said 'George, any chance of you staying open so the boys can come down?' and he said 'yeah, no problem'. And so they went down there. He rang us up the next day and said 'don't bloody do that again. All they had was a glass of milk!' So it wasn't really worth his while, to put it mildly.

The Links burnt down in the Seventies, which was a great shame. The entrance now is into what was the Royal Links caravan park, in the grounds of the original Royal Links Hotel. The main entrance now is into the Cromer country club, built on the same premises. There's a total of seven acres there all told. And the pavilion was at the entrance.

EXETER UNIVERSITY

17 MARCH 1967, EXETER

I WAS THERE: PAUL WALTERS, AGE 17

The Who played in Exeter at the university and our band The Velvet Touch backed them. We expected to be playing in the Great Hall, which is where most of the bands played. We played there with Tina Turner, the Bee Gees, loads of them. We were quite in with the university because Neil, our bass guitarist, still worked there as a lab technician. So we automatically got all the gigs up there.

We were playing in the refectory, which was like a big canteen and much, much smaller than the Great Hall. It's like a long rectangular hall and there are two stages that are opposite each other. The halls probably about two hundred feet long, but a hundred feet wide. We played on the right hand side and The Who were on the left. We were on the same level as them and only about twenty feet apart.

They set their gear up while we were setting our stuff up. It was done by their roadies and they were showing us how they put the smoke bombs in the fake speakers so that when everybody starts smashing stuff up, the smoke goes up everywhere. It was one of the roadies' jobs to go up and light the smoke bombs. It looked like part of the PA but it wasn't. It was quite funny, watching the road managers when they set the stuff up and putting these little smoke bombs, these little fireworks, everywhere and telling us their little tricks – how most of the guitars they smashed up they actually changed so there wasn't as much damage going on as you think.

They were actually late getting there and we were going on probably a bit longer than we should have done. Then The Who came in looking a little bit like they'd had a few drinks. But they got up and started doing their thing and at the end of their set they started smashing their gear up and the drummer started throwing his kit around and Entwistle looked like he was totally disinterested.

The problem was, because they were playing the short way of the hall, people couldn't really see. There was a couple of thousand people in a room that should have held a thousand. Health and safety would have a field day these days. So everybody got up onto our stage. We had stayed on the stage and watched the show.

Their drum kit was being smashed up, which wasn't really that spectacular because all Moon did was push it over while Townshend smashed his guitar on the floor. And these smoke bombs were going off with sparks and stuff everywhere, making it look more spectacular than it actually was.

But the drunken students started to smash our gear up as well. So we got our drum kit smashed up and part of the PA. We'd just got a new Orange PA, which we were very proud of. It weighed a ton, I remember, and that got pushed over. And of course the concert finished and, as we were packing up what was left of our gear, we were all talking to the university guy who was in charge of the gig. We said 'this isn't good enough. We're playing in a band, semi professional, and we've now got no gear to speak of'.

So they said they would go down to the local store in the morning and sign the stuff off. Because, sometimes when The Who were smashing stuff up, although it was mostly fake what they did, if they did damage some of their gear, they had an open account with whatever record company they were with. Our drummer's father was a solicitor, and he was really mad that his son's drum kit was wrecked, and he turned up at Bill Greenhalgh's, which was our local supplier of equipment. The Who's stage manager, Roger Daltrey and John Entwistle all turned up. While they were playing around with different instruments that Bill had, they signed up to let us have the equipment. So we got an upgraded Orange PA system and a much better Premier drum kit than we'd actually had, all written down to The Who's record label. And the university signed it off as well. So if there were problems with the label, the university would pay for it. We weren't held liable in any way.

About ten years ago, I was measuring up a kitchen for this couple in the centre of Exeter and they said they recognised me from the band. They had met me at The Who concert. They said it was one of the most exciting nights of their lives and remembered that the audience got a bit over fraught and had thrown our drum kit around. They met at that gig and had since got married and had a kid called Roger and a kid called Pete!

FLORAL HALL

3 JUNE 1967, SOUTHPORT

I WAS THERE: CAROLE NAYLOR, AGE 15

I was lucky enough to see The Who at the Floral Hall in Southport. I chatted to Roger Daltrey outside who told me that Keith Moon was ill and couldn't appear that night. As he was my favourite, I was devastated! I was 15 years old and he was my crush. That night he was replaced by a certain someone from a group called John's Children and for years I was convinced it was Marc Bolan! It was a fantastic night.

Chris Townson, the drummer from John's Children, replaced Keith Moon on four dates during a 1967 UK tour after Moon had injured himself demolishing his drum kit on stage.

GOLDEN SLIPPER BALLROOM

9 JUNE 1967, MAGILLIGAN

I WAS THERE: BERNARD MCNICHOLL, AGE 21

I was at the Golden Slipper along with my sister, Rose Dorrans. The

Golden Slipper held about 300 and it was packed. The sound was so much different from what we usually heard from the Irish show bands. Rose thought the music was very loud. Some of the songs I recall were 'Happy Jack', 'My Generation', 'The Kids Are Alright' and 'La La Lies'. I'm not sure if they smashed their guitars and drums. The Golden Slipper was demolished about 20 years ago to make way for new houses.

I WAS THERE: BOBBY BRADLEY

It was a big thing The Who coming to Magilligan. I was a keen follower of them. The dancehall probably held about 2,500 people. My brother's band was the back up band for The Who that night – they were called the Bankers Showband and The Who asked if they could use their equipment when they arrived.

The chairs were all over the place when The Who came on, and they wrecked all my brother's equipment. He got compensated but they went ballistic on the stage, they smashed the drums and the keyboards and amplification. I'll always remember that. They were fantastic that night.

I WASN'T THERE: STEVEN McCRACKEN

I'm too young for it, but my granny used to talk about it. The Who stayed in a small caravan at the bottom of our yard. At the time my granny had turned the farm into a big guesthouse, but it was still a farm. At the very bottom of our second yard, the lower yard, we had a small caravan down there for guests. Just a few extra beds, so, when they played in Magilligan, The Who stayed in the yard. The Slipper was at the top of our lane, so it was handy. I didn't know they'd stayed in our farm until I was talking to the neighbours who told me and then I said to my gran 'what's this about The Who?' and she told me all about them.

I WAS THERE: GERARD O BRIEN, AGE 17

I saw The Who perform at The Golden Slipper. I went with two of my friends. We were very excited but too young to realise that this was part of music history. They came on stage around 10pm and played for about one hour. They had a stand in drummer as Keith Moon was ill. I was disappointed about that but the music was brilliant. At the end they did their stage act. Pete Townshend bashed his guitar up and down on the stage floor and smashed it against the amplifier. The drum kit was knocked over and smoke appeared. I thought this was fantastic. I had never seen anything like it. Shortly after they finished playing, Roger Daltrey came down amongst the audience beside me. He was wearing a bright pink shawl and was chatting and asking questions.

The Who travelled to the United States in June 1967 to perform a group of shows, including appearing on the closing day of the Monterey Festival. They played a thirty minute set which featured exploding coloured smoke bombs and saw Daltrey and Moon destroying their equipment, and Townshend reducing his Stratocaster to splinters. Next on the bill, Jimi Hendrix managed a feat that few could accomplish – that of upstaging The Who – by setting fire to his guitar on stage.

MONTEREY INTERNATIONAL POP FESTIVAL

18 JUNE 1967, MONTEREY, CALIFORNIA

I WAS THERE: HARVEY KUBERNIK

I'm an LA native. I first heard music in the late Fifties around town on the AM radio. I was really at the center of the surf music world. There were some hit records from England. We saw acts on the Ed Sullivan show from England and there were disc jockeys that played songs from England. B Mitchel Reed is a disc jockey, who played music from England that we'd never heard before. He played 'My Generation' and I'd never heard anything like this in my life. It

blew my mind.

He started playing The Who a lot. It wasn't just The Beatles and The Rolling Stones, he really leaned on The Who. On radio station KFWB there was a British disc jockey called Lord Tim, Tim Hudson. The Who got their airplay here initially through B Mitchel Reed and Lord Tim. This guy had a test pressing, of a great new tune called 'Pictures of Lily'. I never heard anything so monumental in my fucking life.

June 67 and The Who played Monterey. The reverberations of Monterey were something. The impact of The Who and Jimi Hendrix playing Monterey were that more airplay happened, and then they were on *Shindig* doing 'I Can't Explain'. It vaulted them right up there with The Beatles and the Stones. LA went mad in 67 for these groups.

BOUTWELL MEMORIAL AUDITORIUM

29 JULY 1967, BIRMINGHAM, ALABAMA

I WAS THERE: BILL HENDERSON

I went to the show with a college friend, who was from Birmingham, and our girlfriends. This was the summer between our sophomore and junior years in college. I lived in Mississippi and had to travel about

200 miles to Birmingham. Birmingham had a lot of steel plants and I remember the smog hanging over the city. This was before there was much concern about clean air and the environment. This was my first trip to Birmingham and it was quite an adventure for someone from a small Mississippi town.

A local radio station put these shows on several times a year. Usually they were called the 'Shower of Stars' but they may have used other names as well. The show would normally have six to eight acts with each doing two or three songs. In the 1950's the performers were country music stars, but they had shifted to pop and rock by 1967.

Herman's Hermits were the headliners at the show I went to. I remember Lou Christie singing 'Lightning Strikes'. Lou had a very distinctive voice and singing style. I think I read somewhere that he had a three-octave range and he must have used all three on 'Lightning Strikes'! I had not heard of The Who and was surprised by their performance. I don't remember what songs they did but I do remember them smashing their instruments at the end. I didn't 'get' this and it made no sense to me. You can imagine the contrast between the soft, smooth sound of Herman's Hermits and the raw style of The Who.

In 1967 it was rare to get to see the stars in person or even on TV. Of course, there was no YouTube, internet, or music videos. For the most part, all we knew about the bands was how they sounded on the radio and records and how they looked on album covers. So when you heard that one of your friends had been to a concert, you wanted to know all about the show. I remember telling my friends about the show in Birmingham, including The Who smashing their instruments. I had to start leaving this part out of my description of the show because I couldn't answer the inevitable question 'why did they do that?'

BALTIMORE CIVIC CENTER

11 AUGUST 1967, BALTIMORE, MARYLAND

I WAS THERE: BILL KNIPP, AGE 11

My brother took me to Baltimore Civic Center in 1967 for what was labeled The British Invasion. The opening act was the Moody Blues, then The Who and the headliner was Herman's Hermits! Two years later, Herman Hermits was playing Holiday Inns and The Who were huge! The biggest thing I remember was The Who breaking up their equipment.

CONSTITUTION HALL

13 AUGUST 1967, WASHINGTON DC

I WAS THERE: PATRICIA MARX, AGE 15

The first time I saw The Who – by accident, when they played as one of the supporting bands for Herman's Hermits tour in the US in the Summer of 1967 at Constitution Hall in Washington D.C. I was hooked. Their second album, *A Quick One*, which was called *Happy Jack* here in the States, had just come out but I hadn't heard it. I hadn't heard 'My Generation' either. I was completely wowed by the music and the lyrics, the crazy drummer who drummed so fast he was a blur and the rock singer who could actually sing beautifully. The carefully controlled chaos, the strong individuality of each member, their colourful costumes and each one competing for full attention of audience members. As they swung into 'My Generation' for the finale, I finally realized I had heard that song at least on the radio, but I didn't know Pete would smash his guitar at the end, which I thoroughly enjoyed. I loved the entire set but especially remember 'Boris the Spider', 'Pictures of Lily' and the mini-opera. In fact I thought at the time, as I am sure every Who fan has, 'God made this band for me.' Hermann Who? I was 15 and my life had changed forever.

MEMORIAL AUDITORIUM

17 AUGUST 1967, CHATTANOOGA, TENNESSEE

I WAS THERE: LESLIE LADD, AGE 14

They came to Chattanooga, Tennessee for the local radio station show, 'The JetFli Spectacular. I went with my older sister Glenda and our neighbor and her mom. I was most thrilled to see Herman's Hermits, but when The Who came on stage and smashed their instruments at the end of 'I Can See For Miles' I was mesmerized! I still get a thrill when I hear that powerful song.

After the show, my neighbor's mom took us to meet them where they were staying, the Downtowner Motel. They were all sunning by the pool. I was so shy to meet these older and famous guys. But Keith broke the ice when he told me he had a sister also named Leslie! I thought Roger was the cutest and gave us a sweet smile and Pete didn't say much. They proceeded to ask the neighbor's mom if she would go buy them some Bourbon since they were underaged to buy in Tennessee, which she did. I had them all sign my autograph book, although sadly I lost it, and somewhere there are pictures the mom took. What a thrill and what an influential moment in my life as a rock fanatic!

SMOTHERS BROTHERS COMEDY HOUR

17 SEPTEMBER 1967, LOS ANGELES, CALIFORNIA

I WAS THERE: HARVEY KUBERNIK

There's another key moment in Who history when they had a TV booking on *The Smothers Brothers Comedy Hour*. They destroy their instruments on stage and Keith destroys his drum kit with a cherry bomb. That thing was filmed eight blocks from where I live and down the street from the high school that I was attending – Fairfax High School, where Shel Talmy went to high school.

That show on TV was the talk of the town. That was like The Beatles on *Ed Sullivan* when The Who destroyed their equipment. Why are you destroying your equipment? There's smoke bombs. There's craziness. What a way to make an impact on people. I don't know if it was about Gustav Metzger and all that art stuff that Pete Townshend talked about, the art of the destruction of the instruments. It was hard enough to find money for petrol out here.

BALLERINA BALLROOM

6 OCTOBER 1967, NAIRN

I WAS THERE: ANNELLA FLYNN, AGE 15

It was a Friday night and there was a special bus running from Tain to Nairn to the gig, picking up in towns and villages along the way. I got on the bus in Invergordon with my friend.

We were both 15 years old and I was wearing a gold lurex halter neck mini dress. I remember it as it wasn't actually my dress – it belonged to my friend. As we were still at school we didn't have much money and used to swap clothes. She was wearing something of mine. Little did we think that, almost fifty years hence, The Who would still be around. We were just on a night out to see a chart group. They weren't called 'bands' in those days.

When we got to the Ballerina the dancehall was heaving. The group had already had about ten chart hits so they were a big draw. I remember the ladies toilets were up some steps and, because of the massive crowd and all the pushing and shoving, the door to the toilets came off the hinges – no health and safety in those days!

I WAS THERE: ROB MILNE, AGE 17

The Ballerina in Nairn was my favourite music venue when I was growing up in the North of Scotland. I saw lots of great bands there including Cream, Juicy Lucy, Status Quo and the Herd. When the Cream turned up to play their gig on a Friday night, the van with their equipment never arrived. They were offered the use of the support band's gear but they refused. All three of them appeared on stage to explain the situation, stating they would return to the venue on the following Tuesday to play. This they duly did.

The Ballerina was a converted church with an artificially lowered roof making it a very intimate venue. Whilst small, with a capacity of maybe two to three hundred and a tiny stage, it was great for getting up close to the band. The Who were no exception. There was no bar in the Ballerina, only a small place for soft drinks. Just after the support act finished, which was a local band, I remember standing next to Roger Daltrey and a gorgeous blonde.

When The Who came on, I was about two rows back from the stage and I remember Pete Townshend plugging in and windmilling his Gibson. The volume was incredible! Townshend wore a gold Regency style jacket with a frilly shirt and Daltrey was in a fringed leather jacket and wearing bright orange trousers. I couldn't work out if he had a bit of hose pipe down his inside leg or if he was particularly well blessed in that department. I think John Entwistle was wearing a denim style dark green leather jacket and Keith Moon was in a t-shirt.

The band had just returned from their first American tour and went through their normal repertoire of songs. I recall Pete telling us he had written a rock opera and the band would play some tracks from it, which they duly did. This was not *Tommy* but *Rael*. This was the first time I had ever seen a double necked Gibson SG. It was black but the thing I remember is that it was split in two. It was held together by two bolted stainless steel plates on the front, having obviously been smashed up by Pete at an earlier gig then patched up by the guitar roadie so that it could still be used. I also remember Keith Moon breaking loads of sticks but some he just sent spinning, unbroken, into the crowd. They were fought over by the crowd as souvenirs. A girl I had been in school with, Marlene Dodd, managed to get one and she brandished it triumphantly on the bus on the way home to Inverness. I don't know where she lives these days to find out if she still has it. She did well to get one, as she must have been the smallest person at the gig! My all time favourite Who song, 'I Can See for Miles', was particularly memorable. I was standing so close to the band and hearing the guitar intro at that sound level along with the drum intro was incredible. Keith was using his twin bass drum Premier kit with the coloured fluorescent 'The Who' logo, with 'The' on one bass drum and 'Who' on the other.

My one other memory of The Who gig took place before the actual gig itself in a local pub called the Star. As no alcohol was on sale in the Ballerina, The Who's roadies were out for a couple of beers after the sound check and I happened to be in the same pub at the same time. There was an upright piano in the corner of the lounge bar and one of the roadies pulled up a chair and started to play some tunes a la Chas and Dave. So we had a right good sing song before going to the gig. Great memories!

BEACH BALLROOM

7 OCTOBER 1967, ABERDEEN

I WAS THERE: JIM STRACHAN

I took my new girlfriend to see The Who at the Beach Ballroom for what proved to be an unforgettable gig. I was amazed at Townshend's electrifying guitar playing on a Rickenbacker and Entwistle's thunderous bass sound. I've never heard anything like it before, or since! By the way, my girlfriend became the wife and we're now in our 49th year of wedded bliss.

I WAS THERE: ARTHUR WYLLIE

I was one of those lucky enough to see The Who at the Beach

Ballroom, Aberdeen. The tickets cost 15/- (75p)! I was there with three friends, two of who I have lost contact with. The Who were meant to be on stage for an hour to close the night, but they stayed on stage for at least one and a half hours. They played all their hits at that time, and several album tracks very loudly. After they had been on stage for about an hour they started playing 'A Quick One' – which I had never heard before – and this lasted about half an hour. At the end of the night, Pete Townshend smashed his guitar over his knee and Keith Moon kicked over his drum kit. To this day, I class this as the best performance that I have ever seen – and I have seen a lot.

KINEMA BALLROOM

8 OCTOBER 1967, DUNFERMLINE

I WAS THERE: LINDSAY CARMICHAEL, AGE 18

I was fortunate enough to see them perform at the Kinema and their performance that night has stuck with me to this day. It was around Christmas of that year, as I can recall a story of the band staying in the City Hotel in Bridge Street in Dunfermline and Keith Moon being arrested. He was using an air pistol to shoot out some of the old style Christmas lights which were stretched out between the lamp posts at that time. It was an evening to remember.

NEW CENTURY HALL

21 OCTOBER 1967, MANCHESTER

I WAS THERE: STEVE BERNING, AGE 15

At school in Bury in the 1960s, pupils were either Beatles or Stones fans. However, as soon as I heard 'I Can't Explain', The Who became my band. So the 15 year old me was thrilled that Friday night as I set off for Manchester. I had managed to get about 20 feet from the stage as The Who came on.

Townshend had his twin-necked Gibson SG and Moon his Pictures

Steve Berning and his brother Pete

of Lily Premier kit. When they started, the sound was unbelievably loud. Not only was it loud but you could feel Entwistle's bass thumping your chest. Their set consisted of their third album *Sell Out*, earlier hits, 'Heat Wave' and – I think – Stevie Wonder's 'I Was Made To Love Her'. When I got into school on the Monday my ears were still ringing!

I WAS THERE: TED TUKSA

The second time I saw them was at the CIS building in Manchester. The Who did a great set, but were being hurried up by the manager to finish the night. He was shouting from the side of the stage. Pete then used his guitar as a cricket bat, and one by one smashed all the lights at the foot of the stage.

COVENTRY THEATRE

29 OCTOBER 1967, COVENTRY

I WAS THERE: RAFFERTY BATES

Before they came on the Jimi Hendrix Experience were on and I think The Yardbirds were on as well. Nobody expected what would unfold at the end of the show. The Who were at their brilliant best. It was an amazing performance by the band. All of a sudden the stage manager drew the stage curtains while The Who were still playing and announced on the tannoy for the band to stop as the show had to stop at a certain time, 10.30pm I think.

Pete Townshend was not amused. He said 'you don't draw the fackin' curtains on The Who, we are the fackin' Who'. Pete and Roger then swung on one side of the stage curtains and ripped them down and John Entwistle and Keith Moon did the same to the other side. They then smashed all the stage scenery and set about all their equipment. The stage looked like a bomb had hit it. The crowd could not believe what they had seen. They had witnessed the best and most destructive band on earth living up to their reputation that night.

I WAS THERE: DAVE JONES

They were top of the bill on a Sunday night. Before their act reached its smashing finale it was cut short. At 10.30pm, power to the stage was cut and the safety curtain came down, leaving the audience somewhat bewildered. Sunday night in the 60's – that was the curfew for entertainment to cease! I don't think there was any fuss or protest by the audience, just a bit of moaning. It was what happened at the time – like last orders in the pub!

TOWN HALL

6 NOVEMBER 1967, BIRMINGHAM

I WAS THERE: LIZ WOLSEY

They were supported by The Tremeloes and third on the bill were Traffic. The Who were brilliant. Lots of energy and Keith Moon was on form. At the end of the concert Pete Townshend smashed his guitar and Keith kicked over the drum kit.

David Robinson playing in the woods

GRANADA CINEMA

8 NOVEMBER 1967, KETTERING

I WAS THERE: DAVID ROBINSON, AGE 18

I saw them at Kettering Granada, and it was probably the first of the two houses they played that night, as buses home to the steel town of Corby did not run particularly late. In retrospect, the bill of The Who, Tremeloes, Traffic, Herd and Marmalade – all with their definitive line ups – was solid gold. There were no weak links in that chain!

I'd decided at the time of the *My Generation* album that The Who were my favourite British band of the 60's, ousting Gerry and the Pacemakers and running alongside The Byrds and the pre *Pet*

Sounds Beach Boys. One of the things that appealed about The Who's songs was that, while 'pop' music generally had been about love and relationships up to and including that time, Pete wrote about other stuff in 'I'm a Boy', 'Happy Jack', 'Pictures of Lily' and the subsequent rock operas.

Some of their songs I found straightforward to perform using three guitar chords. A mate and I were asked to do 'Substitute' at a church service (don't ask!) and 'I'm a Boy' was the first track our modest local 'beat group' attempted – we didn't last long.

On stage at the Granada, the boys still had the tail-end of their Mod look. We had quite good seats in the circle but, as was par for the course in those days, could hardly hear a thing due to the screams of teenage girls. Luckily for me, I could lip-read most of the setlist and it included one or two of my favourites, including 'Happy Jack'. I seem to remember that they might have included 'Rael' in that set, too, although the logical side of my brain suggests that they wouldn't have included two elongated tracks at that pre-stadium stage of their careers, and they definitely did 'A Quick One'. My girlfriend, Sue – now my wife of 44 years – was quite awestruck, and a colleague of hers was impressed when she revealed that she'd seen The Who live.

I remember the ads in the local paper printed the title of a high profile hit for each act above the name of the band and thinking these were unsubtle, as though we wouldn't know who they were! But I don't think any of the audience cared. For me, it was at least a double header, and probably more.

GRANADA CINEMA

9 NOVEMBER 1967, MAIDSTONE

I WAS THERE: DAVID STAFFORD

I saw The Who at the Granada Cinema in Maidstone. I sat politely through The Tremeloes and Marmalade – 'Ob-La-Di, Ob-La-Da', their big number, was never a cue for dangerous over-excitement.

Then The Who came on. I'd never been to a proper rock concert before, but I knew straight away that this was a proper rock concert. It was like attending a small war. They were thugs – thugs dressed in satin and lace, but still unmistakably thugs.

Roger's voice hadn't yet reached its full Rock God potential, but it could menace. He spat 'I Can't Explain' and 'Substitute' all over the audience. There was no sense of fun in Pete's windmilling. It was a job that had to be done, as if the only way to build enough momentum to hit the strings properly was to start high. I'd worried about Keith's defective motor functions and unblinking eyes when I'd seen him on telly. That night, I swear, the eyes had crosses in them, like Tom's after Jerry's smacked him on the head with a bowling ball. I don't recall any of the more restrained numbers like 'Happy Jack' or 'Pictures of Lily', but they finished the set with 'My Generation'. It started like a jet engine and then got louder. The small war escalated into something that was genuinely scary. It was to me, anyway.

Bits of wood from Pete's splintered guitar flew around like shrapnel. Smoke was pouring out of one of the speaker cabs. Cymbals got frisbeed. Eventually, Keith managed to kick the entire kit first off the riser then into the orchestra pit while stage hands ran on to sort the carnage out. I don't remember what happened after that except I was deaf for three days.

COW PALACE

18 NOVEMBER 1967, SAN FRANCISCO, CALIFORNIA

I WAS THERE: BOBBY ASEA

By the winter of 1967, I was somewhat of a veteran concert goer mostly due to the fact that my older sister would let me tag along with her and her girlfriends when they went to see The Beach Boys in concert. After two or three Beach Boy concerts between the years of 1964 -1965, I was fortunate enough to see The Rolling Stones in December of 1965 with my best friend and we were all on our own. It was a wonderful feeling to be able to do this at the not so ripe age of 12 years!

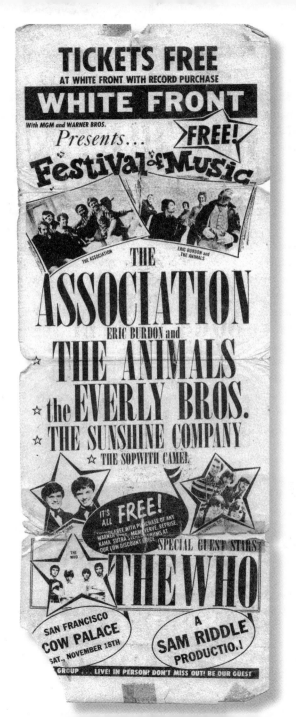

Fast forwarding to the Christmas holidays of 1967, my Christmas wish list consisted mostly of records by some of my favorite bands. I remember one night my family and I were Christmas shopping at a department store called White Front. Naturally, I had to drag my parents to the record section to show them what record albums that I wanted for Christmas. Lo and behold, once we arrived there, we discovered that the store was having a special that offered a free concert ticket with a purchase of a record album. The concert was to be held at the Cow Palace in San Francisco, which was 50 miles from where we lived. On the bill were The Sunshine Company, Sopwith Camel, The Association, The Everly Brothers, The Animals and The Who.

Originally I was just going to show my folks what records that I wanted and they would possibly purchase them at a later date so I could be surprised on Christmas morning. That plan got shot to hell when I begged them to buy a couple records so that my twin sister and I could go to the concert. To our delight, our parents agreed to buy two albums right then and there so my sister and I could score two tickets to the show. We were thrilled to say the least and somewhat surprised that our folks were going to allow us 14 year olds to go to a show so far away from home.

When concert day came, it was my older sister (who used to take me to see The Beach Boys in concert) and her boyfriend who drove us from San Jose to the Cow Palace in San Francisco to drop us off at the venue. Even though I had heard of all of the groups, I was most excited to see The Animals and The Who. When the British Invasion happened a few years earlier, I was completely smitten by all of the bands from across the pond. It wasn't until years later that I appreciated some of the American artists who actually influenced the British bands. One of those artists was the Everly Brothers who was on the bill. Looking back, I feel very fortunate to have seen them live in their heyday.

I vividly remember that we had some very good seats on the main floor. The show opened up with The Sunshine Company then The Animals followed. This wasn't the original Animals but none the less, Eric Burdon was there and he was fabulous!

The Who followed The Animals and they were on fire. Among the songs that they played that I can remember are: 'My Generation', 'Happy

Jack', 'I Can't Explain' and 'Substitute'. The one song that stands out the most in my memory is, 'I Can See For Miles'. It was their latest hit from their most recent album, *The Who Sell Out*. It was a short set but filled with high energy. Pete was doing his trade mark windmill motion, Roger was tossing his microphone in the air and catching it, Keith was recklessly pounding on his drums like a madman while always staying in time, and John stood firmly in place holding it all together with his dynamic bass playing. There were many highlights during their set but it was the climax that stole the whole show. This was still the period when the band would destroy their equipment at the end of the set and lucky for us we were treated to their display of violent madness. It was quite entertaining to watch Pete and Keith go ballistic on their instruments. Broken drums and guitars littered the stage as they stormed off in victory.

In the years that followed, I attended many Who concerts including the one where Keith Moon passed out during the show and the rest of the band had someone from the audience come up on stage and finish the show with them. As great as each and every one of them were, the first time that I saw them at the Cow Palace will always remain my favorite.

HOLLYWOOD BOWL

19 NOVEMBER 1967, LOS ANGELES, CALIFORNIA

I WAS THERE: HARVEY KUBERNIK

In 1967 they're coming to town. I go with my friend David Wolf and we get tickets in the days before the world was rigged and we get second row box seats at the Hollywood Bowl. That would never happen today. It's kind of a blur to me, but it was frantic. After seeing the Everly Brothers and The Association and their very well constructed, beautiful harmony pop songs, here comes The Who and it's 'My Generation' and Roger Daltrey's doing that microphone deal. And Pete Townshend – I'd never seen anybody be so aggressive and strident in his playing. Keith Moon was in hog heaven because he was playing in Hollywood. He's playing in a venue with 18,000 seats.

They're on the stage where Sinatra and The Beatles and everybody had played. It isn't like you're seeing Oasis in a club in Manchester. They're starting off in an 18,000 seater on a package show out here. It was really something.

1968
The Who began 1968 continuing to support *The Who Sell Out*, which had been released in late 1967. A short 6 date tour of Australia and New Zealand with Small Faces and former Manfred Mann vocalist Paul Jones was marred by bad press and poor sound, leading Pete Townshend to vow the group would never return (they eventually relented, but not until 2004).

The year also saw two long stints in North America, the second US tour featured performances of the newly recorded 'Magic Bus', which was released in July and quickly became a fan favourite; it was also during this time that Townshend began giving interviews related to his visions of the concept album that would become *Tommy*.

The band played over 130 live dates in 1968, and one of their last appearances of the year occurred at The Rolling Stones' *Rock and Roll Circus*, a circus-themed rock and roll special intended to air on the BBC. Although The Rolling Stones were dissatisfied with their performance, The Who's performance of 'A Quick One, While He's Away' was seen as a highlight, resulting in its appearance in *The Kids Are Alright* biographical film and its soundtrack in 1979.

SILVER BLADES ICE RINK

8 JANUARY 1968, BRISTOL

I WAS THERE: JOHN MOGER, AGE 16

I was a massive Who fan and saw them about five times during the 1960's. I saw them perform at the now demolished Silver Blades Ice Rink in Frogmore Street. I was still at school but any pocket money I had went on watching bands, especially the old 'package' tours. The Bristol Locarno Ballroom and Silver Blades Ice Rink were part of one complex and were relatively new, so hadn't established themselves yet on the gig circuit, although I do recall seeing The Yardbirds and The Move at the Locarno, which had a revolving stage and (then) state of the art lighting. I've no idea who thought it would be a good idea to stand hundreds of people on an ice rink, but it's possible the gig may have been moved from the Locarno Ballroom, which was situated in the same building, due to technical problems.

Anyway, this was pre-health and safety days, so we all gathered round the stage at the side of the rink and waited for our rock heroes to appear. They were late starting – no surprise there – but once they did they were brilliant. Amazingly, there were no covers on the ice so the combined body heat of the crowd started to melt the ice. By the end of the gig we were standing in an inch of freezing water but it didn't matter – we'd seen The Who! It certainly goes down as one of the most unusual gigs I've ever been to. It was wintertime and it was just as cold in the ice rink as it was outside, although we warmed up as the show progressed!

I WAS THERE: JOHN RUDGE

We couldn't understand why the ice rink was used but there was a rumour that they'd trashed their dressing room the year before and so the Locarno manager banned them from ever appearing there again. I've since heard the Locarno was double booked that night but I prefer to believe the trashing ban story! My mate caught a drumstick at the ice rink.

Moonie was always breaking them and throwing them at the crowd. I remember the ice was bloody cold to stand on. I don't think they wanted people on the ice with no skates but we went on anyway.

ASSEMBLY HALL

11 JANUARY 1968, WORTHING

I WAS THERE: JOHN FEEST

My friend Pete Wadeson was in a band called Total that supported The Who on this occasion and Pete Townshend wanted to borrow his guitar, pledging to pay for any resulting damage. My friend sweated throughout the act and fortunately Townshend didn't damage the guitar, much to the other Pete's sanity!

STARLIGHT BALLROOM

11 FEBRUARY 1968, CRAWLEY

I WAS THERE: DAVID GOODWIN

We saw them at Crawley Starlight. That was *Tommy* era and they were exceptionally good. They came off the stage and walked across in front of us. Moon's eyes were staring everywhere. He just bumped into us and had a laugh and said 'come on lads, come and have a drink' but the whole thing was gobbledegook really.

ROYAL BALLROOM

12 JANUARY 1968, TOTTENHAM

I WAS THERE: PAULINE LEVER

I can't remember where I saw them but it may have been the Royal in Tottenham. I do remember I had Keith's drum stick with teeth marks on it. He just lobbed it straight into my lap and I shoved it down my dress for safe keeping.

SHEFFIELD UNIVERSITY

16 FEBRUARY 1968, SHEFFIELD

I WAS THERE: PAUL BRUCE HADEN

Because I was brought up in Sheffield, the only way to find out what was happening on the music front was by reading music papers like *Melody Maker* and *NME*, which were weekly, and *Beat Instrumental* which was monthly. I'd been going to gigs from quite a young age as my dad took me to a few of the rock'n'roll package tours that went around the country in the late 1950s and early 1960s.

My first gig was Gene Vincent and Eddie Cochrane. Radio Luxembourg was a source of 'new' music and I used to listen nearly every night. I was by then playing guitar although I'd played classical violin from the age of seven. I think it was the overall raw sound of The Who, and particularly the guitar, that drew me to them. I first saw them in Chesterfield in a small club in early 1966. My girlfriend's older brother could drive and was also a fan. We next saw them at Barnsley town hall and then in 1967 at Sheffield City Hall on a package tour, where the support acts included Traffic and The Herd.

At the uni gig, because the stage was quite low and we were sitting on the floor quite near the front, the whole experience seemed much more intense. The sound was better, presumably because we were hearing a lot of the stage sound and not the PA sound.

WINTERLAND BALLROOM

24 FEBRUARY 1968, SAN FRANCISCO, CALIFORNIA

I WAS THERE: NEIL FAUGNO

It was an interesting line up – The Who, Cannonball Adderly and The Nice who were boring, Cannonball was cool and The Who were fantastic. An interesting thing about this show was that it was set up like a dance with a very large dance floor. The Who, of course, finished with 'My Generation' and people were urging them to destroy their equipment. Pete made a comment about 'how much this stuff cost' but that only made the crowd cheer louder.

Well, Pete complied but really looked pissed off and he walked off leaving just Keith playing his drums like only he could. Keith eventually kicked over his drum set but I really felt that his actions were a big 'fuck you' to the crowd urging him on.

MARQUEE CLUB

23 APRIL 1968, LONDON

I WAS THERE: GERRY ALLINGTON

I saw them three times at the Mecca in Stevenage – nobody local called it by its correct name, the Locarno Ballroom. I was in my last year at school. They were my idols and didn't disappoint. Their records were good but live they were fantastic.

I seem to recall an article in the *Melody Maker* or *Sounds* that, after one of those gigs, John had injured his hand punching a framed picture of Joe Loss in their dressing room. Aah – happy days! They often kicked off a show with 'Substitute' which got everyone rocking from the start. I saw them about fourteen times in all up to about 1971, including at Civic Hall in Dunstable, at Brunel University with The Crazy World of Arthur Brown, The Alan Bown Set and others, at the Roundhouse and at the Saville Theatre, when Vanilla Fudge were second on the bill. Best of all was at the original Marquee Club in Wardour Street, which ended with equipment wipe-out and Pete shoving two guitars at the same time into the very low stage ceiling. It cost 25/- (£1.25) entrance. My ears were ringing for days afterwards.

Pete Townshend told Melody Maker: 'I smashed up two guitars at the end of the show, because one I was using had recently been repaired and broke as I came on stage, so I played another one I used for recording. At the end, I thought 'what the hell...' and smashed them both.'

STAMPEDE CORRAL

10 JULY 1968, CALGARY, CANADA

I WAS THERE: KEITH ROWLEY

The Who headlined the Calgary Stampede in 1968 and my brother John and his wife Rita went backstage to meet up with Roger. They had filthy old ice hockey dressing rooms to change in and there was no security to stop anyone wandering around backstage. John and

Rita went a few years back to see The Who in Winnipeg and tried to see him again but this time there was major security in place, so no luck.

SINGER BOWL

2 AUGUST 1968, FLUSHING, QUEENS, NEW YORK CITY

I WAS THERE: JOHN KOEGEL

The Doors, who performed on a revolving stage, which broke down partway through their performance, headlined the show with a wild performance that led to a well-documented melee when the security staff and police tried to end the show early. The opening act was a band called Kangaroo, which featured Jon Hall (later of the band Orleans) and some hippie girl singer.

I remember The Who opened with a song about angels and devils I had never heard before. Of course, it was 'Heaven and Hell'. They also played 'Summertime Blues', 'Young Man Blues', 'Magic Bus' and 'My Generation'.

JAGUAR CLUB

10 AUGUST 1968, ST CHARLES, ILLINOIS

I WAS THERE: DANIEL TEAFOE, AGE 13

If one saw them in concert in the late Sixties or Seventies, it's possible you had a 'profound experience', of the transcendental kind. The Who could take you to places your mind didn't usually go. Having seen the band many times over the past 50 years, and in many incarnations, the show worthy of claiming bragging rights for took place at the Jaguar Club in St. Charles, Illinois – my home town.

The Jaguar, once a roller rink and then a used car dealership, was a popular music venue at the western outskirts of the Chicago area. It was a groovy place to hangout, where acts on the summer concert circuit with a hit single or two appeared. It also served as a showcase for local talent. The intimate space was festooned with florescent coloured murals, psychedelic posters, strobes, and black-lights.

The announcement of The Who playing there drew great excitement. I couldn't believe it! In my little town? I heard them on the radio. Saw them on TV. They touched a nerve in me. 'My Generation' was an anthem. 'Magic Bus' was cruising up the charts.

On show day, I was among the first in line at the door, with my hard earned four dollars. Once inside, I went straight for the stage, firmly planting myself on the cold hard concrete floor. Front row centre, within arms reach of the three-foot high stage.

After the two opening acts finished their brief sets, their stage gear was taken away, revealing The Who's equipment. I thought how cool Keith Moon's double bass drum kit looked. But it was Pete Townshend's scorched and battered stack of Marshalls that startled me a bit. As in 'I think this is going to be intense.' Otherwise, the staging was unadorned save for a few flood lights and a follow spot. Very basic. There were no monitors. The only microphones on stage were for vocals. That is, no microphones for the stacks of speakers, no microphones for the drums. So what you got in the end was in-your-face, grab you by the throat, kick you in the groin, straight-from-the-source, raw and un-filtered Who. All within spitting distance. This is about as close as you would ever get to seeing The Who play in your garage.

Without fanfare, after a polite introduction, the band took to the stage. The latest sensation from the British Invasion was here. Roger Daltrey, looking dandy in velvet trousers and a suede shirt, said 'thank you. Just getting the balance sorted out. We're not used to playing in places with quite such low ceilings. We'll play for ya, anyway.' On behalf of the audience, Townshend's tendency to 'turn up the amplifiers so they can't hear themselves think' was obvious at the very first chord he strummed. 'This one's called 'Can't Explain.' For the next 66 minutes, the band was in full throttle, focused and ferocious, well orchestrated, youthfully defiant and exuberant. Punks. Taking no prisoners. Apologizing to no one for nothing. The set list was a collection of rarely played tunes, then current crowd pleasers and new songs. The set included 'I Can't

Explain', 'Fortune Teller', 'Tattoo', 'Heaven 'N Hell', 'Young Man
Blues', 'Daddy Rolling Stone', 'Summertime Blues', an 18 minute long
'Magic Bus', 'Boris the Spider', 'A Quick One (While He's Away)' and
'My Generation'.

There was also relaxed and humorous band member banter in
between songs, whether it was to introduce the next one, or Pete's
explanation of his mini-opera. Visually, the band was thrilling. Having
only seen them perform a song or two on television, suddenly there they
were in full feature-length mode. By then their meaty, beaty, big and
bouncy stage personas were becoming legendary. I was gob-smacked
by their presence from the get-go. It was all a heavy dose of sensory
overload, sending quivers down my backbone. I wanted them to play all
night.

If you listen to a bootleg of the show, in a quieter moment during
'A Quick One' you can hear a girl in the crowd say 'uh-oh.' I'm
guessing that was her response when she saw the cops come into the
club. Through the side door on the left came a battalion of the local's
finest, lining up in front of the stage. The police presence was puzzling,
distracting and a bit unnerving, given the climate of the time. In 1968,
the world was in turmoil. Townshend announced 'we've been asked to
finish now, so we'll play our last song, called 'My Generation'.

In an instant, the audience rose to their feet and rushed the stage.
Simultaneously, the cops leapt up and locked arms. I became pinned
against the stage but managed to wedge my head between two of
the uniformed guards to get an unobstructed view of band and of
the wreckage about to take place. 'My Generation' was played with
a vengeance. And in the end, amid the smoke bombs, strobe lights,
feedback and mass hysteria, there was Daltrey helping to kick over the
drum kit as Moon firmly planted his boot through the bass drum heads.
Entwistle, meanwhile, continued playing off to the side. As for the coup-
de-grace, the cheap plywood stage floor was no match for Townshend's
guitar as he tried to desecrate his instrument. So, like a slugger in the
batter's box taking a few measured half-swings, he took aim at an
overhead pipe with the body of his Les Paul knock-off. Chunks of wood
went flying, Pete did a pull up on the pipe and rammed his foot into the

crumpled ceiling. Before we knew it, The Who were gone, thank you
and good night.

As the stunned crowd, including myself, started to slowly file out of
the club, I nonchalantly reached over onto the stage. I got my hand on
a splintered chunk of broken guitar just sitting there. But the roadie guy
came up to me and said politely, 'oh no ya don't'. Shucks, that would have
been a treasured belated birthday present to myself. If turning 13 years
old involves a rite of passage of some sort, then seeing The Who at the
Jaguar was one hell of an initiation.

YORK UNIVERSITY

11 OCTOBER 1968, YORK

I WAS THERE: BILL HARDING

By the time I heard about it the tickets had all sold out. Luckily for me
the girl next door had a cold and couldn't go. Two or three hundred of
us piled into Derwent dining room. I met up with a couple of friends
and we supped a few Newcastle Brows. Big mistake! 'Magic Bus' had
just been released and I distinctly remember Moonie's magnificent
drumming in the wonderful live version. Townshend kept looking at
him nervously, as if he expected him to fall off his drum stool. My
bladder held on as long as it could and finally gave out.

I rushed to the loo and could hear the yells as the concert ended.
Bugger. I ran back down the corridor just as the band was leaving
the stage. Daltrey was first, followed by Moonie. I stopped dead and
realised I was standing next to the dressing room door. I was a few
feet from Daltrey and was about to speak when he said: 'what the
fuck do you want?' He thumped my chest and turned to his left into
the dressing room. I said something like 'what did I do?' Moonie gave
me a huge grin and spread out his hands as if to say 'it's nothing to
do with me, mate!' He disappeared into the dressing room, followed
by Pete and John. It was more of a thump than a punch, but I always
tell Who fans about it. I'd love to buy Daltrey a pint and find out if he
remembers the incident. I don't blame him as he obviously thought a

bloke running towards him presented a threat. My diary entry for that day reads: 'Good day, except for the weather. Spent most of afternoon in refectory. In evening, Stella's ticket for THE WHO! FANTASTIC! Tried to catch a Moonie stick during 'Magic Bus'. To bog after floods of Newcie Brown. Missed last song. Face to face with band as they came off. Roger thumped me in the chest! What!? Moonie gave a cheeky smile and big shrug. Should have said something! Bugger! Bed at 1.'

I WAS THERE: JOHN HARRIS, AGE 18

This was in my first week as a first-year student at the university. The university had only been founded five years earlier and was still very small. Langwith College dining room was also very small for such a major band. My diary entry for 11 October 1968 reads:

'An absolutely outstanding evening. The set list included 'Shaking All Over' with three-part harmony on the chorus lin e, and the whole of 'A Quick One While He's Away', as well as most of their hits. During 'My Generation' Daltrey slipped and the music temporarily halted before Townshend led them back into an amazing climax: he raced athletically up and down, forwards and backwards; shook the lighting staging behind Moon; threw his guitar spinning into the air, then caught it neatly and continued playing; and finished by throwing his guitar against the wall behind him, kicking his amplifier over it, and jumping on top before walking off. Moon kicked his drums over; Daltrey smashed his mike against the cymbals. Entwistle, after an hour of truly excellent bass playing, left the stage calmly. A great fifteen shillings (75p) worth – the most incredible group performance I have ever seen.'

I WAS THERE: CHRIS MASON

I was an undergraduate, studying history at the University of York and went to both of The Who's concerts at the university. At the 1970 concert – and I should have had more sense by then – I managed to position myself rather too close to the speakers and was suffering from partial deafness for the next two or three days.

They were already a big name. It now seems truly remarkable that, with an act which more befits a stadium, they should be doing gigs in a hastily converted college dining room. What was then Langwith College Dining Room was the venue for numerous concerts involving big names. In October 1967, for example, I attended a Freshers Week concert

Chris Mason (centre)

performed by Peter Green and Fleetwood Mac, who were last minute stand-ins for John Mayall and the Bluesbreakers. Although I enjoyed the music of The Who, I was not a particular fan. In the cosy confines of Langwith Dining Room, their seemingly anarchic guitar smashing finale seemed pretty over the top and I did wonder about illegal substances.

However, when I saw the band for a second time in 1970, the same routine was reproduced and was clearly tightly choreographed. It was a bit of a USP! That aside, such standards as 'Substitute', 'My Generation' and 'Pinball Wizard' were delivered with great power. They were just very good. And Pete Townshend's nose looked just as impressive as it did on television.

After my student days, I moved to Brighton but eventually returned to York to follow a marketing and public relations career. Quite recently, I was walking with my wife past the former Langwith College Dining Room and regaled her with the story of The Who performing there.

I WAS THERE: TONY SHAWE

I was often in York for half-term holidays from boarding school in Richmond, Yorkshire. One half term, my father showed up, which was rare. He was always travelling. One evening he suggested we go to the cinema and handed me the York Evening Press to check what was on. On or near the cinema page I spotted a tiny classified advert – in summary 'for one night only, The Who, York University.' I was already a huge fan and could hardly believe it, so I went with my father, who was full of scepticism and dressed in his military blazer and regimental tie.

The concert took place in a very large lecture hall with the seating on a steep slope. My father and I took seats at the back. Roger swirled his mic high into the air and caught it on the way down. He was going through his goldilocks phase with a suede, heavily fringed jacket and bell-bottoms while Pete was in a white boiler suit with DMs, playing the red Gibson SG. Keith and John were in their usual roles, left and centre back. The music was a blend of familiar *Tommy*, a few singles. I never saw them live again, although I did bump into Pete at record label party at the Venue in Victoria in London many years later. I often wondered why they showed up in York almost incognito when they were such a big band. A friend says it was a rehearsal for the *Live at Leeds* tour.

I WAS THERE: PETE WRIGHT

I had a car by the time I attended this gig, and I parked outside. A bloke came on stage and said 'would the owner of car registration number so-and-so,' which was mine, 'please move it.' I thought sod it, I ain't going out there now. Afterwards, I went to get in my car and there was a policeman standing there and I got done for all sorts of things – wrong side of the road at night, no lights. I got fined £7, which was more than a week's wages.

The Who embarked a nine-date UK theatre tour with a changing bill that included Free, Yes, Joe Cocker, headlined by the Small Faces. The week started with Keith appearing at Clerkenwell Magistrates Court charged with being drunk and disorderly. The magistrate told Keith 'now we don't want you playing in the traffic anymore, Mr Moon.' Keith's riposte? 'Absolutely. They already have a drummer.'

ADELPHI CINEMA

9 NOVEMBER 1968, SLOUGH

I WAS THERE: DENISE HARPER, AGE 16

I had my first pop concert experience at 15 watching The Monkees at Wembley in July 1967, then went to a few concerts at the Slough Adelphi. I lived in a small village, so attendance at these shows depended on whether I could still catch a bus home afterwards, as my parents didn't drive!

I saw The Who at the Slough Adelphi in 1968. I know we were all waiting to see if Pete Townshend smashed a guitar on stage, as per his reputation at the time. I went to the Adelphi a few times in the late Sixties, seeing The Tremeloes, Spencer Davis Group and some others. I can't remember them all now, sadly! But I do remember thinking what good value it was seeing several groups all in the one night, as my only previous experience had been seeing The Monkees at Wembley in 1967.

COLSTON HALL

10 NOVEMBER 1968, BRISTOL

I WAS THERE: WAYNE PURSEY, AGE 12

I'd heard that they were going to be on at the Colston Hall and told my friends, who told me that I'd missed it. I told them 'let's go to the Colston Hall anyway. There may be posters or something.' When we got to the hall, chalked on an a frame blackboard was 'The Who, The Crazy World Of Arthur Brown'. They were playing two houses that day. It was ten shillings (50p) a ticket.

I now had a big dilemma. That was a lot of money to me and I was sure my parents wouldn't be able to afford it. To my surprise, my mum gave me the money straight away. When we got into the hall, there was what seemed to be a chrome drum kit that went right across the stage. In front of it was a normal size drum kit. I later found out it was played by Carl Palmer (later of ELP fame) when he was with The Crazy World of Arthur Brown. I really can't remember seeing the other members of the band because when Keith Moon started playing I had never seen anything like it. I've studied many drummers over the years but none have been quite like that. At the end he kicked the whole kit over. When I got home I made a pair of drum sticks out of some wood from my mum's clothes horse and I have been messing about with drums ever since.

CITY HALL

18 NOVEMBER 1968, NEWCASTLE

I WAS THERE: JILL MORRISON

My friend Lesley and I went to Newcastle City Hall to see a group we both loved – The Who. The main event were the Small Faces. We were sat on the balcony which seemed miles from the stage and from what I remember we were the only people screaming for The Who. Keith Moon was trying his hardest to throw his drumsticks at us but just couldn't quite reach – if only. At the end of their set all the equipment was demolished, which was a shock – but great entertainment!

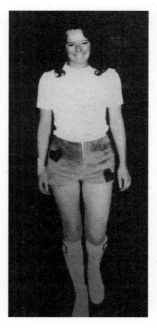

I WAS THERE: RUSSELL WILKES

I saw the group several times in the late Sixties and early Seventies. In 1968, I saw them as part of a very big tour at Newcastle City Hall with the Small Faces, Joe Cocker, Arthur Brown, The Mindbenders (no Wayne Fontana, but including Eric Stewart and Graham Gouldman, later to form 10cc) and an unknown band called Yes. Everyone only played two songs. There were two shows that night. It was probably the last big tour ever undertaken and the place was packed. It was a great atmosphere. I can't remember what they played but I do remember it was a great night and there were other good turns on. Apart from it being stunning visually, the City Hall is a good venue.

PAISLEY ICE RINK

19 NOVEMBER 1968, GLASGOW

I WAS THERE: JAMES BADDOCK, AGE 18

The Who were the headline act in what was probably one of the last package tours, where you had several bands on the same bill, in the UK. They were supported by Free, The Mindbenders, Joe Cocker and the Grease Band, The Crazy World of Arthur Brown and the Small Faces. Each band was limited to about 25-30 minutes on stage, although The Who probably had nearer 45. It still meant about three hours' worth of music, though, which wasn't bad at 12/6 (62p) for a ticket. I travelled up from Ayrshire with about half a dozen mates, one of whom had brought along his younger sister, who was a rabid Small Faces fan and who had threatened to tell their parents what he had been doing with his girlfriend unless he took her along.

The actual ice rink had been mostly covered over in front of the stage, but the venue was still pretty cold, especially at rink level. We were up in the gallery to the left, looking down on the stage from about thirty yards away. Thinking back on it, the line up was pretty impressive, although none of us had heard of Free at the time – they had yet to release their first album. The stage was set up with every band's equipment on it, one in front of the other, so that at the end of each set their amps and speakers were removed, enabling the next band to go straight on. This meant that Paul Rodgers was balancing right on the front of the stage with only three or four feet between him and Simon Kirke's drums, and less than that in front of him, which added to the difficulty of having to try and grab the attention of an audience who weren't there to listen to Free at all.

The Mindbenders minus Wayne Fontana were in the process of evolving into Hotlegs and 10cc and were much more rock oriented than expected, finishing with a long version of 'Da Doo

James Baddock saw The Who at Paisley Ice Rink

Ron Ron' that featured twin lead guitars. Joe Cocker performed 'With A Little Help From My Friends' while Arthur Brown had his flaming head dress on for 'Fire'. There was a short break before the Small Faces came on and that's when the screaming kicked in, especially from my mate's sister, who deafened us all. I especially remember a rocking version of 'Tin Soldier'.

And then – finally – it was The Who. They did not disappoint. Even then they were an amazing live band. They'd been touring for most of 1968, gradually writing the songs that would form *Tommy*, but I don't remember any of them being featured at Paisley. Songs that I do remember were 'Substitute', 'I Can't Explain', 'My Generation' and an extended version of 'Magic Bus' to finish with, where they were joined onstage by the Small Faces who, to be honest, mostly just hit various percussion instruments. Pete Townshend was in classic arm windmilling mode. Roger Daltrey had honed his microphone whirling act to perfection, swinging it around his head on its lead and sending it curling out over the audience before pulling it back just in time to sing the next line. John Entwistle just stood over on the left hand side of the stage playing rock solid bass while Keith Moon's arms seemed to be flailing everywhere without ever missing a beat – and yes, he did destroy the drum kit at the end.

Talking of Keith Moon, apparently the police were waiting to interview him after the gig. The Who had been performing in Newcastle the night before and Moon had taken it into his head to steal a mannequin, as you do, and stuff it into the boot of his Rolls Royce to drive over to Paisley. But he'd left one of the legs dangling out of the boot and the police had received phone calls about a dead body in a car boot. I don't know if this story is apocryphal or not – we certainly knew nothing about it at the time – but it does seem typical of Keith Moon.

BRISTOL UNIVERSITY

7 DECEMBER 1968, BRISTOL

I WAS THERE: JOHN FLETCHER

I saw them at Bristol University Union where they put in a very presentable but not amazing performance, and I speak as an admirer of their LPs of those days. I had already seen groups like the Stones, John Mayall, Cream, Yardbirds, Hollies, Animals and Them. Of course, they finished with the usual destruction of guitars!

BUBBEL'S CLUB

14 DECEMBER 1968, BRENTWOOD

I WAS THERE: JOHN HALES

I was a drummer back in the Sixties. We used to be on a college circuit, playing progressive rock. At the same venue we supported The Herd, The Nice, The Easy Beats, and the Small Faces with Peter Frampton as special guest just before they broke up and formed Humble Pie. A band called The Gun who went on to form the Baker Gurvitz Army with Ginger Baker. And then obviously we had The Who. It was about the time of 'Magic Bus', because they did that in their set.

Bubbel's was an old converted cinema next door to the railway station in King's Road Brentwood, Essex and this guy had converted it into a nightclub. I do know he got The Who ridiculously cheap that night on an old contract and so he got them for next to nothing. It was a good gig. I stood in the wings about ten or fifteen feet away

Drummer John Hales watched Keith Moon from the side of the stage

just watching Keith Moon from the side. When our road crew set up all our stuff, a couple of them knew The Who's road crew and they came back and said 'you want to keep your eye out because I know a couple of them blokes and I know they make their money up by nicking other people's equipment, like mics and stuff like that'. And sure enough the lead singer had bought a couple of new Shure mics and we did have one go missing.

Roger Daltrey's mic used to look like a massive great ice cream cornet that he would swing round his head and chuck it out into the crowd. Well, when the band finished he put it down on the stage and someone we knew cut the lead and had it away. Later on in the evening when everyone was getting packed up, we went to get our stuff back and let him have that mic back.

WEM TOWN HALL

DATE UNKNOWN, 1968, WEM

I WAS THERE: RON PUGH

I was in Wem Town Hall when The Who came to town. They arrived quite late with instruments already on stage. Their turn lasted about 30 minutes. At the end they trashed the instruments. We were told that they had also performed at Whitchurch, ten miles north of Wem, earlier that evening. I had the same local as Keith Moon for a couple of years when he lived down in Chertsey in Surrey in 1972 and 1973. I played for the pub football team. The pub was called the Golden Grove and we were called the Golden Grovetrotters. I remember him asking once 'how did you get on on Sunday?' He lived just behind the pub about a hundred yards away and would drive to the pub in his V8 hot rod. It had chrome trumpets on the cylinders and no bonnet. It was barely street legal. When he was showing it off, people would make remarks such as 'does it float?' and 'mind the pool.' He just laughed it off.

I WAS THERE: TERRY CONNOLLY

I remember my mates and I were riveted to the spot as they blasted out all their hits of the day. For their finale the smoke and fireworks started in earnest, culminating with Townshend smashing his guitar and Keith Moon hurling his drums into the audience. This was a first for me and my mates and we gleefully threw them back at Moon, much to the hilarity of the rest of the band.

I WAS THERE: DES CLORLEY, AGE 22

I remember them coming to Wem in what I think was 1968. I was home on leave from the RAF. The day of the event, which was a Saturday, myself and a couple of pals were in a café in the town playing on a pintable. We had just had our lunch when six guys walked in. It was The

Who! They ordered food and sat in an adjoining room. We didn't have tickets for the event as I only arrived home from leave earlier in the day. The guys had their food and then, as they were paying Mrs Obertelli, a lovely lady who was known as Ma, was asked by Roger Daltrey which was the nearest garage to the town as they were returning to London after the event. By this time it was 2.30pm. She didn't know as she didn't drive. I said 'Mr Daltrey, there are no garages open in the town as they all closed at 1pm on a Saturday afternoon.' There were only three garages in town that served petrol in the town at that time.

I knew of a garage I used regularly when at home which was only four miles from Wem on the main A49 London to Liverpool trunk road, so I gave them instructions on how to reach it as it was six miles nearer than Whitchurch or Shrewsbury. As they left, they said 'thank you' and went to their vehicles. A few minutes later, Keith Moon came back and said 'we have forgotten the route and would one of you go in the first vehicle and show us the way?' Myself and Jack said we would both go, one in the first vehicle and one in the second.

When we got to the Town Hall rear, where they were playing that night, parked there were two Rolls Royce cars and a beaten up large white Ford van. I agreed to sit in the first Rolls Royce, (the first time I had ever sat in a Roller in my life), and Jack sat in the second. The van also came along for petrol.

We got the fuel and they signed autographs for about ten minutes and then we returned to Wem. I must say I was glad to get back as Keith was driving and he wasted no time with his foot on the pedal! We go out of the cars and Roger and Keith plus the other four guys said 'thank you' and they would see us that night. But we had no tickets as they were all sold out. Roger said 'wait a minute' and he went inside the town hall and came out again with four tickets. He also said that if we went back at 6pm, security would let us watch the sound check, which we did. They bought myself and Jack a drink at the bar and gave us a mention when they appeared on stage at 8.45pm after the supporting group came off stage. They were a fantastic group of lads, as were the roadies.

It has not been possible to determine the date, or even clarify which year, The Who appeared at Wem Town Hall. One contributor believes it was 1968.

1969

The Who had begun recording the rock opera *Tommy* the previous autumn and for the first part of the year, the group alternated between recording in the studio during the week and performing live dates on the weekends. With recording completed in March, the rock opera was reportedly performed for the first time on 22 April at Bolton Institute of Technology. By the time the group travelled to North America for a tour in May and June, they featured roughly 40 minutes of *Tommy* during certain shows. Meanwhile, the instrument smashing that had characterised their performances for several years diminished considerably.

MOTHERS CLUB

19 JANUARY 1969, BIRMINGHAM

I WAS THERE: MAUREEN STOBBART

I grew up in Erdington, Birmingham where there was a club called Mothers. It was a music venue between 1968 and 1971 over a furniture shop on the High Street in a shopping area called the Village. At the time it was the best club in Britain. Over 400 acts performed there including Pink Floyd, Family and Led Zeppelin. In 1969, The Who were appearing at Mothers. I had a boyfriend, we were both still at school and we had very little spending money.

We were too young to get into Mothers but of course admission was not so strict then and there was definitely no security. We sat in the Milk Bar which was on the High Street, opposite Erdington Parish Church and adjacent to Mothers. The Who were notorious for loud music so we listened to them all evening in the Milk Bar, or at least as late as we could, as I had to be home before 10pm. In 2013 a blue plaque was placed on the former Mothers building, a permanent reminder of Erdington's contribution to rock music.

NEWCASTLE UNIVERSITY

1 FEBRUARY 1969, NEWCASTLE

I WAS THERE: RUSSELL WILKES

I wasn't a Newcastle University student but on two or three occasions I managed to get tickets for the student union. It was a very small and intimate venue and I was only a few feet from the small stage. They put on a great show and it's the only time I can definitely remember Townshend smashing a guitar up and Keith Moon kicking the drums over. Those in the very front had to get out of the way because the drums came out into the audience.

I had a pint in the bar beforehand and I can recall Roger Daltrey also being in the bar and chatting to people. Remember the outfits Roger used to wear, with all the tassels, and the long hair and him swinging the mic about? Well, he was just standing at the bar dressed in that jacket, just leaning against the bar having a chat with whoever it was.

CENTRAL LONDON POLY

8 FEBRUARY 1969, LONDON

I WAS THERE: NIGEL MOLDEN

In 1969 I was studying at the Polytechnic of Central London and had been elected Social Vice President. I booked the band to appear for a 45 minute set for a fee of £450. The event took place in the gymnasium of the main extension building in Little Titchfield Street and was completely packed. The date was less than three months before the launch of *Tommy* and their set included all of the hits, plus the classic rock and roll numbers that they always performed towards the end of the show.

I introduced the band and had the opportunity to talk to Roger Daltrey briefly in the toilet just before the performance. Not many people can say that! I have also been told that a recording on a reel to reel tape machine was made but that it has been lost to posterity. Certainly I have never heard it. The tickets for the appearance at The Polytechnic were eight shillings (40p) in advance and twelve and sixpence (63p) on the door.

LANCHESTER COLLEGE

14 FEBRUARY 1969, COVENTRY

I WAS THERE: GRAHAM AUCOTT

They were very good at the Lanchester Polytechnic in Coventry. There was a lad sitting in front of the speakers when they were the loudest band in the world. And he was shouting 'Smash! Smash! Smash!' And when the number finished Daltrey went over to him and said 'I'll fucking smash you in a minute.'

Peter Woor, (left) with hair, outside the Corn Exchange

CORN EXCHANGE

14 MARCH 1969, CAMBRIDGE

I WAS THERE: PETER WOOR

They were just bringing out *Tommy* and played some material from that ground-breaking album. I can remember Pete Townshend coming into the hall and making an acid comment about the lack of people in there. A year or so later they would be packing out stadiums all over the world. I also saw them a year earlier at the Gaiety Ballroom in Ramsey. A very low ceiling was a feature of this old dance hall and we came out afterwards deafened. I remember a very chilly ride home on my friend Ray Banyard's scooter from the Fenland town back to Cambridge.

CASINO CLUB

22 APRIL 1969, BOLTON

I WAS THERE: DAVID ALMOND

It was Bolton's student rag week. The Casino Club was on Crompton Way. It was an old cinema type building. They were on the verge of bringing *Tommy* out and they played one or two of the songs off *Tommy*. Daltrey had that jacket with all the tassels on.

I WAS THERE: TOM CASEY

I was a drummer in a band called The Answers. During my time in The Answers whilst semi-pro I was also working for the L.E. Agency at Hindley and it was me who booked The Who to play at Bolton Casino for the Bolton Students Union annual bash. Not being totally stupid, I had the presence of mind to put The Answers on with them as support group. Wow, what a night.

Townshend broke a G string part way through a number, although I can't remember which, and he actually changed it during the song whilst Moonie, Daltrey and Entwistle carried on regardless and without the audience ever noticing. This confirmed to me then that John Entwistle was the best bassist in the world – next to our own bass guitarist Dennis Shuttleworth! I also had the presence of mind to wrap up my own Ludwig set of drums following our set before Moony started his antics in destroying drum kits.

I WAS THERE: CARL RUSSELL, AGE 21

I went with a couple of mates. Pete had the white boiler suit and the flailing arms on the guitar and there was Roger with the permed locks, throwing the mic out to the crowd that were round the stage.

In fact, I think he hit somebody with it. He kept doing that. They played 'Pinball Wizard' but the showstopper for me, which they liked to do on live shows, was 'Summertime Blues'.

The Casino Club was a cinema originally. It had a balcony, but they'd taken out the downstairs seating and there was a bar at one end and a stage at the other end. It was quite near private houses. When Slade played there, they actually stopped them from playing because they had that many complaints from neighbours nearby. In the end it got turned into a supermarket.

The Who also appeared at the Cromwellian Club on Bank Street in Bolton prior to that, probably in the early to mid Sixties. I didn't see them there then, but a friend of mine did and got one of Keith's drumsticks.

STRATHCLYDE UNIVERSITY

25 APRIL 1969, GLASGOW

I WAS THERE: JOHN CHARLES MORTON

I played with them at Strathclyde University. It was the start of the *Tommy* rock opera tour. The name of my band was Happy Ever After but we were changing our name to Snow, so I'm not sure which name we were billed under. We were up there in the afternoon and we were sharing

John Morton, playing with his band Happy Ever After, is second from left

a changing room. Daltrey was there in the afternoon. We spoke to them all. Obviously Keith Moon was crazy. We had a four-gang plug adaptor we'd made out of wood. Our road manager was a joiner and his electrician mate had made it. We'd had it for six years, it was six double sockets, and they pestered us all day to buy this from us. We were a professional band. We lived in Newcastle. We were a Scottish band but we'd moved to the north east to get more gigs and we needed it for ourselves.

We were set up at the other end of the hall from them. We did our set and they asked us if they could come and play our last song with us. So I had Pete Townshend, Keith Moon and John Entwistle backing me while I sang 'People Got To Be Free' by The Rascals. At that time, I didn't think it was a big deal, but now I do.

COMMUNITY CENTRE

26 APRIL 1969, AUCHINLECK

I WAS THERE: JEAN FERGUSON, AGE 18

People came from all over and the hall was packed full. One thing I remember is that no one was dancing. Everyone was so engrossed with The Who, they just stood and listened. You could have heard a pin drop. People still talk about that night yet my family find it hard to believe that it happened, or that I was there!

The Merry Macs, The Who's support act at Auchinleck Community Centre

I WAS THERE: ROBIN LEES

I was lucky enough to play lead guitar in the Merry Macs band, which was the warm up act in April 1969. We were a large band, probably termed a show band like some of the Irish show bands of the Sixties. The venue where The Who performed also had a lot of other Sixties acts perform including The Troggs, David Bowie, The Tremeloes, The Hollies, The Move, Herman's Hermits, The Searchers, Dave Dee, Dozy, Beaky Mitch and Tich, The Love Affair, Amen Corner, Marmalade, and Cream.

The acts included some one hit wonders and some artists from America. What struck me was that most groups sounded as good as their records – there was no computer enhancement of recordings back then. My stand out memory is the amount of amplifiers and speaker cabinets that were on the small stage. They were Marshall cabinets – two high and four per instrument. They took up the full width of the stage. The sheer volume was tremendous. I used a Vox AC30 which generated 30 watts. The Who must have had hundreds of watts!

I WAS THERE: RAY LORIMER, AGE 17

I was home on leave in Cumnock as a junior boy soldier, having joined up two years earlier as a 15 year old. I remember getting a ticket locally and went along with a now deceased friend after some pre-gig under age tanking up on the McEwan's Export. The Community Centre was packed, it was a Saturday night and the teens came in from all over Ayrshire.

The Who were unbelievably brilliant and I can still remember 'I Can't Explain', 'My Generation', 'Substitute', 'Happy Jack' and 'I Can See

Ray – in his civvies – with his sister

For Miles' being blasted out. The noise was deafening and the atmosphere in the absolutely packed centre was incredible. I also vividly remember them smashing up their kit, which was just unbelievable. That night there was no room for dancing, which was the norm on Saturday nights – it was truly a gig!

There was also a big police presence as these Saturday night concerts at the Centre attracted local gangs and much fighting with knives at the time between Cumnock and Auchinleck youths. I remember getting a late bus back to Cumnock in the early hours, calling in at the back-door bakery for warm rolls and making myself scrambled egg at about two in the morning. I was still pinching myself and couldn't wait to get back to Aldershot to tell my mates I had watched The Who live in Auchinleck.

I WAS THERE: JAMES NICHOL

I was there that night to see The Who along with my girlfriend Catherine Andrews, my twin brother George and his girlfriend Grace McNiesh. It was a fantastic evening, The Who were brilliant and they did smash up their equipment after the gig. Auchinleck was a major venue and a lot of big bands played at this community centre like Hot Chocolate, Love Sculpture, the Poets, the Dave Clark Five and many other groups.

I WAS THERE: ALEX WILSON

I was a miner but also played drums for local band the Merry Macs, who opened the show. At that time the Merry Macs were the resident twelve piece band with three brass, piano, bass, two drums, two guitars and four vocals. It was a great time at the Community Centre with not only The Who but all the big name groups at the time appearing there – The Tremeloes, who were at Number One in the charts at the time, The Searchers and Dave Dee.

I knew who the group were – I'd seen them on TV – but it wasn't really my kind of music. Fans came from as far away as

Glasgow and paid ten bob to get in. The Who were excellent in terms of sheer stage presence. I can't remember the entire set but they played all their hits and it's impossible to forget the single 'Pinball Wizard'. We were waiting to see what happened at the end because they had a reputation for smashing up their stage equipment. We weren't disappointed. At the last number they knocked over their PA speakers and smashed their guitars and drums.

Keith Moon had a really unusual technique. Normally you'd hit the top of the cymbals but he'd strike the edge and sticks would fly everywhere. He went through dozens of drumsticks during the gig, while I'd make one set of mine last months.

At the end of the night I was speaking to Keith Moon and he asked if I needed any sticks or drum parts so I said yes. At that time he was being sponsored by Premier Drums who supplied him with all his gear. He gave me about 30 pairs of sticks and some accessories and a bass drum pedal. Both lasted me for years. Playing with them brought back memories of that great night. I still have the bass drum pedal to this day.

I WAS THERE: WILLIAM LOGAN, AGE 18

I went with friends. It was a wonderful night. There was supposed to be a support band but The Who played all night, playing all their hits including *Tommy*. Some people may wonder why a wee mining village like Auchinleck could attract such big name bands, but I recall that there was a lot of gangland trouble in Glasgow at the time, and as a result it was deemed off limits to touring bands.

Knowing they wanted a venue in the west of Scotland, a Mr Rafferty from Auchinleck saw an opportunity to bring them to our village community centre, where they wouldn't be exposed to any trouble.It certainly paid dividends for us young guns in East Ayrshire, as we were privileged to see many groups from the Sixties on our doorstep. I first saw The Searchers, for 3/- (15p), and many bands followed.

KINEMA BALLROOM

27 APRIL 1969, DUNFERMLINE

I WAS THERE: ALAN HILL

I saw The Who in 1969 at the Kinema in Dunfermline, and I'm pretty sure it was one of the very early occasions when they performed songs from *Tommy*. The Kinema was absolutely packed and there were a number of busloads through from Glasgow. The Kinema's bouncers did not stand for any nonsense and a few of them were ejected in the customary Kinema manner. Pete Townshend effectively ran through the *Tommy* story with a short monologue between each song. I can remember him introducing one song with an anecdote about Tommy's conception and a quip about Tommy's father being like British Rail and 'not pulling out on time'.

RONNIE SCOTT'S

1 MAY 1969, SOHO, LONDON

I WAS THERE: NIGEL MOLDEN

As a result of booking The Who at Central London Poly, I received an invitation to the launch reception and first public performance for *Tommy* at Ronnie Scott's in Frith Street. The event was notable for two very different reasons as far as I was concerned. The first was that it was my introduction to Ronnie Scott's, which I thought was an excellent venue and somewhere that I very much like to visit to this day.

The second was, as so many other attendees have recollected, that the volume of the music was extraordinary. I was seated in the middle of the club on the front row of the raised level but, in fact, only a few yards in front of Pete Townshend and his stack of speakers. It was quite a long performance and I remember the rock and roll finale. After the show, I actually went to Klooks Kleek in West Hampstead to see Deep Purple. I can clearly remember that my ears were ringing for two days!

TOMMY

THE WHO RELEASED THE ROCK OPERA ON 17 MAY 1969
(USA/ 23 MAY 1969 (UK)

I WAS THERE: HARVEY KUBERNIK

I thought the drums were under-recorded on Tommy. I was impressed by the scope of it but I'd already heard *Village Green Preservation Society* by The Kinks and I thought Ray Davies was already doing this kind of themed rock opera work.

That's not to take anything away from The Who. But I thought there was something wrong with my AM or FM radio when I heard *Tommy* the first time, at least side one of it. The drums weren't prominent. And there were horns and all kinds of things. Now I'm older I realise someone was trying to tell a story and the guitars and the drums were a tad 'unrecorded' because it was supposed to be done that way. That front cover was all over town.

Townshend wouldn't even be able to put out an album like *Tommy* in the politically correct world we live in now. He would be accused of exploitation of challenged people, where he was showing the heroic journey of Tommy. I remember it confused the media initially and he had to really keep talking until people understood he wasn't exploiting or mocking or making fun of the hero in his story. He was showing us the victory lap. We didn't give a fuck about any of this. We thought the music worked. It leapt out of our car radios and our transistor radios. And *Tommy* sounded great.

MERRIWEATHER POST PAVILION

25 MAY 1969, COLUMBIA, MARYLAND

I WAS THERE: CHRIS ALVORD, AGE 18

I was a senior at Wakefield High School in Arlington, Virginia and travelled about 40 miles to attend the concert. I had been a Who fan since first hearing 'I Can't Explain' on the radio and then their following hits 'My Generation', 'Substitute' and 'I Can See For Miles'. The Who were among my favorite listening choices along with The Kinks, Beatles, Dave Clark Five and other British invasion groups along with 1967 psychedelic groups like The Doors and Jefferson Airplane.

Chris Alvord and his friends thought the early Led Zeppelin couldn't be outdone... until they heard The Who

Merriweather Post Pavilion is an open-air venue with a covered area and massive lawn seating. My friends and I were on the lawn close to the stage and had a great view of the band. The sound was perfectly balanced and loud. My friends and I all buzzed to see the 'new' Yardbirds (Led Zeppelin) who had an incredible rousing opening set and we shared the sentiment that no one could top that performance. Boy, were we wrong. The Who followed and opened with 'I Can't Explain' and ended with 'My Generation' and then 'Magic Bus' with the destruction act.

We heard a lot of the *Tommy* album performed. 'Pinball Wizard' was a standout along with personal favourites, 'Happy Jack' and 'Boris the

Spider'. Pete was wearing a white jump suit and impressed us with his
jumping leg kicks, windmill guitar strumming and other antics. Roger
was wearing a fringe vest, which was open with just his bare chest
under it. He did his famous microphone swirling over his head. John
was rather subdued and not moving much except during his bass riffs.
Keith was behind his drum kit so we really didn't see much of him
but we sure did hear his drumming. We had been impressed with Led
Zeppelin's performance but The Who took it to another level. They
were much tighter and polished but still had the raw energy and knew
how to play to the audience.

ROYAL ALBERT HALL

5 JULY 1969, LONDON

I WAS THERE: ROBIN BELL, AGE 22

I was studying engineering at South East London Technical College
and I had been to the free Stones concert in Hyde Park that afternoon
before going to the Albert Hall with a couple of house mates. We could
only get in to the very top of the hall, right up in the standing circle, so
we could move around a bit up there but it was a very long way down!
I don't remember much from the actual concert apart from peering
through the balcony railings and seeing Roger's buckskin fringes and
Moonie' mad drumming.

I WAS THERE: GORDON HEATH

After seeing them at the Trade in Watford in the early days, I saw
The Who live on two more occasions. While I was at university
from 1965 to 1968 they appeared at the Student Union dance one
Saturday night, heading the bill. I bought my ticket and looked
forward to a good night. People danced to the warm up groups and
then The Who came on and started their set. But because their
music was not really stuff that you could dance to, the dance floor
slowly emptied and I was left standing there with only a couple of
dozen others, such was the lack of enthusiasm for the boys. They still

gave a great, professional performance but my own enjoyment was diminished.

Then in 1969 they appeared at The Royal Albert Hall sharing the bill with Chuck Berry. Chuck closed the first half and was well received by an audience that included large numbers of rockers in black leather biker gear. When The Who came on, these rockers were still chanting 'we want Chuck' and it was clear they were not going to go away. They roamed around in the aisles and threw coins at the group and abused some fans who were head-shaking in the boxes higher up in the hall. I was down in the stalls, as were the rockers. It got quite ugly and the police arrived in force and spread out around the place, which calmed things down. All the while The Who carried on performing although I thought a few times that they were going to have to run for it!

I WAS THERE: MICK NORWELL

I was sitting just to the left of the stage. Chuck Berry was the group to perform before The Who. He played a few songs and all of a sudden Hell's Angels, helmets and all, lined up along the front of the stage. Chuck came on for an encore and the crowd loved him.

The Who came on and the crowd wanted more of Chuck. Coins were being pelted at The Who. Daltrey swung his mic the way he does at the fans and they eventually were escorted away and out of the venue. The Who carried on performing a perfect set and one to remember.

I WAS THERE: GUÐBJÖRG ÖGMUNDSDÓTTIR

We had been to see the free Rolling Stones concert in Hyde Park which became a memorial concert for Brian Jones. My Danish friend and I had tickets to see the Chuck Berry and The Who double bill at the Albert Hall, tickets we had bought months in advance when the idea of the not to be missed free Stones concert wasn´t even born. We arrived at our entrance to the Royal Albert Hall at least 20 minutes late and the men at the door seemed agitated. But to our relief a lot of people were late arriving from the park so the concert had not started yet.

We found our seats upstairs with a great view of the stage. It wasn´t long until Chuck Berry started playing. We were amazed that a man in his forties was still rocking out like that. He played all his hits one after another and kept doing the duck walk across the entire length of the stage. The audience was rocking and rolling with him. After his set there was an interlude before The Who. Many people downstairs with floor seats started protesting as soon as Chuck stopped playing. It turned out there was a large number of Teddy boys who all had floor seats and wanted more old time rock and roll.

It became clear when The Who took the stage that the Teddy boys and their girls were not going to stand for 'long haired hippies' playing and they started shouting and screaming. There was pandemonium downstairs and I thanked my lucky stars I didn´t have seats there. It got worse. They threw things at The Who and began ripping up the chairs and throwing them about too. Roger Daltrey got something thrown at him and was injued on his forehead. The Who tried to calm people down by stating Chuck Berry was their hero too and they had roots in old time rock and roll. They played 'Summertime Blues' by Eddie Cochran to prove their point. It took a long time to calm things down but eventually The Who were able to continue with their set.

When The Who finally could get on with their set they performed with great intensity and professionalism. I was enthralled, listening and watching their fantastic performance of their best songs, among them the mini opera 'A Quick One While He's Away'. Then they launched into *Tommy* and played their great opera almost in its entirety.

I'd never seen such a performance as theirs. Roger Daltrey in his suede fringed pants and jacket, swinging the microphone around him like a circus entertainer. Pete Townshend's fantastic hand swings while playing his guitar fantastically and energetically, now and again jumping straight up into the air underlining his powerful playing. John Entwistle playing the bass impeccably and singing high note back ups but not moving around as much as the others.

And last but not least there was Keith Moon. I had never seen drumming like he did drumming. And he also sang! He had the biggest drum set I had ever seen and the biggest grin on his face. He played the drums intensely and like a mad man. I loved watching his different expressions as he pounded the drums. At the end of the set he kicked and threw all of his drum set all over the stage.

PIER BALLROOM

20 JULY 1969, HASTINGS

I WAS THERE: ANDRÉ PALFREY-MARTIN

The Happy Ballroom was just that. I well remember the night of 20 July 1969, when The Who had just released their album *Tommy* and came back to Hastings to play a warm up show for their appearance at Woodstock. They were fantastic and loud and I wandered home in a bit of a daze. When I arrived home about one o'clock on Monday morning I found my parents still up and watching a live television broadcast from Cape Canaveral. Two men had landed on the moon. No one had mentioned it and I could hardly believe it. Afterwards, it was strange to think that this historic event was being witnessed all round the world and we were on the pier, not giving this momentous event one thought.

WHITBURN BAY HOTEL

28 JULY 1969, SUNDERLAND

I WAS THERE: KEITH SCOTT, AGE 20

Pete Townshend to me is one of the top four or five songwriters this country has ever produced. He's a genius. There were four of us, me and my three mates from work, who went. When we first got there, about an hour before the show was to begin, we got in the door and there was a big reception area with a lot of people standing about chatting. We were standing talking and somebody said 'ah, there's Pete Townshend coming through the door.'

Pete walked in with one or two of his entourage and they were standing chatting about ten or fifteen yards away from where we were stood. I said 'I'm going to go over and shake his hand and just say hello.' So I went over and we had a quick hello. And he said 'do you live locally?' I said I did. And he said 'do you know anybody who's selling anything?'
I instantly knew what he meant, we knew a lad who was also called Peter. He was a student at Leeds University and we used to buy some stuff off him. I said 'aye, as a matter of fact I do. I know somebody who might be able to help you out if you want something.' He said 'I would appreciate that' and I said 'just give us five minutes.'

Now I knew Peter was in because I'd seen him earlier. I ran through the reception area and into the stairwell and he was halfway up the stairs with his bag, a rucksack affair, on his shoulder. I told him what had happened and I took him back down and got them together as it were. I introduced them and I just left them to it. I spoke to Peter about an hour later and I asked him how things had gone. I said 'did you make a few bob?' He said 'I've got nowt left. They took everything.' I said 'what? Everything?' He said 'aye. Just about. They emptied the bag.'

That night they did a 15 or 20 minute version of 'Magic Bus' and Pete dedicated that song to me. Not by name. But at the start he said 'the next song we're going to do is the 'Magic Bus'. And it's for our mate over there in the corner' and he pointed across to where I was standing. Obviously nobody in the audience knew what was going on, but we did.

There was one other highlight of the night, performance wise. Keith Moon had a white t-shirt on with a bull's eye on and, halfway through the gig, the t-shirt was literally saturated in sweat and sticking to him. He pulled it off over his head, held it at full arm's length above his head, wrung it out and proceeded to drink the sweat out of the t-shirt. The roar in the crowd nearly took the roof off.

Gerry Balcikonis, a true Mod with the wheels and the badges to prove it

WINTER GARDENS

2 AUGUST 1969, EASTBOURNE

I WAS THERE: GERRY BALCIKONIS

Myself and my friends Ray and Gary saw The Who at the Winter Gardens. In those days we were not earning a great deal of money. In fact, being on apprenticeship wages meant that most of the time we were skint, plus I was paying for my Lambretta on HP at the princely sum of £2. 2s (£2.10) a month! I wore the parka a lot of scooterists wore in the era, with an army issue roll cap and scarf.

The scooter was yellow and midnight blue with gleaming chrome crash bars and, because the GT had a quick turn of speed, I wouldn't load the bike with a load of mirrors as some of 'the lads' had, due to wind resistance. But, despite having no money, we were desperate to see The Who.

Ray came up with the idea of arriving backstage at the venue and asking the roadies if we could help carry in the equipment, securing places to watch the group in return. On the day we duly turned up at the venue, spoke to the roadies and, to our amazement, they agreed to our suggestion. After lugging in heavy boxes, etc. we were told to hang around backstage whilst the concert started and, when the curtains had been drawn, go to the front of the stage and jump into the crowd.

We decided instead to climb up the spotlight gantries and watch the concert from there, hidden by the glare of the lights. However, we weren't prepared for the sheer volume of the noise the speakers blasted out. So, when The Who opened up with 'I Can't Explain', I remember nearly losing my grip whilst holding the gantry. We were very relieved to climb down at the interval and jump into the crowd. The ringing in my ears lasted for days. But that hour watching, listening and clinging on for dear life was brilliant – and unforgettable!

ASSEMBLY HALL

7 AUGUST 1969, WORTHING

I WAS THERE: JON SAVAGE

I saw them in a small church hall in Worthing the day before the Plumpton Festival. They were so loud they took the top of my head off for three days.

Steve Davy's band, Steamhammer, who reputedly upstaged Family

NINTH NATIONAL JAZZ AND BLUES FESTIVAL

9 AUGUST 1969, PLUMPTON

I WAS THERE: STEVE DAVY

I remember it as an outstanding and breathtaking performance. They played a lot, if not all, of *Tommy*. Daltrey was wearing a light coloured leather jacket with long tassels and swinging the microphone by its lead a lot. I sat out on the ground not too far back and had a good view of the stage. I remember the weather being very good and it was one of those performances that had an exceptional magic about it. At the time I played bass with a group called Steamhammer, who played a set on the Sunday. The band were more successful at the 1970 Plumpton Festival when, according to press reports, we upstaged Family.

I WAS THERE: IAN EVEREST

I was at the Plumpton gig in 1969. My first ever music festival and what a performance by The Who! As I recall, they did all or most of *Tommy* and Roger Daltrey sang 'from Soho down to Plumpton….' during 'Pinball Wizard'!

I WAS THERE: ANDREW WELLS

At the time my parents had a house in a small village about three miles further west and, if I was in the garden, I could hear the festival. It was that loud. My friend and I went to see The Who. They were the star act. You know that line he has in 'Pinball Wizard' about 'from Soho down to Brighton, he must have played them all'? Well, he changed Brighton to Plumpton!

I WAS THERE: SANDRA HARDY

I was 17 or 18 years old and went to this three-day festival with my first proper boyfriend. It was miles away for us at the other end of the country. Also appearing were Pink Floyd, Roy Harper, Family, Soft Machine and others. The Who sang through the whole *Tommy* stuff and I remember Roger Daltrey in his fringed jacket swinging the microphone round.

I WAS THERE: KEVIN MARCH

I remember it being a warm evening and standing at the back on an incline looking down on the stage. Roger was strutting his stuff in his tassels. I also had the honour of seeing Chicken Shack on the same evening. Tickets for the whole weekend were two pounds and ten shillings (£2.50)!

I WAS THERE: GUÐBJÖRG ÖGMUNDSDÓTTIR

Me and my French boyfriend decided to go to the Saturday concert. I still have the pink pamphlet so I can tell you the afternoon session cost 10 shillings (50p) and the evening session cost £1! We chose to go on the Saturday because The Who were headlining in the evening. My boyfriend had a little yellow sports car so we drove down there and of course managed to get lost on the way. We stopped for directions and finally found the festival grounds. A lot of people were camping out there and there were also lots of tents with all kinds of groovy merchandise and even one with a fortune teller. It was a hot, sunny day and people were sitting on the grass enjoying the music and we soon joined them.

During the set of one of the bands, I think it was Jigsaw, there was a mystery drummer who joined the band unexpectantly and incognito. He had a large brown paper bag over his head. Everyone soon realized due to his antics and playing that this was none other than Keith Moon! He did some fantastic drum playing but mostly fooled around, running in and out of the stage.

At one point he came on stage with a bucket full of water and threatened to empty it over the heads of the band members. After he'd finished playing, he pushed and kicked the drum set all over the stage and emptied the water bucket over himself. He still had the paper bag on his head at this stage. Then he was led to the front of the stage by one of the band members and introduced with great bravado as 'Peter Townshend!' Then he finally took the brown paper bag off his head. It was the highlight of the day. Talking to some people around us who had been camping there since Thursday, we were told that Keith Moon had come along with his own tent and had been drinking and enjoying himself with the other campers for a couple of days.

The evening line up for the festival featured twelve acts. As a result, nobody apart from The Who played a long set, but I especially remember King Crimson and Yes. There was a seated enclosure right in front of the stage and my boyfriend knew the people at security. They let us into the enclosure and we managed to get front row seats. The Who astounded me with their professionalism and pure quality of performance. In my memory they played only music from *Tommy* that night, but I was over the moon to witness that and haven't forgotten it to this day. As when I saw them at the Royal Albert Hall in July, Roger Daltrey was again wearing his now legendary fringed suede pants and jacket, singing his heart out and doing amazing tricks with the microphone line. Pete Townshend was at his best playing the guitar like a madman, swinging his arm and jumping into the air. John Entwistle played great bass lines and Keith Moon was no worse for wear after his afternoon adventure and played incredibly. They just launched into *Tommy* and played without any interruption at all. It was an unforgettable event to witness. At the end they smashed up their gear, hurling their drums and amplifiers all over the stage! After the festival and late in the night, we drove on to Brighton and got a room for the night – exhausted but very, very happy.

I WAS THERE: ALAN POWELL

A minibus went from our youth club in Ellesmere Port, Cheshire. The bill was fantastic and comprised The Who, Chicken Shack, Yes, The Bonzo Dog Doo Dah Band with Viv Stanshall and Neil Innes, Family, The Strawbs, Roy Harper and many supporting acts. We had a great day and The Who were astounding and in top form.

In December 1998, we went to see Stan Webb's Chicken Shack in a small club in Chester. After the gig, we were lucky enough to have a drink with Stan who was great company. He told us that he, Viv Stanshall and Keith Moon went out on the town in Brighton that night. All three of them were famous party animals and he said that they got into all sorts of trouble, each egging the other on in to more and more outlandish behaviour. Sadly, both Keith and Viv are no longer with us. Maybe Stan will write his memoirs one day and let us know what went on!

In August 1969, The Who played Woodstock. During the set, Abbie Hoffman took the stage and protested the imprisonment of MC5 manager and White Panther leader John Sinclair on charges of marijuana possession. Hoffman was met with a few unfriendly words from Townshend and a guitar clout to the head. A clip of this can be heard on the Who compilation *Thirty Years of Maximum R&B*.

WOODSTOCK

17 AUGUST 1969, BETHEL, NEW YORK

I WAS THERE: STEVE DOCKENDORF, AGE 17

My first exposure to The Who was when 'I Can't Explain' rattled my little GE clock radio. They seemed to have the energy of The Kinks, but with smoother vocals. Shortly after I acquired the *Tommy* album, I discovered that my local library had high-end phonographs and headphones, presumably for listening to the classical music in the library's collection. So I got the bright idea of taking this new double Who album off my stereo that only played the left channel, and listen to the whole thing straight through at the

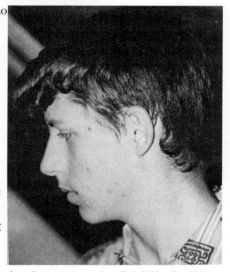

Steve Dockendorf remembers 'Pinball Wizard' and 'We're Not Gonna Take It' being Who highlights at Woodstock

library. It was as close to heaven as I'd ever been, although I do remember being afraid that people walking by would hear what was coming out of the headphones and send me home. In May of 1969 I saw them at Merriweather Post Pavilion in my home state of Maryland. I was positioned about 25 rows back and directly in front of the stage right PA speaker stack. It was the loudest sound I'd ever heard. I recall being thrilled to hear a number of songs from *Tommy* in concert.

In August of 1969 I took the five-hour car trip to Woodstock with my then girlfriend and I was again thrilled to hear *Tommy* played live. The spell was momentarily interrupted when Abby Hoffman took Pete Townshend's microphone to plead the case for imprisoned revolutionary John Sinclair 'rotting in prison.' Pete Townshend manually forced him off the stage. And just as abruptly, the show went back on as though nothing had happened. My favorites, 'Pinball Wizard' and 'We're Not Gonna Take It' helped to make The Who's performance one of the most exciting of all the acts at Woodstock as well as one of my fondest musical memories.

ISLE OF WIGHT FESTIVAL

30 AUGUST 1969, ISLE OF WIGHT

I WAS THERE: GERALD CLEAVER

Between 1969 and 1970 I saw them about six times. The first time I saw them was the 1969 Isle of Wight Festival which was the one where, according to the story I'd heard, they'd asked for more money, and the promoters wouldn't give them any and so they said 'ok then, so we want to play in the afternoon so that we can go back to the mainland and play another gig in the evening.' And so they flew in by helicopter on the Saturday afternoon and played what for them was a short set.

They were only on for about an hour. They flew in by helicopter and flew out by helicopter. They'd just played Woodstock and they spent their whole set talking about Woodstock and the fact that Joe Cocker was on the bill later and how he was fantastic and so we should all stick around and watch him.

I WAS THERE: MIKE TUCKER

Memories are a bit dim but there were an overwhelming number of people and few facilities. I'd never experienced anything like that before, with a far distant and not very big stage. There were no screens in those days and nor was there a PA system that could reach everyone. Daytime performances were difficult to see unless you were in the front third of the crowd, which was pretty much impossible. Night-time was better. The memories I have are images of Pete in his trade mark white boiler suit and an amazing amount of frills on Roger's clothes.

COSMOPOLITAN CLUB

7 SEPTEMBER 1969, CARLISLE

I WAS THERE: JOHN BELL

All the men had to form a security cordon around the stage to stop the chicks from rushing the stage. The real fans could not get in because of the strict suit and tie policy that was in force at the Cosmo at the time. Roger Daltrey came out closely followed by Pete Townshend. Roger had a quick chat with us and wished us a pleasant evening! Keith and John must have been engaged with the Carlisle chicks as there was no sign of them. The sound outside was excellent!

FAIRFIELD HALL

21 SEPTEMBER 1969, CROYDON

I WAS THERE: CHRIS SMITH

After seeing them in Leeds in 1966, I saw them again in London when I was a student at Ealing Art School. I'd formed a band called Smile with a fellow student called Tim Staffel. We had a band outing to see The Who perform *Tommy* in Croydon.

The other guys in the band were Brian May and Roger Taylor and we took along our other college pal, Freddy Bulsara. There was a lot of constructive criticism of the gig on the way home in the van. Personally, I thought The Who were magical and it was amagnificent performance. As musicians, I'd say we all learned a thing or two that night.

GRANDE-RIVIERA BALLROOM

11 OCTOBER 1969, DETROIT, MICHIGAN

I WAS THERE: DENNIS DUNAWAY

As a high school teen in Phoenix Arizona, I was lying on my family's

Dennis Dunaway (centre) onstage with Alice Cooper. Right: a poster advertising the upcoming gig

living room floor and The Who came on television. Pete threw his guitar into the crowd and my parents went on and on: 'how could he treat a perfectly good instrument that way?' I thought it was the coolest thing I'd ever seen.

On 11 October 1969 the Alice Cooper group, which I was a member of, opened for The Who. We had chickens onstage and created a feather storm with pillows and a fire extinguisher. The song was 'Black Juju' and when we were walking offstage I told Neal Smith that his drums sounded exceptionally thunderous. Then our roadie told us that Keith was backstage, playing his kit along with Neal!

The venue was an old movie theater that had a perforated screen, which you could hazily see through. So I squeezed behind the screen and sidestepped over unused stage lighting until I was directly behind Keith, who was set up at floor level with no drum riser. Nobody could see me but if the screen weren't there, I could have placed my hand on the back of Keith's head.

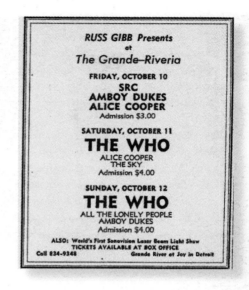

RUSS GIBB *Presents*
at
The Grande–Riveria

FRIDAY, OCTOBER 10
SRC
AMBOY DUKES
ALICE COOPER
Admission $3.00

SATURDAY, OCTOBER 11
THE WHO
ALICE COOPER
THE SKY
Admission $4.00

SUNDAY, OCTOBER 12
THE WHO
ALL THE LONELY PEOPLE
AMBOY DUKES
Admission $4.00

ALSO: World's First Sonovision Laser Beam Light Show
TICKETS AVAILABLE AT BOX OFFICE
Call 834-9348   Grande River at Joy in Detroit

With my face pressed to the dusty smelling perforated screen, I watched The Who play their entire set. They were on fire that night. Between songs I could hear them talking to each other, but it wasn't about the show. They were cursing at each other.

GEORGETOWN UNIVERSITY

2 NOVEMBER 1969, WASHINGTON DC

I WAS THERE: PATRICIA MARX, AGE 17

I was about to see The Who for the fourth time in two years, this time at McDonough Gymnasium at Georgetown University, and this would be the second time I saw them perform *Tommy* that year. It was hot, humid and raining, but inside it was standing room only and abuzz with excitement. My friend and I had excellent seats in the center, fairly close to the stage. I counted 14 amps and 24 speakers and it was loud. Keith Moon was using his silver drum kit.

When The Who came on stage after 10pm, they were obviously in a very good mood, so much so that throughout the set when Roger wasn't singing he was laughing, and Keith and Pete did a Laurel and Hardy routine. As usual The Who took command of the stage immediately and went straight into the John Entwistle number 'Heaven and Hell', which they used to start their concerts with in those days. This was the first time I saw Pete in his white boiler suit, also the first – and probably the last – time I saw Roger in his spectacular buckskin outfit with fringe, fringe and more fringe. Some of the fringe looked to be three feet long.

They played for an hour and 35 minutes and in addition to doing nearly all of *Tommy*, including 'Sally Simpson', they played their versions of 'Young Man Blues', 'Summertime Blues' and a very delicious 'Shaking All Over'. At our concert, there were quite a few people outside the gym trying to break down the doors to get in and Pete dedicated *Tommy* to them. At the end everyone was dancing and the aisles were packed. The concert did not end with 'My Generation' but a long jam session that included parts of *Tommy* and other songs.

And, most notable perhaps, Pete did not smash his guitar! The crowd wanted 'MORE!' but in those days they usually did no encores. The Who always left the audience with its appetite whetted for the next Who concert. After this one I was flying high on natural adrenalin and went to school Monday morning without having slept a wink.

BRISTOL HIPPODROME

4 DECEMBER 1969, BRISTOL

I WAS THERE: NIGEL CORTEN

The Who tour was unofficially billed as 'The Last Big Gig of the Sixties', and my wife, Pat, and I saw it in Bristol, England. We queued for about an hour outside the Colston Hall to get in. There was not much pre-booking in those days. We got in and had a balcony seat overlooking the stage. On the support bill were The Crazy World of Arthur Brown, Joe Cocker and the Grease Band, and The Mindbenders, who in a month or two turned into 10cc. When the roadies were setting up The Who's stage kit, I remember one fellow nailing down about eight tom toms in front of Keith Moon's drum kit.

Once on stage, they played for over an hour, which was pretty unusual for those days, and weren't as loud as The Kinks, whom we had seen at the same venue. There was not a lot of screaming from the crowd; I think that we were all a bit awestruck to see such a big band of the times. They did all the singles, and I remember Townshend saying 'On our next number Keith is playing lead drums', it was 'Happy Jack'.

They also played a few album tracks; Entwistle's 'Boris The Spider' was memorable. Moon was magnetic and played the drums like he did on the TV, with that high wrist style and, most stunningly, the whites of his eyes were super white. They didn't wreck their guitars at the end, but Moon jumped from his kit and ripped a few of his nailed down tom toms from the stage and tossed them around. I had the ticket for that gig for a few years in a jacket, but it disappeared with time. Shame, as entrance was 19 shillings and 6 pence or 97p. That's pretty good value by today's standards for a line-up like that.

I WAS THERE: WAYNE PURSEY

I remember Pete Townshend in white boiler suit apologising because he had a cold. During the show somebody threw an orange smoke bomb onto the stage. Then someone in one of the boxes took his trousers down and showed his bottom to everyone. Pete said 'so, did you see the pimples?' Beforehand, you could hear the bass tuning up on Queen's Square, which is a fair distance from the Hippodrome.

I WAS THERE: LEO MULLEN, AGE 14

A member of the audience did a 'mooner' over the side of a box! I saw this quite clearly from where I was sitting in the balcony. It was on the right of the stage and I still remember it now. There was uproar in the Hippodrome when security, were going to eject the culprit. Eventually the situation settled down, the culprit returned to his seat and the concert carried on. I remember the concert being very loud and absolutely brilliant. Roger Daltrey was in his jacket with the long fringes and somehow swinging the microphone at length on a cord whilst singing. I also saw The Who at Bath Pavilion and was taken with my friend by my dad in his black Morris Minor car. I can't remember the date of this concert but I do however remember not having a ticket and climbing in through the toilet window at the side of the Pavilion. That was in the days when I could fit in through a small window! Again, I remember the concert being extremely loud and fantastic. We climbed up on top of the speaker stacks!

Leo Mullen remembers an audience member baring his bottom to the stage

PALACE THEATRE

5 DECEMBER 1969, MANCHESTER

I WAS THERE: STEVE BERNING

This was the second time I had seen them. They were supported by the James Gang, with Joe Walsh. They played in effect what I now think of as their *Live at Leeds* set – *Tommy* in its' entirety, 'Summertime Blues', 'Shakin' All Over', 'Young Man Blue's and an extended version of 'Magic Bus'. As an aspiring guitarist, Townshend was my hero. But what strikes me retrospectively was that my eyes kept getting drawn back to Moon. He was arguably then at his peak and drove them on like a madman. Even when he wasn't drumming he was acting out each song. Having seen hundreds of gigs in my life, this remains number one.

I WAS THERE: TONY MICHAELIDES

Growing up as a teenager in the mid 60s I wasn't starved of great music! Seeing The Who perform what was the first and still the best rock opera, *Tommy*, was indeed a piece of history. Even though there were some amazing bands around at that time, it remains one of the finest shows I ever attended.

I saw The Who another three times over the next 18 months and they never disappointed, yet the show they put on that night performing *Tommy* was so different to anything else I'd ever seen. Just for a band at that time to attempt anything like that was unique in itself. A 'Rock Opera', what the hell was that? They had a unique way of giving the same powerful show no matter what size the venue was.

The thing I remember the most about seeing The Who was the sheer power of the band and how much they looked like they were loving every minute that they were onstage. That has such an affect on an audience – it's infectious. I remember, after seeing the show, standing in from of my bedroom mirror trying to emulate Pete Townshend's whirling arm movements and cutting the end of my fingernails. My guitar playing years from that day on were numbered! I remember how amazing their stage presence was that night. Roger Daltrey and Pete Townshend were great front men.

You couldn't take your eyes off them whilst at the same time their sound was being driven by a powerhouse of a rhythm section in Keith Moon and John Entwistle. Although they initially appealed to Mods, they also gained a huge following from people like myself who were progressive rock fans. Their songs were so catchy and they had so many classic hit singles. For the next ten years, and up until the death of Keith Moon, The Who were one of my favourite bands and certainly one of the most original. Their music has stood the test of time and I'll always be forever grateful that I was able to be there at such an incredible live show.

REGIONAL COLLEGE OF TECHNOLOGY

12 DECEMBER 1969, LIVERPOOL

I WAS THERE: PAUL BARTLETT

I went to Liverpool Regional College of Technology to study for a degree and got involved with the student union. It was based on the top floor of a 1960s built block that faced on to Byron Street, which is a very wide road linking the old and new Mersey Tunnel entrances. The refectory was also on the top floor and was where the gigs were staged. A number of us students did the setting up – clearing tables, building the bar and the stage and so on.

To set up for gigs we used very good quality desks borrowed from various senior staff offices in the building to form a stage! The refectory had a relatively low ceiling. (The following spring Paul Rodgers of Free smashed a ceiling tile when he swung his mic stand, as he still does). It hadn't been replaced when I went back in 1977 to give a talk at the Biology Society. The refectory had a fire certificate for 700 occupants. In exchange for free entrance, security was provided by a hired team whom wore proper old-fashioned uniforms and usually there was one dog available. I don't remember there ever being any trouble.

On this particular evening, the Bonzo Dog Doo-Dah Band were playing the refectory. The Who were also in Liverpool, to play at the Empire. The Bonzos arrived unusually early, and with a considerable quantity of stuff, including two drum set-ups. We quickly learned that, unexpectedly, Aynsley Dunbar was to use the extra drum set up. I remember Neil Innes hammering a wooden foot stop into the top of this very fancy desk and swearing about not expecting to play in such 'fucking awful places'.

The Bonzos then asked if they could play late as they wanted to catch the first half of The Who gig at the nearby Empire. This was fine as we had our regular support act – Stackwaddy. We knew they would play for hours if asked. They were very heavy and were a brilliant band associated with John Peel.

Anyway, the Bonzos returned as promised and did their usual set, full of playfulness with Viv Stanshall's beautiful lead. It was probably less than one hour as sets in those days were, like the recordings, quite short. And then most of The Who turned up, minus Pete Townshend. The Bonzos stayed on stage. The Bonzos second drummer was Sam Spoons (Martin Ash) and he readily gave his seat to Keith Moon as Sam preferred larking about. And then we were off – for some hours! I'll admit I don't remember much detail, apart from a drum battle between Moon and Dunbar which lasted, if I recall correctly, about 25 minutes.

I don't know when it finished but I remember it was very late, with all the band and few of us helpers having a drink in the bar until gone 2am. What we did about security I have no idea. They were paid by the hour and, apart from the bands, were the major expense of these gigs. On Saturday the LRCT was closed, but we were able to go in to clear up and return the desks to the various floors.

We also learnt from the college security that the residents of the adjoining Gerard Gardens were very angry, not appreciating the amount of noise that had come from the largely glass walled eighth floor refectory until the small hours. Years later I learnt that Stanshall and Moon were good friends, often drinking together in the Sgt. Peppers club in Staines, which co-incidentally was my parental home town, although I never went into such an expensive club, not even to deliver Schweppes – my regular holiday job. I also read that the Bonzo Dog Doo-Dah Band and The Who only ever played together once. I think that was Canada. Well, admittedly not all The Who played our college. But did they battle Aynsley Dunbar anywhere else?

COLISEUM THEATRE

14 DECEMBER 1969, LONDON

I WAS THERE: JOHNNY FOLLON

What a colossal performance it was! Daltrey's voice singing *Tommy* was mesmerising. 'Pinball Wizard' and 'See Me Feel Me' were incredible sounds. And it was probably revolutionary at that time, them appearing at an iconic theatre world renowned for mainstream opera.

Quadrophenia. Now I always thought that Ken Russell must have been in Brighton when the second Mods vs Rockers bank holiday riot took place because the film he directed was nigh on right to the point. I say that due to being a unintentional participant in the first Clacton riot of 1963. My friends and I regularly went to Clacton for bank holidays during the early Sixties and it was in 1963 when we inadvertently started a riot by charging the pier turnstiles.

We had jokingly – and with no malice intended – backed up a few yards to pretend to run and jump over the turnstiles, the council workmen having just refused us entry to the pier. This caused a ripple effect and a surge of holiday makers pushing back onto the pavement. Those around thought a fight had broken out and then all of a sudden all hell broke loose, with Mods attacking Greasers, Greasers attacking Mods, and ordinary folk caught up in the middle.

The tinderbox bad atmosphere between local Greasers, which is what we called Rockers at the time, and the invading mass of day-tripper Mods all having congregated around the pier entrance, was suddenly ignited and the battle began. It's sad that an innocent bit of fun should lead up to subsequent yearly rioting. But that's the honest truth of what happened.

I WAS THERE: MICHEAL O'GEALLABHAIN

I saw The Who at the Coliseum. It was good music, well played with a very strong rhythm. But it was very, very loud. Uncomfortably loud. And unfortunate subject matter.

CITY HALL

19 DECEMBER 1969, NEWCASTLE-UPON-TYNE

I WAS THERE: JOE CHIPCHASE

It was a packed Newcastle City Hall during the tour they did promoting *Tommy*. All of the members of the group were on top form, with the vocals being outstanding. You could tell later that evening as people were heading for home who had been at the concert – as they were conversing in shouts! This was no doubt due to the banks of speakers on the City Hall stage. What sticks in my mind is that Keith Moon stotted (ie. bounced) a cymbal edgeways

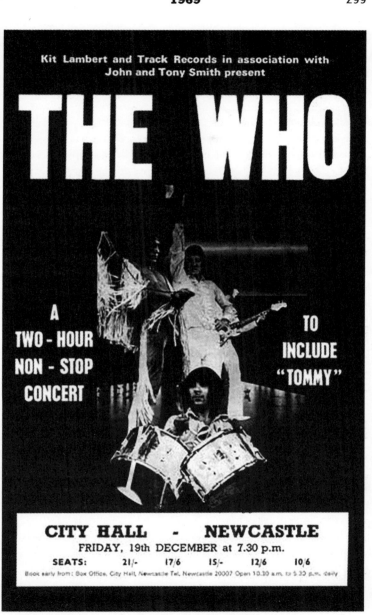

off the stage into the audience. Hopefully, nobody was hurt but it did have the potential to have caused a serious injury. Despite their reputation, no guitars were smashed up, though I think Keith Moon kicked his kit over at the end of the concert.

I WAS THERE: ROB GRIMES

I saw them at the City Hall just as *Tommy* was released. It was mid week and I had a ticket in the cheap seats which were upstairs in the balcony. They were not the best but standing up along with everyone else you got a good view. I can remember a huge wall of amplifiers and Keith Moon sat in front with the biggest drum kit you could imagine.

For my money, 'I Can't Explain' was the best record they did in the early days. They are the loudest band I have ever heard and I used to frequent the City Hall often to see groups. I remember seeing Jethro Tull, Deep Purple, Grateful Dead. But The Who? Wow. I remember nicking a huge poster advertising the concert off a nearby building. It went on my bedroom wall. Halcyon days.

1970

1970 began with the group bringing *Tommy* to various European opera houses, a trend they had begun in December 1969 when they performed at the London Coliseum. The band then focused again on recording a live album, having abandoned the idea of wading through the hours of tape they had from shows during their North American tour the previous autumn.

Both the 14 February Leeds University and 15 February Hull City Hall shows were recorded, but only the Leeds recording was deemed suitable for release, as the bass track was inadvertently not captured during the first few songs at the Hull show. The result was the legendary *Live at Leeds*, which became a hallmark live rock album.

WINCHMORE HILL

I WAS THERE: JOHN MEARS, AGE 20

Keith moved to Winchmore Hill towards the end of November 1969 and bought a house directly across the road. When I first met him, it was snowing and I heard a load of bottles being smashed outside and wondered what it was. I went to look out the window and there was this guy standing in the middle of the road wearing leopardskin underpants and nothing else. A woman at the front door of the house was throwing bottles at him. It was Kim (Keith's wife) and they'd had a row and it had got a bit out of hand. So I opened the front door and he saw me and said 'do you mind if I come in for minute?'

My old man was in at the time and he was a bit like Moon in that he loved his booze, and Keith told us how they'd had an argument and things didn't look too good and Dad said 'well, come up to the bar and we'll have a drink.' We had a bar at the top of the house. Dad gave him a dressing gown and he went up there and spent virtually all night talking to Dad. And as a result of that he got to know Dad well. After that, he had a few parties and we went over there and got to know him. And then Neil died.

On 4 January 1970, Keith's driver Neil Boland was accidentally killed when Keith, Kim and others were visiting a pub in Hatfield and their car was attacked by local youths. Neil got out of the car to remonstrate with the youths and was dragged under the vehicle. Keith was reportedly at the wheel of the car but the death was later judged to be an accident.

They went to an opening at a place in Hatfield that was down to my Dad. My Dad knew the owner and he wanted someone to open it and Dad mentioned Keith Moon and they said 'great'. And they went down there and that's when the accident happened.

Neil got dragged under the car. I'd left a note on Keith's front door saying 'party time', thinking he'd come over and celebrate the pub's opening. And when they eventually got back, I heard a big commotion outside and wondered what was going on so I thought I'd leave it. And next day it was front page news.

About two weeks later he was he was having his first party with the same old mates – Legs Larry, Jimmy McCulloch, Jack McCulloch, Thunderclap Newman and a few other people - and he came over the road and invited my old man across. And

Keith Moon and John Mears' dad, who became friends

my old man was out so I said I'd go over.

I was working for my old man at his furniture factory in Hatfield, which was a long way away. I was sick of it and I spent half the night telling Keith how bored I was with it all and he said 'well, we'll see what we can do.' And the next morning he was kicking everyone out and he said 'look, I've got to get into the office and you've got a motor. Would you mind taking me in?' I said 'no, not at all.' It was a Saturday so I didn't have to go to work and so I drove him in.

We got to the Track office and he said 'come up and meet some people.' So I went upstairs and met all the guys up there. And he said 'could you do me a cheque for about three thousand five hundred?' The guy did the cheque out, gave it to Keith and Keith gave it to me. He said 'listen, if you fancy a job, you can drive me if you go and buy me a Roller. I want a Silver Cloud Mark 3.' It just knocked me

Keith and his wife, Kim

for six. I said 'I'd love to work for you.' 'Well, go and buy a Roller and bring it round to the house. I'll get one of the guys here to take your car back home and take me home with it.'

So I went up to Owen and Son. They only had one in there for three grand - a green one. I took the car back and Keith took one look at it and said 'I don't like the colour. Do you know anyone that does spray jobs?' I said 'yeah, I know a couple of people in Southgate that have got a garage' and he said 'well, take it there and get it sprayed.' I said 'what colour?' He goes 'er, lilac.' I had a bit of a laugh and said 'no, what colour?' He said 'lilac. Get it sprayed lilac.' So that's what I did. That night I had to tell the old man that I'd finished working for him. He didn't mind, because the business was going downhill. And that all conjoined into him wanting to get something else and ending up with him buying a hotel with Moon.

A couple of weeks after I'd been working for Keith, Dad had a party. He always had parties at the weekend, with people back from the pub, and he invited Keith over. Keith was talking about hotels all that day, saying 'it's about time I had one of my own.' And he started talking to the old man 'do you fancy going in on a hotel with me?' So they started looking and visiting places together and they came up with the Crown and Cushion (in Chipping Norton).

When I was working for Keith, we went there once or twice a month because at the time he was doing a lot of gigs. He was either

Right: Keith, behind the bar at the Crown and Cushion, the pub he bought, and (above) with Ronnie Lane, Viv Stanshall and Chris Welch

in the States, or that year was the university gigs all over the country. Live at Leeds and all that sort of stuff. But when we had a spare weekend we'd take Mandy and Kim and go and spend the weekend down there.

And of course he had loads of parties. That's the reason really why the hotel ended up having to be sold. Because he never paid his bill. He'd invite all these people down, free drinks and all that, and it would take months to get the money from Track.

The normal routine if he had a day off was that he'd get up at about twelve, go into London to get some money from Track, go to the A&R Club in Wardour Street and meet all his mates up there and start drinking. I didn't drink so much because I had to drive, obviously, but I'd have a few. That would go straight through to knocking out time and then we'd all

Keith's wife, Kim Moon

go down the Speakeasy until that shut at about four o'clock and then I'd drive him home. And if he had another day off he'd go through the same thing again. It was constant party time. He hardly spent any time at home. He was always out on the razzle.

The first few weeks I worked for him he was still getting over Neil and it was playing on his mind something chronic. The depression was terrible. He'd get back from a club and then he'd disappear into the front room. I was in the kitchen making a cup of coffee one time and I went in the front room and he was lying on the floor, mouth half open and frothing, with this white stuff coming out of this mouth and a bottle of pills by the side of him. Kim had warned me that he did things like that for attention and when I got to him I opened his mouth and the pills were all in his mouth. He hadn't swallowed them. I thought then 'she's right what she's saying.'

I had to get him up, get him to drink water and walk him round. It was Mandrax in sleeping pills and they were deadly if you had too many of them. He did that twice over that month. He didn't know what to do with himself. He was a different man. The jokiness in him didn't come back for about another month. Those times were very dark for the first two months after Neil died. But when he perked up he was back to his old self.

One day, we'd gone somewhere for a few drinks - I think it was with the McCulloch brothers and Legs Larry - and he took us into a costumiers. We all got dressed up. Legs Larry and the two boys were dressed up as hoods from the 1930s with hats and plastic machine guns. He gave me a gorilla outfit, so I was driving the car in a gorilla outfit. And he did himself up from head to toe as a vicar. He had the bald head, the dog collar, the bible and everything. The gag was that he would walk down Shaftesbury Avenue and I was supposed to drive up, screech to a halt and the boys would get out, drag him to the car and drive off. Shaftesbury Avenue at that time of day was packed, with all these people looking round. So we drove off and Keith had his head out of the window, shouting 'Obscenities! Obscenities!' We got to the end of the road and there was a copper standing there, with his hand out to stop us. He obviously knew it was Moon's car, because everyone did in London in those days, and the window came down and he goes 'hello, Mr Moon, I thought it was you. We've had reports that a vicar was shouting obscenities out of a car having just been abducted.' On the third day I was working for Keith, he said 'we'll go and meet a mate of mine.' And my eyes nearly popped out of my head when we got there because it was Ringo. We got invited into the house. Ringo was in the front room, laying floor tiles.

I ended up meeting Ringo's driver and PA at the time, Martin Lickett, and we became really good friends. He knew I was going through a lot with Keith. It was having a devastating effect on me, trying to keep up with him. I wasn't getting sleep. I lost a lot of weight. It was very difficult and I was only 20 - I didn't have the skills that I've got today. So, at the end of that year, Martin said to me 'if you've had enough, why don't you come and work at Apple? I've got a spot for you driving if you want it.' So I spoke to Keith when we were at the Crown. He said 'dear boy, if that's what you want, no problem. I can always get someone else to drive me.' And that was it. It was just before the end of 1970 and I went straight into Apple and started there. I did a lot with Keith over that year. We went to Copenhagen. And then there was Live at Leeds and the Isle of Wight. So I got into all the really good gigs that they did and I think they were the best gigs that they'd ever done. Especially *Tommy* – it was fantastic.

BREMEN

27 JANUARY 1970, WEST GERMANY

I WAS THERE: STEPHEN DAVY

I briefly met Keith Moon. It was whilst my group were in Bremen, Germany recording some numbers for the TV programme *Beat Club* around 1969 or 1970. The Who were also there recording parts of *Tommy* for the same TV show. We went to a nearby night club and were sitting there upstairs, sipping some lagers. During the evening, in walked Keith Moon and John Entwistle. They sat down at the next table and recognised us from when they arrived earlier at the entrance to the studio. They both came over and sat at my group's table, bringing a bottle of wine which Keith had brought into the club hidden under his coat. He introduced himself as Keith, speaking in a very educated voice and shook each one of us by the hand. He made conversation while John sat there in complete silence. This lasted for a little while and then we went on our different ways.

LEEDS UNIVERSITY

14 FEBRUARY 1970, LEEDS

I WAS THERE: GERALD CLEAVER

I went to Leeds University. Daltrey knocked me gently out of the way when they had done their sound check at Leeds University for the Live at Leeds concert. They came marching out through the crowd who were queuing to get in. It was a good humoured exit. But they did move us out of the way.

The person I was sharing a room with at that stage at the university was a drummer in a band. He was adamant he was not going, because Keith Moon was 'a bloody rubbish drummer.' Afterwards, he wanted to know what I thought of the concert and he said 'well, I have to admit I walked around the back of the refectory and they were playing some song about Christmas' – it was the track

'Christmas' from *Tommy* – 'and I was listening to the drumming and I have to admit it was bloody good.' He apologised.

Keith Moon, backstage at Leeds

The Leeds University social secretary that booked them for the 1970 Valentine's Day concert got into trouble with the students union. The termly gigs had an overall price ceiling of £5.00, ie. around ten shilling (50p) average price. The Who cost around ten shillings and sixpence (52.5p), which was above that. I recall some really cheap gigs after that – Mott The Hoople and Elton John were both 3/6d (around 17p) to bring the average cost of tickets for the term down.

I WAS THERE: DENNIS APPLEYARD

In the mid Sixties the university's student union had Saturday night gigs all through term time in the Refectory and the smaller Riley Smith Hall. I saw up and coming bands like Elton John, Joe Cocker and a very early gig by the Faces. The main hall featured bands like Free, The Move and Fairport Convention. The bookers were really astute and we heard lots of cool music. This was in the days when music had an underground quality and before the big names like Leonard Cohen or 10cc played there. The admissions policy varied every year. Some years it was open and on others it was students only or guests signed in by a student. As a junior clerk in an insurance firm, this could be problematic and I admit I resorted to forgery and blagging on occasions.

When The Who were booked, we acquired our tickets and waited for the band to appear. In those days long waits were normal. I went for a pee and heard a commotion from one of the stalls. And then Keith Moon tumbled out. I do not know if he was pissed, on something or just clowning around but he thought it was hilarious. As the night wore on, we heard that it had been cancelled and was going to be rearranged and so we shuffled off. That was the night Pete says he ran out of petrol! Would you believe the garage attendant wouldn't take his guitar as payment? A while later, we queued on a Sunday morning for tickets for the gig which was recorded as *Live at Leeds* but they sold out before we got to the front of the queue.

CITY HALL

15 FEBRUARY 1970, HULL

I WAS THERE: SHEILA STARK

My husband and I saw The Who at Hull City Hall: the two hour non-stop pop opera featuring *Tommy*. I still have my original ticket. We remember how original the music and band were at the time. The hall was packed, standing and balcony. We were front row balcony, above the stage and with a good view. We have great memories of the night – our ears were buzzing for about two days afterwards.

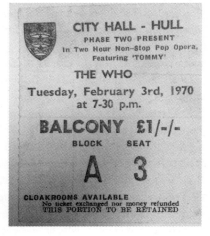

I WAS THERE: TONY WARD

I remember the recording vans outside recording the concert, which I believe was mixed as The Who *Live at Leeds* album as the recording at Leeds wasn't too good. I sat on the balcony and thoroughly enjoyed it as that was the real Who with Keith Moon and all.

CIVIC HALL

27 APRIL 1970, DUNSTABLE

I WAS THERE: PETE WRIGHT

I took this girl with me and we parked my car and we were walking across this car park. There was a massive juggernaut there and Roger Daltrey was walking back from it. All I had to do was walk over there and shake his hand and I just didn't feel I could, and this girl with me, she would have given anything to give him a hug or something. I just regret it so much, not meeting them when I had the chance.

It was all sitting on the floor that night. They came on and it was Roger Daltrey in his tassels and Pete Townshend in his white boiler suit and all the Hi-watt amps. Pete leapt in the air and his guitar was as dead as a dodo. But the rest of the band sounded very good, and Daltrey started singing 'Can't Explain' and Townshend realised his guitar was dud and he slung it on the floor and kicked all three of these Hi-watt stacks over. Someone came running on stage to try and calm him down and he took a swing at them.

They managed to grab his arm and then three or four people came on and they just manhandled him off the stage. The rest of the band walked off. They got all the gear set up again and Roger, Keith and John came back on stage and Pete came on a bit later. They had a bit of a sound desk on stage and he went over there to the sound desk and threw a few fucks into him, and then came back and picked his guitar up and carried on. That was the very, very best I ever saw the band. They played a blinder.

UNIVERSITY CENTRAL HALL

16 MAY 1970, YORK

I WAS THERE: STEVE ROGERS

I was in a band and doing theatre work
at the time and I heard The Who were
on at Central Hall at York Uni. I had
a night off so had to go. They were on
with Wishbone Ash so it was going to
be a good one. After Ash had done their
gig it was The Who's turn. They just
strolled on, picked up their instruments
and started. It was bloody loud! It was
deafening. Their set was the whole of
Tommy and several old hits. They were
on for about three hours and it was one
of the best concerts I've seen. They were
definitely on form and you could tell
they were enjoying it and playing well.
Roger Daltrey was top man in his fringed
jacket and big hair. He was superb, as was
Keith Moon. It was a superb show and a
pleasure to hear and see.

*Steve Rogers, remembers The
Who playing for three hours and
being 'bloody loud'*

I WAS THERE: JOHN SIMPSON

It was one of the venues on their tour of universities including the
Refectory at Leeds University where they recorded The Who *Live at
Leeds* album, a concert at which I was also at. At the Leeds concert,
my friend caught and kept one of Keith Moon's drumsticks. At the
York concert, The Who played the same set as is on *Live at Leeds*.

They were superb and sounded much like the album. I remember
walking to the venue and passing Keith Moon's psychedelic Rolls
Royce, which I think was previously owned by John Lennon, being
filled up with petrol at a garage on Lawrence Street.

MERRIWEATHER POST PAVILION

29 JUNE 1970, COLUMBIA, MARYLAND

I WAS THERE: DENIS GOULET

MPP is a cool little amphitheater that probably holds 14,000 including some fixed pavilion as well as lawn seating. The venue was overrun and 20,000 people showed up. We probably paid $15 for the seats. They were good, center stage and about 30 rows back on the aisle. We were totally stoked. I bought the tickets with the expectation that my very pregnant wife would have dropped our baby on the date due (26 June) and that she'd be sufficiently recovered to go with me.

I got off work and made it back to the apartment and my wife, my cousin and good friend piled into the car for the normally quick trip up Route 29. It was hot, very hot, and my wife was extremely pregnant. I must have asked her fifty times if she really wanted to deal with the walk once we got there, given the heat and the crowd. But there was no way she was staying behind. We got to within a mile of Merriweather and traffic came to a standstill. But we were still 45 minutes early and there was no concern at the time that we'd miss anything. After sitting in the car and not moving an inch for ten minutes, we noticed people walking up from behind us and there was no doubt that, if we wanted to see The Who, we were going to have to hoof it from that point.

I wedged the car onto the shoulder and off we set. It probably took 30 minutes to get close to the gates. When we got close enough to see the fence that surrounds the center, it was apparent that the crowd was having none of the fence and ripped it down. It was at that point a free concert.

I was constantly worried that my wife was going to start downloading that baby. She was already three days overdue and all of that excitement couldn't help. But she was relentless. She led the way past the mob on the lawn. Police estimated that 20,000 people showed at a place that holds 14,000 maximum. When we finally got there and of course they were occupied. She looked at the two people and said 'out!' They said 'right, where are we supposed to go?' Then they saw her giant pregnant belly and got up and moved on.

We missed maybe half of the first song and were treated to the best Who show I would ever see. Show over, we marched back to the abandoned car and went home. Our daughter was born eight days later. If she was a boy I would have named her Tommy!

AUDITORIUM THEATER

4 JULY 1970, CHICAGO, ILLINOIS

I WAS THERE: NICK VERBIC

I saw The Who seven times between 1968 and 1970. The first time I saw them they were the opening band for Herman's Hermits, which is almost as crazy as when Hendrix opened for The Monkees. Seeing them at the Chicago Auditorium on 4 July 1970 is one of the top three concerts in my life. I've seen more bands than I can remember and none of them played with the energy of The Who with Moonie.

ISLE OF WIGHT MUSIC FESTIVAL

29 AUGUST 1970, ISLE OF WIGHT

I WAS THERE: GERALD CLEAVER

When they returned to play the Isle of Wight festival a second time, one of the reasons they played a long set was to make up for the previous year. They seemed to go on forever. And they sounded superb. I was there with my girlfriend and she just couldn't believe what she was seeing. She'd never seen anything like that before.

If you hadn't already realised why The Who were so popular in the 1960's and 1970's and why nerds like me would see them up to four or more times in any one year, as I did in 1970, quite simply The Who were an exciting live band. They put on a stage show to entertain their audience, and engaged their audience by talking to them, by looking at them and giving the audience something to look at on stage. I do recall at that time there were many other bands on the road, but many were scruffily dressed, some did not talk to or look at the audience, and some had zero stage presence.

ISLE OF WIGHT FESTIVAL

AUGUST 28th, 29th & 30th

----------- FRIDAY -----------
CHICAGO
FAMILY
JAMES TAYLOR
ARRIVAL
LIGHTHOUSE
TASTE

--------- SATURDAY ---------
DOORS
JONI MITCHELL
WHO
SLY & THE FAMILY STONE
CAT MOTHER
FREE
JOHN S. SEBASTIAN
EMERSON
LAKE & PALMER
MUNGO JERRY
SPIRIT

----------- SUNDAY -----------
JIMI HENDRIX EXPERIENCE
JOAN BAEZ
RICHIE HAVENS
MOODY BLUES
PENTANGLE
GOOD NEWS
LEONARD COHEN

Tickets: Friday 20/- Saturday 30/- Sunday 40/-
Weekend Ticket £3

FIERY CREATIONS LIMITED
P.O. Box 1, Freshwater, Isle of Wight
Telephone Freshwater 2162

Light shows and effects were sometimes used to entertain the audience, but The Who did not need these: they were showmen and were leaping about and showing off, etc. The only big effect they used at that time was a big searchlight shining out over the audience at the 'listening to you' refrain at the end of *Tommy*, which always got a big response.

I think they used it at The Isle Of Wight in 1970 for the first time. I can still recall how entranced my then girlfriend was by the sight of Roger Daltrey, long curly hair, dressed up in his cowboy fringed jacket, swinging his microphone on a long lead out over the audience like a lasso. Nobody else was doing this at the time. No one else still is. Keith Moon was playing the drums as if he was an octopus, arms flailing everywhere. Eyes bulging, cheeks puffed blowing away. As for Pete Townshend...well, you know about him!

I WAS THERE: PAUL BRUCE HADEN

My girlfriend and I had been to a couple of smaller festivals with a group of friends before but the Isle of Wight was on a whole different scale. It was a bit of a trek so we took my girlfriend's car and made our way down there, setting off a few days before to make sure we got on a ferry.

The scale of the festival was mind blowing. Supposedly there were more people there than Woodstock, which was 500,000. I think we just about managed to see every act, or at least hear them, as we lay in our tent. Fortunately the weather was fabulous. I dread to think what it would have been like if there had been Glastonbury style downpours and mud.

The Who came on very late. It must have been the early hours of the morning. Because the air was still at that time of night, the sound was crystal clear with none of the wind blown phasing that often occurs at outdoor gigs. My favourite memory of the set was the intro to 'Pinball Wizard'. When John's bass came in, the ground seemed to shake.

I've been a sound engineer both live and in studios all my life so it's sounds that move me. In comparison with today's sound systems, the PA at the Isle of Wight was tiny but for the time it was enormous and also made by WEM who were pretty good. The atmosphere when The Who were on was fantastic. Everyone seemed to be singing along and it was as though they lifted the crowd who had sat there patiently for hours. I know there were some great acts on, and I was looking forward to seeing Hendrix who I'd seen the week before, but The Who's set was one of the best I'd seen from any band and certainly the best I'd seen them play. I've got a copy of the gig on DVD and, good though it is, it doesn't entirely capture the visceral sound of the band or indeed the atmosphere of such a huge crowd. It really was a case of 'you had to be there'.

I WAS THERE: MICHAEL STOKES, AGE 16

I have seen The Who many, many times and April 2017 was the 100th. One of the many gigs I remember with great fondness was the 1970 Isle of Wight Festival. I had persuaded my parents to let me go.

I said I was going with two friends – little did my parents know I had lied. I had been a fan since the age of 11 and had seen them a couple of times by then, but this was the big one so I travelled from Bristol to The Isle of Wight.

I'd never seem so many people at a gig before and I was so far back they were only just visible but boy could you hear them! The sound was out of this world. Loud would be an understatement. They started with 'Heaven and Hell', John Entwistle in his bones costume, Daltrey looking cool and mean, Moon looking like Moon and Townshend looking mean with his white boiler suit and Doc Martens. It was loud and full of energy until the third song and then, somehow, they stepped up a gear. 'Young Man Blues' was so good I honestly thought my lungs were going to explode. I could not get my breath – this was something else. It was aggressive and so full of energy. I remember looking around me at the time and seeing that people were just mesmerised by the sheer power that was coming from all four members of the group.

Later they went into *Tommy* and again held the audience in the palm of their hands, and when it got to 'See Me Feel Me', a massive searchlight came on and it was an amazing moment. I believe this was a defining moment of the band's career; they were at the top of their game. I went back to my tent only to find it had been stolen along with all my stuff, so all I had was my train tickets back home, a small amount of money and the clothes on my back. I did stay to watch Jimi Hendrix but was so exhausted I fell asleep and slept through the whole performance, but that's another story.

I WAS THERE: RICHARD DIXON

I lived in Belgium until 1970 so my first live concert was the Isle of Wight with my cousin. *Tommy* was playing as the sun came up whilst my cousin slept next to me in his sleeping bag. He has always maintained that The Who were amazing!

I took my daughter to Hyde Park some years ago, having given her *The Who's Greatest Hits*. Whilst waiting for them to come on, Lucy asked me when I first saw them. I was telling her about the Isle of Wight and was overheard by a forty something couple who started bowing to me. My street cred with my daughter rose astronomically!

I WAS THERE: MARTIN JONES

The Isle of Wight concert was proof to me that they were the best live group in the world bearing in mind over a period of time I saw all the top groups apart from The Beatles. They played around 2am at the festival and played a set which included most, if not all, of *Tommy*. Given the sound system, the quality of performance was staggering. I do remember paying £4.50 for a weekend ticket, which was never checked and which I wished I'd kept!

FALKONER CENTRET TEATRET

20 SEPTEMBER 1970, COPENHAGEN, DENMARK

I WAS THERE: JOHN WADLOW

I saw The Who for the first and only time at the Falconer Centre in Copenhagen. It was part of a 28 date European tour they did that year. I've always remembered the classic look of the band at that time – Townshend with his paint splattered white boiler suit, Entwistle with his famous skeleton suit and Daltrey with his long fringed jacket. It was a long set; they played 29 songs that night. 17 of them were from the album *Tommy* which they'd released the year before, but they also played some of their big hits, including 'I Can't Explain' and 'My Generation'. I remember being shocked by the sheer volume of the band. I think it must have been the loudest gig I'd ever been to up till then, as well as one of the most energetic. The band were incredibly tight and all of them were superb, particularly Pete Townshend. It's one thing to hear him on record and quite another to see him live. It's definitely one of the best gigs I've ever been to and that includes seeing Jimi Hendrix at the Royal Albert Hall a couple of years earlier in 1967.

FREE TRADE HALL

7 OCTOBER 1970, MANCHESTER

I WAS THERE: COLIN JOY

A totally different Who played the Free Trade Hall in 1970 – they were bloody loud! The main emphasis of the tour was to capitalise on their appearance at Woodstock and the Isle of Wight Festivals, and to bring their showpiece *Tommy* to the stage. The album when originally released was not to everyone's cup of tea, but, live, it was a masterpiece mixed in with The Who's back catalogue of stage favourites.

Townshend had his trademark hand swinging guitar playing down to a tee, Daltrey was throwing his microphones high in the air at every opportunity, Moon's drumming was over the top and Entwistle occasionally moved. Not too much – but he moved! The problem was the band got louder and louder, but the set seemed to go on forever as they played the full *Tommy* album, with all the instrumentals. It was a good night which took no prisoners. They did 34 songs in all. It was a long, long deafening night.

UNIVERSITY OF SUSSEX

10 OCTOBER 1970, BRIGHTON

I WAS THERE: JOHN SCHOLLAR

A few times, Keith Moon would ring me up and say 'what you doing tonight?' I'd say 'not a lot' and he'd say 'come up and see the gig' and I'd drive up there in my little sports car. When they did the university tour, when they recorded Live at Leeds, we went to the show at Sussex University outside Brighton. I rang Keith up and he said 'come down in the Rolls with us.' So we drove over to his house and he'd left a great big note on the front door saying 'sorry, mate. I've got to pick somebody up. See you in Brighton.' We got there and walked up to the main entrance and said 'we're with Keith' and the bloke said 'yeah, everybody says that mate. No ticket? You're not getting in.' Then Keith turned up in his Rolls and gave me a big hug and I said 'we've got a problem, mate. They won't let us in because we haven't got tickets.' He said 'what?' and called for the manager.

The manager came out and Keith said 'my mates can't get in without tickets and they haven't got tickets. Well, if they don't get in, I ain't coming in. Have you ever seen The Who without a drummer? They're crap.' So the manager agreed to let us in. Now, a crowd had gathered by this time and Keith said to the crowd 'has anybody here not got a ticket?' And half a dozen said 'we ain't got tickets.' And Keith said to the manager 'and they're my mates as well.'

LOCARNO BALLROOM

13 OCTOBER 1970, LEEDS

I WAS THERE: GERALD CLEAVER

As soon as they got *Tommy*, Pete started playing in the boiler suit. I think for the Locarno gig he got it tie dyed. I think it was tie dyed at the Isle of Wight festival by John Sebastian. It was quite a shock. I'd only ever seen him in this plain white boiler suit and there he was looking quite garish. They'd start with the singles and 'Young Man Blues' and then do *Tommy* and then come back for 'Summertime Blues'. I never saw them smash up their equipment. The James Gang were the support act. I can't remember much about it other than the people I went with, who I also went to see the other two Leeds dates with, were a couple and they'd had a row and he'd ripped the tickets up in a fit of pique. So they turned up at the door with these sellotaped bits of paper that they had to blag their way in with.

I WAS THERE: JOHN OLDROYD

The gig was set up in the Mecca ballroom, which was situated in the Merrion Centre, Leeds. The support act were a band called the James Gang, whose leader was none other than Joe Walsh, now firmly ensconced as a member of The Eagles. They must have been good because it encouraged me to go and buy their LP *The Games Gang Rides Again*, which I still have.

John Oldroyd and his homage to Eric Clapton reading The Beano on the cover of Blues Breakers with Eric Clapton

Anyway, the Mecca being a ballroom had this huge wooden dance floor with seats around the outside and a seated balcony. There was no hysteria and no rushing towards the makeshift stage. Everybody just sat on the dance floor or sat in a seat and enjoyed the music. Although the content of the gig has been lost with age over the years, the quote of the night came from Pete Townshend just before they were to play songs from *Tommy*. He said 'and I as a composer', which sounded unusual coming from a rock star. You normally think of them as songwriters.

TRENTHAM GARDENS

26 OCTOBER 1970, STOKE-ON-TRENT

I WAS THERE: ALAN GOODWIN

My wife and I went to one of their gigs at Trentham Gardens, in what was then the ballroom. It was standing room only. On the night

Alan Goodwin with his wife Jean

Keith Moon's drums remained intact. During the interval we went for a drink in the upstairs lounge bar and found ourselves sitting on the next table to the group and their entourage.

Contrary to their perceived image, they were in fact very well behaved and apart from their star status you wouldn't have realised they were one of the country's leading groups.

HAMMERSMITH PALAIS

29 OCTOBER 1970, LONDON

I WAS THERE: GREG COYNE, AGE 15

I saw The Who the first time at the Hammersmith Palais for a gig that was limited to just 300 tickets, or so we were told. I paid black market prices to get the tickets, which was a lot of pocket money! Me and three other mates got there early and were right at the front of the stage and, as the concert began, I climbed up on to the stage far right. I was recording the gig on a small tape recorder – yes I know I shouldn't have done – and the gig was amazing.

It opened with 'Heaven and Hell' and went right through *Tommy* and finished with 'Magic Bus'. Pete even shouted some obscenity into the tape recorder microphone for me. At the end of the gig, Pete smashed up his Cherry Red SG guitar right next to me – amazing – and with the SG body lying next to me on the stage I made a grab for it and got it but an eagle-eyed roadie grabbed me and ripped the body out of my cradled arms. You can't imagine the disappointment of being so close to acquiring a Pete Townshend smashed guitar body only to lose it to the roadie!

I subsequently wrote to Pete to tell him but unfortunately never got a reply. I was hoping he would take pity on me and send me a smashed up body but he didn't. If you are reading this, Pete, I would still love one. That one gig made me a Who fan for life. As for the recording of the gig, it came out really well and I subsequently lent it to a mate and never got it back. Such a shame. I bought a t-shirt of the gig from a seller outside and still have it somewhere. God knows how I fitted into it. I wouldn't be able to get it over my head now.

LEEDS UNIVERSITY

21 NOVEMBER 1970, LEEDS

I WAS THERE: GERALD CLEAVER

I think they were better the second time I saw them at the university than the year than when they recorded *Live at Leeds*. But it's subjective. The first time I went with fellow students. The second time I went with my then girlfriend who became my first wife. So she was coming up to see me at the university and I managed to get tickets by a fluke. I'd gone down to see her when the tickets went on sale and they sold out. And the next day they found they had ten left that they'd forgotten to sell so they made an announcement in the students union and I just happened to be there walking past the counter. So of course I was first in the queue. It was very lucky.

The second time I saw them at the university was probably the loudest I ever saw them. I can remember my ears were ringing as I was walking back to where I was staying and they were still giving me some discomfort several days afterwards. Since then I've started being more careful about where I stand. They were all standing venues with no seats. It was only after that that I started seeing them in seated venues. It wasn't the same. It was problematic. Sometimes if you got excited and stood up you were allowed to and sometimes if you got excited and stood up they weren't having it. I don't think their music is music for sitting down and nodding to.

MAYFAIR BALLROOM

26 NOVEMBER 1970, NEWCASTLE-UPON-TYNE

I WAS THERE: IAN DALGLEISH

I saw them at the Mayfair. On the date they were first due to play, only two of them turned up so the support act, Curved Air, did an extended set. However it was announced that, as we left, we would get a ticket for the rearranged date. So the wide boys left early, got their tickets and then ran round the back and sneaked in the fire escape door and left again with a couple of extra tickets!

THE LADS CLUB

5 DECEMBER 1970, NORWICH

I WAS THERE: DAVID NOBBS

I remember they played their latest single, 'Won't Get Fooled Again'. I'm not sure if it had actually been released at that stage because when I tried to buy it later, the shops didn't have it. The venue was fairly small and was actually wider than it was long. The music was so loud you heard it twice – once when it came towards you and then again when it bounced off the rear wall!

I actually met Roger Daltrey earlier that day. I worked just down the

road from the Lads Club and when I went to the local corner shop to buy some tobacco for my boss (I was an apprentice engineer so was the company dogsbody!) Roger was in there buying some cans of coke. He was my hero at the time but I was too shy to speak to him. We just nodded to each other! I can't believe I didn't speak to him, something I regret to this day.

I WAS THERE: TONY LANGFORD

I saw The Who at the Lads Club. It was a very high energy gig with a lot
of the stuff from *Live at Leeds*. I have always been a music fanatic and The
Who were one of my favourite bands from their early days. The abiding
memory of the gig was the volume. I don't think I ever went to a louder
gig. The Lads Club was a bit of a strange venue. I don't think it put on

too many gigs and I don't know why they didn't use the University of East Anglia LCR.

I used my beloved Lambretta LI125, which I purchased in 1970 for £50 saved whilst working in London for a year previously, to go and see my girlfriend (later my wife) most nights, which was a 50 mile round trip on some dodgy roads to Cromer. I remember one dark night, on my way home, hitting a pothole and my spare wheel going flying off the back with a bag of singles that I had borrowed from my sister. When I went back the following day nothing could be found and I got into my sister's bad books because I couldn't afford to replace her records.

I WAS THERE: ROB CRANTHORNE

I was a student at the UEA from 1968 to 1971. I was at the The Lads' Club concert in December 1970; it was a brilliant performance – with no guitar smashing! I was, and still am, an amateur photographer and in 1970 I had a Zenit E camera with a 58mm Helios lens, which I took to the gig loaded with high speed Ektachrome film. I shot a number of photos from the audience, some more successful than others.

I WAS THERE: ROBERT KELLY

I bought a ticket in 1970 for a gig at the University of East Anglia, which was due to be held on 5 October. A short time later it was postponed and rearranged for another venue, the Norwich Lads Club. But I made a mistake and thought it was a week later! So I missed the gig – but I still have the postcard sized ticket. It cost one pound and five shillings (£1.25).

FUTURIST THEATRE

6 DECEMBER 1970, SCARBOROUGH

I WAS THERE: DIANE BAILEY, AGE 16

I went with friends to see them. We were seated in the second row directly in front of the band, and what an experience it was! I think that set me on the road to seeing bands live, and I was lucky enough to see many, many more. I remember how exciting this all seemed.

Roger Daltrey had a habit of swinging his microphone around in the air. I could not believe it when it actually landed in my lap! I was stunned, and my friend and I actually did a little scream into the microphone before Roger hauled it back on stage, grinning at us as he did so. As you can imagine, we were so excited by this and the very electrifying atmosphere in the Futurist. I remember a lot of screaming and Keith Moon going at 100 miles an hour on the drums, his face completely wrapped up in what he was doing. It would be true to say that he really did have a wild man look about him.

Sadly, as is usually the case, it was over all too soon, but not before they trashed all the equipment, sending us and all the other people lucky enough to see them wild. What a night it was. I saw The Beatles before The Who, but I was too young really for that, and I saw Black Sabbath and Deep Purple when they were just starting out. But the concert by The Who has always remained in my mind and even though I have seen the likes of the Police and U2, I think The Who was the most exciting of all. I can still see a young girl giggling into a microphone looked on by Roger Daltrey grinning!

I WAS THERE: IAN DAWSON

I was at university at the time but some of my peers were at the Tech and I went along with them. For me it was quite a big gig to attend having generally missed out on attending the Sunday night one night stands of the early to mid Sixties that used to be held at the Futurist – the Beatles, Stones, etc. Young teenagers did not have the cash for such events though my sister and my wife both managed to get to many of those events through complimentary tickets given to theatre staff and shopkeepers carrying publicity posters! It was also priced at a comparatively low level for the time, costing me no more than I was paying to see lesser bands like Renaissance, Caravan, Hardin and York.

At the time the Futurist Theatre was owned by the Robert Luff Organisation, the people who ran the Black and White Minstrel Show. They generally ran the summer season shows and an occasional out of season week long booking. The Who were not booked by them but the theatre was hired by the Scarborough Technical College student body. It was effectively an FE college running vocational, O and A level courses particularly – but not exclusively – for the more able secondary modern students to move on to in order the raise their qualification levels.

The student body ran regular dances and concerts at both the college and outside venues. These were very profitable and they booked The Who and the theatre for the concert. The concert was, I believe, effectively subsidised by accumulated profits. The concert was well attended but far from being a sell out in what was for the time a large provincial auditorium with a 2,150 capacity that was geared up for high season tourist shows rather than for events out of season in a modest sized town. Pete Townshend did comment on the enthusiastic and appreciative response from the audience. The set was the standard one for the era and enthusiastically received.

I WAS THERE: CHRIS HAMLIN

I was at the gig as a student of Scarborough Tech and as a roadie for the night! The story of the booking is more about the Tech than the Futurist, as I remember it. My group of friends at Tech included Paul Woodhead, then Social Secretary and in charge of entertainments for the College. I remember being in the small group of people influencing Paul in decisions about Tech dances and this one was the climax. The budget was the largest ever – I remember £4,000 for some reason – but to economise on costs the arrangement was to provide a number of students to roadie and I was an eager volunteer as a budding guitarist myself. So along with some extremely hard work lugging amps, cabs and flight cases up the back stairs, we six or so got tickets and seats for a rendition of *Tommy*. Memories include

Keith Moon's entrance in a full gorilla outfit, and the stage strewn with plectrums and broken drum sticks afterwards. I had many souvenirs of the night and still have a couple of plectrums bought from Manny's Music in New York.

I WAS THERE: MIKE HOLLIDAY

The drink beforehand was probably in the Toby Jug, a bar on The Crescent, now long gone. I went to the Futurist with fellow students Rod Parker (sadly no longer with us) and Rob Hart who, last I heard, was living in USA. We sat on the right hand side of the stage, three rows from the front, and in the seats somewhere around D6. Entwistle was his usual calm self. Townshend was fairly reserved with just a few guitar 'bounces' off the stage.

Moon was spellbinding and absolutely brilliant and Daltrey did his usual stage show. But he did lose the mic off the end of the lead whilst doing his trademark microphone swinging and it hit a young lady in front of us on the front row fair and square in the stomach. I think she thought she had bagged a good trophy but it was retrieved within seconds by a couple of roadies. Afterwards we went to the Minstrel Bar – a bar that was part of the Futurist Theatre.

I WAS THERE: PAUL MURRAY

I've still got the newspaper clipping. There was The Who and there was a support band called Spread Eagle and of course it said underneath 'and Scarborough's top DJ Paul Murray' and it was 17 and a tanner (87p).

It should have been in October when it was originally booked. It was a pal of mine that used to run the technical college. He was the main one in the student union, and they did quite a few gigs over a period of a couple of years. They had Black Sabbath on and Free. The Who was the biggest one that they did cost wise, and apparently to this day there's still talk at the college of the loss that there was. They weren't going to go on stage at one point, Pete Townshend kicked off because it wasn't a complete sell out.

All the four band members turned up in different vehicles. I can't

remember which one was in which but there was a Citroen – I think
that Entwistle was in that and there was a Range Rover, an old Jag and
another one.

They had a 2,000 watt PA system. It was WEM. I've got an amp
which is 2,000 watt on its own now but back then the biggest amp
you could get was 100 watt. What they did was they looped them
from one to another to another to another and they had 20 with
20 sets of speakers from either side of the stage. I remember the
rider was amazing, it was all booze. They had a bit of an argument
because on the contract they said they wouldn't play within 50 miles
of Scarborough and they'd been in Middlesbrough. They reckoned
that Middlesbrough was 53 or 54 miles away, well the argument was
that it was 48 miles away.

I WAS THERE: DENIS PICKUP

The concert was organised by the then Scarborough Technical
College student union and as far as I know they hired the Futurist. I
went into Bernard Dean's music shop on St.Thomas Street the day
before the concert to see if there were any tickets left. I remember
saying exactly that to the assistant who replied with a laugh 'how
many do you want?'

There were about six of us seated about ten rows back, with
nobody in front of us and very few around us. The gig had no
advertising as I remember so looking back I think there was
something like three or four hundred there in the 2,000 seater
Futurist. It was obviously a financial disaster. Paul Murray was the
MC. The Who were great as you would expect but I wondered as the
concert proceeded what were they thinking as they played to a near
empty hall after all the massive gigs they had performed during that
time.

I WAS THERE: ASHLEY SMITH, AGE 17

It was a strange gig, because so few people turned up. I couldn't
believe it because they were massive. They'd done Woodstock and all
that sort of stuff. I kept the ticket and I pinned it to a copy of *Live at*

Leeds. It was so surreal, when you looked back behind you and saw all those empty seats. It was unbelievable. It was in the miners' strike, but you were given warning of when the electric was going to be off. Personally, I think the main reason people didn't go was because there wasn't a bar.

MAYFAIR BALLROOM

15 DECEMBER 1970, NEWCASTLE-UPON-TYNE

I WAS THERE: RUSSELL WILKES

The Mayfair in Newcastle, which is no longer with us, was a club and I remember they generally had a small circular stage. In the early Seventies, they got some really big acts on, like Led Zeppelin and The Who. For those bands they had a specially constructed stage, which was huge and took up half the dance floor but nobody was interested really in just the normal club activities. Everyone was just there to see the group. I remember they went on for just about two hours. I can't really say what they started with or what they finished with, I can remember a song they did which was 'Ohio', which was about the National Guards shooting in America and I'm sure they sang that. I think they did all their hits. I remember it was a great night!

1971 With the band's 69 and 70 performances dominated by Tommy, Townshend and the group were ready to infuse their act with new material, with Townshend having written a number of songs around the 'Lifehouse' concept. Several songs performed for the first time in 1971 would become staples in the band's act, including 'Behind Blue Eyes', 'Baba O'Riley', 'Bargain', and 'Won't Get Fooled Again'.

'My Wife' also appeared in many subsequent tours as the featured John Entwistle number in the show, right up until his death in 2002. 1971 was also the first year the group performed with backing tapes, which allowed them to include the synthesizer tracks from both 'Won't Get Fooled Again' and 'Baba O'Riley' onstage.

HURST

20 APRIL 1971, BERKSHIRE

I WAS THERE: VAL MABBS

I went to interview Roger at his house, the interview appearing in the *Record Mirror* on 8 May 1971. He had a nice house down in the country. This would seem to have been before he bought and moved into Holmshurst Manor in East Sussex.

I travelled up there by train and then was picked up at the station by one of the guys that worked with him. I loved it at the time because he had a Jensen Interceptor, which was a beautiful car. I went down to his home and we had a chat and sat out in the garden there. He was a very nice guy.

TOP RANK SUITE

7 MAY 1971, SUNDERLAND

I WAS THERE: BILLY HUTCHINSON, AGE 19

I was with five friends. They were playing at the Rink and it was a packed house with everyone sitting on the floor. In my estimation, there were approximately 7,000 people in the dance hall. I cannot remember clearly who was supporting them. It might have been Jethro Tull with Ian Anderson. Pete smashed his guitar into Keith's bass drum. They sang 'Substitute', 'Magic Bus' and 'My Generation, to name a few.

I WAS THERE: HENRY RACE, AGE 17

I saw them at the Top Rank Suite but everybody knew it as the Rink. It was just next to Park Lane bus station. Everybody played there in their prime – the Stones played there in the Sixties, The Beatles played there twice, Deep Purple and Free played there.

The other big venue in Sunderland was the Mecca ballroom. Local promoter, Jeff Docherty put Sunderland on the map because he used to promote bands. He actually put on The Who at the Bay Hotel in Whitburn, just outside of Sunderland. It was the back room of a local hotel and Jeff Docherty used to rent it out on Friday nights. He had been working there as a bouncer. I didn't go because it was three or four miles out of Sunderland and it was a bit of a logistical nightmare to get there. Then Jeff Docherty moved to the Mecca Ballroom, which was bigger than the Bay Hotel. He brought Led Zeppelin to Sunderland, Pink Floyd, Ginger Baker's Air Force.

I was still at school. You just piled through after school. It was very much a communal, social kind of thing, going to see bands. For the Mecca and the Rink you could just turn up. I went with my girlfriend at the time, Alison.

We went in the pub first even though we were only 17. We'd seen the Woodstock film and saw phenomenal scenes of The Who live and were thinking 'will Townshend smash up his guitar at the end?' We were really quite gassed at the prospect of seeing The Who.

We'd gone into the back room of the pub, the posh bit, and we were sat there just being daft teenage kids, drinking our lager and lime, when in walks Daltrey and Entwistle with their guys. There was probably five or six of them. We were completely overawed and we didn't go and say 'hi' to them. Daltrey was asking at the bar if they could buy a bottle of brandy. They wanted to try it first, and Daltrey took a swig from a glass and he said 'this isn't good stuff. Go into the cellar and get me out a bottle of good stuff. I'm not paying for that.' So a group of them just sat in the corner and drank their brandy, having a good crack. This was in a pub only three minutes away from the venue. We didn't say a word to them. We were frightened to even make eye contact.

When they left, we left soon after and we walked back down to the Rink where their was a fairly hefty queue and we realised that the white Rolls Royce being driven backwards and forwards was Keith Moon's chauffer-driven Rolls Royce. Keith had his body out of the back window and he was waving and shouting. 'Fucking hell, it's Keith Moon!'

I remember Townshend was being quite rough with his SG, but he didn't smash it. He had his white boiler suit on and his monkey boots. They were still playing bits of *Tommy*.

I WAS THERE: JOHN SANCASTER

I was lucky enough to be one of the few to see The Who at Sunderland Top Rank Suite. 50p – that's what it cost to see the greatest ever rock band. I was about three feet away from the pure unadulterated rock music and my friend John managed to grab Keith's drum stick as he flung it and I managed to get John Entwistle's plectrum.

The teenage John Sancaster

As if that was not the ultimate way of ending the night, it got even better. My friend and I went round to the back of the Top Rank which then led to the back of the Odeon. It was there we saw Keith, Pete and John and were lucky enough to get their autographs. Roger had gone off before them so we could not get his. But the best bit was yet to come. The pen I gave to John was spring loaded and, yes, it sprang just as John was going to sign. What a nightmare! But to my ultimate surprise, John opened a car boot, proceeded to look for a torch and then looked on the ground for my pen top which he found! He then gave me his autograph which I still have to this day.

MAYFAIR SUITE

13 MAY 1971, BIRMINGHAM

I WAS THERE: GERALD CLEAVER

The only one I saw where any instruments got broken was at a ballroom in Birmingham in the city centre. It was a lot of new material which became *Who's Next*. I think Pete probably broke the neck of the guitar while he was playing it, or it was already damaged.

But he just dropped it when he finished and it just broke across his knee. I never saw them smash their instruments apart from that. It was the first time I'd seen them do some different tunes. It was interesting because they were doing things like 'Behind Blue Eyes' which no one had heard before. They did 'Water', which they'd done at the Isle of Wight. And they did 'Don't Know Myself'.

CAIRD HALL

23 MAY 1971, DUNDEE

I WAS THERE: IAN DOBSON, AGE 16

My memory is that the Caird Hall gig was a warm up show for a forthcoming British tour. The Who had recently released *Who's Next* and were going on the road on the back of this album. A number of songs on *Who's Next* used synthesiser and performing these live involved using pre recorded passages which I believe The Who wanted to test out on stage before embarking on the main tour. What better venue to do this than a backwater like Dundee?

CAIRD HALL SUNDAY 23 MAY at 7.30 PM
DOORS OPEN 7.00 PM
IN CONCERT.....
WHO £1.00
10

I attended the gig with my friends Graham and Harry, both sadly passed on now. Although the Caird Hall was on the tour circuit for most bands, this was special and caused massive excitement among

Ian Dobson and friend,
holding their gig tickets

us when the gig was announced. Graham in particular was a massive Who fan and he was beside himself at the thought of his heroes playing the Caird Hall. The ticket price was £1.00, which was a fair outlay for a schoolboy at the time. I borrowed the money from my father and had to pay him back at five shillings per week out of my pocket money. Hence it took me a whole month to fund the ticket price – but it was worth it!

The show was on a Sunday night and prior to the gig we went to Forte's Cafe decked out in our flares, t-shirts and greatcoats. This was the event of the year and we were buzzing. I still have a very bad photo of us in the cafe holding our tickets and beaming broadly. I don't remember a great deal of detail about the show itself other than it was fantastic. I don't recall there being a support act and I think The Who played mostly the new numbers from *Who's Next* in the first half of the show and then followed this with excerpts from *Tommy* and a couple of numbers from *Live at Leeds*. I have a memory of them playing 'Magic Bus', which was a real highlight.

In those days security wasn't what it is today and if you knew your way around the Caird Hall it was possible to get down to the dressing room area. After the show the three of us blagged our way backstage

and I managed to get the autographs of Townshend, Daltrey and
Entwistle. Keith Moon wasn't there but when we left and went round
the back of the Caird Hall we spotted a pink Rolls Royce parked
in Shore Terrace. On approaching the car, there was Keith Moon
sitting in the back with his driver/minder in the front. We went over
and Keith rolled down the window and signed autographs for us to
complete the set. He was quite chatty and took the time to speak to
us, which made our night.

I sold the autographs a few years ago to a memorabilia company
and got £300 for them. Little did I know at the time that my £1
ticket outlay would prove to be such a lucrative investment?

At the time, the *Melody Maker* used to have a letters page and they
would give an album to the author of any letter published. I had
drafted a letter to them slagging off The Who for various things. I
had mainly written the letter to annoy my mate Graham (the massive
Who fan) as it was all about 'favourite band' rivalries in those days.
I hadn't sent the letter but I had it in my pocket that night and it
was on the back of this letter that I got The Who autographs. I
remember being terrified that they might turn the paper over and
spot the nasty things I was saying about them.

I WAS THERE: RODDY FERGUSON

It was May 1971. It was the day after Scotland got beat 3-1 by
England. It was a wet Sunday night in Dundee. Heavy, heavy rain.
The reason I remember it is that I was actually standing on stage.
Townshend had a white boiler suit on with big brown boots. Moon
at the back of his kit had a big gong. In the 1960s, most cities had
Mods and Dundee, just like any other city, had a lot of Mods. The
boys in Dundee used to go to a coffee bar and they'd played Small
Faces, The Who. But this mob seemed to enjoy the B side of 'My
Generation', which was called 'Shout and Shimmy'. And these guys
were going in the town and they were singing it all the time and
people assumed there was a gang.

I got to know quite a few of these guys and we went to see The
Who and me and some of the yobs, as you might call them, went and

sat right in the front seats. The people were coming in and saying 'excuse me, that's my seat.' And we were telling them in no uncertain manner to 'eff off.' So the doormen came over but they didn't know what to do because one of the guys I was with, his brother had a bit of a reputation in Dundee. They didn't want to eject us because they didn't want to fall out with his brother. So as a compromise one of them came up with the solution: 'do you want to stand on stage?' 'Yeah, nae problem.' So me and me mates were standing right beside them. Actually on the stage watching The Who!

I WAS THERE: GERRY FORTE

In 1971 I was 19 years old and very much into 'underground' music as it was called back then. My favourite band at that time was (and still is) Led Zeppelin, who we also saw a couple of times at the Caird

Hall. The Led Zep albums 1 and 2 blew me away.

My good friend's favourite band, though, was The Who and although I liked them, they were basically a Sixties pop band to me, and not an underground band like Led Zep, Deep Purple, Tyrannosaurus Rex, Jethro Tull, Genesis, Yes, etc. We got all the good bands at the Caird Hall around that time. I liked all the 'flashy' guitarists of that era and to me Pete Townshend was basically just a chord thumper. But my mate loved them so I decided to go with him when it was announced that they were coming to the Caird Hall.

We solicited another of our mates' mums (who became my mother in law) to stand in the queue for tickets at Larg's music shop in Whitehall Street for us as we were all working the day they went on sale. She stood in line for hours for us and got the tickets for my mate, my other mate and his sister – now my wife of 44 years!

The tickets we got were up on the second tier level of the Caird Hall, and we were right above the right hand side stage as you faced the stage. In fact it was directly above the amplifiers, speakers and other sound equipment on the stage which was manned throughout the concert by a dedicated sound engineer who we could see and watch easily. As it turned out, he was an integral part of the concert.

This was the *Who's Next* tour and some of the material had not been released yet. It was evident to me from the get go that this was not the pop group Who of the 60s – they were doing something different. They went on to play a lot of their well known songs and all of the tunes that went on to become classics from *Who's Next* which has become one of my favourite albums of all time. It was the first time that I had seen and heard the sound engineer use the equipment to play back the recorded loops of music simultaneously as the band were playing live. In fact that loop of recorded music turned out to be 'Won't Get Fooled Again', as we all became familiar with very soon afterwards.

I was, as we all were, blown away by The Who's performance. It is one of the best concerts that I have ever witnessed to this day and Pete Townshend's (chord thumper) compositions and use of sound were ground breaking for the time in my honest opinion. We all thoroughly enjoyed their performance and it became a benchmark for us throughout the years. I still can't listen to anything from *Who's Next* without a fond memory of that concert, and the older I get, the greater the nostalgia.

I WAS THERE: JACK LORD, AGE 18

The concert I saw was part of their 'small city' short UK tour to phase out *Tommy* and introduce new material from *Who's Next*, and was a major surprise. I still recall sitting at home on study leave, with Radio 1 on, and the DJ saying 'The Who have announced a short tour of smaller venues, and will be playing X, Y, Z – and Dundee.' His voice implied 'where?' and I was wishing 'pause and rewind' was available!

The Caird Hall (2,300 seat auditorium, perfect acoustics) was a very busy venue in the early 70s with a regular flow of good artists of the day, mainly those on an early upward spiral. But the bigger artists didn't usually come further north than Edinburgh and Glasgow so this was a major event for us.

With no mobile phones, no internet, and hardly any of us even having a landline, a gathering in our local was required to allocate responsibility for the box office visit. I worked 100 yards from the Caird Hall, so it may have been me. My pals were all students. I'm sure the concert was a Sunday night, and that weekend I had a '24 hour venture scout challenge hike' event from Saturday through the night, during which we walked almost 70 miles.

My memory of the packed concert is perhaps blurred by the interim 45 years, but I recall the immediate feeling of a huge level of energy from the band (probably only ever replicated by the punk phase in smaller venues), and of hearing a few of my favourite tracks from *Live at Leeds*, still a couple of songs from *Tommy*, and The whole of *Who's Next*, especially the magical 'Baba O'Riley'. The encores were a blur of old hits, but they (almost predictably!) went well over the normal 'lights out' time.

Our last bus home was 10.55pm and at 10.45pm my pals all got up to go. But I said 'they're doing another encore – I'm not leaving yet' and so I stayed. This final number was 'Water', the perfect number for Daltrey swinging the mic about his head, Townshend's flailing right arm and Moon spraying himself, the stage and front rows with water fountains from huge gulps of bottled water, while half a dozen sets of sticks flew through the air. Guitars and drums remained undamaged, as I recall.

As soon as it was over, I ran for the exit, down the huge sandstone steps, through the underpass and down the street to see my bus pull out of the terminus. I had no money for a taxi, so had to walk yet another five miles home. My blistered feet were very sore, but I was absolutely convinced I'd made the right decision to stay to the end.

After this tour, The Who rapidly became a huge arena band, and I've never again been anywhere close to where they've played, but of the dozens of concerts I was lucky to see in my youth, that raucous night at the Caird Hall was easily the stand out for me. 'Baba O'Riley' was my first mobile ringtone. It used to drive some colleagues bonkers if I'd left my desk and my phone rang, as it played the entire track – all seven minutes of it!

I WAS THERE: IAN MCALLISTER, AGE 20

There are two specific things that I've always remembered about that gig. There were coloured lights on the lighting rig on the stage behind Keith Moon. He had bottles of water by the side of him and I remember him tilting his head back during a song, taking a big swig of water and spitting it quite high up into the air. As the water then cascaded back down through these coloured lights it was like a rainbow effect and it was very effective. The water was then landing on his drum skins and as he was playing the drums this water was then bouncing back up. So there was this colourful rainbow type effect with all this water that he was cascading about.

They obviously felt obliged to sing 'My Generation' because that was one of the big hits that helped make them. Townshend pointed out that he hated the song. Whether it was because they'd played it that often I don't know. But I remember being a bit disappointed that he felt that way about it. But they felt obliged to do it because that's

Ian McAllister remembers Townshend being less than enthusiastic about 'My Generation'

what the fans wanted to hear and he introduced it by saying 'this is my fucking generation.' I remember thinking 'oh, that's not very nice.' They didn't play the whole song. They just played a few verses. So they felt they'd done their bit for the fans. Even at that young tender age of 20 I thought it was a bit dismissive. Other people might have thought it was funny. I didn't think that was very nice. They were a rock band. Townshend – he was quite coarse. But as a rock band perhaps they thought the audience wanted them to be coarse.

I WAS THERE: JOHN WALLACE, AGE 20

I was first and foremost a Beatles fan but I absolutely loved the music of The Who. My favourite track is the album version of 'Won't Get Fooled Again', because Townshend was getting into sociopolitical stuff and it's the most amazing track. I saw them at the Caird Hall. It's a lovely building. It's got all these cornices and all that sort of stuff. Since the days when we used to have the rock concerts there, they've made it a bit more sophisticated. But it's a venue that has had criticism over the years from rock bands about its acoustics because it was built in the days when you had orchestras. The acoustics in the building, if you're playing acoustic music with a 60-piece orchestra, are beautiful.

But if you're listening to a rock band, you have to be facing the stage to appreciate the music. Because there's a balcony and I've been on the balcony when there's been a rock band. I saw Led Zeppelin twice. The first time I was in the auditorium and it was great and the second time I was on the

No Vespas or sports cars for John Wallace, however...

balcony and it wasn't, because the PA system phases out.

It was the original band. It was Moon, Townshend, Entwistle and Daltrey. They did the trademark stuff. The jumping up and down by Townshend and the windmill chords that he was famous for. Daltrey throwing the mic up in the air, swinging it around and all that sort of stuff. And Moon just going absolutely mental on the drums. He was crazy.

And there was some humour. Moon actually stopped a number. I couldn't tell you what the set list was, but they did stuff from *Tommy*. There was one point where they were starting up on a number and Moon said 'excuse me, Mr Townshend, what key are we playing in?' And they had to stop the number. And I'm sure Townshend said 'B flat.' A drummer doesn't need to know the key. It was a piece of theatre.

And there was another point where Townshend actually unplugged his guitar and said 'we're going to do an acoustic number.' Now, how do you do an acoustic number in a venue that seats 2,400 people with an unplugged electric guitar? Those are the kind of things that I remember from the gig.

Post-Woodstock, people were getting into festivals and bands were having to have big PAs. And I suppose the word at the time was that The Who were one of the loudest bands in the world, the PA system was something like 10,000 watts. Now I saw The Beatles at the Caird Hall in 1963, and they were playing with eight Vox AC60s and a 100 watt PA system. I was only 12 years old. It was my birthday. And there was too much screaming going on.

ASSEMBLY HALL

1 JULY 1971, WORTHING

I WAS THERE: JOHN PARSONS

I was there introducing them when they did their trial run, the first time they ever played 'Won't Get Fooled Again'. I was doing the records and announcements. The first time I saw them was in the Florida Rooms at Brighton Aquarium before they were well known. I think they were called The High Numbers then.

The next time was at the Assembly Hall when Fred Bannister was putting them on. I think I worked with them about three or four times at the Assembly Hall and

Compere and booking agent, John Parson

it always used to be absolutely packed. It was 7/6 (37p) to get in. He used to put the bands on there and I used to do the announcements. It wasn't a disco. There was no such word as disco in those days.

We used to go in the dressing room and have a chat. Fred used to leave four bottles of drink in the dressing room and they were all gone by the end of the show. I had the Assembly Hall booked that night in 1971 for myself but Fred Bannister got in touch and said 'look they want to get out and do one gig. They've always liked Worthing. Can you let me have the hall?' So I did. I forget what band I'd booked but I managed to rearrange it. Fred booked The Who.

My ears were still whistling for about three days afterwards. I'm sure that's what's given me a hearing problem. They were very loud. They had a whole new set of WEM amplification. It was massive. It took the whole stage up. They had a reel-to-reel tape recorder which they used for the intro and that wasn't live at the beginning of 'Won't Get Fooled Again'. I remember the manager going on and switching it on. I reckon there were about two thousand people in that hall that night. It was only supposed to hold one thousand. There was water running down the walls because it was so hot. It was probably the best night ever there.

CENTER FOR THE PERFORMING ARTS

2 AUGUST 1971, SARATOGA SPRINGS, NEW YORK

I WAS THERE: KEVIN M KNAPP, AGE 13

I went with my brothers. The Who broke the attendance record with 35,000 people there, a record that still holds today. They were touring right after they put out *Who's Next*. The crowd was shoulder to shoulder and they were the first band to play there where they had to put a big screen outside so that everyone on the lawn could see the stage. It was an excellent show. Pete had his Esso jumpsuit on and, of course, smashed one of his guitars.

PUBLIC MUSIC HALL

12 AUGUST 1971, CLEVELAND, OHIO

I WAS THERE: ANDREW MIKULA

I saw The Who for the first time at Cleveland's Public Hall, which is still there, only blocks from the Rock Hall of Fame. It was my first major concert and The Who were absolutely my favorite band, touring in support of *Who's Next*. It was pretty early in the tour. Cleveland was one of their favorite places to play in the States and they gave a show to beat all shows. They started out with 'Love Ain't For Keeping' with Townshend jumping around all over the place, Daltrey doing the lasso whip with his mike cord and Moon flailing away liker a madman.

I was in the upper balcony and you could feel the balcony vibrating, both from the loudness of the band and people stamping their feet and screaming. In the encore, after they closed the regular set with 'Won't Get Fooled Again', Townshend smashed his guitar on stage during 'My Generation', something I read he had stopped doing for a while. Moon kicked his drum set over and there was smoke everywhere. It really looked a lot like the closing of their set at the Monterey International Pop Festival movie. It was the wildest thing I ever saw in my life and I was absolutely physically drained from the experience.

MR DEE'S MUSIC CLASS

AUGUST 1971, BOSTON, MASSACHUSETTS

I WAS THERE: BARRY BELOTTI, AGE 12

I was in seventh grade and my music teacher, Mr Dee, had an old reel-to-reel tape deck. We'd go into his music class and he used to play music. He was an old hippy. He wore a flowered tie and a three-piece suit and was bald as a cue ball, and the kids would make fun of him. But I listened. I liked him. Music was a big part of my life and I went on to play drums myself.

He put this reel-to-reel on and he said 'now, you kids, I'm going to play something from a British band called The Who. This is a record that just came out and it's called *Who's Next*'. He introduced the members and did a little background, and he pressed the button and played the whole thing. He would stop the song and explain about the ARP synthesiser. He was really into it.

Barry Belotti, meeting his hero, Pete Townshend. Right: the 12-year-old Barry with his treasured Who's Next

I listened to the whole thing, the class ended and I walked out to the door – and he used to stand right at the door as the kids would exit – and I said to him 'Mr Dee, where can I get this record?' He said 'Lechmere Sales, Barry.' Back then, that was it. There was only a couple of places you could buy a record, so I ran home and told my mom.

My father worked for the *Boston Herald*, in downtown Boston, and Mom said 'call your dad.' So I called my dad: 'Dad, on your way home can you go to Lechmere Sales and pick up this album? It's by a band called The Who and it's called *Who's Next*. So he gets home, with the record and we had spaghetti dinner, and then I put it on the big stereo console that my parents had. That was my introduction to The Who. And there's a photo of the twelve year old me holding my copy of *Who's Next*.

Another class, a few weeks later, Mr Dee plays the whole of *Tommy* and he explains it. 'So this is the wicked uncle Ernie…. This is where the followers start to rebel…' He was such a story-teller. I went back to thank him years later, after I got in with the fan club. He was still there, at the school. And I was able to thank Pete one night as well. I always felt like they were writing about me. But Townshend more than anyone, especially *Quadrophenia*.

Plans for a free concert in Hyde Park on 4 September 1971 in front of an anticipated crowd of over 200,000 were scuppered by the Greater London Council, leading Roger to comment 'it's bloody tragic that free shows are being sabotaged by authority.' Two weeks later, The Who performed to an audience of over 30,000, donating their fee to the Bangla Desh Relief Fund. The show was badged as Goodbye Summer.

OVAL CRICKET GROUND

18 SEPTEMBER 1971, LONDON

I WAS THERE: ROBBIE LATHAM

I was about 22 or 23. It was a packed house and at the time I was very, very lucky to get a ticket because my friend's mum worked for EMI in London and that's how I got the tickets. It was a brilliant night. The stage was at one end. The Oval holds quite a few thousand people. It was an evening performance and the weather was fine. From what I remember they all wore white boiler suits.

I WAS THERE: RONALD D. ROWLANDS

This charity gig also featured The Faces, Atomic Rooster, Eugene Wallace, America, Mott The Hoople, Quintessence, Lindisfarne, Grease Band and Cochise. Keith Moon came onstage brandishing a cricket bat. He then proceeded to use the bat as a drumstick for the first number. I was up on stage and have never seen a group work a crowd like that.

The smashing of the guitar was the only way to bring concert to an end. I was lucky enough to get a large chunk of Pete's Gibson SG guitar.

The crowd at the Goodbye Summer festival at the Oval cricket ground, 1971.

I WAS THERE: PAUL BASS, AGE 16

The first time I saw The Who was at a concert in aid of Bangladesh. This was my big outdoor concert. It was a great day and I enjoined most of the acts. The Faces were brilliant, playing Rod's new song 'Maggie May' and really getting the crowd going. Rod even auctioned his leopard skin suit. I thought 'nothing can follow this' and then the announcement came 'all the way from Shepherd's Bush' and The Who came on stage.

I think Keith played the first number with a cricket bat. They ran through some of the early singles, which really got the crowd going. By the time they played 'Won't Get Fooled Again' I had forgotten there was a band called the Faces. The Who were in a different league altogether.

I WAS THERE: MIKE WINTERS

I hitched it from Southport to London with a mate late summer 1971 to watch The Who at the Goodbye Summer concert held at the Oval Cricket Ground in Kennington. The concert was in aid of famine relief for Bangladesh and also to provide some much needed cash for Surrey County Cricket Club. The journey down was great, as after making our way to Knutsford Services, we got a lift on an empty coach that dropped us off in the centre of London. It was in the early hours so we found an all night cafe before heading off to the Oval later that morning.

The tickets were ridiculously cheap, about £1 from memory, bearing in mind that The Faces, Mott the Hoople, Atomic Rooster, Lindisfarne and others were also appearing. Introducing the acts was Jeff Dexter who was

a London club DJ. We were told that The Who had a new sound system and, after The Faces set, Jeff Dexter said 'if you think that was loud, wait until you hear The Who. They'll be rocking to them in Paris' and he must have been right.

They were of course brilliant. They played several songs from *Tommy* with 'Pinball Wizard' going down a storm along with 'Won't Get Fooled Again'. I think that Townshend had stopped smashing his guitar for a while but in answer to requests from the crowd he shouted 'you want my guitar? Alright then you can fuckin' have it' and

Mike Winters hitched from Southport to London to see the Goodbye Summer show at the Oval cricket ground

totally wrecked it. Pretty much as soon as he started, Keith Moon, who Townshend always said was a 'great joiner-inner', simply stood up and walked through his drum kit as though it wasn't there. Pure mayhem and everyone loved it.

I can't remember what time it all finished but everyone left the ground peacefully which, given the numbers – it was later reported that there were over 30,000 there. It was late afternoon the next day before we got back home to Southport, having spent most of the night at Scratchwood motorway services. I've seen The Who since but that was the only time I saw them with their original line up. Although I'd seen the Stones (who were also brilliant) in Liverpool only a week before, they were completely outshone by The Who.

UNIVERSITY OF READING

2 OCTOBER 1971, READING

I WAS THERE: NIG GREENAWAY, AGE 20

My mates and myself all lived in Reading and went along to a lot of gigs at the university. We were all just starting work and were not flush with cash. Some of us were doing further education so NUS rates were welcome. People from the town could go to events anyway, but had to pay a higher price. I had a mate who was a printer and the NUS cards didn't have pictures on them, so we all became

Nig Greenaway, leaning on the back of the car, has a quiet ponder

'students', even those who only studied music at the University on a Saturday night and sometimes at the disco on a Friday!

Who's Next had been out for a couple of months. I recall having the single of 'Won't Get Fooled Again' in a picture sleeve which I purchased after seeing the single performed in the 'album spot' on *Top of the Pops*. I didn't have the album until later due to the aforementioned cash shortage.

For once, the curtains over the large windows down one side of the student union hall were left open so those that couldn't get in could see from outside. We heard some commotion from outside and didn't know what was going on but later heard that someone had come up behind the crowd outside saying 'The Who are a load of shit.' This caused the fans out there to turn round to set about this guy, and then they realised it was Keith Moon!

Inside the hall, we were all waiting for the band to come on when a hand with a hammer appeared over the wall of amps and started laying into them – that was Keith again. I've seen them at least eleven times since but that was the only time with Keith and the band has never been so effectively introduced on any of those later occasions!

ODEON

20 OCTOBER 1971, BIRMINGHAM

I WAS THERE: GERALD CLEAVER

I can remember one of the times we saw them in Birmingham. We were right down the front on the left hand side. It was the Birmingham Odeon and there was obviously a problem that we weren't aware of, which was that the PA wasn't working. Because we were down the front anyway, it was so noisy that we didn't notice. So we were looking round saying 'what's the problem? It sounds perfectly good to us.'

And then the PA kicked in and we were almost knocked over. We then realised you didn't need the PA. You could see this big grin on Keith Moon's face because he knew what had happened.

OPERA HOUSE

22 OCTOBER 1971, BLACKPOOL

I WAS THERE: NICK MOORE

Me and my mate Phil Crowther went to see The Who playing their last ever gig in Blackpool. We had managed to blag two tickets from a lad at Blackpool Tech, by swapping them for my original copy of Black Sabbath's first album! The gig was absolutely fantastic. Daltrey was lashing his hair and jacket fringes around in gay abandon, Entwistle actually moved once or twice, and Moonie was an absolute thrashing loon.

Townshend was strangely subdued for the first 15 minutes, but after exchanging 'pleasantries' with two or three ignorant, swearing hecklers, he told them to go fuck themselves and then instantly switched to his imperious, windmilling best!

The whole gig was utterly superb and all of us in the crowd worked up a proper sweat by dancing like idiots – much to the chagrin of the house staff. My everlasting memory has to be when Moonie launched a drumstick into the crowd and I caught it. That stick took pride of place on my misused homework desk for at least three weeks. Sadly, the lure of a copy of *Live at Leeds*, signed by all four lads, and complete with all the original tickets and memorabilia, proved too tempting and I swapped it. And, NO, the album ain't for sale. I swear that my ears didn't stop ringing until we saw Led Zeppelin at Preston Guild Hall in 1973.

I WAS THERE: JEFF CALVERT

I was at the Opera House concert in 1971. I lived in Morecambe then and a group of about 15 of us got tickets but, as we couldn't drive, we travelled on public transport – Ribble Buses as it was then – to Blackpool. I remember wearing my brand new Ben Sherman shirt which, for those who remember that brand, were usually stripe or sometimes check in design. This was plain white and I thought I looked 'the business'. Not everyone believed it was genuine as it was plain so I repeatedly had to show the label to convince them.

The concert was superb and Roger Daltrey with his flowing long hair was incredible as was the volume! I remember seeing something fly through the air so I ducked out of the way, not realising that Keith Moon had launched one of his drumsticks into the audience. Someone three rows back got a great souvenir! A great day out and a fantastic concert for my first gig. Incidentally, I now live in the Isle of Man and saw Roger Daltrey a few years back, when he hit the road doing the *Tommy* tour. He can still do it and was again fantastic!

TRENTHAM GARDENS

24 OCTOBER 1971, STOKE-ON-TRENT

I WAS THERE: MICK FARR

We were a group of four lads age 14 and 15 who attended Who concerts in 1971, 1973 and 1975. We were working class lads who happened to pass the 11 plus so went to grammar school. We had very little money in comparison to some at 'Grammar' so we tended to excel in sports and trying to out do those with plenty of money and assets. As a kid I had heard 'Substitute' circa 1966 on the radio and was always fascinated by the lyrics, never quite working out what sort of 'suit was made out of sack'. I always found the stuttering in 'My Generation' slightly weird, probably because there were a couple of kids at junior school who did stutter. However it was 'Pinball Wizard' which got me hooked.

Were we Mods in 1967 and 1968. We had, a couple of years earlier, seen the fighting at Brighton and elsewhere and I had two older uncles who spoke about it. One was a Teddy Boy and the other a Mod. From what I saw and heard I felt more inclined to be a Rocker. However, then the parka appeared in the provinces. We bought them purely because of the fur around the hood and they were warm. Going to football games in those days was a cold affair. A parka, and plastic bags inside your socks, kept you warm.

Everyone had a parka and then the trouble started. The school confiscated anyone who turned up in one. 200 were impounded in one day out of 600 pupils. My mother was furious, mainly because of the cost and because she had bought it in the belief that it was a useful piece of clothing and nothing to do with gang warfare.

The parka quickly disappeared to be followed by the 'original skinheads'. These were lads from the local secondary modern. They hated us and we hated them. They liked music performed by black artists, which, morphed into Northern Soul and we decided we hated black artists and chose a more 'psychedelic' code of dress with a lot more denim and leather. Well, what we could afford which wasn't much. I would have died to be able to afford to buy a pair of Levi jeans or Stayprest. We could not, however, have our hair long. School had its own barbers for those that did! Finally the original skinheads ended up on the football terraces and became proper nasty skinheads and we spent two years running from them until Slade came along and gave them a band to latch onto.

We were shocked when one of us acquired a *Backtrack* album featuring The Who on one side and Slade on the other. For my 14th birthday my mum and dad bought me *Live at Leeds* out of a catalogue. I played it a lot and in particular 'Magic Bus'. From the paraphernalia inside the *Live at Leeds* album, I learned who The Who were. There was even a copy of their Woodstock contract. I had never been to a concert before and we read The Who were coming to Trentham in October 1971.

We walked. It was almost five miles but this was nothing to us as we regularly walked to Stoke City home games, which was three miles and we would do anything to save what money we had. We were eventually let in. It was a Sunday, so we had been queuing outside the Gardens for some time. We walked past three or four huge lorries, which must have brought the band's equipment, and a very large Bentley motor car parked almost outside the main entrance. The statue on the front grille of the car was missing and I thought 'were all Who fans thieves?' In later life I learned the statues on Bentleys and Rollers were retractable.

I had been to Trentham Gardens before to pick up sporting

awards but I had never been in the ballroom. It seemed huge. It quickly filled up. It was hot and the crowd noisy. Then they came on. Christ – the noise. The energy! It was louder than a plane taking off. They played a lot of *Tommy, Who's Next* and *Meaty Beaty*. The latter came out at the same time and I bought it some weeks later. I had a part time job, cleaning glasses at the bar at Port Vale Football Club, so for once I had a little bit of my own money.

Townshend, wearing white overalls, kept putting his microphone on the floor and dropping from a jump fully onto his knees with an almighty bone crunching thud. Was he nuts? Towards the end he pulled his trouser legs up to reveal two large knee protectors. Roger was all fringes and hair and microphone spinning and it took me a couple of Who concerts to realise the microphone was stuck on with a great deal of tape and that there were always a couple of spare microphones laid across the front of the stage in case they broke.

It was the energy I remember the most, and the smashing up of equipment at the end. Funnily, it seemed the right thing to do. The only disappointment was that they either did not do 'Magic Bus' or it was not as good as on *Live at Leeds*. And I thought there was a bit too much *Tommy* in the set.

ODEON CINEMA

30 OCTOBER 1971, NEWCASTLE-UPON-TYNE

I WAS THERE: HENRY RACE

We got tickets in advance. The Odeon was then a cinema. It wasn't a proper concert venue. It's all boarded up now and they're just about to pull it down. I'd just bought myself a portable tape recorder with the shittiest microphone ever and I recorded the show, (although I missed the last fifteen minutes because the tape had run out, I could only afford one tape). I sellotaped the little mic to the armrest.

I was there with two pals from school and we were on the front row of the balcony. On the tape you can hear a 17 year old me say, just before they came on, 'it's fucking marvellous when they start'.

I digitised the recording and uploaded it to a file sharing site and about 10,000 people grabbed it.

It was The Who's Next tour. They played numbers like 'Won't Get Fooled Again' and 'Baba O'Riley'. Moon was playing with the backing tracks in his headphones and Townshend, taking the mickey, said 'Oh, Keith finished before the tape. Most nights the tape finishes before him. So well done Keith.' I think he was playing Les Pauls by then. He had five customised Les Pauls numbered one to five. I think he was wearing his white boiler suit again. That's the benefit of being a certain age. You got to see all these cool bands.

RAINBOW THEATRE

4 NOVEMBER 1971, LONDON

I WAS THERE: VINCE JORDAN

It was the opening night at the Rainbow and The Who were the first band to play the theatre when it changed its name. I was sitting 13 rows from the stage, bang in the middle of the auditorium. Can Can girls brought The Who onstage after support act Quiver had finished.

The Who played a great set, including many tracks from *Who's Next*. 'See Me, Feel Me' had the customary searchlight illuminating the theatre and my ears were ringing for three days after the concert. It's still the best gig I've ever been to.

I WAS THERE: VAL MABBS

I was lucky enough to meet The Who and see them in later years, primarily through my work. I was working for *Record Mirror* and I started there in 1968. I saw them when they opened the Rainbow Theatre (formerly the Astoria) in Finsbury Park. That's one I know I definitely went to – a great concert.

In later years, Keith used to spend time at the London pubs that we frequented. For all that he could be crazy, I thought that he was a really nice guy. He taught me how to play drum paradiddles, which I had no idea of before. That was nice.

INGLEWOOD FORUM

9 DECEMBER 1971, LOS ANGELES, CALIFORNIA

I WAS THERE: PAUL JOSEPH

I was in High School at the time and living in Glendora, so it took about an hour to get there. I was totally blown away at how these four guys sounded. It was if the heavens opened up and poured forth an indescribable energy. Keith Moon was a show unto himself, a blur of motion and joy. Pete Townshend seemed to be upset with a roadie near the top of the show as he was yelling at someone off stage. It went on for a couple of minutes, with Pete looking displeased about something, pointing at this or that on the stage while he was yelling.

Other than that, it was The Who, as you'd expect them to be, astounding in every way. I know that I'll not witness again, anything that even comes close to what I heard and saw that night. They were truly amazing.

CIVIC AUDITORIUM

12 & 13 DECEMBER 1971, SAN FRANCISCO, CALIFORNIA

I WAS THERE: JIM FORSTER, AGE 14

It was the first concert I attended in the big city. I was a huge Who fan and this was shortly after the release of *Who's Next*. I remember threatening my father that I would ditch school to get a ticket. He went on his lunchtime and got me what may have been the last ticket available because he could only get one. I think the cost was $5.50. I saw them more recently in 2006 and paid $225!

Back then I was too young to drive so I convinced my brother to drive. I don't believe there was an opening act. The show was incredible and Keith was a jovial acrobatic clown. Pete was still into jumping high in the air and often landing on his knees. Roger had mastered the mic swing and his voice had not begun to show the slightest wear. I think they were probably at the peak of their ability to perform at a very physical level of high energy. This show still rates in the top five of all the concerts I have attended. My brothers both saw The Who in the late 1960s. My mom was an opera fan so one year my brother gave her the *Tommy* album for Christmas!

1972–74

1972 began quietly for The Who as a performing outfit. John's son Christopher was born in January and he was working on his second solo album in April and May. In late May and early June the band were recording at Olympic Studios in London. In August, the band embarked on a European tour, commencing with dates in Germany. On 3 October 1972 Roger's partner Heather gave birth to a daughter, Rosie Lea, at Pembury Hospital in Kent.

1973 was also a quiet year for The Who. They bought an old church hall in Battersea, London and started recording their new album, *Quadrophenia*, whilst Ramport Studios was taking shape. The Who toured *Quadrophenia* in late 1973, but problems with the sound system were evident to the audience.

HOLMSHURST MANOR

OCTOBER 1972, EAST SUSSEX

I WAS THERE: KEITH ROWLEY

Me, and my brother John, who was on holiday from Canada and our wives Beverley (she's my ex) and Rita (John's wife) were invited to Holmshurst Manor, Roger's mansion in West Burwash, East Sussex just after his daughter Rosie Lea was born in 1972. As I recall, Roger had paid £30,000 for it.

It must be worth several million pounds today. I remember that Roger needed a pen for something but couldn't find any in the house so we all had to troop down to his local pub, The Kicking Donkey, to borrow one! I don't know if he still has it but he had a room set aside at the time which was open house for the local kids to come in and paint, make a mess and generally do whatever they wanted to do.

MORGAN STUDIOS

NOVEMBER 1972, LONDON

I WAS THERE: DENNIS DUNAWAY

Keith came to the recording sessions at Morgan Studios in London, where we were recording the Alice Cooper album *Billion Dollar Babies*. Keith was wearing novelty glasses like the Groucho Marx model with the big eyebrows and moustache. But the nose was a limp penis. Lots of other musicians showed up – Donovan, Harry Nilsson, Rick Grech, Marc Bolan, and Flo and Eddie – and it turned into a super jam. Harry was too drunk to walk a straight line but he was playing piano and singing surprisingly well.

Everyone sounded great except Keith, who kept falling off the drum stool and couldn't come close to keeping time. However, he did manage to keep it together enough for great renditions of 'Bang a Gong' and Harry's song 'I Want You To Sit On My Face'. Everything else was sloppily incoherent, although Keith had everyone dying laughing.

TRENTHAM GARDENS

28 OCTOBER 1973, STOKE-ON-TRENT

I WAS THERE: STEPHEN BOSSON

I went to the concert with my best friend Neil Buckley. We were both in our early twenties and enthusiastic music lovers. I had seen many bands live, including Fleetwood Mac with their original line up including Peter Green, The Nice, Them with Van Morrison and the Small Faces. Both Neil and I loved The Who and had bought *Tommy* and *Who's Next*.

It was a cold, dry midweek evening in Stoke and the concert was a sell out. This was the first Who venue of the UK *Quadrophenia* tour – other legs included Wolverhampton and Manchester before dates in London. Pete Townshend had already stated in the press, prior to the release of the album and the start of the tour, that he wanted to fine-tune their performances by first visiting the 'lesser provinces' so that when performing in London they would be at their peak. This was a typically caustic Pete comment and controversial at the time. Trentham Gardens was quite an intimate venue, The Who's massive PA system being quite intimidating. The show opened up, highlighting Roger's long all blond curls, whirling mic and tassles, Pete's windmill guitar actions and attitude, John's stoic but brilliant bass and Keith's quite sombre but eye catching drumming.

After the first *Quadrophenia* album songs, you could sense the frustrations of the crowd and the band, who it seems were having problems translating the complex structure of the studio sound and performing it live. I clearly remember Pete changing his multitude of guitars very frequently. The crowd were by then calling out for more familiar Who songs, including 'Magic Bus', a song I personally wasn't aware of.

Townshend got so fed up with the interruptions that he abruptly stopped mid song and, very angrily and swearing loudly, said 'we are not playing 'Magic Bus'. We are trying to educate you Philistines!' They carried on playing a selection of songs from *Quadrophenia*, finishing with 'Bell Boy', with Keith Moon's vocal solo being sarcastically applauded by Townshend.

The second half of the set started with The Who playing their back catalogue, which received a very enthusiastic response from the crowd. They ended the set with 'Magic Bus', and I saw for the first time why the big concert song, that included solos from all the band members, was such a crowd favourite – a brilliant end to a controversial concert. Simply the best live performance I've ever seen in over 50 years of going to gigs.

I WAS THERE: MICK FARR

We were the guinea pigs. We would be the first people to hear

Quadrophenia at Trentham. By now I had bought a few Who albums and learned about their so-called Mod roots. This was a painful, muddled concert because we didn't really understand what Townshend was on about. It took years, until the film came out, before we did. There were no breaks in the music. There was a weird backing tape with sounds of the sea and seagulls which reminded me of Sgt Peppers. And that was crap as well. One of our brethren had bought the Beatles' famous album and we could not understand why anyone thought it was any good – we wanted short rocky songs, not long-winded stories.

The tape kept breaking down and we all found out who Bob Pridden was. He was being tortured on stage by Townshend as band and sound technician were not in harmony. A couple of years ago my Dad, in his mid eighties and still with us, spotted and bought me *The Who Live at Hull*. It was made the night after *Live at Leeds* as a back up. Hull, had been kept by Bob Pridden all those years and it was he who released it. He was right – it was better than the Leeds concert.

CIVIC HALL

29 OCTOBER 1973, WOLVERHAMPTON

I WAS THERE: GERALD CLEAVER

One of the best times I saw them was on the *Quadrophenia* tour. I know they didn't like it as much, but I saw them at Wolverhampton with a group of friends. One of the reasons that set them apart is they were very, very funny. They were usually quite chatty but very good at deflating each other or pricking any pompous comments from each other, usually Townshend. But whoever was being pricked didn't mind. It was part of the show almost.

The way that Moon used to rattle the drum kits and pretend he was introducing the orchestra and wave his arms about. And he'd always play up. If he threw the drumsticks in the air and actually caught them on the way back down, which was rare, he'd always have a big grin on his face and they'd all look at him. They had a tremendous banter. They were very, very funny. On stage they had a good joke, a good laugh.

We had to hang around afterwards until the bus came back to pick us up. That was the time I spoke to Entwistle, he had a chauffeur who looked quite like him.

They'd got three or four limousines outside – they obviously travelled in limos separately and went off separately. Entwistle came out first and we were all chatting to his chauffeur and he came over and joined in the conversation. I can't remember anything about the conversation other than that he was very friendly. People were very polite and there was no screaming or shouting. So he was quite affable and quite happy to come and join in the conversation. And then he got into the back and off he went at great speed.

I WAS THERE: ROB TITLEY

In the 1970's I had the privilege of seeing The Who three times in concert in consecutive years. On the first occasion, the ticket cost £2.20 and I had front row balcony seats.

The *Quadrophenia* album had been released three days previously and the band played a large amount of material from what was at that point in time a relatively unknown album. It didn't matter as the crowd went crazy right from the beginning.

ODEON CINEMA

5–7 NOVEMBER 1973, NEWCASTLE-UPON-TYNE

I WAS THERE: BRIAN DICKINSON

Myself, and some friends queued all night outside the Queens Cinema where the tickets were on sale the next day. It was a bitterly cold night and I recollect stealing early morning milk from the adjacent office doorways. My then girlfriend brought us soup on her way to work – the least she could do in view of the fact that I was getting her a ticket! Our tickets were for the second night but I believe that there had been an altercation between Pete Townshend and one of the roadies on the first night. Great concert!

I WAS THERE: BILL MONKS, AGE 18

I saw them for the first time at Newcastle Odeon on Bonfire Night 1973. There weren't just fireworks outside that night but fireworks on stage too when problems with the backing tracks on some of the *Quadrophenia* songs led to Townshend hitting one of the sound engineers and walking off stage! After a short delay, they were back and performed a blistering set.

I WAS THERE: IAN POTTS, AGE 14

I met the band outside their hotel in Gateshead on the same night that Pete Townshend went on to famously smash the stage up. Me, and a mate, both 14 years old at the time, heard they were staying at the Five Bridges Hotel just up the road from where we lived. As we had tickets for the Tuesday gig we thought we'd pop along. There was no one around but just as we were about to leave a guy came out and asked if we were waiting for the band. We said 'yes', and he said 'do you want to ride in their car?' pointing to a big Jag in the car park. Dead right we would!

ODEON THEATRE
NEWCASTLE ON TYNE

THE WHO

EVENING 7-30 p.m.
MONDAY
NOVEMBER **5**

REAR STALLS
£1·50
AA 41

No ticket exchanged nor money refunded
THIS PORTION TO BE RETAINED

It turned out he was only going around the corner to get petrol but we couldn't believe it, riding round the block in The Who's motor. It turned out the guy was the road manager. Five minutes later we were back round the front of the hotel. We got out and he opened the boot and then dished out these posters of Keith Moon lying naked on a bed. Then, best of all, the band came out, all four of them chatting away and signing the posters along with my ticket for the 6th and my *Who's Next* tape cover which I had brought with me. Sadly, two of them are no longer with us and the hotel is no longer a hotel, but my memories are still with me all these years later.

I WAS THERE: COLIN PETERSEN, AGE 15

I've seen The Who a number of times, most recently in 2014 at Newcastle Metro Arena on the 50th anniversary tour, the first big gig my son went to; he was transfixed, especially as the tickets were four rows from the front.

However, I saw the original *Quadrophenia* tour. In those days there was no internet, social media, etc. as we have now and no buying tickets a year in advance. You found out who was touring by word of mouth or via *Sounds, Melody Maker* or *NME*. You normally had to buy your ticket in person at the box office so for a group like The Who this meant an early start.

Colin (left) and his mate Jim.

I was still at school. I'd started going to gigs at 13, my first being Free at Newcastle City Hall. I'd seen the likes of Deep Purple and Led Zeppelin, and although Free are still my favourite band, The Who would be the biggest band I'd seen at that time of my life. I remember

my friend Jim and I caught the first number 39 bus from Washington
to Newcastle at about 4:45am but when we arrived at the Queen's
cinema where the tickets were being sold, there was already a vast
queue snaking away from the entrance. As we walked along the queue
we saw a group of school friends including Dave, with whom I still
attend gigs today.

We stopped and talked to them and, as no one protested, absorbed
ourselves into the queue, significantly forward from where we should
have been. Dave being Dave, he bought tickets for all three nights.
Jim and I plumped for the third night. I think our rationale was
that Newcastle was the beginning of the tour, or very early on, and
any glitches would be addressed by night three. Little did we know
about what glitches would occur on night one and how prophetic our
thoughts would be!

On the morning after gig one, we attended school avidly awaiting
a report from Dave. He told us about the backing track problems and
the fight between Townshend and the sound engineer, with Moon
joining in. He said the gig was great in some parts, shambolic in most.
On the morning of gig three we awaited his report from the previous
night. A bit subdued, he said, as if they were playing it ultra-safe and
not what you expected from The Who. Off we went on the Wednesday
evening, a quick pint or two in the Man In The Moon (or whatever it
was called at the time) and then off to our first ever gig at Newcastle
Odeon.

I can't remember the set list other than I believe all of *Quadrophenia*
– which I hadn't heard before – was played, plus the other tracks you'd
hope for or expect: 'Won't Get Fooled Again' et al. The atmosphere
was electric and the audience so, so excited. The band? Awesome. It
was if they'd thought about the previous two nights and said 'fuck it,
lets go for the jugular.'

They were very much in their prime at that time; Daltrey shouting,
screaming, caressing the lyrics, prowling the stages. Townshend; pent
up anger, aggression, a vast array of emotions absolutely flooding
out in his playing and singing. Moon; mesmerising, a whirlwind, still
the most exciting drummer I've ever seen. Not the best – the most

exciting. Entwistle, an un-moving presence for much of the time but with mesmerising bass runs. Probably the best Who gig I've attended, a few others run it close. Finally, the support band Kilburn and the High Roads – who we thought were poor. Later they morphed into Ian Dury and the Blockheads!

I WAS THERE: JOHN ROBSON

The first time I ever heard The Who was in the junior school when 'I Can't Explain' came out and I thought it was The Kinks and I remember saying to a lad in my junior school 'that The Kinks new record – great, innit?' and he said 'it's a band called The Who.' It was the final night of the *Quadrophenia* tour in 1973. I queued all night and it started to rain about 6 o'clock in the morning. There was a guy who got right to the front and he started pushing in and a copper got him by the hair and dragged him out. I thought 'you've waited all night for a ticket and you've let yourself down like that.'

On the night itself, we were eight rows from the front and all of a sudden we found ourselves on the grand piano in the orchestra pit right at the front. Me, and one of my pals got a drumstick each. We nearly got Pete Townshend's guitar because it was smashed to bits and lying on the stage. My mate leant across the stage and he nearly got his fingers on it when a roadie came on the stage and kicked it away. I've got the drumstick framed with the tickets at work. I run a barber's shop and I've got it framed on the wall. My mate hasn't got his drumstick any more. His mother threw his out. She thought it was just a scrap bit of wood.

I WAS THERE: JIM ROBSON

All appeared to be going well for the first part of the show. The Who came on and kicked off with 'I Can't Explain', 'Summertime Blues' and then 'My Generation. But we knew something was going wrong as they started to play tracks from the new album *Quadrophenia*. We heard later that the backing tapes weren't working correctly causing Pete Townshend to lose it.

You could see him shouting at a soundman at the side of the stage, (Bob Pridden), which turned into a scuffle with punches being thrown. Pete just went mad. He smashed his guitar on the floor of the stage and then ripped wires out of the mixing desk and amps. As all this was going on up on the stage, the fire curtain was brought down and we all sat in darkness for 20 minutes or so until The Who reappeared. They played a few songs but you could tell Pete was still furious and was swearing at the audience calling us 'fucking bastards'. He then smashed his Gibson SG guitar, threw one of his amps to the ground, and Keith joined in knocking his drums all over the stage. Quite a night!

LYCEUM

11–13 NOVEMBER 1973, LONDON

I WAS THERE: WAYNE PURSEY

Me, and my friend Malcolm queued outside for fifteen hours to get in. The queue became massive as the day went on. In the queue were some girls who had come from Australia to see Yes but couldn't get tickets. When the doors opened, the queue became wider and dangerous. People were pushing and if you fell you would have been crushed to death. That's not an exaggeration. People were looking out of surrounding office blocks to see what the commotion was about.

We eventually got into the Lyceum and I remember Roger Daltrey saying that if the crowd didn't move back and stop pushing, the show would be stopped. The lighting rigs were moving. I decided that I wanted a closer look at Keith Moon and managed to get to the front of the stage. I was staring at Keith Moon and he was staring back. He looked rough and unshaven, like someone who hadn't slept for days. I noticed drum sticks all over the floor. I was disappointed as I thought he caught the ones he threw in the air. He then did a very impressive paradiddle around the kit. At that point, I thought I'd better not get separated from my friend so I made my way to the back of the hall.

COW PALACE

NOVEMBER 20 1973, SAN FRANCISCO,

I WAS THERE: BOBBY ASEA

After seeing them in 1968, I attended many Who concerts, including the one where Keith Moon passed out during the show and the rest of the band had someone from the audience come up on stage and finish the show with them. It was the first stop on their new tour and had been a few years since I saw them last, and I was very excited to hear their new songs in concert. It wasn't too far into the show before it became noticeable that Keith Moon was off. As the set progressed his playing became worse, to the point where it got Pete's and Roger's attention.

They continued to play even when Keith started to wobble in his seat. A roadie appeared and attempted to hold Keith in place and finally it seemed that Keith was ok and the roadie left. At one point, Pete crossed back to the drum kit and it looked like he was trying to help Keith with his playing. It was when they were playing 'Won't Get Fooled Again' that Keith couldn't hold up anymore and collapsed into his drums. He was carried off the stage and left everyone in the house baffled and concerned. Roger and Pete addressed the audience and offered an explanation that Keith must have had eaten something bad that made him sick and that they would come back again in the near future to make up the show once Keith got better.

Apparently that idea didn't seem like it was going to work so instead Pete asked if there was anyone in the audience that could play drums. I had gone to the show with my best friend who happened to be a very good drummer and we thought that this would be an unbelievable opportunity for him to play with The Who. Unfortunately, our seats were not close enough to the stage to make way there before the hordes of others who rushed the stage. It wasn't long before some lucky guy was asked to join the band onstage. For obvious reasons the show lost its spark.

They had to play some songs that were not some of The Who's strongest and, musically the show went downhill. Not long after this, it

became known that it wasn't food poisoning that did Keith in that night. It turned out that his use of drugs and alcohol before the show was to blame.

I WAS THERE: MARTY MATHIS

You know what they say – if you can remember the Sixties, you weren't there. Well, that's the Seventies for me. As an innocent white suburban kid, I remember being wide eyed by the San Francisco culture of freaks and costumed people and open sexuality. I remember too the revolutionary Quadrophonic speaker system set up, with half the speakers located behind the audience. During the intro to 'Won't Get Fooled Again', I swear I could see the notes passing me and bouncing back towards the stage. Impressive!

INGLEWOOD FORUM

22 NOVEMBER 1973, LOS ANGELES, CALIFORNIA

I WAS THERE: MIKE HICKS

I was at the after concert party at the Sheraton Universal. I was management with The Wherehouse Record store chain at the time. My main recollection of that party was having about a five-minute chat with Roger Daltrey in the buffet line up. I recall him wearing a t-shirt that had BB King's album cover *Indianola Mississippi Seeds* on it. Roger was very friendly and down to earth. I told him how much I enjoyed his solo album, *Daltrey*, that had come out earlier in the year and he appreciated that. Also I asked him about a song I hadn't heard at the time that they played earlier in the evening, 'The Naked Eye'.

As *Quadrophenia* had just been released, I asked Roger what the next record might be like. He told me the next release would be a collection of unreleased tracks. Sure enough, *Odds and Sods* came out next summer. It was cool because the next day at the record store I was able to tell a customer that was a Who fan and that 'I was talking to Roger Daltrey last night and he told me their next album was gonna be a collection of unreleased tracks.'

I saw an empty chair at the table where Pete Townshend was sitting with Harry Nilsson, so I sat down for what might have been 30 seconds. I told Harry how much I loved his standards album and told Pete how much *Who's Next* meant to me. They were gracious and friendly and Pete asked my name. Then I got up and left. I vividly recall Keith in his gold lamé suit going from booth to booth, drink in hand, introducing himself. He sat down at our table briefly after welcoming us with "'ello mate!' I don't recall seeing John Entwistle there. The opening act Lynyrd Skynyrd was at the party. I saw Dobie Gray, whose hit 'Drift Away' was current and there were a few other TV celebrities there. I was on the fringe!

I WAS THERE: HARVEY KUBERNIK

I ran into Keith Moon in 1973 at the Century Plaza Hotel. I was doing a little bit of rock writing for the Hollywood press at the time. He was with Dean Torrance, of Jan and Dean, and Harry Nillson. In *Sixteen* magazine or *Melody Maker* he would still talk about surf music. So I bought Keith a t-shirt from the Con surf board company. It was a shop on Pico and Santa Monica Boulevard.

He really flipped out because he was a surf guy. He liked the wild abandonment of surf music. And he wore that t-shirt to the encore to one of the nights when The Who played the Forum out here in 1973. He wore it on stage for the encore! I was invited to the party after. That was kinda cool.

SUNDOWN THEATRE

18, 19, 20, 23 DECEMBER 1973, LONDON

I WAS THERE: DAVE BAGNALL

Probably the best Who performance I witnessed was at a place called the Sundown in Edmonton. It was one of those occasions where everything was perfect and it was only a week or so before Christmas and so everyone was up for it. I was never a student, but my mates were students and they lived in London so I went down and spent the weekend there. Everything just jelled together. It was not a big venue and the floor was stepped, like in a cinema, so wherever you stood you got a great view.

I WAS THERE: IAN MCKEAN

I was living in Farnborough at the time and made my way up to Edmonton via coach and train. We arrived about four hours early. Babe Ruth opened who were great but when The Who came on there was a big rush towards the stage and me and my mate got squashed up in front of Entwistle. It was very hot and Daltrey was handing out plastic cups of water. They played most of *Quadrophenia*, as I remember, which had only just come out. Townshend made some joke about not recognising people and even said he sent his own mother away at the stage door because he did recognise her. He was in his Spike Milligan mode. They actually did an encore (the only time I have ever seen them do one) and Townshend smashed his guitar, (again the only time I ever saw that). The encore went on for about 40 minutes. My parents had driven up to Edmonton and had to wait for ever while they played the protracted encore. I was very excited and was saying how Townshend had smashed his guitar but my dad was none too pleased. He had had an accident in the car just prior to me and my mate coming out of the venue!

In February 1974, nine weeks of production commenced on *Stardust*, the sequel to the film *That'll Be The Day*. Starring David Essex as Jim Maclaine, the film allowed Keith Moon to reprise his role as the drummer in Jim's backing band, The Stray Cats. One of the scenes aimed to recreate the hysteria of Beatlemania, with the Stray Cats in matching suits.

BELLE VUE

17 MARCH 1974, MANCHESTER

I WAS THERE: DONNA SULLIVAN, AGE 12

I was an extra in *Stardust*. David Essex was the lead singer in the band so we all had to dress in Sixties gear. I was at church that morning, so everybody was like 'what's she wearing?' And then I had to go to this gig at Belle Vue. So we're all in the audience and of course everybody's really pent up. And the producers were saying 'don't forget to scream, don't forget to scream!'

Keith Moon came on first. He was the drummer. And then the other people in the band came on. Everybody was a massive David Essex fan and so everybody's going bananas for David Essex and screaming 'David!' The producers are running up and down going 'It's Jim! It's Jim!' So we had to scream 'Jim!' But Keith was throwing his drumsticks into the crowd and then everybody started getting into Keith and going 'Keith! Keith!'

THE VALLEY

18 MAY 1974, CHARLTON ATHLETIC FOOTBALL GROUND, LONDON

I WAS THERE: MICK BROPHY

This was the first time I'd seen The Who and the best £2.50 I ever spent. I had no money, so the concessions running out didn't bother me, and although there was some unrest in the crowd I didn't notice any of the violence. In fact I don't remember much about anything around me – apart from it being sunny – as I found a really good spot, close enough to see the sweat, and was mesmerised all-day by the great line-up. As a Free and Mott the Hoople fan, Bad Company did it for me and Stevie Marriot kicked ass, almost stealing the show.

Come The Who and I was absolutely gob-smacked! I knew most of the songs, worshipped Townshend's song-writing and loved the records. But live they were something else. Tremendous power, uplifting rather than bone-crunching, and I didn't know where to look next. Haymaker-guitars? Whirling-dervish microphones? Every cymbal at once? Or the serene bass man with the mad spider fingers? The whole thing seemed on a knife-edge. Later reports talked of sound problems but I didn't notice any, and I remember some moments when the band seemed like they were collectively mind reading their cues for the changes. It was inspiring. It was exhausting. It sucked me in deep. Then it was over. An hour plus felt like 15 minutes and I was on such a natural high afterwards I can't remember how I got home that day.

A few weeks later a pal suggested my birthday drink location to be the pubs around Twickenham. After a few pints, and much blithering on from me about Charlton, 'would you like see Pete Townshend's house?' seemed like a great idea. So down a path by the side of the Thames staggered the two drunken numptys. 'That's Pete Townshends house!' he slurred. And so it was. Complete with a tall guy with a instantly recognisable proboscis having a chat with next door at the end of their respective gardens. What I wanted to say was 'Mr Townshend, you are God and your band changed my life last month. Please can I shake your hand?' What I actually said was 'oh shit! It's him!' and we legged it.

I WAS THERE: JEFF BERRY

The weather was a little grey going up by train with friends but when we got there it was dry with sunny intervals. The Who were top of the bill with the artists that preceded them including Lou Reed, Humble Pie, Bad Company, Montrose, Lindisfrane and Maggie Bell, who I wasn't the biggest fan of. I can't remember what order the artists played in but it was a fun day out. I was boozed up but not too drunk.

I WAS THERE: ROB TITLEY

The second time I saw The Who was at Charlton's football ground for the 'Summer of '74' show. The price of the ticket was £2.50 and, as a young 16 year-old living in Birmingham, I made the trip to London to meet up with my pal who was studying at Canterbury University. The gig was at the old Charlton Valley ground, in front of an 80,000 crowd. Although my memory of the day is blurred, I recall Roger Daltrey twirling his mic, Pete Townshend dressed in white Oxford bags and Doc Martens and him whirling away on 'Baba O'Riley' and 'Won't Get Fooled Again'.

I WAS THERE: LINDA SWEEDEN

I was a schoolgirl just turned 16. My fellow classmates were into The Jacksons and The Osmonds, swooning over Donny! My friend Denny and I were different. We loved rock music and couldn't get enough of The Who. Denny's older brother said they were appearing at Charlton's Valley football ground. We begged him to get us tickets. They were on sale for £2.50. I only had a pound but promised I'd pay him with next week's school dinner money.

The day of the concert arrived and we caught the train from Hitchin to Kings Cross and the tube on to Charlton. I'd never seen so many people. I was scared but buzzing with adrenaline at the same time. I felt so grown up! We got into the ground quite early, but the football pitch was filling up fast. We sat down on the grass and claimed our space about 10 deep from the stage. We had no food or drink, just a can of Coke on the train. I guess we hadn't thought that one through.

There was a heavy smell of dope in the air and the midday sun was beating down on my bare arms. There was no sun factor protection in those days. On came Montrose. I'd never heard of them and they were loud but good. Next came Lindisfarne and I can remember the crowd getting involved singing 'we can have a wee wee, we can have a wet on the wall' from 'Fog on the Tyne'. Bad Company were next and I loved Free and Paul Rodgers' voice so I loved them. Then there was Lou Reed sporting bright bleached yellow hair but I only really knew 'Walk On The Wild Side'.

Humble Pie and Steve Marriott were amazing. I looked around and noticed the crowd getting thicker and thicker. It was more than ten deep in front of us now and every little gap was filled up. I was desperate for a wee and a drink, in that order, but if we separated we would never find each other again! But we had to go, so went together. Maggie Bell was on and we didn't care about missing her.

When we came back we just had to push and weave our way to the front. There were two huge burly blokes stage centre right at the front. I was a tiny blonde just about five foot and my skinny friend was not much taller. I cheekily asked them if we could sit in front of them as there was no way we would be blocking their view. They agreed and started chatting us up. We didn't mind as we had the best view of all! It seemed to take forever waiting for The Who. They came on at about 8.30pm and we'd been there since midday! The sun was going down as they exploded onto the stage with 'I Can't Explain' and, my God, I was truly in heaven. Tears of joy streamed down my face. Roger was even more gorgeous in real life than on camera! He wore what looked like two chamois leathers laced together, showing off his amazing bronzed torso. At that moment I fell in love!

They did a couple of covers and then launched into my all time favourite 'Baba O'Riley'. I screamed as one of the burly chaps lifted me up onto his shoulders. I was flying high, almost face to face with Roger as he twirled his mic round and caught it every time! The lights turned blue and I guessed what was coming – 'Behind Blue Eyes'. I burst into tears again as I felt every word. The crowd went crazy singing along to 'Substitute' and 'I'm a Boy'.

After 'Tattoo', serious John in his glittering emerald green jacket did 'Boris The Spider', his deep voice matching his bass guitar, which was mesmerising. A few tracks from *Quadrophenia* followed, with cheeky Keith Moon playing his part singing 'Bell Boy'. I remember trying to count his drums. I'd never seen such a big drum kit, complete with gongs! 'Won't Get Fooled Again' was the song of the night for me. The energy on stage was phenomenal. Pete was windmilling like crazy, Roger was marching on the spot and, as the song built up to a crescendo, Roger let out the scream of all screams 'yeeeeaaaahhhhh!' His voice penetrated my every cell as the burly chap behind me picked me up and threw me in the air like a child!

After 'Pinball Wizard' came 'See Me Feel Me' and, as I was only feet away, I imagined Roger was singing just to me. I put out my arms as if to try and touch him. Oh how I wished I could.....

They went off stage and the crowd stomped and shouted 'more more more! Who Who Who!' To the crowd's delight they came back for another six songs including '5.15', 'Magic Bus' and, of course, 'My Generation'. As all good things, the day had to end. We were on a high. It took ages to get out of the ground and when we finally reached the tube station it was gone midnight and the tube station was closed. We were tired, hungry, thirsty and sunburnt and we had to walk across London to Kings Cross station. But we were happy!

In the spring of 1974, production began on the filming of *Tommy*. Roger Daltrey was cast as the lead, Keith played the role of Uncle Ernie and The Who appeared as themselves in concert scenes shot at the Guildhall in Portsmouth.

PORTSMOUTH

MAY & JUNE 1974, PORTSMOUTH

I WAS THERE: GLENN FEARONS

The filming of *Tommy* at Portsmouth was absolutely brilliant. Before we were married, we used to go down and stop in a hotel. As we were driving in the taxi to the hotel, we saw the pier and saw that the end of the pier was missing. It had burnt down, and we mentioned it to the taxi driver and he said 'oh, it's that film crew

Daltrey on location for Tommy and Glenn Fearons (right)

that's here.' As we were walking around the shops, most of the young people had got *Tommy* badges on and I kept looking at them and thinking 'what's this 'Tommy'? What's it about?'

And then one day we were having a walk down to the beach from up near the castle and we looked down and we could see a car with a camera on the top and it was filming. So we walked down and there was Roger Daltrey with Robert Stigwood at the side of him, running along to 'I'm Free'. They were filming that bit in the film where's he's just got denim jeans on. I've got a lovely picture of him with Stigwood. He's just stood in the middle of the photo with his hands on his hips. Ken Russell was directing and he was obviously looking across to Ken who must have been saying something to them. I tried to get Ken Russell's photograph but there was this big guy stood there who said 'no, you don't take photographs of him'.

But I got quite a few photos. Roger Daltrey looked really fit. It was nice to see it happen like that. There were maybe fifty people there watching it. It made the holiday a little bit more exciting. And then we knew what all the *Tommy* badges were and everything. We were only there a week. We just happened to drop in on a lucky day.

THE LAKE DISTRICT

AUGUST 1974, CUMBRIA

I WAS THERE: JULIA PRIOR

I remember a week spent with Roger Daltrey in August 1974. We were on a family holiday. He was in the Lake District filming *Tommy* and, as we were all staying in a small family run hotel, whichever table you were allocated determined where you sat for breakfast and dinner for the duration.

We shared a table for the week. Roger 'fell in love' with our daughter Selina and on the last night he wrote a 'ditty' to her on the back of the menu. We had typical Lake District weather so Roger let us have his poncho!

1975 This was to be an eventful year for The Who, not least due to the release of the movie *Tommy*, leading to Pete Thownshend being nominated for Best Original Score at the Academy Awards. Keith Moon released his solo album *Two Sides of the Moon* in the USA in March. The album was released five weeks later in the UK.

The Who By Numbers tour began in October 1975, and took up most of the band's time in 1976. Record label Polydor wanted the band to promote the album but the set list essentially followed a trusted pattern of greatest hits.

MANN'S WILSHIRE THEATRE

19 MARCH 1975, LOS ANGELES, CALIFORNIA

I WAS THERE: HARVEY KUBERNIK

Keith Moon invited me to the *Tommy* movie premiere out here in the US which happened a week before the UK premiere. I saw Keith Moon and he gave me a big hug.

He was living in Malibu, and I knew Moonie a bit from the scene. I wasn't a party guy. I'd see him down at restaurants. Once Ringo moved to town, there was a party every night. I was invited occasionally as a journalist from *Melody Maker*. I could be trusted, I really didn't do drugs, I never drank and I wasn't there to take their chicks from them.

People like Keith would want to know about import records. I would steer him towards some good record stores. People like David Bowie went to these, they liked seeing their stuff on the walls. They weren't that jaded yet. The American domestic album releases were still a little bit different from the British versions that came out earlier. The extra tracks and different album covers and things like that. In Hollywood you could get both editions if you were a record collector.

I went to some of the recording sessions when Keith did his solo album for MCA Records, I interviewed Keith for a half page in *Melody Maker* in 1975 about his solo album. There was some crazy madness going on there. But I remember hearing a playback of him covering 'Don't Worry Baby'. The guy liked surf music. He wasn't the greatest singer but he had great energy. He really propelled the group.

March 1975 saw the release of *Tommy*, the Ken Russell directed film of The Who's 1969 album. It featured a star-studded cast, including the band members themselves (most notably, Roger Daltrey, who plays the title role), and Ann-Margret, Oliver Reed, Eric Clapton, Tina Turner, Elton John, Arthur Brown, and Jack Nicholson.

NEW BINGLEY HALL

3–4 OCTOBER 1975, STAFFORD

I WAS THERE: MARTIN JONES

They were the first group to play at Bingley Hall and we were able to see them from the balcony, which was subsequently outlawed for health and safety reasons. But it was a fantastic venue. I'm pretty sure they had the first ever laser show that night and despite audience encouragement I don't recall any guitar smashing or drum wrecking. All the top groups played Bingley. In summer, it was the venue for the cattle show of Staffordshire County Show so it was very barn like! The crowd noise banging on the walls inspired Queen to write 'We Will Rock You'.

We could drive by now so off we went to Stafford and a giant cowshed. It was a cowshed – later in life I would become a bank manager in Stafford, and Bingley was used for agricultural shows. It could hold around 8,000 people. I was very near the front. I stood next to a 30 year old guy who was Australian. He told me his family was wealthy and he followed The Who around the world and this had started when he had seen them in Melbourne two years earlier. I thought, 'my God, this was a fan.'

On stage, matters got out of hand. It transpired after a few numbers that the band could not hear each other. Townshend got very, very frustrated and started having a go at Bob Pridden (sound man). Then Roger started singing the wrong song to an intro and to make matters worse Keith was drumming a completely different beat. Townshend accused Moon of being drunk, at which point Keith climbed out of his drums and threw a vodka bottle at him. I know it was vodka and empty – I was that close.

Roger broke up the ensuing melee and they carried on. To me it was disturbing. These were my working class heroes. They had gone to grammar school like me (except for Roger) and they were arguing and drunk on stage. Although we had seen many bottles and other things thrown at football matches, on stage this was seriously dangerous. Bizarrely, towards the end of the concert Moon apologised to Townshend and us, and it was as if nothing had happened. I have been a Who fan since 1965. My youngest son and his best mate, both 28, are very keen fans and see them a lot. It was the sheer energy at the concerts which was the draw and which is still evident today. They tore down the perspex drum guard at Glastonbury and Hyde Park because they could not hear Zak, a lesson learned many years earlier at Bingley. I have always liked their anti establishment stance and Townshend's songs, as Roger always now says, were a joy to sing.

BELLE VUE

6TH OCTOBER 1975, MANCHESTER

I WAS THERE: COLIN JOY

This concert was a bit of a disappointment as the crowd were hoping

The Who would play their *Quadrophenia* set but only songs from *Tommy* were played. It was the last time I saw Keith play. The King's Hall was inside the Belle Vue Zoo Gardens, located within the fairground complex. It was a popular venue and attracted the likes of The Rolling Stones, Status Quo, Deep Purple, Bowie, T.Rex, Jackson 5 and David Cassidy – all top guns – but was better known for its weekly Saturday ITV *World of Sport* wrestling programmes and the Christmas circus!

The Who opened-up with 'Substitute' at full volume and a blinding strobe light display and continued knocking out their catalogue of hits, before entering their *Tommy* opera suite, much to the disappointment of the crowd. Pete Townshend was getting angry and was being heckled by the audience, but he kept his cool. Keith Moon was his usual flamboyant self-emphasising drumming of all the words to the songs in his trademark style and even at one stage decided The Who didn't need him for some of the songs and walked off the stage! It was that kind of night but they should have played *Quadrophenia* as we all expected. Only 'Drowned' and '5:15' made the set. A very noisy night!

I WAS THERE: MARK ELLISON, AGE 15

The first time I saw The Who was just before my 16th birthday, and it was my very first gig as it happens. Times were very different then. People go to gigs at 5 years old now! It would have been announced in the *NME* about tickets going on sale. Whatever day the *NME* came out I think it was the day after that, tickets went on sale and, given my age, it must have been school holidays. Either that or it was a weekend because I went along with my cousin, Jeffrey who is a year older than me. I called him and said 'Who, Who, Belle Vue' because somewhat naively, or maybe not in the event, I kind of assumed that we needed to go an queue up for tickets now, rather than tomorrow morning or they'd all be gone.

So, that same day, whatever day it was, I was supposed to do the household shopping. My parents went to work and had left me a shopping list and some money and some shopping bags. So basically I left a note for my parents saying 'I've gone to Belle Vue to queue up overnight for tickets and I'll see you tomorrow. I've taken the shopping bags with me to do the shopping.'

So we hopped on the train, went o Manchester and I did the bloody weekly shop. So I'd got two old granny shopping baskets full of stuff – fruit and veg and stuff – and took the bus to Belle Vue. I had the stuff with me as we joined the queue. There was about six people there before us and I think it was late afternoon when we arrived there. So I was in the queue with these shopping bags full of stuff, full of groceries, and then just hunkered down for the rest of the night. 15 years old and daft, you know? I suppose, if nothing else it were bloody cold overnight, so it wouldn't go off quickly.

We had a bit of a chat with the other people who were there before us, not much, just hello because we were young and gauche and not really able to have a conversation with people who were much older and hairier! And then over the rest of the evening and overnight the queue started to grow and grow and at some point, around about 10 or 11 at night, the local radio turned up and had a little interview with a couple of people. Not us. And I remember asking the guy immediately behind us in the queue about the buses carrying on all night. Being a local provincial lad, I was used to the buses stopping at 10 or 11 o'clock at night, so I said 'when do the buses stop?' and he said 'no, they carry on all night' and I thought that was amazing, that big city sort of thing.

I don't remember a lot then, just being absolutely bored out of our minds for the rest of the night and it getting bloody cold. Across the road there must have been an alley way or a ginnel or something, because there was somewhere to stretch your legs but mainly, when you wanted to go for a pee, everyone was getting up and going down the alley throughout the night, including me at one point because I just couldn't hold it any longer. But that was a bit weird because I remember it was absolutely pitch black.

Anyways that was the night – absolutely no sleep or anything like that. The box office opened at 9 o'clock in the morning. I went in and got the tickets but that's when I realised that I don't do sleep deprivation well, because by that point I was barely conscious and I had no idea how I managed to pass over the money for the tickets. If you'd asked me my name, I wouldn't have known it. So that's a common thing for my two Who gigs – a lack of sleep. I couldn't think straight at all. When we left, there was a chip shop nearby who'd obviously seen a chance – 'hundreds of people during the night queuing, they'll all be starving' – so this chippy was open at nine in the morning so we called in and got chips and gravy.

The support on the day was The Steve Gibbons Band and I thought they were just awful. They were pedestrian and lacking in variation but that might have been really unfair because I didn't know any of this stuff.

Now The Who, by contrast, just exploded. I've got in my head that they started with 'Heaven and Hell' but I know that's wrong. They would have started with 'Can't Explain' and then 'Substitute' and then 'Heaven and Hell' but in my head 'Heaven and Hell' was first and I don't know why. Absolutely classic set of the period.

And in those days of course they were very famous for not doing encores but at the end there was still this absolutely massive clamour. I mean, I had nothing to compare it with, but people were saying afterwards that this was the best they'd seen them for years. So there was this massive clamour for a encore at the end, and you could see off the side of the stage, Keith Moon was kind of gesturing as though he was ringing a bell. Obviously he was trying to get 'Bell Boy' chants up or whatever going and there was every indication that they would actually, unbelievably, play an encore. That's how good it was. But they didn't and the house lights went on. I'd arranged a lift home and in the car the local radio that was reporting on the gig was saying that apparently the band had wanted to play an encore which was very, very unusual, but that Belle Vue management wouldn't let the back on because they'd run over time. Which is a bit sad, isn't it?

APOLLO THEATRE

15 & 16 OCTOBER 1975, GLASGOW, SCOTLAND

I WAS THERE: MICHAEL MALONE

I'd been listening to The Who since 1972. When I heard that tickets were going on sale for the October gigs at The Apollo I queued out all night listening to bootlegs on cassette with a great feeling of anticipation as the doors opened. I purchased 2 tickets for each night for £8.00.

On the night of gigs the support act was The Steve Gibbons Band who had a hit with 'Tulane'. On the first night The Who played 24 songs. Highlights for me were Pete using a music stand during 'Squeeze Box' and then Keith standing on his drum kit conducting fans shouting for 'Bell Boy' and Pete telling him and us they were not singing it tonight.

After the second gig, I waited round the back and shook hands with Roger, Pete, John and Keith as they came out a door and went straight into a limo. Roger asked if we had been at the previous night's show and, if so, what night did we prefer? I told Roger how, from my vantage point on the famous Apollo balcony, I saw him throw the mic stand into the backstage area and a roadie having to duck as it just missed him. Since then I've seen The Who at Parkhead, The SECC, The Hydro, The O2 Arena, and Hyde Park but non of these can beat the first time.

I WAS THERE: JOHN WILSON

It was the greatest concert I have ever been to. Keith was immense that night. They all were. However, he appeared to be in a huff because, even though there were lots of folks shouting for 'Bellboy', Keith said to stop shouting for it because 'that particular number isn't in the show tonight.' I remember laughing loudly at that. It was just a truly magical night in Glasgow.

GRANBY HALLS

18 – 19 OCTOBER 1975, LEICESTER

I WAS THERE: DAVE BARBER

They were appearing at the (now long gone) Granby Halls Leicester as part of The Who by Numbers tour. They were late coming on stage. They had appeared two nights earlier in Glasgow and apparently Keith Moon had been arrested for driving his car into the hotel lobby! Several announcements were made saying that there were doubts as to the band performing because of Moon's absence. Then it was announced that he was on his way and the helicopter had just landed. Rock 'n' roll lifestyle or what?

I WAS THERE: IAN SMITH, AGE 19

I will always remember Keith Moon arriving late on stage and saying 'I've just been to see my probation officer!' He had in fact been apprehended in Scotland after assaulting a coffee machine at the airport and was then flown down to Leicester by helicopter!

EMPIRE POOL

23 OCTOBER 1975, WEMBLEY

I WAS THERE: ROB TITLEY

This was the final time I saw The Who. It was the Empire Pool, Wembley. The ticket cost £2.25 and I made the train journey from Birmingham to London. What a gig! They had just released *The Who by Numbers* album and it was a superb show, my main memory is of Townshend whirling away on his Gibson. Unbelievable memories.

I WAS THERE: KEVIN RICHARDSON

This gig was one of the first I had seen in London and it was fantastic. We drove up on the day and picked up two hitch-hikers en route. These guys were huge Beatles fans and we had a big discussion about who were the better band. They had to agree with us in the end that The Who were better as otherwise we were going to make them get out and walk!

At the gig, I remember Keith

Kevin Richardson proudly brandishing his ticket on the day of the gig

being suspended in a harness and swung round the auditorium. I can't remember what he was shouting but I think it was something about how uncomfortable his testicles were!

PHILIPSHALLE

31 OCTOBER 1975, DÜSSELDORF, GERMANY

I WAS THERE: CHRISTIAN SUCHATZKI

I'd been a Who fan for six years when the band came to Germany in the autumn of 1975 for a few gigs. Still a pupil, I was barely able to afford a ticket for 18 DM (approx. 9 Euro). When I told my friends and school mates that I wanted to go to a Who concert and be in the front row, they replied 'are you crazy? In the front row you'll get hurt by a broken amplifier.' So I took a seat in the second row.

Right after school I hurried to the concert hall and waited outside excitedly for it to open. Finally the doors were opened. A giant man – I think he was a member of the Hell's Angels who were hired for security reasons – made the single entrance with his huge body even smaller so that everyone could get in only one at a time. Of course, pushing and shoving from all sides towards the only entrance began immediately. This was really a dangerous situation and for everyone involved it was difficult not to tumble and fall as they tried to get in. Somehow I managed to be one of the first to get in.

Inside the hall the atmosphere calmed down until The Who entered the stage with a steamrolling performance of 'Substitute' followed by an equally powerful 'I Can't Explain'. I was staggered how four musicians were able to produce such a loud and enormous power. Keith Moon bashed his drums like there would be no tomorrow, Roger Daltrey's voice was loaded with huge energy while John Entwistle stood in his corner playing a thunderous bass and now and then took a nip from the two beverage bottles which were mounted at his microphone stand. Pete Townshend was in a slightly bad mood, not regarding his guitar playing but his temper. During the show, he got more and more offended by a few people, probably press reporters or security staff members, chatting in the pit right in front of him. Finally he took a cup and poured the contents over them while making some enraged gestures in their direction. With 'Squeeze Box' and 'Dreaming From The Waist', The Who played only two and virtually unknown songs from their new album *The Who By Numbers*. A set of nine numbers from *Tommy* followed and was accompanied by a stunning green coloured laser show. When they continued with 'Summertime Blues', finally everyone in the audience climbed on the seats and went berserk. The Who's performance culminated in an electrifying version of 'My Generation' and at the end of 'Won't Get Fooled Again', Roger Daltrey and Pete Townshend and a superior motivated Keith Moon destroyed some pieces of their equipment. The whole stage floor was covered with broken drumsticks, damaged tambourines and bits of wood. Roger threw some parts of them into the audience and one of Keith's broken drums sticks right in my direction where I luckily caught it. The drumstick was not the only reminder of my first Who concert. I also had a ringing in my ears, which lasted two more days and an everlasting enthusiasm for an awesome, powerful and incomparable rock band.

THE SUMMIT

20 NOVEMBER 1975, HOUSTON , TEXAS

I WAS THERE: JOHN RAMSEY, AGE 17

A few days before The Who's opening American tour gig, we – OK, my Mom actually – called the Summit in Houston, Texas to see if any tickets were available. As it turned out, a lady who worked at the Summit had reserved a bunch of seats on the floor near the front for her daughter and her friends for her daughter's birthday. The party fell through, so we scored four 7th row tickets at the last minute. Pure dumb luck. Thanks, Mom! And Summit lady with her daughter, who we waved to. It was the greatest rock show I have ever seen. I remember that when The Who took the stage, people from the back came rushing up the aisles past us in our reserved floor seating. This freaked out my 15-year old brother, who thought it was very dangerous. I dismissed his concerns, but of course the Cincinnati disaster occurred four years later. The concert has been released on DVD recently, some forty plus years later. The Summit had a policy of filming all performances.

PONTIAC SILVERDOME

6 DECEMBER 1975, PONTIAC, MICHIGAN

I WAS THERE: CAROL DRABEK MOGGO, AGE 18

The place was packed with over 75,000 fans and festival seating and they refused to come on until the crowd backed off in the front of the stage. Once they came on they rocked the house! It is one of my top ten concerts. Keith Moon was a wild man on those drums!

I WAS THERE: DENNIS PUTNAM, AGE 19

A few friends and I went together from Royal Oak, Michigan, which was about an half hour away. It was a cold day, because I remember standing outside the venue for a while, along with all the other concertgoers. After a time, the lines of people started to move slowly as we were let inside. All of a sudden the waves of fans began to part to the left and the right. I soon saw why: There was a guy bent over and vomiting onto the snow-covered cement. Too much to drink I expect! We finally got inside and found our seats. The Silverdome is huge and it was jammed full! Eventually the show started with the reggae group Toots & the Maytals. I remember that my friend John was really into them. He stood and danced for most of their set. John recently told me that I smuggled in test tubes of alcohol into the building. I don't remember this, but it is plausible.

The Who eventually took the stage and the show was great! The only song I have a specific memory of was the last one, 'Won't Get Fooled Again'. When Roger Daltrey screamed 'Yeeeeeaaaaaah' towards the end, all these laser lights shot out from the stage in an arc. Tremendous! The band linked arms, bowed, said 'thank you' and left the stage. Sadly there were no encores but the show was fantastic!

CIVIC CENTER

13 DECEMBER 1975, PROVIDENCE, RHODE ISLAND

I WAS THERE: BARRY BELOTTI, AGE 16

The Who is my band. I worked for a fan club fanzine in the late Seventies which was called *Who's News*. It went from 75 until The Who decided to do their first farewell tour in 1982. I had two friends who started up the magazine. They approached The Who and said that they wanted to start this fan club, this magazine, and The Who said 'oh sure.' And they were dealing with the New York office mainly, here in the States.

And The Who said 'what do you need? We'll gladly fund it.' My friend Mark Cohen was 'no, we don't want any money. We're going to do the whole thing ourselves. We just want tickets whenever we want them and a pass to get backstage.' He was an auditor at the time, in downtown Boston and making very good money. He was just doing it out of fandom. Any of the early shows we saw, we were always in the front and at the parties after the show. Keith was my favourite. They came here in 73 and my mom wouldn't let me go to the show. They came in 75. I was 16. I still didn't have a driver's license but I said 'I'm gonna go see them.' Me and my friend Richie bought tickets and we took a Greyhound bus down to Providence, Rhode Island. It was general admission seating and the first time I was going to see my favourite band.

It was *The Who By Numbers* tour. The show was amazing. Keith Moon came out and did a somersault. My dream had come true. We stayed so that we were almost the last people in there after the show and we watched them break down the whole stage. We were so excited that by the time we left the venue the buses had stopped running back to Boston and we couldn't get home. So I called my dad from a phone booth and said 'Dad, the buses have stopped running.' He said 'call Uncle Louie.' Luckily his brother Louie lived down there and so his brother came and picked us up and we spent the night there and he drove us home the next day.

HAMMERSMITH ODEON

21 – 23 DECEMBER 1975, LONDON

I WAS THERE: KEITH CARPENTER

I saw them at Charlton football ground in the mid 1970s. Roger Daltrey and Pete Townshend stole the show that day. It was pouring down and they both used the rain to slide around the stage. I also saw them at a Christmas party concert at Hammersmith Odeon. It was a really raucous concert right from the off, with Keith and Pete appearing to have an argument during the concert. Keith was really on form that night – he was a complete legend.

I WAS THERE: GERALD CLEAVER

I went to a couple of their Christmas shows. At one of them they had Graham Chapman, of Monty Python fame, as the support act. He got a lot of stick. He either wasn't very funny or people were expecting The Who. He wasn't on long. Keith Moon came out, picked him up and carried him off. I think the two of them were friends. The programme was a calendar. I've got another Who

programme which is made up to be like a *Playboy* magazine. And of course the centrefold is Keith, stark naked.

1976–77

1976 was Keith Moon's final year touring with the band. The first show of the group's first North American tour of the year in Boston began disastrously, with Moon collapsing on stage after only two numbers. The band's second North American trip featured Moon's final US concert at the Seattle Center Coliseum in Seattle, Washington on 14 October, as well as his final concert before a paying crowd at Maple Leaf Gardens in Toronto on 21 October.

BOSTON GARDEN
9 MARCH 1976 AND 1 APRIL 1976, BOSTON, MASSACHUSETTS

I WAS THERE: BARRY BELOTTI

Six months after I saw them in Providence, they came to the famous Boston Garden, which has been torn down now. There was a late snowstorm going in. A water main broke, up on the second floor men's room, and it leaked all the way down, right into the lobbies. And these guys are throwing sawdust down so people didn't slip.

Toots and the Maytals were the support band. And Jamaican music in 1976, with the anticipation of a Who crowd, just didn't work. All of a sudden, fruit and everything else is thrown at the stage and poor Toots, who I became a fan of years later, was behind Pete's Marshall amps and he's waving a white towel. He was booed off. And then, waiting for The Who to come on, there's a fire in the loge section. Back then, you could still smoke indoors, so some popcorn wrappers caught on fire or whatever. They pulled the seats out and they put the fire out.

Finally, The Who come on stage and they jump into 'I Can't Explain' and 'Substitute' and Moon passes out over the drums. He's out! I was in the promenade section, just about four rows up off the floor. I could see up above everybody's head. Everybody's wondering what's going on and Townshend comes up to the microphone and says 'our drummer's sick.' He's out of it.

And Roger comes out and 'we're gonna have to come back tomorrow.' And all of a sudden the Boston crowd starts booing. 'Noooo! Whaddyatalkinabout?' 'Well, our drummer can't go on.' And this kid behind me is really swearing: Fuck you, you'd better play.' So Daltrey throws the mic down and says 'fuck you, we won't come back.' He got pissed off at people booing. And I turned around to this kid and I said 'see? See what you did? This ain't fucking Kiss, you know. This is the bloody Who.'

They cancelled the show. So it was 'hold onto your ticket stubs'. And back then you had the mini little ticket stubs – they weren't the full ticket – and everybody's going through their pockets. My friend Tommy had lost his stub and he was drunk and he was all upset. And then I had another friend, Keith, who found a cigarette packet as he was leaving the show and it had fourteen stubs in it and so he was happy because he could trade those in and get fourteen tickets! So it was a long three weeks but they rescheduled for April 1. They said Moon had a 'viral flu infection'. And we knew it was a little more than that. I guess Keith was one of those guys who took things first and asked questions later.

So they came back on April 1st and to this day, and I've seen a lot of rock concerts, but it was the most amazing rock concert I've ever experienced. Non-stop energy from the minute they started. They came running on the stage and Roger said 'we won't get fooled again, Boston.' Because it was April Fool's Day.

They just launched into 'Can't Explain' and 'Substitute' and they played the whole show and at the very end of 'Won't Get Fooled Again' – there were no encores in those days – Townshend just raised his guitar. Moon was going crazy and he smashed it to smithereens. He threw it way up into the rafters and it came down and he just totally annihilated it. And then Moon kicked over his drums to join in. We were walking back to the train, me, and my buddy, and we didn't say a word to each other. That was either because we were deaf from the show or we were in shock. Probably a little bit of both. It was just quite amazing.

SEATTLE CENTER COLISEUM

25 MARCH 1976, SEATTLE, WASHINGTON

I WAS THERE: BRIAN ZELMER

I had just finished my high school baseball game when one of my teammates, whose family was filthy rich, asked me if I wanted to go. I showered and headed to the concert. We got to the concert about 30 minutes before it started. The ex-girlfriend was there with her other drunk friends and when she saw me she staggered over. She sat down in the chair next to me and started talking but I couldn't understand what she was saying. She proceeded to throw up on her shoes and the next thing I know she's passed out in my lap.

The concert started and I was stuck in my chair. Everyone around us was on their feet for the entire concert so every time I tried to stand up to see, she would dig her fingernails into the back of my leg, so I just sat there and enjoyed the music. I remember hearing Keith Moon just beating the heck out of the drums. The most memorable song was 'Won't Get Fooled Again'. I did see the girl one other time about a year later. I later heard she became a flight attendant but I haven't seen her in 40 years.

The Who performed three shows at football stadia around the UK on successive weekends under the 'Who Put The Boot In' banner. The gig at Charlton Athletic Football Club on 31 May 1976, gave The Who a place in the *Guinness Book of Records* as the loudest rock concert ever: 126 decibels measured at a distance of 32 metres (105 ft) from the speakers.

THE VALLEY

31 MAY 1976, CHARLTON ATHLETIC FOOTBALL GROUND, LONDON

I WAS THERE: SUE STOW

Over the years I went to see them numerous times. Seeing *Tommy* performed live even impressed my then boyfriend (now my husband). Charlton Football Ground was amazing with one of the first ever laser shows.

I WAS THERE: SIMON WRIGHT

I still have the ticket for this show, which reminds me I paid £4 to see (in reverse order) The Who, Sensational Alex Harvey Band, Little Feat, Outlaws, Streetwalkers and Widowmaker. A half-dozen of us arrived early via Mark's Escort van. We had been warned about forged tickets of which there would turn out to be 5,000 in addition to the agreed capacity of 60,000. Our mums had dutifully provided us with cheese-and-pickle sandwiches and a local off-licence had furnished a diverse selection of bottles. Problem: taking booze into the ground was forbidden. As the most respectable

looking it was decided that I should be the designated booze smuggler. This proved ill-advised when after we successfully entered the already overcrowded ground I got parted from the other five. It also began to rain. So with impeccable teenage logic I decided that if I was going to be wet on the outside I would be wet on the inside too. By the time the others found me the booze was gone and so was I.

I sobered up as the afternoon wore off, taking in Little Feat, who should have been great but weren't and Alex Harvey, who should have been great and were. By the time The Who appeared I was sober and ready to be impressed by my first-ever Who gig. This was before video screens, so we couldn't see much but the sound was commendably clear and loud. At 120 decibels the gig made it into the *Guinness Book Of Records*.

Only three songs were featured from the bands most recent LP, 1975's *The Who By Numbers*. The rest of the 90 minute set comprised some early singles, half of *Who's Next* and a great dollop of *Tommy*, the latter introduced by Keith Moon to great effect.

We were about halfway back, so missed the rucks that were happening down the front. Listening today to The Complete Charlton 1976 bootleg confirms that my teenage self was right to be impressed. The band were on prime form – inventive, concise and enthusiastic. The most memorable part of The Who's set were the lasers. No-one had seen them at a gig before and they were used sparingly on 'See Me, Feel Me' and 'Won't Get Fooled Again'. Green and red beams arced over our heads, almost adding a roof to the tatty stadium. I suspect the GLC put the boot in on the lasers, as I never saw them again at a 1970s gig.

VETCH FIELD

12 JUNE 1976, SWANSEA FOOTBALL GROUND, SWANSEA

I WAS THERE: GERALD CLEAVER

I saw them at Swansea football ground. I think they had Alex Harvey on the bill, and Little Feat. They were just tremendously good and there were thousands of people there. What I remember is that I was working and, because I didn't want to worry about missing the last train, I booked into a hotel. The hotel had locked all the doors so that no one could come in for a drink. Of course they had to let me in and they were very unhappy about it. Most of the people next morning had been to the concert. And we were all talking about it and what a great show it was.

I WAS THERE: MARK ELLISON

This was the third of three weekends when they'd played football stadia. I think they'd done Charlton Athletic one week and Celtic the following week and then the third and final one was Swansea. I travelled down overnight on the train to Swansea. I remember there were only about six other people, all males in their teen and twenties, in our carriage, all going to see The Who. And when we got there, we were joining the throng to get into the ground. We'd got half a dozen tins of dandelion and burdock each and some sandwiches to see us through the day and we were all getting frisked and we all had all of our drinks confiscated. Well, the deal was, go over there and drink them or they're going in a skip and there was these half a dozen skips and they were already overflowing with booze and drinks.

We were relatively early in the queue and we learned later that it was because at Charlton and at Celtic there'd been truckloads of fights fuelled by booze so they were just confiscating it all and they were stopping people lobbing cans and bottles as had happened at the other two. And we just thought, well you can't just drink a load of tins of fizzy pop and then go into a football ground for the rest of the afternoon, so we just chucked it in the skip.

We chose to stand pretty far from the stage because we were young and nervous about things. With hindsight that worked well for us I think, so we were near the back really. And the bands came and went. There was Widowmaker. Ariel Bender from Mott the Hoople – it was his band and they were just dull but we knew nothing of their stuff. The Outlaws, a kind of Southern boogie and boring and not for us, Streetwalkers – we'd kind of been looking forward to them because we know some tracks by Family and Roger Chapman's new band but again they didn't really do anything for me. That might be because tiredness was setting in or, in those days, PA's just weren't up to it and unless you really knew the material you were struggling with a haze of fuzzy noise really. I felt really sorry for them actually at the time.

And then there was Little Feat, who were an *Old Grey Whistle Test* favourite at the time but nothing that worked for me so again it passed me by and I was just getting semi conscious by then from lack of sleep.

Then the Sensational Alex Harvey band, much better as a mate of mine was a fan so I'd heard some of their stuff so I knew some of what was going on in their set. So that actually lifted me a bit out of the semi consciousness although even though I was thinking, because Alex did this thing where at one point in the set he'd dress up as Adolf Hitler and burst through a polystyrene ball, then after the track he felt absolutely compelled to lecture the audience about how Adolf Hitler was not funny and I remember thinking at the time, well why do you do it then? What's the point of that?

Then there was a lull before The Who and I just started fading really badly then. I think I was just sat on the floor and looking to prop myself up and have a nap or something. I could barely think, barely speak and I remember in the back of my mind thinking – I'm just fucked here because this'll just happen and I might just about recognise that they're on stage but the reason that I'm here is going to pass me by because I'm just too tired. I was probably also dehydrated because I'd had nothing to drink all day. It must have been 24 hours by then.

Then I heard the opening chords to 'Can't Explain' – wham! Bloody hell, I'd never heard anything as loud in my life. It was just meltingly loud. I mean, just two weeks before at Charlton, they'd been clocked at 220 decibels 20 yards from the stage, which at the time was the loudest on record and it would have been about the same, but thankfully I was a lot more than 50 yards away from the stage but even so it was just devastatingly loud. But it worked for me because it actually woke me up so it was absolutely fantastic.

Halfway through they turned on the lasers, which at the time were very new and very cool and very green. And it was just another great set, a couple of tracks from *The Who By Numbers* dropped in and for me 'Dreaming From The Waist' was a real, real highlight of that gig.

The other things I remember are that there'd been sporadic fights throughout the day, and violence always upsets me so I was not happy about those things, even though it was a fair distance away from me. That's why I was glad to be at the back, because it was less volatile over there. I remember Pete Townshend bollocking a bunch of people from the stage because a fight had started in front of the band and I think he threatened to bring the road crew in to sort them out if they didn't stop. One way of stopping fighting is to introduce more people into the fight! But the thing is, it was fantastic as it immediately stopped and that marked a transition to much more together crowd.

The other thing is, it rained. It was in June, but it rained a lot for the first few acts. It was dry for The Who and when they came on stage, cause Moony was always in the habit of cartwheeling or careering on stage as they came on, I've got this memory that he came careering on and just skidded all over the place on his arse because it was just wet. And when they did 'Squeezebox', he was dedicating it to the people who were leaning out of the windows opposite, because I hadn't realised at the time but there was a prison straight opposite so the prisoners got this gig, this whole day of entertainment.

What I loved, even to this day, is that John Entwistle could play better than anybody. He was just absolutely non-stop and varied and wonderfully musical in that sense. Moony was – well, most people thought Moon was great. I did. I thought he was fantastic. Pete Townshend was never the greatest guitarist on earth, but what he did do was make a virtue of his shortcomings, of his inabilities in some sense and that is remarkable. Hardly anyone does that and he's made a career of it and that is absolutely fantastic. But Entwistle – his hands were flying and the band were just phenomenal.

I WAS THERE: BRIAN PLEASS

It was, I believe, a sunny June day in 1976. The venue was the Vetch Field, aka Swansea Town football ground. The prelude to The Who was Alex Harvey and his sensational band. Understandably, 'Delilah' went down an absolute storm. Along and behind one half of the touchline was a cell block of the Swansea jail and in the setting sun the arms and wrists of the inmates waving through the bars of their cells to the backing of 'Won't Get Fooled Again' was a poignant sight. A little later, in the twilight, the twin floodlight towers flanking the stage had maroon smoke canisters activated at their bases producing thick purplish red clouds rising slowly, through which brilliant green lasers from the floodlight gantries at the other end of the ground pulsated in time to the beat of 'Baba O'Riley'.

I WAS THERE: DAVE SMALE

My first memory of the show was the task in actually getting from Bristol to Swansea! My car back then was a rust-ridden 1965 Austin 1100, which had a permanent oil leak and, around the time of the Swansea gig, a leaky radiator as well, but two mates of mine still decided to risk it with me! We packed the car with as much water as we could carry – gallons and gallons of it in what was a half-size barrel like you see in pubs – and about 8 litres of oil as well, just in case! But as it happened, the old car got us to Swansea without letting us down even once.

We got into the stadium, we were almost immediately offered, shall we say, some dodgy substances (which we all declined) and then we sat in the middle of the football pitch for the whole of the gig which started at around mid-day, if I remember rightly. One thing I recall was that Swansea Prison overlooked the Vetch Field & you could see movement in some of the prison windows, as the in-mates tried to catch some of the gig!

The bands that came on before The Who were Widowmaker, Streetwalkers, The Outlaws, Little Feat and the Sensational Alex Harvey Band, who were all superb. I had already discovered the Florida band The Outlaws and already had their first LP, so seeing them as well as The Who was a real bonus. I had sneaked a small portable cassette recorder into the gig in my rucksack and I recorded the Outlaws as best I could, before the batteries ran out. I recall that the recording came out very muffled and was not really listenable. I've no idea where the tape is today.

And then, maybe at around 9pm or 9.30pm, The Who came on stage, kicking off with 'I Can't Explain' and 'Substitute'. It was awesome to see them there on stage and they were just how I'd imagined. Keith Moon was a totally nutcase behind the drums, while neither Roger Daltrey nor Pete Townshend stood still for very long. Only John Entwistle stood motionless, watching the others go about their manic moves, as he plucked away on the bass, his fingers constantly moving.

We had a wide variety of tracks in the set list, from right across the band's back catalogue, ranging from some of their other 1960s hits to early

70s tracks from albums like *Tommy* and *Who's Next*. But as darkness fell on this summer evening, The Who's light show brought an even greater reaction from the crowd, because they began using laser beams which danced around the four floodlight pylons of the football ground and across the pitch with the crowd below just looking up totally amazed. It was all done in time to the music. This was state of the art technology in 1976. They ended their show with 'Join Together', 'My Generation' and 'Won't Get Fooled Again', which was absolutely fantastic with the laser beams in full flow by then.

I WAS THERE: CHRISTOPHER WHITE

I hitch hiked from Sheffield and slept on the beach. I remember plenty of *Tommy* and it was the first time I had seen lasers, which were bounced off mirrors on the floodlights. We managed to get

Onstage in Miami, 8 August 1976

some students to let us sleep on their floor after the concert and we hitch hiked back to Sheffield the next day. The only thing I had with me was cash and a toothbrush. I still remember it as though it was yesterday.

MIAMI STADIUM

9 AUGUST 1976, MIAMI, FLORIDA

I WAS THERE: GRIZZ GROSSWALD

My uncle had a friend by the name of Skitch who got my cousin, brother and myself back stage passes. We were 15 to 17 years old. It rained heavily the night before the morning of the show and the infield was a muddy mess. We walked into the backstage area and within minutes someone came up to us and asked 'where the hell did you get those?' Then he took the passes from us and made us go into the general admission area. We still got to see the show, and it was awesome! It was Keith Moon's final tour, and I am very glad I got to see all original members perform together.

NORTHLANDS COLISEUM

16 OCTOBER 1976, EDMONTON, CANADA

I WAS THERE: SEAMUS BRADY

It was quite an adventure for a couple of 18 year olds. We drove to Edmonton from Saskatoon, which is a seven-hour drive in a 1973 MG Midget. The car, to put it plainly, wasn't very road worthy. We had purchased tickets in a bar in Saskatoon from a persuasive young woman who had a whole handful of them at $5 apiece. Lots of people snapped them up. When we arrived at the show we were quite devastated to learn that the tickets were all counterfeit.

Turned away at the door, we were outside with the many people who had bought these tickets in Saskatoon. It would not have been pretty had the young lady who had sold them shown up at that time. So we did what we had to do and bought scalper tickets. Just as Mother's Finest took the stage we made it into the show. I remember The Who as being athletic and funny and it being the greatest concert I had seen at the time or have seen since. The laser light show was state of the art at the time. And the Orange double barrel – a type of LSD that was floating around at the time named for its potency – only enhanced the experience. I saw them last year in Saskatoon with the same guy I had seen them with 40 years previous. They were very good but I missed John and Keith.

I WAS THERE: BRIAN D. EDWARDS

I couldn't get a ticket to see them here in Edmonton in 1976, but when we were leaving the arena area we just about got run over my Moonies limo. The car stopped by us and Keith Moon stuck his head out and yelled 'You scallywags!' to us and laughed. And the limo drove off.

SPORTS ARENA

7 OCTOBER 1976, SAN DIEGO, CALIFORNIA

I WAS THERE: MARC DAY

Beneath Keith Moon's drum kit that evening was a Persian rug that the day before had graced a reception area near his room in a Phoenix hotel. Apparently Moon was 'accused by another hotel guest of urinating on the expensive carpet...easily seen by anyone walking past the room.' Moon told hotel management that the wet spot had been caused by a spilled drink.

When told the band would be billed for the full value (of the rug), Moon moved some furniture off the carpet, rolled it up, slung it over his shoulder, and took it immediately to the band's tour bus, using it that night and over the next few dates to anchor his notoriously unstable drum kit.

The 21-song set included cuts from their newest album, *The Who by Numbers*, including 'Squeeze Box' and 'Dreaming from the Waist', as well as an eight-song medley from *Tommy*.

The 1976 tour concluded with a show at Toronto's Maple Leaf Gardens before an audience of 20,000 people. No one who was there that night realised it, but it was to be Keith's last appearance before a paying audience.

The Who were off the road during 1977. Pete had decided that his family, hearing and sanity should come first. Work began on *The Kids Are Alright*, an authorised biopic of the band which aimed to mix archive footage with newly filmed material. A private concert was held at the Gaumont State Cinema in Kilburn in North London to generate footage for the film, but the performance from a road rusty band was deemed too poor for most of it to be used.

1978–79

1978 saw John mixing *The Kids Are Alright* soundtrack and the band preparing to release *Who Are You*, their first new album for three years. After the Kilburn failure, another private show was arranged for the cameras at Shepperton Studios.

SHEPPERTON STUDIOS

25 MAY 1978, SHEPPERTON

I WAS THERE: RUSS PAGDIN

I saw The Who in May 1978 with my mate Adam Hope. We were both big Who fans and he somehow got us invited through, I think, the fan club for a 'secret' gig. We were taken by coach with about 200 Who fans to Shepperton film studios. Well, as you can imagine, we were gobsmacked. We got fed like film extras and then were taken into a giant hangar where, sure enough, The Who appeared. They were filming for *The Kids Are Alright* and played 'Baba O'Riley' and 'Won't Get Fooled Again'.

They did a few versions and at the end Pete Townshend said 'fuck it, we're gonna play for the kids' and they did so for about an hour more. It was truly amazing and the memory hopefully will stay with me forever. After the gig, we were all taken outside for a photo, which was supposed to be for the cover for *Who Are You* but sadly it wasn't used. A few months after that, Keith died, which was a massive shock. I saw them a few times after that with Kenney Jones, but it was never as good. I once knocked on Pete's door in Twickenham and he invited us in, which was amazing.

Those gathered at Shepperton that day were not to know it, but Pete's impromptu decision that the band should play more than just the scripted numbers for the invited audience, combined with the events of just a few weeks later, ensured that these lucky few fans were to witness the last ever performance by The Who with the irrepressible Keith Moon on drums.

Keith Moon died on 7 Sept 1978 of a overdose of heminevrin prescribed to combat alcoholism. A post-mortem confirmed there were 32 tablets in his system, 26 of which were undissolved. He played on all The Who albums from their debut, 1965's *My Generation*, to 1978's *Who Are You*, which was released two weeks before his death. His legacy is outstanding: Keith Moon is said to have named Led Zeppelin when an early version of the band was being discussed that would have had himself, along with John Entwistle on bass, Jimmy Page on Guitar, and an undecided vocalist, as members; he stated the potential supergroup would 'go down like a lead Zeppelin'.

When touring with The Who, Keith used to enjoy flushing cherry bombs down toilets. His repeated practice of blowing up toilets with explosives led him to be banned from several hotel chains around the world for life, including all Holiday Inn, Sheraton, and Hilton hotels. He died in the same flat in Curzon Place in London's Mayfair (belonging to Harry Nilsson) that Mama Cass had passed away in during 1974.

On the eve of his death, Moon had been at a screening of *The Buddy Holly Story* during the Paul McCartney-sponsored, annual Buddy Holly Week.

Moon had been set to have a part in Monty Python's film *Life of Brian* and was with the Python members in the Caribbean as they wrote the script, but Moon died before it began filming. The published edition of the screenplay to *Life of Brian* is dedicated to the Who drummer.

I WAS THERE: JOHN SCHOLLAR

The last time Keith spoke to me, his mother rang me up when he came back from California. He was staying at the Royal Garden Hotel. His mum said 'ring him up.' I wondered if it was a call for help. He was in such a bad way. I got on the phone and had a chat with him and it was just like old times. He said to me 'I'll get over this problem I've got and we'll get our old band together.' And I said 'yeah, we'll go out and have a drink.' He said, 'no, we'll get a pub and go and do a night for them.' He wanted to get back with the old band, just for one night.

I WAS THERE: BOBBY ASEA

Keith continued to carry on with the drugs and alcohol lifestyle, which ultimately led to his demise. When it finally caught up with him, and attributed to the end of his life, I wasn't surprised. In my opinion, The Who were no longer the band that I had come to know and love. Keith's contribution to the music and his drum style could never be replaced.

I WAS THERE: MIKE JONES

When I heard about Keith's death I was naturally shocked, but bearing in mind his lifestyle over many years I honestly thought it was just a question of time. When I first saw The Who on *Ready Steady Go!* I was simply blown away by Keith. He came along and simply ripped up the rulebooks of drumming with a unique style that no one I've ever seen since has managed to match or improve. He was a truly amazing character and drummer who has never been equalled. I don't think I've ever really seen anybody imitate him.

I WAS THERE: ROBBIE LATHAM

It was terrible when Moon went. I did meet his sister. She had a pub and on the wall there was all these drum sticks. She didn't want to talk about him, which was understandable because it was just after he died.

I WAS THERE: KEVIN RICHARDSON

I was in Majorca on a lads' 18-30 holiday. I had met this girl but she was sadly taken very ill and had to be admitted to hospital. I went to visit her and whilst I was there I managed to get hold of an English newspaper where I learnt of the news of Keith's death. I was so devastated they nearly had to find me a bed in the same hospital while I recovered.

I WAS THERE: LINDA SWEEDEN

I remember the day Keith Moon died vividly. It came on the 6pm news. I was hoovering at the time, when out of the corner of my eye the headlines said 'member of the rock band The Who found dead!'

I dropped to the floor and switched off the hoover to hear, but the BBC were running through the rest of the day's headlines. I felt sick to my stomach. Who had died? How? When? I had to wait for the other 'more important' news to be read before the details of Keith Moon's death were told. They said he died in his sleep, found by his girlfriend. I was in shock! That's not how he was meant to die.

He should have died doing something crazy. He should have at least gone out with a bang! In my opinion The Who have never been quite the same. They were like four very different legs of a table, each one in their own way holding the table up. The four faces of *Quadrophenia*.

I WAS THERE: DERMOT BASSETT

Seeing Keith up close for the first time at The Marquee in 1968 was special, but it wasn't until the latter end of 1968 during the run in towards *Tommy* and beyond that he really came into his own. That The Who managed to bring *Tommy* to the live stage with just three instruments was a staggering achievement and couldn't have been done without Keith. Taking nothing away from Pete and John, Keith was a phenomenon, filling out the sound in a way no other drummer could have done. Also, the onstage repartee between him and Pete was worth the entry admission alone. Listen to *Live At Leeds* for proof of both.

Eventually, though, we came to the long decline. Keith was always as famed for his excesses and antics as he was for his playing, which is a great shame. Of course, I used to laugh as much as anyone else, but there came a point where I stopped. I started seeing him as a tragic figure and it made me sad to see his powers gradually leaving him.

One afternoon I received a phone call from a friend. 'Have you heard about Keith?' She didn't really need to say anything else – I knew what was coming. I felt the tears in my eyes. I think for the first time in my life, certainly outside of family, I was crying over someone dying.

I only met him a couple of times. In Le Chasse in Wardour Street, a club – well, a room – above a bookies that was frequented by musicians and roadies. As I walked in Keith, who was standing by the bar, spun round and started shouting at me 'get out, go on get out! We don't want your sort coming in here causing trouble.' We then had a laugh and a drink. Of course, his outburst wasn't aimed at me, just at who walked through the door next. On another occasion, he pushed me off the jukebox, which was in the gap between the two front windows, which were open. The sun was streaming in. Keith said 'just want to do a bit of promotion.' I said 'not that Seeker rubbish.' He replied 'no this' and selected his and Viv Stanshall's version of *Suspicion*. I always remember that day and it always makes me smile.

Following Keith's death, the band resolved to carry on, initially with Kenney Jones, who had previously drummed for the Small Faces and Faces, occupying the drummer's stool. Keyboardist John 'Rabbit' Bundrick was also added to the line-up for live performances. The post-Moon incarnation of The Who played as a five-piece for seven shows, the first occurring on 2 May at the Rainbow Theatre in London. On 18 August, a horn section was introduced to the band's act for the first time for their show at Wembley Stadium in London which would be retained through 1980.

WEMBLEY STADIUM

18 AUGUST 1979, LONDON

I WAS THERE: PHIL BRENNAN

It was the first day of the new football season and, as the traffic down to 'that London' was always going to be hectic on the day of the gig, we set off during the afternoon of the day before. Ten of us in an old transit van, with a few mattresses and plenty of booze in the back. Having survived the journey, we parked the van in a side street in nearby Brent and shuffled off to find some food before ensconcing ourselves in a little pub for the evening.

The weather the next morning was good so we decided to leave the van where it was and walk over to the stadium. Having found a little café where we enjoyed a half decent fry-up, we topped up our bags with more booze from a local off license, knowing that prices nearer the stadium would probably treble in price. There were already several people staggering around drunk when we got to the ground

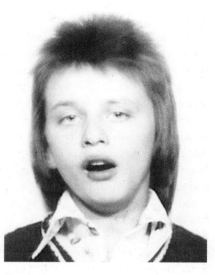

Ziggy Stardust eat your heart out: a young Phil Brennan, with a very Seventies feathered mullet

around midday, but we enjoyed a little kick about in the car park with a group of lads from Leeds.

As the game started to become more serious, with a few tasty tackles flying in, there was a huge roar, as the gates were declared open, fortunately bringing a premature end to the football match and ensuring that the two groups wandered over to the stadium in good spirits. As the ground filled up and people were pushing to get as close the stage as possible, there were a few sporadic fights in the crowd, with a couple of people carried out by St Johns ambulance staff. Fortunately, as we were about 20 strong between the two groups, we were never really under threat.

There were several people lying on the Wembley pitch who had passed out due to their over indulgence, which didn't help matters in terms of the pushing and shoving.First up on stage was former Springsteen sidekick Nils Lofgren who Pete, one of our group, had been excited to see. If I'm honest I didn't really rate him, although his trick of carrying out somersaults whilst still playing his guitar was pretty impressive.

I was really looking forward to Australian rockers AC/DC. I had seen Angus and the boys several times over the years including places like the Marquee and Manchester's Electric Circus. This was the first time I had seen them in a stadium and they didn't disappoint. I felt that AC/DC grew their English fan base that day. The Wembley crowd were bouncing around throughout the set.

Another one of my favourite bands of recent times was next up. But The Stranglers alienated a large section of the crowd by playing pretty much all of their latest album and didn't play 'Peaches' or 'No more Heroes', which I knew would get people up on their feet. Still, it was The Who that we were there to see and, as this was their first big gig since the death of Keith Moon, there was a sense of the unknown about how the set would go down.

Any fears I, or indeed the rest of the crowd had, disappeared as the strains of 'Substitute' began. The crowd were up and singing to every word as the band raced through the first few songs in true rock god style. 'I Can't Explain', 'Baba O'Riley' and 'The Punk and The Godfather' were met with enthusiasm around the stadium and Roger Daltrey had the audience in the palm of his hand.

The band slowed things down with a superb version of 'Behind Blue Eyes' before John Entwistle took over vocal duties for 'Boris The Spider'. 'Sister Disco' from *Who Are You* was followed by a couple of slow songs, with Pete singing 'Drowned' and Roger performing 'Music Must Change'. The hits returned with 'Magic Bus' and 'Pinball Wizard' and superb versions of two of my personal favourites 'See Me Feel Me' and '5.15' either side of *Trick of The Light*. The band turned up the noise around the stadium as they rocked their way through 'Long Live Rock', 'Who Are You' and 'My Generation. I then went to the toilet and the band were well into 'Won't Get Fooled Again' by the time I found my way back to our gang. The band departed the stage and then returned for a two song encore which for me was the highlight of the show.

They played truly magnificent versions of 'Summertime Blues' and 'The Real Me' before taking their bows. It was a triumph in every sense of the word – a gig that lived up to all the hype beforehand, albeit tinged with the sadness that I hadn't managed to see them with Moon behind the drum kit.

ZEPPELINFELD

1 SEPTEMBER 1979, NUREMBERG, GERMANY

I WAS THERE: VIOLA BOGARD, AGE 17

I had been listening to The Who since I was 10 or so. It was their first tour after Moonie died and my first open air concert. It was a big deal to drive 275 kilometers to see a concert when all other venues were between 20 and 80 kilometers away. It took some time to convince my parents to let me go since it meant camping for two nights and I was the only girl in the group. My dad finally said OK after he found out that one of his apprentices was part of the group. He made him responsible for my well being – and most likely threatened the poor guy! My

Viola Bogard, back in the days when dungarees and white vans weren't just for painters and decorators

Inside the programme for the 1979 Wembley Stadium show

favorite album was, and still is, *Live at Leeds* and in particular 'Magic Bus'. To see that song performed live is still one of my best memories. There are no words to describe that feeling.

MADISON SQUARE GARDEN

13–18 SEPTEMBER 1979, NEW YORK CITY

I WAS THERE: JOHN MOGAVERO, AGE 18

We were dead centre of the stage but all the way up at the top tier. What stood out for me that night was that these were the first shows to promote the album *Who Are You* after the tragic loss of Keith Moon. Another highlight for me was the horn section behind the drum kit, which was awesome when The Who played classic songs like 'Pinball Wizard'. I'd become a fan of The Who since I saw the movie *Tommy* back in 1975 and from that point onwards I have bought every Who album, CD and DVD.

BRIGHTON CENTRE

10 & 11 NOVEMBER 1979, BRIGHTON

I WAS THERE: KEVIN RICHARDSON

After the opening couple of numbers, Roger said 'good evening, Brighton'. He then looked around and said, disappointedly, 'sorry about the sound quality. They don't make places for rock'n'roll anymore, do they?' This got an extremely loud cheer because of course, he was so right.

The history of popular music is dotted with individual tragedies and fans dying as a result of drug overdoses and random attacks on concert goers. But events in Cincinnati, in which eleven fans were crushed in the stampede to enter the venue – general seating had been made available on a first come, first served basis – marks an unwelcome note in the history of The Who. The band were entirely blameless, but the tragedy marked the single biggest loss of life at a concert until the terrorist attack on the Bataclan nightclub in Paris in November 2015.

RIVERFRONT COLISEUM

3 DECEMBER 1979, CINCINNATI, OHIO

I WAS THERE: MICHAEL STEELE

I saw The Who in December 1979 in Cincinnati. It's what we here call 'The Who tragedy'. It changed concert going forever. Eleven people were crushed when the huge crowd on the plaza rushed the doors. A friend and I were running late because of work. We got there and went in on the other side not knowing what was happening. We saw a great show and left the way we came in.

We got to the car, turned on the radio and that's when we heard what had happened. The feeling of shock and disbelief was overwhelming. There's a memorial there now and survivors from the night hold a service there every year on the anniversary. The Who have never returned.

THE 1980s

1980 saw Pete Townshend release a solo album, *Empty Glass*, which reached No 11 in the UK charts and hit the top 5 in the US. Pete later admitted to using cocaine during this period and suffering from alcoholism. At a February 1981 show at the Rainbow, Finsbury Park, he drank four bottles of brandy whilst on stage. Pete later admitted 'I just ceased to care.' Still, the band's legendarily powerful volume was clearly undiminished: their performance at the 8,000 capacity Deeside Leisure Centre was described by one fan as 'much too loud for a place that size!'

DEESIDE LEISURE CENTRE

28 FEBRUARY 1981, NORTH WALES

I WAS THERE: RICHARD DIXON

I took my girlfriend, now my wife, to Queensferry Ice Rink to see them. I can still remember the long queue snaking around the building and we probably paid on the door. It was standing only, so you can imagine my excitement when we had pushed forward to the stage.

There was a great crush but the band was right there. After the first song, my girlfriend felt faint so we had to push out to the back. It has been difficult to forgive her even now! I live in Carlisle so seeing them anywhere apart from Newcastle involves some effort. Plenty of people will have seen them far more times than me, but they have been the background for my life, for which I am eternally grateful.

ARTS CENTRE

16 MARCH 1981, POOLE

I WAS THERE: PHIL CHAPMAN

It was the last date of their *Face Dances* tour and their first UK tour since the death of Keith Moon. I wondered whether the post-Moon line up, with Kenney Jones on drums and John 'Rabbit' Bundrick on keyboards, would still pack a punch. I needn't have worried; right from the opener, 'Substitute', through new and old material to 'Won't Get Fooled Again', they were an immense unstoppable force and one of the loudest bands I've ever heard. Townshend chucked in a fair few windmills, Daltrey did his full microphone hurling act, Entwistle put all his energy into searing bass lines rather than leaping about the stage and Jones was fully committed behind his kit.

The highlight for me was the build up of atmosphere and energy through the last four songs: 'Who Are You', '5.15', 'My Generation' and 'Won't Get Fooled Again'. What a treat! The encore seemed to go on forever although it was actually just three songs – 'Summertime Blues', 'Twist and Shout 'and 'See Me Feel Me.' One hell of a concert and my ears are still ringing decades later.

CAPITAL CENTRE

22 SEPTEMBER 1982, LANDOVER, MARYLAND

I WAS THERE: KIM COOLEY BARKER, AGE 16

I'd only been a fan for a few years. Music was and still is an important part of my life. I felt like less of an outsider. My father started taking me to shows when I was 14 and I felt alive. I remember that feeling from The Who show. I saw them on what they were calling their farewell tour. I must've gotten three of the last tickets for the show because I went with my father and brother and we had nosebleed seats and we weren't sat together.

The show was great but I always remember my father saying he had someone sitting behind him who chanted 'Who' through the whole thing. He said it was like having a damn owl behind him. I walked away in awe that I'd seen legends play.

JFK STADIUM

25 SEPTEMBER 1982, PHILADELPHIA, PENNSYLVANIA

I WAS THERE: ARUN JOHN GOTT, AGE 16

It was an outdoor concert with about 90,000 people. I actually got to the fence in front of the stage and it felt like there were 90,000 people pushing. I helped save a woman who passed out as a wave of people started to crush us. We picked her up and put her on the stage. Remember, this was after Cincinnati where people died.

I remember The Clash and Santana but little of The Who. I might of had a little heat stroke. I was worried, by all the pushing so it was no outdoor general admission concerts for me after that, which meant I missed the Stones.

SHEA STADIUM

12 & 13 OCTOBER 1982, NEW YORK CITY

I WAS THERE: TROY MITCHELL OWENS, AGE 20

I saw The Clash open for The Who at Shea Stadium. I remember that traffic getting to Shea Stadium was incredible and we had to park relatively far away, by the ice skating rink. The place was completely sold out and my friends and I had seats along the first base side and felt like we were a hundred miles from the stage. It was a very cold and wet night and no-one had dried off the plastic seats, so everyone was trying to find tissues, napkins or anything else to dry their seat. If anyone would have had a roll of paper towels they could have charged a fortune per sheet.

There was an aura of this event being more than a concert. Maybe it was the weather, maybe it was the fact that this was a pairing of the Old Guard and the seemingly New, but whatever it was, being there was special. I don't really remember any songs that particularly stood out – it was more that the concert on the whole was an event.

I WAS THERE: JOHN MOGAVERO

I guess what stood out for me that night was the rain that was coming down, and Roger singing 'Love Reign O'er Me' – it was just magical! All the songs were great, but when they performed 'Eminence Front', I swear it echoed throughout the whole stadium!

ALAMEDA COUNTY COLISEUM

23 OCTOBER 1982, OAKLAND, CALIFORNIA

I WAS THERE: RACHEL NISELY, AGE 19

I lived in Hayward, just a few miles south of Oakland. We took the BART to the concert, along with thousands of others. I had been a fan of The Who for about five years, every since hearing 'Pinball Wizard'. The Day on the Green concerts, promoted by Bill Graham in the mid Seventies and Eighties were legendary. You could go see bands like The Who and The Clash with T-Bone Burnett opening for less than $15.

The day-long shindig culminated in the headliner taking the stage around the time the sun went down. There was this massive party atmosphere and the music was the centerpiece of the vibe. I remember Roger Daltrey's signature vocals, especially as the crowd sang along with 'Baba O'Riley' and 'My Generation'. Pete Townshend's guitar licks ripped through the haze of smoke above the crowd. I have such fond – albeit foggy – memories of those concerts.

Rachel Nisely, who has fond memories of attending several Day On the Green festivals

SUN DEVIL STADIUM

31 OCTOBER 1982, TEMPE, ARIZONA

I WAS THERE: ELYSE HENDRICKS

My boyfriend was reluctant to take me to see The Who. I was very into art rock at the time and he thought I would spoil the experience for him. I protested that I had heard The Who and liked them, so he took me, and I was blown completely away. We were close to the stage and I could feel the power of Roger Daltrey's voice pour through me, and see the intricacies of Entwistle's playing and marvel at Townshend's riffs and poetic words. An unforgettable experience.

TANGERINE BOWL

27 NOVEMBER 1982, ORLANDO, FLORIDA

I WAS THERE: CARLA MCLENDON, AGE 26

I have been a Who fan, ever since the album *Tommy*. I wore out a couple of copies of *Who's Next* in high school. I loaned that album out to everyone I knew and unfortunately some weren't good at taking care of LPs. I listened and caught up with and purchased all their older material.

My first chance to see them live was November 1975 but I was in the army at Fort Campbell, Kentucky. I chose to come home to Florida to see my fiancé the week of Thanksgiving that year. My next chance was on their 'farewell' tour, just before my 27th birthday. Living down the road in Lakeland made it only a 45 minute ride back then. Along with over 50,000 other fans we eagerly awaited The Who.

On the bill were Joan Jett and the Blackhearts and The B52s. Joan Jett was perturbed at the audience chanting 'Who' The whole time. The B52s didn't even make it through their third song before being pelted off the stage by the crowd throwing paper cups. They had come to see The Who and they were not disappointed!

MISSISSIPPI COAST COLISEUM

1 DECEMBER 1982, BILOXI, MISSISSIPPI

I WAS THERE: KENT BRUCE, AGE 15

Two friends and myself set off to see them on what was to be their final tour. I checked out of school because I was 'sick'. We had a three-hour drive to get to the Mississippi Coast Coliseum in Jackson, Mississippi. The show was sold out and the parking lot was full of fans getting ready for the show. News media were there. I don't know why, but the Clarion-Ledger, the biggest newspaper in Mississippi, asked me if I would do an interview. I did the interview and didn't really think about it.

I got separated from my friends trying to get a good spot to watch from as I made it to the front barricade right at center stage. I was playing drums at the time, so I really wanted to see Kenney Jones up close. I was waiting for the drums in 'Won't Get Fooled Again'. The floor was packed and it was tough down there. Midway through their set, The Who played 'Baba O'Riley.' After the harmonica part, I felt something hit me. I thought it was just somebody being a jerk. Turns out Daltrey's black harmonica had landed in my arms. People were on the floor scrambling to find it. I just stood there holding it, acting like I didn't know a thing. After the show, I met back up with my friends and they were talking about how good the show was. I pulled the harmonica out and they were stunned. I still have the harmonica to this day.

At some point, I had told my mom I was not coming home that night. So the next morning she called the school and made an excuse as to why I was not there. Unfortunately for me, the Clarion-Ledger published the article with my interview in the next morning's paper. It had my name, where I went to school, and what I was doing. My mom was not happy.

ASTRODOME

3 DECEMBER 1982, HOUSTON, TEXAS

I WAS THERE: LEANNE BANKS, AGE 19

My birthday was eleven days later and I was going to turn 20. What a great early birthday present! I had won an album a week for a year at KLBJ radio in Austin but I couldn't find an album that I was interested in. Peggy Simmons, one of the DJs, asked if I would be interested in free tickets to see The Who. She told me the party bus was full but I could drive to Houston so of course I said yes!

I called my parents to have them pick my son up from daycare. Then I called work and told them I had to take the afternoon off – and hit the road! I made it from Austin, Texas to Houston, Texas in record time! I'd been a fan since I saw the movie *Tommy* when I was in 6th grade.

Stand out songs were 'Behind Blue Eyes' and 'My Generation'. I remember crying because it was supposed to be their last tour and I had never seen them live before. The place was totally rockin' and we got out thinking we would hit Cardi's or somewhere on Westheimer Road but cops had people pulled over up and down the street so we drove straight back to Austin after the show. I still have a handkerchief from the show, which is one of the very best shows I've attended – an awesome show and an awesome memory.

The Who's 22nd anniversary tour in 1989 – marking 25 years since Keith had joined the band – was their first tour since 1982. Kenney Jones was replaced on drums by Simon Phillips. Citing difficulties with his hearing, Pete wanted the band to play at lesser volume than in previous years and to play mainly acoustic guitar, meaning the band had to draft in a second guitarist.

CARTER–FINLEY STADIUM

27 JULY 1989, RALEIGH, NORTH CAROLINA

I WAS THERE: ANDY CLENDENNEN, AGE 19

I was in the Navy, stationed in Norfolk, Virginia. Some fellow shipmates and I saw that The Who would be playing at Carter-Finley Stadium, about a three-hour drive away. I was too young to have seen The Who in their heyday but thought that, even without Keith Moon, it would be awesome to see them. So we all got tickets.

The plan was to meet in the stadium parking lot – remember, this is before cell phones – and hang out for a bit and drink a few beers before going in. I was only able to take a half-day off, so I was going to drive separately. Now, I was no gear head – I had an 1980 Impala but no clue about oil changes, radiators, air filters or any of that stuff. Get me from Point A to Point B and I'm happy.

So I started my trip on a nice sunny afternoon, giving myself plenty of time for the drive. About halfway into the drive, I noticed my thermostat start to rise. And it kept rising and rising. If you've ever been in that part of the country, you know there is not much in terms of civilization along the way. I was basically in the middle of nowhere when my radiator blew out on me. Luckily there was a tiny town, if you could even call it that, just up ahead. You know the kind – five or six houses and a couple of businesses on one side of the road, and nothing but farmland and forest on the other side.

Andy Clendennen, who had radiator trouble en route

It was a late Thursday afternoon by now, so most businesses that run on small town time weren't open, but there were a couple of older dudes hanging out outside of one of the bars. I told them my story and, just as every other small town has an auto repair shop, so did this one. They older dudes knew the owner of the repair shop so gave him a call from the bar and he said he could patch me up even though he was technically closed. A couple of hours later, I was on my way again with a 'new' radiator.

I pulled into the parking lot at the stadium and didn't hear any music. 'Whew,' I thought, 'made it just in time.' And just as I started walking across the lot, they broke into 'Overture' and 'It's A Boy'. I found my seat, and my friends, just as '1921' was starting. I caught the rest of the show after telling my story – to which everyone had a good laugh – and it was amazing. I wish I could remember the name of the town where I broke down, but I still have a tour poster from the sponsor, Miller Genuine Draft, hanging on my wall.

I WAS THERE: JAMES NIXON

The tour poster was this godawful rendering of them 'in action'. I was in undergraduate school at North Carolina State University. The area was hosting a lot of big outdoor gigs at the time, ranging from Paul McCartney and Wings through to The Rolling Stones and even Pink Floyd. It was the real onslaught of getting everything through Ticketron. But as a student camping out in line was nothing new.

I had always been a huge fan of The Who and Pete Townshend. They were at one end of the stadium and I was on 'the hill' at the other end a hundred and ten yards away, but they were still fantastic. The highlight of the concert for me was 'Eminence Front', which had been released not long before and which remains one of my favourites of theirs.

There was a rumour after the show that Pete and Roger got into a huge fight during the first set break and that Pete had locked his mate in his dressing room. To be honest, no one really bought it but it made for a good excuse for a bad drum solo lasting too long! John even moved a few steps, probably for a smoke.

1990s AND BEYOND After The Who were

inducted into the Rock'n'Roll Hall of Fame by Adam Clayton of U2 in January 1990, Pete began the decade thinking about retirement. Roger was busy with his trout farm. In 1993, the musical *Tommy* opened on Broadway at the St James Theatre. In June 1996, The Who played live in Hyde Park, performing parts of *Quadrophenia* with guests including Dave Gilmour of Pink Floyd. The Who toured *Quadrophenia* later that year.

CONTINENTAL AIRLINES ARENA

19 NOVEMBER 1996, EAST RUTHERFORD, NEW JERSEY

I WAS THERE: EVAN MICHAEL, AGE 21

I was with my friend Jon Blinn. This was the first and only time of seeing The Who with Pete, Roger, John and their backup band, including Ringo Starr's son Zak Starkey on drums and Pete's brother Simon on guitar. We sat in the nosebleeds. We were so high up, in fact, that I thought I was going to fall forward to my death. But that all went away when they hit the stage. The power! The volume! They performed all of *Quadrophenia*, including Billy Idol as The Ace Face on 'Bell Boy' and Gary Glitter as The Godfather on 'I've Had Enough'. The encores included an acoustic version of 'Won't Get Fooled Again' performed by just Roger, Pete & John, 'Behind Blue Eyes', 'Substitute' and 'Who Are You'. An awesome show.

MANCHESTER EVENING NEWS ARENA

11 DECEMBER 1996, MANCHESTER

I WAS THERE: PHIL CHAPMAN

I saw The Who about halfway through their thirteen month *Quadrophenia* live tour. Zak Starkey was already doing a good job in Keith Moon's role. The band of around a dozen musicians included a full brass section and backing vocalists and they sounded great. The line up was topped out by two special guests: PJ Proby as The Godfather and Billy Idol as The Ace Face. I'd always loved the album and this concert really did it justice. Pete Townshend kept to acoustic guitar for the entire performance but for the encore strapped on the required electric as the band delivered a storming rendition of 'Won't Get Fooled Again'.

An unexpected bonus for me was the inclusion of 'Behind Blue Eyes' from *Who's Next*. I've really liked the song ever since I first heard it back in 1971 and I never expected to get the chance to hear it live. The show was closed with 'Who Are You' and given a suitably big finish by the full band. It was a great end to a memorable night.

FESTHALLE

6 MAY 1997, FRANKFURT, GERMANY

I WAS THERE: ANSGAR FIRSCHING

I saw The Who when they still had three of the original band members. They played The whole of *Quadrophenia* and more. I was there together with my Swedish wife and our oldest daughter, who was in her belly. It was a great concert. In 1980, as a 13 year old boy, I already had all The Who albums. And then they took time out until they came back to play at the end of the 1980s. I am very glad that I made it to a Who concert. Pete taught me how to play electric guitar long before Keith Richards taught me the rest.

I WAS THERE: KAI OLIVER KYPKE, AGE 24

I became a fan when I saw the film of the 1968 Rolling Stones *Rock 'n' Roll Circus* which featured The Who's performance of 'A Quick One While He's Away', which blew me away. So I had to see the *Quadrophenia* tour in 1997. I was worried I'd be disappointed – Pete was just playing acoustic, it was their first tour for eight years and I might be the only one below 40 in the audience.

When 'The Real Me' started, I had doubts it was really live. It was so powerful, flawless and well-timed that I really asked myself whether this was pre-recorded and they were just miming. I'm so glad I was proven wrong when the odd wrong note was slipped in much later. Roger wore the target eye patch.

My favourites were – and, 20 years on, still are – 'The Real Me', 'I've Had Enough' and '5:15'. To me, the context of the rock opera justified the big band style the concert presented. I didn't like the encores a lot, mainly because I would have preferred them to be played by the four-piece and not the entire orchestra. But that's just me doing what we call in Germany *jammern auf hohem niveau* – whining at a high level!

ICE PALACE

15 AUGUST 1997, TAMPA, FLORIDA

I WAS THERE: FABRIZIO MARCILLO

I live in Ecuador but in April of 1997, a friend of mine who used to live near me, told me about this concert. I immediately told him to get the best seats he could, programmed my vacations, bought the tickets and had everything ready. I even planned a Disney/Orlando trip with the family.

The Who, have been my favourite band since I first heard them in 1970. I really had a connection with *Quadrophenia*. Every year in the mid 1980s, I used to go to the beach in the cold season before sunset with a parka, two bottles of booze a Walkman and one 90minute Maxell cassette with *Quadrophenia* on it. I would stay at the deserted beach all night long, singing stuff like 'the beach is a place where a man can feel, he's the only soul in the world that's real' and playing the same cassette again and again until sunrise. Then I would go home, sleep and, after that, return to my daily duties until the next year. It was my escape valve.

I remember on one of these occasions, I was much too sleepy so I entered a cemetery and fell asleep in a grave. A few hours later, I was awoken by some people at a neighbouring grave and I came out of the grave – and they had the scare of their lives!

I had great expectations for my *Quadrophenia* concert but in July my Dad had a routine gallbladder operation and something went wrong. He had several more operations and finally we decided to take him to a hospital in Miami, USA. When I arrived in August, I went to see my Dad at the hospital and I told him I could stay with him and skip the concert and the vacation I had planned. He told me he was OK, and that he didn't want to hear any nonsense and to go to my Who concert. So I went.

There is only oneway to hear a *Quadrophenia* concert: With Dr Jimmy and Mister Jim. So I bought two bottles of Gilbeys Gin, put them in plastic bags and smuggled them into the concert. When I arrived at the concert, I found out my friend was an asshole. He had booked the cheapest seats, although I had told him not to worry about expense and that I would pay for the seats. I told him to fuck off, bought a soda to mix with my gin and – I don't know how – ended in front stage when they started playing 'The Real Me'. I remember seeing Pete's boots two metres away, as he was jumping and soloing away. That is something that I'll never forget.

After 'The Punk and the Godfather', a usher found out I wasn't supposed to be there and I got thrown out so I went back to my 'friend' and his wife's seats, very far from the stage. Somehow we managed to come back a little closer, and saw the concert almost decently. Although I really would have liked to see Keith, Ringo's son's Zak was an excellent replacement. He almost played like Keith. He was no Kenney Jones light version. I really got wasted on my gin and could almost feel I was Jimmy in the boat, as the band played 'Love Reign O'er Me.' I could almost smell the sea and hear the waves.

After *Quadrophenia*, they played many of the other classic songs, and I really enjoyed every bit of them. I really was immersed in the music and the show. The day after the show, I called back and found out my Dad wasn't doing very well, so I returned to Miami. He was still alive, and I asked him why had he told me to go to the concert and lied to me by telling me he was OK. He told me he knew that was something I always wanted to see and so he wanted me to go. A couple of days later, my Dad died. So for me, that concert was the last and most interesting gift my Dad could give me. Every time I hear *Quadrophenia*, I remember my Dad. And remember his gift, and wish I could be like that with my kids when the time comes.

MADISON SQUARE GARDEN

4 OCTOBER 2000, NEW YORK CITY

I WAS THERE: TROY MITCHELL OWENS

After seeing them at Shea in 1982 I saw The Who again at Madison Square Garden. Jimmy Page and the Black Crowes were going to open but Page had to back out due to back problems. Jakob Dylan and his band opened instead and while they were good I am a huge Zeppelin fan so not seeing Page was very disappointing. However, I have to say that The Who were incredible. Daltrey hit all the notes and Pete was on fire on guitar and windmilled his ass off. Everyone clicked that night. 'Won't Get Fooled Again' was the stand out song but there wasn't a dud all night. To see them 18 years after Shea and them be as great as they were back then blew me and my friends away. The mood of the crowd walking out of MSG that night was pure exhilaration, which is always the sign of an amazing concert.

After a handful of UK dates at the start of the year, The Who Tour 2002 was scheduled for the second half of 2002 encompassing a series of North American dates. The band's plans were thrown into chaos on the eve of the tour when, on 27 June 2002, John Entwistle was found dead at the Hard Rock Hotel in Las Vegas, Nevada. The coroner concluded that he died of a heart condition brought on by taking cocaine during a night of debauchery with a Las Vegas stripper after spending the evening in the hotel bar with Roger and Pete. He was 57 years old.

I WAS THERE: BARRY BELOTTI

I miss John Entwistle. John was the closest I got to out of the three. He was such a nice person. He loved to hang out after the shows. He founded the band. Without him, that full sound is really missing.

I WAS THERE: RICHARD DIXON

My parents went on a guided bus tour of the Cotswolds and whilst driving along the guide pointed out a mansion belonging to John Entwistle. This elicited puzzled looks from all the elderly passengers, apart from a smug looking couple who were my parents and who were able to inform the rest who John was. I am a vet in Carlisle and a late client of ours was a Miss Linton, whose friend was Miss Hartley – a sister of the novelist LP Hartley – who wrote *The Go-Between*. They bred deerhounds and John Entwistle used to come up here to visit and buy dogs from her. Sadly, I did not know this until after Miss Linton died. How wonderful it would have been if I had got a call to see the dogs on the day of one of his visits!

In Keith's case, and in view of his lifestyle, there was a degree of inevitability, although great sorrow, when it was actually confirmed that he had died. It didn't come as a great surprise. That was in stark contrast to my feelings when John died. He had reached middle age and as far as I knew was settled in his life in the Cotswolds.

I was aware that he had heart problems but I just assumed that they were under control and he wouldn't do anything stupid. My overall feeling when I heard of his death was actually a selfish one. When Keith died, I assumed that the rest of the band would find a replacement drummer but when John went I thought that would be the end of the band and that I would never see The Who again.

We actually had a family holiday in Orlando whilst the tour was on. It was unlikely that I would have been able to see them in the States but I do remember the pennants hanging from a row of street lights in Universal Studios with 'RIP John Entwistle.' A nice tribute, but I found it rather depressing as it reminded me that it would be the end of the band. Fortunately I was wrong.

Without John Entwistle, the band drafted in bassist Pino Palladino and Simon Townshend, Pete's brother, on rhythm guitar and backing vocals.

MADISON SQUARE GARDEN

1 AUGUST 2002, NEW YORK CITY

I WAS THERE: SARA M NOVELLI

At the age of five in 1980, I heard my very first Who song, 'You Better You Bet', on the radio. But it wasn't until they announced their 25th anniversary tour in 1989, age 13 that I slowly became interested. *VH-1* showed a handful of videos from The Who's early career and particularly 'Pinball Wizard', 'I'm Free' and 'See Me, Feel Me' from *Tommy*.

Self-confessed fangirl Sara Novelli finally gets a hug with her crush

Having fallen for Roger Daltrey that April, I was excited to hear the tour was coming to Rich Stadium but my protective family, assuming I just wanted to be a fan-girl over him and not enjoy the material, forbade me to go, even though no one knew about my crush at the time.

This pattern would go on until 2002 when I was finally able to see The Who at Madison Square Garden! Alas, my excitement turned to grief when the news broke that The Ox had left the building on June 27. I was a tad bitter, having been deprived of past opportunities to see them whilst John was alive. I've seen about seven shows since, mainly in the Boston area – eight if you count the MusiCares benefit in New York May 2015. And I've seen four solo Daltrey shows between 2009 and 2011. I hope Pete and Roger keep on keeping on.

THE JOINT

14 SEPTEMBER 2002, PARADISE, NEVADA

I WAS THERE: JEFFREY EVANS

How absolutely chaotic it was when John Entwistle died. CNN in the lobby of the Hard Rock, interviewing everybody they could.

My casino host – because I gamble a lot there – filled me in on the real cause of his death: cocaine and hookers. The show was cancelled and rescheduled on my 30th birthday. I had 12 tickets in the fourth row in this tiny venue.

The band played incredibly well, surprising since Daltrey's voice is usually shot by this time in the tour. They played that show for Entwistle and were absolutely fucking amazing. Pete and Roger were inspired; they blew the doors off the building. The fill in on bass – Pino Palladino – was superb. You could feel Entwistle in that space – it was a celebration of The Ox. I would put this show in my top five of all the shows I've seen, the energy was electric. During 'Love, Reign O'er Me', Pete just kept looking up and while belting the words from his soul.

The Who Tour 2006-2007 was the group's first worldwide tour since 1997 and was supporting the *Endless Wire* album, their eleventh studio album released on 30 October 2006.

PIMLICO RACETRACK

23 SEPTEMBER 2006, BALTIMORE, MICHIGAN

I WAS THERE: MEGAN TAYLOR, AGE 22

I went for my birthday. I was drunk by 10am, tailgating in the parking lot, and had a hangover by noon. I was then completely sober for the concert. The Who were amazing live and I had the best time, despite the company I was with. I also got to see my favourite band of all time – the Red Hot Chili Peppers. They took the stage after The Who ... I think!

HOLLYWOOD BOWL

5 NOVEMBER 2006, LOS ANGELES, CALIFORNIA

I WAS THERE: SHAWN PERRY

I cruised down the 101 on an uncharacteristically warm Sunday night, psyching myself out for my tenth Who show. Arriving promptly at 7pm, I sipped on a $9 cup of Heineken and watched a 45 minute set by a Boulder, Colorado based power trio called Rose Hill Drive. They played an energetic selection of old school hard rock before acquiescing to the fact that it's a tough assignment opening for legends like The Who. A polite reception, no encore, and at 8pm the lights came down for the headliner.

Kicking into the durable opener 'I Can't Explain', Townshend and Daltrey took command of the stage and never let up. A five-screen backdrop playing old film footage of the original four lifted the performance to new heights of merriment and pageantry. 'The Seeker' and 'Substitute' followed, and it was as if The Who, even without John Entwistle and Keith Moon, had set their sights on becoming the hottest band on the planet.

Townshend, sporting dark glasses and a fez to hide his follicly challenged scalp, still swings his arm as wildly as a New York Yankee southpaw warming up for the World Series. Daltrey, even youthful behind the granny shades, has toned down his growl and minimised the microphone lassoing, at least for now.

The old made way for the new as 'Fragments', its opening sequence borrowing heavily from 'Baba O'Riley', spread its heavy breathing vibe over the 18,000 or so crowded onto the benches and bleachers of the Bowl. But that was just a taste of things to come as we slipped back into the time machine for routine workouts of 'Who Are You', 'Behind Blues Eyes' and the ever predictable but always delectable power chords of 'Baba O'Riley'.

Then it was time for a slew of more new stuff that enigmatically fell out of the sky and massaged the eardrums like a vamp of unexpected houseguests. A slice of 'Wire & Glass', the new mini opera, implored and sniffed out its admirers, supplemented by a heavy dose of visuals that didn't so much explain the tale as exhort its virtues and timelessness. Other tracks from *Endless Wire* were offered up and copiously consumed by the audience, many of whom could probably care less what they played as long they could say they saw The Who before they died. And while I could argue that no one has actually seen

The Who — at least The Who I saw — since 1978, for once I took a beat seat and strapped myself in for the long haul.

Coming down the home stretch, Townshend ditched his fez and Daltrey anxiously paced the stage, possibly in anticipation of screaming his climatic 'yah!' during 'Won't Get Fooled Again'. Although I was mildly thwarted by the absence of Thunderfingers apocalyptic bass runs on 'My Generation', the ensuing jam section and video clips featuring a variety of dancers were enough to make me forget Entwistle's immortal presence, if only for a moment. Repeated video clips of Entwistle and Moon in their heyday reminded everyone that The Who of yesteryear is the one everyone should remember and respect.

The encore was all *Tommy*, something I never tire of. 'Pinball Wizard' made way for 'Amazing Journey' and the extended 'Sparks' instrumental, where Daltrey voraciously slapped two tambourines together while Townshend, Starkey, Palladino, rhythm guitarist and Pete's younger brother Simon Townshend and understudy keyboardist Brain Kehew engaged in a spiral of musical warfare.

Then the familiar lexis of 'See Me, Feel Me' fluttered in and gripped the captive witnesses transported through the peaks and valleys that *Tommy* endured for the sake of sanity. As the crowd chanted, 'Listening to you, I get the music, gazing at you, I get the heat…' from 'We're Not Gonna Take It', I started to exit, not realizing that The Who, who used to shun encores entirely, would be back with another 'new' song, 'Tea And Theatre'.

The mellow notes flew through the air as I walked out of the Bowl and down the hill. I was glad I had changed my mind. Perhaps another album will get me to an eleventh show and then…who knows?

ARENA DI VERONA

11 JUNE 2007, VERONA, ITALY

I WAS THERE: CHRISTIAN SUCHATZKI

After 30 years of absence from Italy – their last concert there was in

1967 – The Who returned for a single concert, at the famous Arena in Verona, a location where usually classic operas are performed. This was absolutely fitting for a group like The Who, and what a joy for all the Italian Who fans, young and old, who at last were getting a chance to hear and see their favourite group perform live. Despite an average price of 80 Euros, the 12,500 tickets were sold out quickly and being a Who fan for 38 years, for me it was an obligation to attend this unique event.

It was a sunny day in Verona and in the arena some dealers tried in vain to sell ordinary rain capes for 2 Euros. When The Who entered the stage at 9:20pm the Italians received them with overwhelming jubilance and, from the first notes of 'I Can't Explain', on they went fanatically and cheerfully along with the group they'd waited for 30 years to see.

Suddenly, after 20 minutes, in the middle of 'Who Are You', an unexpectedly heavy rain and thunderstorm beat down on the open air arena. It was so heavy that the show needed to be stopped and the audience took shelter in the underground arches of the Roman arena, waiting until the storm calmed down to a degree where The Who's performance could be continued.

It was still raining when, after nearly an hour, the fans were allowed to re enter the arena. The rain capes could be acquired for 10 Euros now and nonetheless were sold out as fast as the ticket presale. The Who proceeded with 'Behind Blue Eyes'. But when Roger Daltrey sang the first verse he suddenly interrupted and said 'My voice has gone cold' and, frustrated, left the stage. The others stopped playing and, after a short internal discussion, Pete Townshend told the audience that they were unable to go on with the show because Roger had lost his voice.

The concert teetered on the brink of collapse a second time. What should be done? Disappoint the Italian fans who came here full of expectation? Continue with the show somehow? It was almost 11pm and The Who had played only five songs. After a short discussion with the local promoter, Pete decided to carry on with the concert and told the audience if they were willing to support him and the band he could sing most of the songs. Roger was called back on stage and the original set list was slightly shortened and quickly adjusted so that Pete could do most of the vocals, although Roger tried to sing a couple of songs with a raspy and hoarse voice as well as he could. Even Pete's unloved 'Magic Bus' was included in the rearranged set list. Against all odds and the continuing rain, the Italian fans accompanied The Who's continued performance with loud cheers and singing refrains.

Twenty minutes after midnight, the show ended with 'Won't Get Fooled Again' where Roger once again gave his best and, when he made his famous scream at the end of the song with evidently damaged vocal chords, I thought this would affect his voice forever.

Although this sole Italian Who concert in 30 years was almost a disaster, The Who demonstrated a remarkable professionalism and made this an enjoyable event for the Italian fans. At the end of the show Roger promised to come back with his voice. He did, when The Who returned to Italy in 2016 for two concerts in Bologna and Milano.

ENTERTAINMENT CENTRE

24 MARCH 2009, BRISBANE, AUSTRALIA

I WAS THERE: CHRIS HALES

I saw The Who at the Pier Pavilion and Town Hall in Worthing during the Sixties, which cemented my pure appreciation for their energy, their passion for alcohol, music and beating up their instruments – not necessarily in that order! My memories, which are probably no different from hundreds of thousands of others at the time, are of spectacular energy from both the band and the fans. Pete smashing his guitar was simply expected and Moonie exploded out of his drums. John just seemed to disappear and Roger was brilliant at banging out the lyrics.

When seeing them last in Brisbane it was like seeing something that had evolved into perfection. Modern technology and sound reproduction has helped groups like The Who become the consummate artists and musicians their passion was pointing them towards.

I had the privilege of being at their last concert in Brisbane where the boys showed that they had reached the top of the mountain. We all know that you don't fall to the top of a mountain.

The *Who Hits 50!* tour commenced in 2014 and marked the 50th anniversary of the band. Roger Daltrey referred to this tour as the band's 'long goodbye' hinting that it would be the final tour for The Who. The tour dates saw the band performing in Asia, Europe and North America.

SCOTTISH EXHIBITION AND CONFERENCE CENTRE

30 NOVEMBER 2014, GLASGOW

I WAS THERE: MIKE WILTON, AGE 30

Being the support band on four shows throughout The Who's 'The Who Hits 50' tour, we showed up to the first show feeling very nervous. A member of The Who crew pointed us in the direction of the stage and The Who were soundchecking on the stage. It was an unbelievable experience as *Live At Leeds* is the biggest influence on myself in terms of guitar playing and how a band should sound. They were soundchecking with 'A Quick One While He's Away', hich was even more mind blowing as I don't think they'd performed it on stage since 1970. They even had Bob Pridden working on the sound!

After we'd played our set to a very lovely Glasgow crowd, we waited at the side of the stage for The Who to come on. When Pete Townshend went for his first windmill of the night, it all suddenly kicked in what was happening. I was supporting one of my favourite bands of all time. Dreams can come true.

FIRST DIRECT ARENA

2 DECEMBER 2014, LEEDS

I WAS THERE: JASON BARNARD

I saw The Who at Leeds Arena on the *Hits 50* tour. My main memories of that is that Pete and Roger's show was so long that my wife, who is in her late 30s, was tired watching them – a bunch of guys pushing 70!

MORTLAKE CREMATORIUM

8 OCTOBER 2015, LONDON

I WAS THERE: JOHN CHARLES MORTON

I met Pete Townshend at Jim Diamond's funeral. Jim joined my band Happy Ever After in 1966 and he played with us for three years. Then he went to London and had success with PhD in the Seventies and on his own. Pete was a friend of Jim Diamond's. They all live around that area, all the rockers. So Jim used to meet Pete walking along the Thames, or in the local café for lunch. He knew him well from gigs and things. And Jim was a big fan of The Who.

So I'm standing at Jim Diamond's funeral and we're at the buffet and he's looking at the sausage rolls and the chicken drumsticks and all that. And it's just me and him and I said to him are you Tony Hymas?' who was Jim's keyboard player. He says 'no mate, I'm Pete.' 'Oh sorry. So you are. I'm very sorry.' It was Pete Townshend. How embarrassed was I?

MOTORPOINT ARENA

15 DECEMBER 2015, CARDIFF

I WAS THERE: PHILIP GOODRIDGE

I saw them in Cardiff. Zak Starkey was on drums. Roger Daltrey had laryngitis and he couldn't sing. And they got by on a wing and a prayer. They were still brilliant.

Linda Sweeden finally got to meet Pete and Roger, her lifetime heroes, in 2016

SSE ARENA

13 FEBRUARY 2016, WEMBLEY, LONDON

I WAS THERE: LINDA SWEEDEN

Seeing The Who at Charlton changed my life forever. 42 years and 41 Who gigs on I'm still smitten. My ultimate dream came true at Wembley in 2016 when I finally met Roger and Pete. They didn't want to do the normal 'meet and greet' reserved for those few that can afford it or those part of corporate events. They were looking to meet a real fan. I was totally unaware that my partner was trying everything he could think of to make my wish come true. He contacted anyone that had any connection to The Who via social media, etc. The sponsors of Wembley SSE Energy picked up on some of his tweets and secretly arranged for me to be a special guest at the Wembley gig. What a surprise! We were greeted by broadcast cameras, and a clamour of people interviewing me.

We had complimentary food and bubbly and went to the sound check

before finally ushered into a small room where Roger and Pete appeared
without fanfare. And there I was in the same room as my lifetime heroes!
And what does a woman like me say to her idol after all these years?
I said to Roger 'can I have a nose kiss?' He laughed and said 'why
not?' and put his arms around me, gave me a big hug and we rubbed
noses! I still ask myself – where did that come from? They were both
so warm and friendly. I had my photo taken with them and they signed
autographs and chatted about the sound check and stuff. My bucket list
is complete and I can die a happy woman.

JOE LOUIS ARENA

27 FEBRUARY 2016, DETROIT, MICHIGAN

I WAS THERE: BETH BATTJES

I was a late bloomer to The Who. I saw *Tommy* on cable in 2012 and
have been hooked ever since. I saw them for the first time ever in
Detroit. It was special because it was their first stop on the re-scheduled
American tour. Roger was sounding wonderful. I took lots of pictures.
It was my belated Christmas present from my best friend. I loved every
minute of being at a Who concert. We were on the main floor of the
arena but several rows back. One thing that stood out is, before 'My
Generation', Pete Townshend told a story about the song and how he
would riff away and eventually Keith would say 'Pete, for fucks sake!
Stop!' It was an amazing experience.

In late 2016, The Who appeared for the first time in South America playing
to almost 18,000 fans at the Palacio de los Deportes in Mexico City.

PALACIO DE LOS DEPORTES

12 OCTOBER 2016, MEXICO CITY, MEXICO

I WAS THERE: BERNARDO RAMÍREZ, AGE 20

Mexicans had to wait a very long time to see The Who. I was waiting

The audience at Palacio de Los Deportes – Bernardo is sporting his Rolling Stones t-shirt

in the sun and rain for ten hours with a large crowd, waiting for the doors to open so that I could ensure a good place to see that legendary band The Who. I got to be in the centre and at the front of the stage. Before the concert began, people went crazy with the photos of the old members of the band and the audience shouted 'Who, Who, Who.' Then the lights were turned off and the first chords of 'I Can't Explain' started, which marked the end of a very long wait.

The crowd responded with a shuddering roar to 'Who Are You' and, on 'My Generation', everyone jumped around frantically before singing along to 'Behind Blue Eyes'. During 'Join Together', Pete was dying of laughter listening to people singing. When the song ended, he told to the audience that the lyrics of the song was not 'join together in the band'. After that they played 'You Better You Bet' the audience was completely delivered, with the crowd chanting 'Olé, Olé, Olé – The Who!' Pete's face was full of emotion, not believing what he was seeing.

The song 'I'm One' has a very special meaning for me, even more so when Pete said, 'This song is for all the young people that I see and it's not me.' The power was rising more and more; Pete was very passionate and excited when playing the songs of *Quadrophenia*.

The climax of the concert was definitely 'See Me, Feel Me'. During 'Won't Get Fooled Again', Roger looked at his watch and his expression was surprising. Pete played with a lot of enthusiasm, stumbling and rolling around the floor. When I thought the concert was over, they returned for an encore to play 'Substitute'. In Pete's words, 'The Who is much higher in Mexico City'.

I WAS THERE: GUILLERMO VIESCA, AGE 14

I live in Mexico City and have been a fan since I was 10 or so. The first song I ever heard by The Who was 'Pinball Wizard' and I fell in love with it. I was losing faith that they would ever come to Mexico City, but I knew that if they came I had to see them. One day I was coming home from school and, when I arrived home, my dad showed me the advertisement – The Who are coming for the first time in their history to Mexico City! The next day, I bought my tickets, super close to the stage, and then it was the longest four months of my life until the big day came.

I remember being super excited on the day. The screens showed various Who stories when, suddenly, the lights went out and the first chords to 'I Cant Explain' started playing. It kept getting better and better. The set list was: 'I Can't Explain'; 'The Seeker'; 'Who Are You'; 'The Kids Are Alright'; 'I Can See for Miles'; 'My Generation'; 'Behind Blue Eyes'; 'Bargain'; 'Join Together'; 'You Better You Bet'; 'I'm One'; '5:15'; 'The Rock'; 'Love, Reign O'er Me'; 'Amazing Journey'; 'Sparks'; 'The Acid Queen'; 'Pinball Wizard'; 'See Me, Feel Me'; 'Baba O'Riley'; 'Won't Get Fooled Again'; 'Encore:'; 'Eminence Front'; 'Substitute'; 'Epilogue'.

ROYAL ALBERT HALL

30 MARCH 2017, LONDON

I WAS THERE: JOHN SCHOLLAR

I used to go and watch The Detours because we used to play on the same circuit. There was a pub just up the road from where I used to work in Alperton called the Fox and Goose, and all the bands used to play in there. That's where I first saw The Detours. Commercial Entertainment, who used to manage us, was based at the Oldfield in Greenford. When we weren't playing, if they were on somewhere, we'd go and see them. Loads of bands worked out of there. Even if you weren't playing you'd go along and have a night out watching the band somewhere, so we all knew The Detours before Keith joined them. And I saw them at the Railway Hotel a few times as well. And when The Detours needed a drummer, because they had a record deal coming up, they grabbed Keith.

He jumped at the chance. Keith's dad got on to Tony, my bass player, and he said 'what do you think about him joining this lot? I don't like the look of them. I can't see them doing anything.' Of course, after a few months they'd brought out their first record and there was no looking back. If you went out with him, you never knew if you were going to get home the same day. We were good mates. If he was still alive today I'd be seeing a lot of him.

The Who were on at the Albert Hall in early 2017 doing Tommy, and a friend of my daughter's who is a really big Who fan had just had his 50th birthday. He was planning to go to the Albert Hall twice and then Birmingham and I said 'I'll see if I can fix something up for you.' I rang Roger's secretary and said 'a mate of mine's had a big birthday and I just want to treat him. Can you get me a VIP pass?' And she said 'yeah.' When I rang up the office there was no 'who are you?' It was 'hello, John.' That's nice. Well, they did nick our drummer, didn't they?

The Who's CV as a performing outfit takes some beating, having been gigging on and off for over 53 years since their formation in early 1964. Since John Entwistle's death in 2002, Roger Daltrey and Pete Townshend have continued to perform as both The Who and separately.

The Who remain in demand as a headline act. There have been

a number of tours of north America and continental Europe since 2002, along with a return to Australia and New Zealand in 2009 more than 40 years after their first visit. They appeared at the Live8 Festival in 2005, the half time Superbowl slot in 2010, closed the London Olympic Games in 2012 and the Glastonbury Festival in 2015. In 2016, they shared the bill with The Rolling Stones, Bob Dylan, Paul McCartney, Neil Young and Roger Waters at the Desert Trip Festival, reaffirming their position amongst rock's elite.

In recent years, health has impacted on schedules, with several shows having to be rearranged because of Roger falling ill. But at the time of writing the band were booked to perform a handful of British arena gigs and then a series of US shows, culminating in a return to Las Vegas in August 2017 some 15 years after John died.

When Pete and Roger announced *The Who Hits 50!* Tour at Ronnie Scott's in London back in 2014, Roger described it as 'the beginning of the long goodbye.' When they do throw down their mics and guitars for the very last time, they will leave an enduring legacy as a phenomenal live act.